The Tuscarora War

The Tuscarora War

Indians, Settlers, and the Fight for the Carolina Colonies

{ DAVID LA VERE }

THE UNIVERSITY OF NORTH CAROLINA PRESS
Chapel Hill

*This book was published with the assistance of the Fred W. Morrison Fund
for Southern Studies of the University of North Carolina Press.*

© 2013 The University of North Carolina Press
All rights reserved
Set in Espinosa Nova by codeMantra
Manufactured in the United States of America

The paper in this book meets the guidelines for permanence and durability
of the Committee on Production Guidelines for Book Longevity of the Council
on Library Resources. The University of North Carolina Press has been a
member of the Green Press Initiative since 2003.

Library of Congress Cataloging-in-Publication Data
La Vere, David.
The Tuscarora War : Indians, settlers, and the fight for
the Carolina colonies / David La Vere. — First edition.
pages cm
Includes bibliographical references and index.
ISBN 978-1-4696-1090-0 (cloth : alk. paper)
1. Tuscarora Indians—Wars, 1711–1713. 2. Indian slaves—
North Carolina—History. 3. North Carolina—History—Colonial period,
ca. 1600–1775. 4. Indians of North America—North Carolina. I. Title.
E83.71.L38 2013
973.2'5—dc23
2013020041
17 16 15 14 13   5 4 3 2 1

For Mycah Mae,
and her parents
Jordyn and Mark Zimmerman

Contents

—

Illustrations and Maps

Prologue

It was a hard place. Geography and climate worked against North Carolina, making it a hot, wet, humid country with more water than dry land. Indians had long adapted to it, but European settlers found it tough going. Down among the pine barrens, dreams that began with so much promise withered in the summer heat. Reality met ideals along the dark rivers and easily trumped them. Cultures clashed and insults could no longer be tolerated. Misery fouled the air and Death stalked all. It brought out the meanness in men, European and Indian alike. Hardscrabble English colonists and hard-pressed Indian peoples found themselves squaring off, each fearing, then hating the other. Then, in September 1711, when the anger and resentment could not be tamped down any longer, they exploded into the Tuscarora War, a notoriously brutal conflict of the American colonial period.

War is a dangerous undertaking and the fortunes of those involved often hang in the balance. This one was no different. The Tuscarora War found a divided and weak North Carolina colony seemingly ripe for the taking. The powerful Tuscarora Indians and their Core, Machapunga, Neuse, Pamlico, Weetock, and Bear River Indian allies appeared unbeatable. And so it degenerated into a war without mercy that pushed both the colony and the Indians of eastern North Carolina to the brink of extinction.

But while nations may wage war, it is fought by men, human beings. And so the Tuscarora War also shaped the fortunes of men's lives. Some found their property, their careers, and even their lives destroyed. Others saw opportunities to increase their wealth, their prestige, their political power, or all three. The eight men in this story—Christopher de Graffenried of Switzerland, King Hancock of the Tuscaroras, Core Tom of the

Core Indians, William Brice of North Carolina, Col. John Barnwell of South Carolina, Thomas Pollock of North Carolina, King Tom Blount of the Tuscaroras, and Col. James Moore of South Carolina—certainly found their fortunes rising or falling as this war went along. Many men played important roles in instigating, waging, and ending the Tuscarora War, but these eight played crucial roles. All eight would be touched by the war, wrestled by it, and their lives would never again be the same. Neither would the colony of North Carolina nor the Indian peoples who lived across its coastal plain.

The Makings of a War

Even God seemed to hate North Carolina. Evidence of this appeared definite by the late summer of 1711. When King Charles II granted the colony to the Lords Proprietors back in 1663, these eight English lords imagined a steady flow of American wealth into their pockets. Now almost fifty years later, North Carolina was one of the poorer, if not the poorest, of England's North American colonies. A major part of the problem was water. On the one hand, the colony was blessed with plenty of it, including several big rivers as well as the huge Albemarle and Pamlico Sounds. Yet it was cursed because the waters were too shallow for large ships. And so North Carolina had no deepwater port. That meant trade and commerce lagged badly when compared to Virginia to the north and South Carolina below. North Carolina's colonial population was small but politically divided, having just emerged from a vicious internal rebellion that stopped just short of civil war. Hurricanes hit in the summer, nor'easters in the winter, while diseases such as smallpox, yellow fever, and malaria frequently visited with deadly results. People did not live long in this hot, soggy country. And though the Lords Proprietors encouraged immigration and settlement, the powerful Tuscarora Indian nation sat just west of the line of settlement and so blocked expansion toward the Piedmont and south to the Cape Fear River.

Nor had the Indians of eastern North Carolina bargained for what they were getting in 1711. Most of the Algonquian-speaking Chowans, Pasquatanks, Hatteras, Poteskeets, and Yeopims, once the masters of the Albemarle, had become defeated tributaries to the colonial government. The Iroquoian-speaking Tuscaroras, Meherrins, Cores, Neuse, Pamlicos, Bear River Indians, and Weetock Indians, most of whom had not yet tasted defeat at the hands of the English, were seeing their lives changed for the

3

worse. Their ancestors, along with the shallow waters of the sounds, had repelled Sir Walter Raleigh's colonization attempts on Roanoke Island in the 1580s. But with the creation of the Carolina colony in 1663, the Indians saw a tremendous influx of English settlers, most moving south out of Virginia. By 1711, the Indians of eastern North Carolina had seen their political independence challenged, their lands taken, their beliefs ridiculed, and their dignity ruffled. They also found themselves slowly drawn into a dependence on English traders and the guns, ammunition, metal goods, rum, and other merchandise only the Europeans could supply. The condition of the colony in late summer 1711, the disunity and turbulent politics, its small but dispersed population, made many Indians think it was a perfect time to right those wrongs.

In a way, the conditions that provoked the Tuscarora War in 1711 were a problem of geology. Over the eons, the land from just south of Chesapeake Bay down to the White Oak River, encompassing all of what was then North Carolina, had been slowly sinking. Rivers such as the Chowan and Roanoke, the Tar-Pamlico and the Neuse, racing off the Carolina Piedmont slowed down when they hit the low coastal plain then widened to create the Albemarle and Pamlico Sounds. As these rivers lost momentum, they deposited silt at their mouths as a series of sandy barrier islands broken by shifting shallow inlets. These "outer banks," as they would come to be called, bottled up the sounds and so created an inland sea of shallow, brackish water that the Roanoke Indians called "Occam." So eastern North Carolina became a water world of soggy land cut by rivers and streams, pockmarked with swamps, marshes, and pocosins. Fertile uplands existed but they sat like islands amid sodden ground and water. And with the waters so shallow, colonial economic development lagged. Conversely, for the Indian peoples of eastern North Carolina, the land and waters provided a bountiful home.[1]

By the 1650s, as Virginia's settler population increased and good lands became expensive, some Englishmen looked south to what would become North Carolina. It could be a difficult trek. One had to struggle through the Great Dismal Swamp and pass through many Indian towns and territories, some not that excited about white people tramping across their lands. But North Carolina's remoteness appealed to some Englishmen. If it was hard to get to North Carolina, then it was hard for authorities back in Virginia or London to get there as well. By the early 1660s, hundreds of settlers filled the north bank of the Albemarle Sound, many buying lands from the Indians and cutting cabins out of the forest. During this same time, a few short-lived settlements were attempted down on the

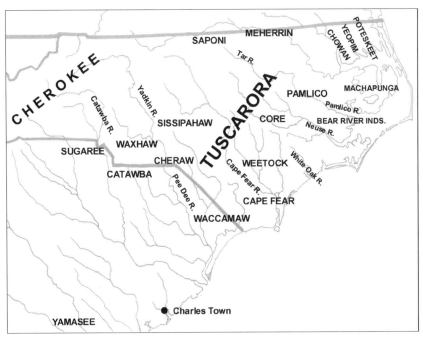

Indian Peoples of North Carolina, c. 1711. Map by David A. Norris

Cape Fear River, the southernmost river system in North Carolina. These failed quick enough and so those interested in that southern area now shifted their attention down to what would become South Carolina.[2]

Most of these early settlers moving to the north side of the Albemarle Sound sought its isolation. The Albemarle sat far from the power centers of Virginia. Men and women on the run from whatever chased them found refuge here. No real government existed to demand taxes or militia service. The Anglican Church barely registered with the early settlers, and they ignored the church's demand for tithes or obedience. With the smoke from the English Civil War barely cleared, men who had drunk from Oliver Cromwell's egalitarian, anti-Anglican cup found like minds here. In the Albemarle they could pursue their own interests, farm, hunt, and trade with the Indians, with little interference from authorities. Shallow waters provided a haven. Then all this freedom ended in 1663, at least in theory, when King Charles II created the colony of Carolina. It stretched from about where the border of Florida and Georgia is today, up to the present-day border of North Carolina and Virginia. As a favor for supporting his return to the throne, he granted Carolina to eight English aristocrats known as the Lords Proprietors. In 1663, they were Edward

Hyde, Earl of Clarendon; George Monck, Duke of Albemarle; Anthony Ashley Cooper, Earl of Shaftesbury; William Craven; John, Lord Berkeley; Sir William Berkeley; Sir John Colleton; and Sir George Carteret. These lords and the men who succeeded them as Proprietors governed Carolina from England, making laws, appointing governors, and resolving disputes, and they did so for the following sixty-five years. Down on the Albemarle, the farmers and Indian traders saw no immediate change in their lives, but whether they realized it or not, they now had masters back in London.[3]

In their plans for Carolina, the Proprietors wanted to wrest as much wealth from their colony as possible while spending as little of their own as they could. But it did not take long for them to realize that riches were not evenly distributed in Carolina. Albemarle County, as the Proprietors now called it, was not that wealthy, and with no deepwater port it did not appear it ever would be. Conversely, several hundred miles south, in South Carolina, where as the residents will tell you, the Ashley and the Cooper Rivers come together to form the Atlantic Ocean, settlers began flocking in from overcrowded Barbados. In 1670, the city of Charles Town, later Charleston, was founded. Blessed with a deep harbor, the city soon boasted a bustling population of rich planters and merchants shipping and receiving goods from throughout the British world. Residents built much of this prosperity on the backs of Indian and African slaves. In fact, slave taking and slave trading became a path to riches for many in South Carolina. The potential for wealth in southern Carolina certainly caught the attention of the Proprietors, and they soon ignored the Albemarle. Charles Town became the colonial capital where the governor sat. But with settlement at the extreme ends of the colony, deputy governors were later appointed for the northern Carolina Albemarle. By the early 1690s, North and South Carolina were unofficially separate colonies, with separate governing executives for each. The separation would become official in 1712. The border between the two was rather nebulous, but roughly the lower Cape Fear River.[4]

The Proprietors began issuing regulations for the Albemarle. Albemarle County was divided into four precincts: from east to west sat Currituck encompassing the coast, barrier islands, and sounds; Pasquotank; Perquimans; and finally the westernmost Chowan Precinct. William Drummond was appointed governor of the Albemarle, the first of many more to come, some good, some bad. An appointed Governor's Council assisted him in running the colony. Consisting of between five and twelve men, the Council was a powerful entity that served as an upper legislative house and so could counter any foolishness that might come out of the people's elected Assembly. Offices such as chief justice, attorney general, surveyor general, justices of the peace, and others were created, then filled by friends of the Proprietors and governors. Consistent with the laws of England, these officials with full Proprietor support levied import and export duties. A process was created for settlers to purchase land and a fee charged at every step. The Proprietors were more than willing to grant a settler a hundred acres just for the asking and then give an additional fifty acres for every person whose way that settler paid to the colony. But nothing was free and on taking the land, the settler needed to pay a quitrent, normally two shillings per one hundred acres of land.[5]

The Proprietors thought themselves most generous and reasonable. Their laws could not go against British law. The Albemarle Assembly was elected by the people, meaning white, adult males, could write its own laws, and expect that the Proprietors would ratify most of them. Though the Anglican Church was the official church of Carolina and settlers were supposed to support it with tithes, few paid. Freedom of conscience was guaranteed and Dissenters, meaning those who did not support the Church of England, served in the Assembly. In fact, since land was plentiful and settlers few, the Proprietors encouraged Quakers and other Dissenters to immigrate to North Carolina. Land grants were liberal, quitrents small, and a settler had as many as five years to pay them. At the same time, the Proprietors provided little actual support, willing to let the colony fend for itself even in emergencies, and pretty much contented themselves with appointing governors.[6]

If those in London imagined that the transition to Proprietary rule was going to be smooth, they were sadly mistaken. Many men and women had purposely sought the far reaches of North Carolina to escape just such authority. Old settlers such as George Durant, Valentine Bird, and others did not welcome the rules now emanating from London. These men and others like them were a touchy, argumentative lot and dead set against the Proprietors getting too involved in local affairs. They disliked taxes of any sort and did not care for government except when they took someone to court or petitioned it for redress. They looked askance at new laws that favored the wealthy or limited their own rights. More than anything they wanted to be left alone and were willing to ignore the Proprietors as far as they could.[7]

Their ranks grew as more people of this stripe immigrated to North Carolina. Some were debtors, some criminals, some on the run from wives or husbands, and some just honest men looking to strike out on their own. But outside the region, Albemarle County garnered a reputation as a haven for pirates, runaways, and illegal traders. Virginia officials called the Albemarle "Rogues' Harbor."[8] Reverend John Urmston, an Anglican minister in the Albemarle, later called these old settlers "libertines, men & women of loose, dissolute and scandalous lives and practices . . . educated at some of the famous Colleges of Bridewell, Newgate, or the Mint," these being some of the most notorious prisons in England.[9] Many may well have seen the inside of an English prison, but that did not mean they were politically naive. They understood the power of the ballot box and quickly began electing themselves or their supporters to the colonial Assembly. In this way, these old settlers formed a distinct, antiauthoritarian political faction in early colonial North Carolina.

North Carolina attracted another group of people who would form a second political faction, and one Reverend Urmston hated as much as the first. These were the Religious Society of Friends, better known as Quakers. The Quakers arose in England in the mid-1600s and emphasized a personal experience with Christ. A clannish religious sect, they seemed about as far from England's official Anglican Church as one could get and still be considered Christian. Besides differences in basic theology, Quaker social ideas also shocked Reverend Urmston and other Englishmen to such a degree that they referred to them as Dissenters. In the Albemarle, Quakers believed in egalitarianism, even among men and women, and refused to tip their hat to their social "betters." Pacifists, they refused to take up arms against anyone, including Indians or England's enemies. This carried over in that they refused to provide supplies or support to military operations. Most were farmers, and in these early years a few even owned slaves. Since they did not consider themselves as part of the Anglican Church, they declined to pay taxes and tithes for its upkeep. They refused to swear oaths: not in everyday life, not in the courtroom, not an oath of loyalty to the English monarch. And this last was usually needed to hold any type of public office or elected position.[10]

By the early 1700s, the Quakers had converted many of the old settlers and so formed a considerable population in the eastern parts of Albemarle County. They did not hesitate to use their political clout to swing legislation in their favor. Reverend Urmston called them "a mutinous and rebellious people" and bemoaned that it was "Oliver's days come again." The nervous reverend feared that the old anti-Anglicanism from when Oliver Cromwell governed England in the 1650s had come to life again in North Carolina.[11] Politically, the old settlers and the Quakers found much in common and often voted for similar policies. Both tended to be anti-government, anti-tax, anti-regulation, anti–Anglican Church and skeptical of the Proprietors' intentions.[12]

A powerful third faction was also rising in the Albemarle, one that countered the old settlers and Quakers. These might be called the Proprietary men. They understood that the British Empire had come to North Carolina. The Proprietors, backed by the English throne, made the laws, but they also distributed money, political appointments, and granted land. So it was wealthy men, at least by Albemarle standards, who backed the Proprietors. Or men who hoped to become wealthy, or who wanted a government salary, or a favor of land or title. So did planters and merchants who hoped to become part of the market economy as much as North Carolina geography would allow. Above all, these men wanted stability, and like Reverend Urmston, they looked in horror at the old settlers and Quakers who seemed so ready to ignore the Proprietors' edicts. Because of this, the Proprietary men were inclined to be law-and-order men determined to enforce the Proprietors' laws and taxes. They also tended to be Anglican, adherents of the official Church of England, and so supported the idea that everyone, even Quakers, should pay tithes for the building of Anglican churches and salaries for its ministers. They expected subjects of Queen Anne to swear an oath of loyalty to her and did not understand those who would not.[13]

In reality, just the pressure of putting food on the table or creating wealth in this backwater of empire meant that politics played only a small part in any settler's life. Though Albemarle County's population swelled, North Carolina was still a watery wilderness of rivers and swamps. A traveler might come across a small farm in a clearing and or a plantation along one of the watercourses. Merchants and stores could be found if one knew where to look, but there were no towns in North Carolina until Bath was chartered in March 1706 at the junction of Bath and Back Creeks on the north side of the Pamlico River. Once on their land, settlers cleared the forest to build a cabin and then planted Indian corn for food. Most settlers ate salt pork, but supplemented it with fresh meat by hunting deer, rabbits, squirrels, and opossum. With few, if any, grist mills, bread was almost nonexistent. Tools were few, so settlers usually made their own hoes, forks, and shovels. More established planters might try to grow tobacco, wheat, oats, rye, and in some instances, rice for the Atlantic market, but failure was common. Those better off might have carts or wagons, but draft animals were scarce as well. On the other hand, hogs were plentiful and settlers let them run wild in the woods, cutting notches on the ears to show ownership. Along the coast, fishing helped, as did scavenging the beaches for shipwrecks or the occasional beached whale. And a man with a boat might supplement his income with a little smuggling, bringing in rum or tools without paying the import duties. A few others turned to piracy.[14]

Social classes and status rankings existed in North Carolina during the early 1700s, and at the lower end sat the hundreds, if not thousands, of men and women, mostly illiterate, working hard just to get by. The men received an undeserved reputation for laziness and indolence, of whiling away the day smoking a pipe.[15] Their social betters said little good about them. Governor Edward Hyde called his North Carolina subjects "naturally loose & wicked, obstinate and rebellious, crafty and deceitful and study to invent slander on one another."[16] Certainly many North Carolina men and women were on the run. These were people who saw bear hunting as a sport and often broke the Sabbath by killing cattle or branding horses. They accused each other of lewd behavior, of killing unwanted children, and of practicing witchcraft.[17] It was tough country. Reverend Urmston despised them, but he acknowledged their hard work. "Men are generally carpenters, joiners, wheelwrights, coopers, butchers, tanners, shoemakers, tallow chandlers, waterman & what not. Women soap makers, starch makers, dyes &c.," he wrote. "All seem to live by their own hands of their own produce and what they can spare goes for foreign goods. Nay many live on a slender diet to buy rum, sugar, and molasses with other such like necessaries."[18]

Some women found life in North Carolina to be liberating. The wilderness gave Dorothy Steel the opportunity to leave her husband and run off with John Spellman. Other women found a measure of economic independence. But most colonial North Carolina women were wives, daughters, servants, or slaves and so legally under the thumb of husband, father, or master. And many perceived freedoms dried up as Proprietary rule tightened toward the end of the seventeenth century. Even Dorothy Steel was forced to return to her husband, where she received thirty lashes. Her lover, John Spellman, received thirty-nine and was banished from the colony. If North Carolina men gained a reputation as lazy slugs, North Carolina women were seen as hardworking drudges. One traveler reckoned that women born in North Carolina tended to be very fair if they stayed out of the sun, but in reality, this was impossible. Women worked hard, had to be rugged, and often carried guns into the fields where they shot deer, turkeys, and wild hogs. When it came time to slaughter cattle or hogs, women were there, tying up the animal and knocking it in the head. Just about every woman possessed watercraft skills.[19] One traveler in

North Carolina pointed out that many "women are very handy in canoes, and will manage them with great dexterity and skill, which they become accustomed to in this watery country."[20]

At the very bottom of this colonial social pyramid sat slaves, both Indian and African. In 1710, about nine hundred African or African American slaves lived in North Carolina, but no counts exist for the number of enslaved Indians. Slave owners often possessed a mix of Indian and African slaves, usually, but not always, Indian women and African men. Nevertheless, Indian and African slaves cost much, putting them out of reach for most North Carolina common folk. Only the more prosperous North Carolinians could afford them. Indian slaves tended to be war captives and North Carolinians often bought them from South Carolina slave traders. Those taken in North Carolina were normally sold out of the colony. On the other hand, as the plantation economy solidified in North Carolina, the colony saw a steady increase in African and African American slaves. By the second decade of the eighteen century, well-off Albemarle and Bath county planters increasingly wrung their profits from black slave labor. It became common for owners to put their slaves to work on public projects, such as the building of forts, clearing of roads, and constructing the construction of bridges. At the same time, slave owners complained about their black slaves, accusing them of theft or destruction of property, of killing or injuring their masters, of running away, and one of the most fearful, of running off to live free in Indian villages, thereby sharing valuable knowledge with the Indians.[21]

For Indians, that was the rub. They increasingly found themselves coming into contact with the men, women, and even African slaves who lived on the many small farms and plantations scattered across eastern North Carolina. Indians and settlers often hunted the same grounds, traded with each other, worked with each other, and brawled with each other. Indians, curious about the English, visited settlers' homes. Coming from a culture in which hospitality was highly valued, Indians asked for food and drink, even personal property, and expected to receive it. Sometimes they just took what they wanted, thinking it an extension of hospitality. Settlers, placing a high value on personal property, became enraged at the Indians' audacity and accused them of theft. Over the years and in hundreds of minor interactions and altercations, the English settlers and the Carolina Indians began irritating each other.

Nevertheless and despite its many hardships, North Carolina was a growing colony. While accurate counts and censuses are in short supply, in 1679 there seem to have been about 1,400 settlers. By 1700 there were about 5,000. And by 1710 North Carolina counted a combined white and black population of 15,120.[22] It had not taken long for Albemarle County on the north bank to fill up. As early as 1675, English settlers had moved to the south shore of the Albemarle. By 1691, some had jumped further south and taken lands on the north bank of the Pamlico River. French Huguenots founded a colony north of the Pamlico River in the 1690s. This left a fifty mile strip of uninhabited land—the Great Alligator Swamp—between the Albemarle settlements and those on the Pamlico. Then as early as 1701, settlers were leaping south to the lands around the mouth of the Neuse and Trent Rivers, leaving another sparsely inhabited area between the Pamlico and Neuse.[23]

The Lords Proprietors strongly encouraged this settlement to the south, and as the population grew, they saw a need for a second North Carolina county. In 1696, the Proprietors created Bath County, which covered everything south of the Albemarle to the Neuse River. It was divided into three precincts eventually named Beaufort and Hyde, both north of the Pamlico River, and Craven Precinct, which covered everything south of the Pamlico River down to the Neuse and Trent Rivers. By 1708, the north bank of the Neuse River near its mouth had been settled, as was the area around Core Sound and along the Trent River. The population in this area continued to grow, and by 1711 the White Oak River south of the Neuse was the southern limit of European settlement in North Carolina. From there, South Carolina lay several hundred miles further south, separated from North Carolina by the Cape Fear River and a tangle of forests, swamps, lowlands, and Siouan-speaking Indian peoples.[24]

However, the settlement of the lands along the Pamlico, Neuse, and Trent Rivers set in motion two forces that directly led to the Tuscarora War. First, when Bath County was created in 1696, it received an inferior political status to Albemarle County. Where Albemarle County elected five representatives to the Assembly from each of its four precincts, Bath County originally had no precincts and could only send two representatives to the Assembly. In 1705, when Bath County was divided into three precincts, it could still only send two representatives from each. This meant that Bath County would be out-voted by Albemarle County twenty to six. This created much resentment among Bath County settlers. Second, as settlers began carving out farms and plantations along the Neuse and Trent Rivers, they were now invading the lands of the Tuscaroras, the most powerful Indian nation in eastern North Carolina.[25]

Down in Bath County, the political resentment caused by unequal representation began to simmer just as the battle between the Quakers and the Proprietary men began to heat up again in the Albemarle. Until then, the old settlers and Quakers had dominated the North Carolina Assembly. Most governors rarely took them on. Even the Proprietors, some of whom became Quakers themselves, had given North Carolina Dissenters much leeway. British law said that those elected to the Assembly were to swear an oath of loyalty to the English king, but Quaker assemblymen would not actually say the word "swear" or would substitute the word "declare" instead. This refusal to swear an oath of loyalty did not pose much of a problem in North Carolina until 1702, when Queen Anne ascended to the throne of England. Strongly Anglican, she felt Dissenters posed a danger to her realm. She now forbade partial oaths and insisted that all holders of any political office actually *swear* the oath of loyalty to her. As she saw it, refusal to do so was akin to treason. This gave the Proprietary men in North Carolina the ammunition they needed to destroy Quaker power in the colony. Governor Henderson Walker, a devout Anglican, and his Council insisted that elected assemblymen fully swear their oath to the queen. No more partial or substitute oaths were allowed. Most Quakers refused and so the governor and Council would not let them take their seats in the legislature. The Proprietary men also pushed the Anglican Church as the colony's established church. Settlers would now be taxed to pay the salaries of Anglican ministers sent to the colony and to build and maintain churches.[26]

The Quakers fought back. They complained to the Lords Proprietors and refused to be pushed out of the Assembly. They shored up their po-litical alliances with the old settlers, but they also made new ones with the disgruntled planters and landowners down in Bath County. In 1708, the Quakers persuaded former governor Thomas Cary to return as governor until the Lords Proprietors could officially appoint another. Cary, who owned a plantation on the Pamlico River in Bath County, had always been a Proprietary man, and in his recent administration from 1705 to 1707, he had been anti-Quaker. But as a Bath County man, he held a grudge against the Albemarle men who gave Bath County fewer votes and so retained control of the lucrative Indian trade. Seeing a chance to strike a blow against the Albemarle Proprietary men, Cary now championed the Quakers. In doing so, he gained the backing of the Dissenters and the old settlers in Albemarle County, as well as of many Bath County men just as angry at the Albemarle Proprietary men as he was. Though Cary soon gained control of the governor's office, the Albemarle Proprietary men cried foul and never accepted him as the legal governor. Neverthe-less, with the backing of the Quaker-dominated Assembly, Cary governed rather well for the following two years, much to the chagrin of the Albemarle Proprietary men.[27]

In 1710, the Lords Proprietors back in London, tired of the squabbling, appointed Edward Hyde, a cousin of Queen Anne, as governor of North Carolina. Proprietary men Thomas Pollock and Thomas Boyd were officially appointed as deputies to represent the Lords Proprietors on the Governor's Council. Hyde's arrival in early 1711 delighted the Albemarle Proprietary men, and they quickly escorted him to Pollock's plantation on the west side of the Chowan River in Chowan Precinct. Once there, Hyde declared himself the true governor of North Carolina, replacing Cary. Though Hyde's official appointment had not yet arrived, Cary peacefully surrendered the government to Hyde. Had things been left there, all might have been well. But in March 1711, Hyde, egged on by Pollock, never one to forgive an enemy, now indicted Cary and his closest supporters on charges of high crimes and misdemeanors they had supposedly committed in office. The charges were baseless, but Cary, fearing arrest, backtracked, claiming that Hyde was not the true governor. He now determined to take back the office for himself.[28]

So began "Cary's Rebellion" and North Carolina sat on the verge of civil war. Hyde led a force of 150 men down to the Pamlico River to arrest Cary, but decided against attacking Cary's fortified position and so retreated to Pollock's house. In June 1711, Cary and his supporters sailed a brigantine up the Albemarle to Pollock's plantation where Hyde and his supporters were meeting. The brigantine fired a cannon shot at the plantation house, the ball ricocheting off the roof. Pollock returned fire with one of his own cannons and so drove off the brigantine. Governor Alexander Spotswood of Virginia, acting on an appeal from Governor Hyde, sent the Royal Marines to the Albemarle to arrest Cary and his supporters. Cary, realizing that fighting the Royal Marines would actually be treason, ended his rebellion and escaped to Virginia. Spotswood arrested him and sent Cary back to London in chains to stand trial. Cary's Rebellion was over. Edward Hyde was governor. Thomas Pollock became president of the Governor's Council. The Albemarle Proprietary men were in charge politically, though Dissenters in the Assembly still constituted a challenge. The hard feelings of Cary's Rebellion had not subsided by late summer 1711 and North Carolina remained heavily factionalized. Cary's supporters wanted vengeance and some imagined the Indians might be used for this purpose. Rumor said that Cary's men visited Indian towns and urged them to attack their political enemies.[29]

If the influx of settlers into the areas around the Pamlico and Neuse Rivers brought bad blood between Bath County and the Albemarle, it did the same with the Indian people in that region. Expansion of European settlement in North Carolina meant a corresponding loss of land by the Indians. Soon, eastern North Carolina Indians found their lands, their culture, their dignity, and even their lives under assault. But the summer of 1711 found the Indian peoples of eastern North Carolina far from the powers they had been back in the 1580s when they encountered Raleigh's colony on Roanoke Island. Then there may well have been a population of more than thirty thousand Indian people in the North Carolina coastal plain, maybe many more. Exact counts of Indian population numbers are unreliable, but by 1711 that number is thought to have declined to some-where between five thousand and ten thousand. War, disease, and rum, one Englishman said, took a terrible toll on the Indians.[30]

As the old settlers moved onto the north bank of the Albemarle and along the Outer Banks back in the 1650s and 1660s, they encountered several towns of Algonquian-speaking Indians: Pasquatanks, Hatteras, Poteskeets, Yeopims, and the largest of the group, the Chowans. Things did not always go smoothly and these early settlers fought a war with the Chowans, which ended with the Chowans defeated in 1677 and placed on a twelve-square mile reservation on Bennett's Creek.[31] After this, the Indians north of Albemarle Sound became tributaries to the North Carolina government, recognizing North Carolina's authority over them. They posed no real threat to the colony, were clients of co-lonial traders, and served as a buffer to protect the English settlements from attacks by other Indians. Despite their tributary status, or maybe because of it, these Indians complained mightily about abuses from English settlers.

Further south along the Pamlico and Neuse Rivers, settlers came across other Indian peoples. Out to the east near Lake Mattamuskeet lived the Machapungas, while on an island in the Pamlico River sat a town of Indi-ans the English referred to as Pamlico Indians. South of the Pamlico River, on Bay River near the coast, was a town of Indians called the Bay River Indians. Because of English accents, they often got mistakenly called the Bear River Indians. A couple of Neuse Indian towns sat alongside that river, while the Core Indians, probably pronounced "Coree," could be found on Core Sound, south of the Neuse River, and then later on both the White Oak and Neuse Rivers. These were rather small Indian nations, each with maybe a few hundred people and none able to put more than fifty warriors into the field.[32]

The real Indian power lay just further to the west with the Tuscaroras. These Iroquoian-speaking peoples boasted a population of well over five thousand, scattered over a dozen towns stretching from Contentnea Creek, a tributary of the upper Neuse River, northeast across the Tar River to the Roanoke River, putting their northernmost towns just west of Albemarle County. A true force to be reckoned with, they could put several hundred warriors into the field. Diplomatically, they had close relations with the Five Nations of the Iroquois in New York, theoretically giving them powerful allies. In a way, the Tuscaroras acted like a cork blocking North Carolina's expansion to the west. They also possessed the potential to block any further settlement south of the Neuse River as the Neuse and Core Indians were Iroquoian peoples and seem to have been merely offshoot Tuscarora villages stretching down to the coast.[33]

As North Carolina expanded, Indians and settlers increasingly came into contact and in due course rubbed each other the wrong way. Complaints among the two peoples increased dramatically during the first decade of the eighteenth century. Settlers complained that Indians killed their cattle and hogs; hunted on settler lands; burned valuable stands of timber as a hunting strategy; were thieves; attacked lone boats on the colony's waters; threatened settlers with violence; and murdered them when they could get away with it. The North Carolina government became so fed up that in 1703 it declared war against the Neuse and Core Indians, but not much came of it.[34]

Indians levied similar charges against the English. They complained that they were beaten by settlers if they appeared in the settled parts of the colony; that the English prevented them from hunting in their traditional hunting quarters; that settlers ignored land boundaries, then squatted on Indian land; and stole from them as well. Traders cheated them and abused them, even sexually assaulted their women. A lone Indian could easily wind up dead at the hands of settlers. As for their killing of English livestock, well, that was what Indian men did, they hunted animals that roamed the forests, whether they were deer or bear, cow or hog. As matters went, it was the Indians who constantly worried that the English were going to attack them. And in a way they were, as Indian slave raiders out of South Carolina targeted their towns, captured their people, and then marched them back to Charles Town as slaves, never to be seen again. Loss of land proved particularly worrisome as the Indians along the Pamlico and Neuse Rivers found themselves hemmed in by settlers. They looked on in alarm when in 1710 several hundred Palatine and Swiss settlers under the leadership of Christopher de Graffenried came to the mouth of the Neuse River. Soon these settlers crowded out nearby Core and Neuse Indian towns and forced them to relocate further upriver. But the North Carolina government did little to address Indian complaints.[35]

So by the late summer of 1711, North Carolina smoldered, just waiting for a spark that could explode the entire colony into war. It seemed, as Reverend William Gordon said, "a country but wild and imperfect in its circumstances."[36] The Quakers, old settlers, and Bath County men fumed at how Cary's Rebellion had turned out. The Proprietary men pushed ever harder to set themselves and the Anglican Church as the political power in North Carolina. All the while, the Indians grew more worried and angry as the abuses against them escalated and their complaints fell on deaf ears. That spark came in mid-September 1711 as two Englishmen decided to take a trip up the Neuse River for a closer look at the land.

CHAPTER ONE

Christopher de Graffenried

The Dreamer

It was a pleasant late-summer day, around the eleventh or twelfth of September 1711. Baron Christopher de Graffenried, John Lawson, the surveyor general for the colony of North Carolina, and Christopher Gale, its chief justice, had decided to make a trip up the Neuse River.[1] Since De Graffenried's colony of Swiss and German Palatines at the mouth of the Neuse River was thriving, expansion up the Neuse seemed a real possibility. Gale begged out at the last minute due to sickness in his family. So De Graffenried and Lawson, along with two black slaves and a couple of Indian guides, set out with both boat and horse up the Neuse River.

They were well into their third day of the trip, maybe thirty miles upriver from New Bern, when everything changed. Suddenly from the forest appeared a large party of Indians. They seemed to come out of nowhere and quickly disarmed De Graffenried and Lawson, taking them as prisoners. Though the two men begged to be allowed to return downriver, in short order the baron, Lawson and the black slaves were forcibly marched away to Catchena, the main town of King Hancock of the Tuscaroras. Suddenly the late-summer days did not seem so promising.

❖ To some, he was the perfect fool. Christopher de Graffenried certainly seemed naive and trusting, the kind of person more worldly men often looked on as an easy mark. He was also snobbish, condescending, given to complaint, and said little good about anyone. Yet he was also brave, resolute, and possessed a keen sense of personal honor that he refused to compromise—all hallmarks of dreamers. And De Graffenried dreamed big. For a man who disliked people on an individual basis, he wanted to save the world, or at least a little part of it in North America. And if he could right his family fortunes while doing it, then all the better. But De Graffenried would soon learn how easily dreams could drown in eastern North Carolina.

Born on November 15, 1661, in the town of Worb, canton of Bern, Switzerland, De Graffenried was the son of Anton, Lord of Worb, a minor Swiss nobleman and government official. They could not be considered a wealthy family, but they were certainly not poor. Proficient in French, German, and English, De Graffenried attended the University of Heidelberg, but his professors saw him as a mediocre student. He caroused, fought a duel, got into trouble for it, and eventually left the university. He next enrolled at the University of Leyden in the Netherlands, where he studied law, history, and math, but he was still an average student. On graduation and hoping to make his own fortune, he struck out for London, where he believed he had a job as an aide to the Duke of Carlyle. In London, the job fell through and suddenly De Graffenried found himself in a foreign city with no money. He survived by hitting up his father for funds, but he also made some connections that would serve him well, such as with Christopher Monck, the Second Duke of Albemarle, and with Sir John Colleton, both of them Lords Proprietors of Carolina. In fact, the Duke of Albemarle pulled strings to get De Graffenried an honorary Master of Arts degree from Cambridge University. But master's degrees alone did not generate income. His father, tired of paying for his son's spendthrift ways, now pressured De Graffenried to come home. In 1683, the wastrel returned to Bern.[2]

He married Regina Tscharner of Worb in 1684 and in 1691 the couple had their first child, a son also named Christopher. A bequest from his mother helped the family financially and De Graffenried and Regina soon had more children. But the money did not last and the costs of supporting his family put him into heavy debt. In 1702 De Graffenried was elected as the governor of Yverdon in Neuchâtel province. He had expected to receive a hefty income, but the duties of governor came with great expenses. When his term ended in 1708, he found himself poorer than when he started. The family moved to Bern trailed by a gaggle of creditors. Desperate to find financial security, De Graffenried's mind turned back to London and his old friends the Duke of Albemarle and Sir John Colleton; the latter De Graffenried once called "my special friend."[3] Though both were long dead, De Graffenried had the outlines of a plan that might well interest the then current Lords Proprietors of North Carolina.

In his original idea, he planned to relocate Swiss paupers and religious dissidents to someplace in England's North American colonies. He would find a financial sponsor, maybe the Swiss government who wanted to be rid of undesirables, or someone in London who wanted to spur immigration to a certain colony. Then De Graffenried would set up the immigration and settlement, being paid so much per head and receiving generous tracts of land as well. It all seemed feasible. Chance encounters over the following few months would make it a reality.

In late 1708 or early 1709, De Graffenried traveled to London. There he was shocked to see refugees from the German Palatinate pouring into the English capital. The "poor Palatines" were Lutherans, along with a few Catholics, from the Palatinate region in present-day southwest Germany. A series of wars during the past century had left the Palatinate in bad shape. French armies had invaded as recently as May 1707. Destruction, famine, and higher taxes trailed the invasion, while the especially hard winter of 1708–9 only worsened Palatinate misery as now many starved. Wanting to help fellow Protestants in need, Queen Anne and the English government encouraged many poor Palatines to immigrate to England. Eventually thirteen thousand Palatines abandoned their homes in the Palatine and headed for London. The city soon teemed with German refugees, many camping out in parks and squares, and most fed at Queen Anne's expense. English authorities began tossing around the idea of relocating these refugees to America. Seeing this, De Graffenried believed his relocation idea would get a much better reception if he centered it on the "poor Palatines."[4]

At about this time, De Graffenried met Franz Ludwig "Louis" Michel, an adventurer who had made several trips to North America in the early 1700s, including to the Carolinas. Michel represented Georg Ritter and Company of Bern, which was already pursuing similar plans to relocate Swiss paupers and religious dissenters to North America. With De Graffenried's connections and Michel's backing of a stable Swiss company, it was natural they should join forces and so De Graffenried became a partner in the company. Up to this point, Georg Ritter and Company, founded by Georg Ritter, a Bern apothecary and member of Bern's city government, and Johan Rudolf Ochs, a stone engraver, had imagined Pennsylvania or Virginia as a place for relocation. But at some point, while De Graffenried was visiting the Lords Proprietors, he met John Lawson, the surveyor general of North Carolina. Back in 1701, Lawson had made a lengthy journey across the Carolinas and had written a book on his travels that included a natural history of the colony. Now he was in London to meet with the Proprietors and get his book, *A New Voyage to Carolina*, published, which served as very favorable propaganda for the struggling colony. Lawson gushed about the possibilities North Carolina offered. He convinced De Graffenried and Michel that North Carolina was the only place for their proposed settlement.[5]

The Lords Proprietors, wanting to spur settlement to a colony with plenty of land but few people, seemed receptive to the idea. So in April 1709, De Graffenried and Michel negotiated a very detailed contract with the Proprietors to create a colony in North Carolina for German Palatine refugees in England, Swiss paupers, as well as for Swiss Anabaptists, an offshoot sect of the Protestant Reformation that did not believe in the baptism of infants. In return, De Graffenried and Michel received land in North Carolina for them and their colony. De Graffenried said he received 15,000 acres at the confluence of the Neuse and Trent Rivers and 25,000 acres further south on the White Oak River. For these lands he was to pay £10 sterling per thousand acres, then after that an annual quitrent of six pence per hundred acres. De Graffenried said he paid £175 sterling cash up front. He also received a reserve of 100,000 acres at the place of his choice between the Neuse and Cape Fear Rivers at the same price of £10 sterling per thousand acres with twelve years to pay it in full. The Lords Proprietors also granted the company a thirty-year lease on all mines and minerals they found, split fifty-fifty between the company and the Proprietors for the first five years, then three-eighths for the company after that.[6]

In return, the Proprietors demanded that De Graffenried and Michel relocate a total of 650 Palatines to their Neuse River lands. Queen Anne would provide 20 shillings worth of clothes to each Palatine and pay De Graffenried and Michel £5 10s. for each migrant to cover transportation and the cost of setting them up in North Carolina. The Proprietors would order the North Carolina receiver general to have supplies ready for the Palatines when they arrived to get them settled on the Neuse. De Graffenried and Michel were to repay the cost of these provisions to the Proprietors at the end of two years. The Proprietors ordered Surveyor General Lawson, once he returned home, to begin immediately laying out the colony's lands on the Neuse River. Once the Palatines reached the Neuse, De Graffenried and Michel had three months to have 250-acre tracts ready for each Palatine family. These would be assigned by lots to the head of family, for whom it would be his and his heirs forever. For the first five years, the landowners would pay nothing, but after that, they should pay De Graffenried and Michel two pence per acre per year. The two men were supposed to provide whatever food, supplies, tools and utensils the Palatines needed, with the Palatines repaying these outlays at the end of three years. Incredibly, the Proprietors also instructed the two men that by the end of the settlers' fourth month after arrival, De Graffenried and Michel should supply each family with two cows, two calves, two sows with their litters, two lambs, a male and female of each. At the end of seven years, the Palatines were to pay De Graffenried and Michel the cost of this cattle and 50 percent of the increase from the original stock.[7] On paper, it looked like a paradise.

The Palatines in England certainly thought so and quickly signed up for a chance to receive a free farm in America with almost everything paid for. One could be a prosperous planter within months after arrival. All this thrilled the Bern city government, the original backer of the relocation idea. It had citizens it wanted to get rid of and was willing to pay forty-five thalers for every Mennonite or Anabaptist who went to North Carolina; it would also pay five hundred thalers for De Graffenried and Michel to take a hundred Swiss paupers off their hands.[8]

In truth, it was a fantasy and a dangerous one at that. The contract shows that neither the Proprietors nor De Graffenried had any sense of what North Carolina was really like or what the colonists would face. One wonders if Lawson saw the contract. Surely he could have set them straight about having unreal expectations. Or maybe Lawson actually imagined it the same way. He was in London, after all, to promote his book on North Carolina, which he believed was ripe for additional settlement.

Just as fanciful, the Lords Proprietors, as did De Graffenried, saw the Neuse River colony as a throwback to a medieval fiefdom. One of the perquisites King Charles II had given the original Proprietors was the right to set up a Carolina hereditary nobility, though the positions could not have the same name as those in England. So now the Proprietors named De Graffenried as a landgrave of Carolina, the peer equivalent of an English baron. For good measure, they also brevetted him as the English Baron of Benberg and a Knight of the Purple Ribbon, and issued him a medal and a set of crimson robes to wear on ceremonial occasions. But titles were cheap and De Graffenried soon realized that no money came with them. Still, as the new baron saw it, he would be their liege lord and his German and Swiss colonists would obey him, repay the money he laid out for them, and look to him as their leader. As their landgrave, he would settle their disputes, marry and baptize them, punish wrongdoers, and protect them. This last—protect them—De Graffenried took seriously. To solidify their relationship to the English, De Graffenried offered to have himself and his Swiss and Palatines convert to the Anglican Church. The Bishop of London agreed and asked the Society for the Propagation of the Gospel

to send a chaplain to the Neuse River who could read the Book of Common Prayer in High German. As De Graffenried would eventually learn, his colonists did not necessarily see themselves as his serfs nor bound to the land. Most expected to quickly become free landholders themselves.[9]

Still, De Graffenried felt confident. The only image we have of him, though some dispute it, may have come from this time. It shows a long-faced, long-nosed middle-aged man wearing a poofy, powdered wig parted in the middle. There appears an assured look to his eyes and a hint of a smile on his mouth, as if he was certain that all would be well. It was just a matter of crossing the Atlantic, docking at Virginia, and then making an overland trek south to the Neuse River at the far reaches of North Carolina. Then the dream would become reality. Not many realized that leaving England was just the beginning of a nightmare.

❖ De Graffenried soon calculated that he was already losing money on his Palatine relocation. The passage for each person to North Carolina cost £6 sterling, but Queen Anne only provided £5 10s. per person. Nevertheless, the baron possessed a definite vision for his colony and carefully chose which Palatines he would take, opting for younger men and women, the healthy, and people who appeared to be industrious. He tried to ensure that his colony would have the proper craftsmen and tradesmen it needed. They only lacked a minister of the Gospel, and De Graffenried received permission from the Bishop of London to serve as one. He selected equipment and tools with equal care. By January 1710, the Palatines were ready to leave. But then De Graffenried made a questionable decision. Instead of personally leading the Palatines to North Carolina, he sent them across the Atlantic without him, escorted by John Lawson and Christopher Gale returning home from London. De Graffenried would remain in the English capital to await the arrival of his Swiss settlers, then being escorted to London by Michel. De Graffenried, Michel, and this second group would head for North Carolina a few months later during the summer.[10]

In January 1710, the Palatines sailed from Gravesend, England, east of London, on the Thames River. It is unclear exactly how many settlers left in this first contingent, but it seemed close to the agreed-on 650. Neither are we sure how many ships it took to carry 650 settlers, their baggage, equipment, and food to tide them over during the trip, but probably several. At the docks, De Graffenried gave a rousing speech while a pastor from the Reformed Church of Gravesend preached a sermon. Then the ships cast off to be escorted part of the way by a squadron of English warships.[11]

Things quickly went sour for the Palatines. The crossing was particularly rough and storms kept the ships at sea for an unusual thirteen weeks. Seasickness, bad sanitation, rotten food, and close quarters took their toll. Ship fever, what sailors called "typhus," hit the Palatines and they died in extraordinary numbers, almost three or four a day. Morale plummeted. Then, just as they arrived at the Virginia coast, at the mouth of the James River, a French privateer attacked them. A British warship sat nearby but was undergoing repairs, so its crew looked on helplessly as the French plundered the Palatines. They took everything, the food and tools designated to get the colony started, all the Palatines' possessions, including their clothes. The Palatines finally limped into port at Hampton, Virginia, a sad, destitute group. A quick count showed that only about half of the 650 who began the journey were still alive. They spent several weeks recuperating in Virginia, but even then the dying did not stop.[12]

Still, the Palatines needed to get from Virginia to their lands down on the Neuse. After recovering as best they could, Lawson and Gale led them on an overland trek south through the Great Dismal Swamp to Thomas Pollock's plantation on the Chowan River. Pollock provided food and supplies for the poor Palatines, keeping carefully itemized accounts of what he supplied and how much it cost. He later billed these to De Graffenried. Eventually, Pollock arranged for several small boats to take the surviving Palatines to their lands on the Neuse River. In May 1710, Lawson deposited about three hundred Palatines on a tongue of land between the Neuse and Trent Rivers. And that was that and there they were. They had expected to see farms laid out and houses being built, but there was nothing. No farms, no houses, nothing except the nearby Neuse Indian town of Chattooka and a few amazed English settlers who called the region home. Destitute, with little food, some Palatines sold what few clothes they still owned to their new English neighbors. Lawson had done what he could and now returned to his official duties, leaving his charges to fend for themselves. So as the weather heated up, the Palatines awaited the arrival of De Graffenried. And while they waited, more died.[13]

Back in London De Graffenried waited on Michel and the 150 Swiss. One hundred of them were paupers, whose upkeep the city fathers of Bern saw as drain on the municipal treasury. The other fifty were Anabaptists, a religious sect closely associated with Mennonites, Hutterites, and the Amish, and so did not fit well with Swiss Calvinism. They had been held as prisoners until they could be transported to England. The Bern government was to pay Georg Ritter and Company 101 thalers for transporting the hundred paupers to North Carolina and 45 thalers for the fifty Anabaptists. De Graffenried calculated it cost £1 sterling per person to move the 150 Swiss and their baggage to England and then the usual £6 to North Carolina. Michel and 150 Swiss immigrants arrived in Rotterdam in April, where they waited eight weeks before they could get transport to England. During the time, Dutch authorities came to the rescue of the Anabaptists and allowed them to take political refuge in Holland. In June, the remaining one hundred Swiss made their way to Newcastle, England, met up with De Graffenried, and prepared for their voyage to North Carolina. On July 11, 1710, De Graffenried, Michel, and their Swiss colonists sailed from Newcastle, rendezvoused with a convoy on July 24, then headed across the Atlantic for Virginia.[14]

Unlike the Palatines before them, De Graffenried and the Swiss crossed fast and rather painlessly, with no reports of disease or death. They arrived in Hampton, Virginia, on September 11 and soon were trudging south to Pollock's plantation on the Chowan. This was a particularly tense time for De Graffenried to be entering North Carolina as Cary's Rebellion was just heating up. Whether De Graffenried realized it or not, he was now an important political player in North Carolina. As a landgrave, he was one of the colony's nobility, and the Proprietors insisted on him being a member of the Governor's Council. So Pollock, president of the Council and an enemy to Cary, tried to persuade De Graffenried to join his faction against Governor Cary. De Graffenried begged off getting involved, saying that as a newcomer to the colony he wanted to remain neutral right now. Besides, he needed to get his Swiss to the Neuse River and see how the Palatines had fared. So he purchased some additional supplies from Pollock on credit and in late September 1710, De Graffenried finally arrived at his colony on the Neuse.[15]

The condition of the Palatines shocked the baron and his Swiss immigrants. This could scarcely be called a settlement, but merely a huddled mass of destitute Germans. Many had died over the summer, but actual numbers are nonexistent. The baron blamed Lawson. As he saw it, Lawson should have surveyed and allotted the lands, laid out the town, and gotten the Palatines working their fields. Instead, he claimed Lawson put the settlers on unhealthy land nearer the Trent River than the more northerly Neuse River. This was unfair, as Lawson was not really part of the relocation, had few instructions on what the baron wanted, and if De Graffenried was truly concerned about getting the colony up and running, he should have come with the Palatines himself. Even worse for De Graffenried was that the Neuse Indian town of Chattooka, where King Taylor and about twenty Neuse Indian families lived, sat directly where he wanted to build his own town. Back in May, De Graffenried and George Ritter and Company had purchased 1,250 acres from Lawson at the confluence of the Neuse and Trent Rivers. The surveyor general assured them that no Indians lived there. Now De Graffenried saw with his own eyes that Indians actually did live on that land. They had not been bought out and if he wanted the land their town sat on, he would need to pay them for it. So De Graffenried paid King Taylor and his Neuse Indians for their land and they moved a little ways up the Neuse River. De Graffenried complained that he paid for the same land three times over: once to the Lords Proprietors, a second time to Lawson, and a third to King Taylor of Chattooka town.[16]

Now with clear title to the land, De Graffenried went to work to save his settlement. He called on Christopher Gale, the receiver general for North Carolina, for the supplies the Proprietors had ordered him to provide. But nothing came of this as Cary's Rebellion severely disrupted the workings of the colonial government. The baron returned to Thomas

Pollock and borrowed additional cash and supplies, amounting to £1,118 18s., possibly more. In a fateful move, he mortgaged ownership of all his lands on the Neuse River as collateral. Unwilling to see his settlement fail, he wrote to Virginia and Pennsylvania for supplies and spent £600 for Indian corn, £80 for wheat, £100 for salt, £250 for meat, then paid £100 to get it all shipped down to the Neuse. De Graffenried's efforts worked and before long these supplies, including lard and rum, were making their way down to the colony.[17]

De Graffenried and Lawson began to survey family lots for the settlers. They also laid out the town the baron called "New Bern," where Chattooka town once stood on that point of land where the Neuse and Trent Rivers flow together. Set up in a grid pattern, since it was on a peninsula, New Bern had town lots on both the Neuse and the Trent. Wanting spacious conditions, De Graffenried ordered three acre lots, enough room so a family could have a house, barn, garden, orchard, hemp field, and poultry yard. He built a proprietor's house, which doubled as a store, as well as a warehouse for provisions. He also brought in equipment for a grist and saw mill. Thinking ahead to their colony's participation in trade, Michel bought a brigantine, the *Return*, for £200. As De Graffenried saw it, the colony's craftsmen and tradesmen would live in New Bern. And the colony seemed well set with two carpenters and joiners, a mason, a locksmith, blacksmith, a couple of shoemakers, a tailor, miller, armorer, butcher, weaver, turner, saddler, glazier, potter, tile maker, a couple of millwrights, a physician, surgeon, and a schoolmaster. Bursting with pride at how things were turning out, De Graffenried boasted that New Bern would one day become the colony's capital. He was prophetically right. Outside the town, farmers would work their 250 acre plots. Soon these were laid out and stretched as far south as the White Oak River near present-day Pollocksville.[18]

Despite De Graffenried's positive spin, it was still touch and go for many more months. Metal tools, clothing, kettles, and goods for the Indian trade were in short supply. Costs were high when it came to purchasing livestock and supplies. Ticks and snakes bedeviled them. And none was used to the Carolina heat. Fever hit and more settlers died.[19] Anna Zant wrote home that her husband, Johannes Zant, "did not stand it but fell asleep in the blessed Lord. . . . My daughter Katherine also desired to go to the Lord."[20] Many Palatines even questioned De Graffenried's leadership. His condescending attitude did not help. He had little good to say about his German settlers. "I found them for the most part godless, rebellious people, among them murderers, thieves, adulterers, cursers, and swearers," he complained. "Whatever care and pains I bestowed to keep them in order, there helped neither strong warning, nor threat, nor punishment. God knows what I endured with them."[21]

By the spring of 1711, the colony seemed to have turned the corner. Much of this could be attributed to the indefatigable efforts of De Graffenried. He had spent £2,228 on provisions to save his colonists, purchasing cattle for them and building New Bern. Soon somewhere between 250 and 350 German and Swiss colonists were settling in. Houses had been built, farms were beginning to thrive, herd cattle were trickling in. Settlers with the last names of Kornegay, Koonce, Wolf, Mueller, Royal, Sheets, Rimer, Bissette, Rugsegger, Engel, Janssi, Wyssmer, and others spread over the land between the Neuse and White Oak Rivers. Things appeared to be moving in the right direction.[22] In April, Benedict Zionien wrote his family back in Switzerland that "I am well and healthy. . . . The quality of the country is sandy, but yet suitable for everything one plants."[23] Anna Wull saw profits to be made. She wrote home that if one "can get in Holland one hundred iron tobacco pipes, knives, iron pots, and copper kettles. He can make on them in America about three or four times the cost."[24] De Graffenried imagined establishing a Caribbean trade, with his colony supplying pork, corn, and indigo to Barbados and Jamaica at high prices.[25]

The baron had also successfully navigated his way through Cary's Rebellion, in full swing by May 1711. De Graffenried had met Edward Hyde back in Virginia and believed him the legitimate governor of North Carolina. Even then, the farthest De Graffenried would go in declaring sides was to have a strong letter sent to Cary and his supporters back in September 1710, urging that they accept Hyde as the new governor and turn over the reins of government to him. Pollock, who wanted Cary destroyed, reluctantly agreed and Cary initially accepted these terms. De Graffenried also claimed neutrality when a delegation of Quakers, and Cary supporters asked him to take over the colonial government. In the spring of 1711, Cary visited De Graffenried at New Bern. Over a bottle of wine, Cary promised £500 worth of cattle and provisions to help get the colony on its feet. He asked nothing in return, but De Graffenried believed his support of Cary was required. The baron refused to come out publicly in favor of Cary and the cattle and supplies never came.[26]

De Graffenried's neutrality could not last long. In June 1711, Governor Hyde demanded that De Graffenried, as a colonial landgrave, take his place on the Council and help find a way to end Cary's Rebellion. De Graffenried traveled to the Albemarle and was in council with Hyde at

Pollock's plantation on June 30 when Cary's brigantine attacked but was driven off. Later, arrested by Virginia's Governor Spotswood and sent to London, Cary successfully defended his actions before the Proprietors and was released. But Governor Hyde and Pollock had won. Cary's Rebellion was over. De Graffenried had tepidly backed the right side.[27]

The baron also congratulated himself for dealing smoothly with the local Indians. Indian culture fascinated him and he often visited King Taylor's Chattooka town to observe his neighbors firsthand. He admired how Indians gave gifts and looked out for the community. He also claimed to have witnessed a flame hovering over an Indian woman's grave and believed that Indians could call up the wind to help becalmed ships. But in truth, he found Indian life sadly lacking, almost humorous. If anything, he believed them helpless pawns of Satan.[28] Still, he was happy that King Taylor had so willingly relocated Chattooka. After the successful negotiations, King Taylor and seventeen of his principal men dressed in their finery finalized the agreement by meeting with De Graffenried in all his. The baron called the Indian dress "grotesque" and felt that King Taylor looked "more like an ape than a man." Still, the baron needed that land and so "made them several small presents of little value, and as purchase price for this land in question, I gave to the king two flasks of powder holding four pounds, a flask holding two pounds, and with that 1,000 coarse grains of buckshot; to each of the chiefs a flask of powder and 500 lead shots. After that I had them drink well on rum, brandy distilled of the settling of sugar, the ordinary liquor in this country, and the agreement was made."[29]

But even this did not end well. De Graffenried's partner, Louis Michel, had gotten drunk with some English neighbors who had come to observe the show. De Graffenried wrote that during the ceremony with King Taylor, a drunken Michel "took the head dress from the king and threw it as far as he could. He entered into the circle and taking by the arm one of their orators who spoke a little too much against our proceedings, he pulled him out of the circle giving him several blows." An appalled De Graffenried ordered Michel forcibly removed. An insulted and appalled King Taylor told De Graffenried that "if the Christians made peace and their alliances after that fashion, he did not want to have anything to do with them." The baron tried to soothe King Taylor's anger and promised nothing like this would happen again. "I would never do them injury so long as they were good neighbors with me." But that night after De Graffenried had gone to bed, Michel returned to the Indian camp and again beat the Indian speaker. King Taylor hurriedly summoned the baron. De Graffenried was amazed that the Indians had not beaten Michel to a pulp. The next day King Taylor again complained about this treatment and again De Graffenried swore things would be different. "I had them drink freely again and sent them away with the assurance that I would have this turbulent fellow sent away and that they would not be insulted any more." He quickly dispatched Michel to survey lands further south on the White Oak River.[30]

Insults did not stop there. Once when De Graffenried and one of his Swiss settlers visited Chattooka, the Switzer spied an Indian effigy—a post with a carved head "with a horrid face painted black and red." Those were the two colors of the flag of Bern in Switzerland. The colonist took this as an insult, grabbed his axe, and chopped the effigy in half. De Graffenried thought the incident funny, but admitted he could not approve of such behavior. King Taylor did not approve either and visited De Graffenried to complain about this insult. The baron tried to jolly him along, "that it was only the wicked idol, that there was not much harm done. . . . And that, in the future, orders would be given in order that no such thing could happen any more."[31] Still, De Graffenried seemed to have forgotten his own earlier observation about Indians: "They are enraged when angry, but, left to themselves in peace and quietness, they are benevolent and obliging after their own way. They seldom offend the Christians, who deal roughly with them."[32]

Nevertheless, by the summer of 1711, De Graffenried truly believed that he and his colonists had good relations with the Indians. But his sense of superiority made him overlook some clues to the contrary. That the Indian orator attacked by Michel spoke against selling the land at the confluence of the Neuse and Trent Rivers was telling. Other Indians certainly shared his sentiments. In fact, Michel may well have been insulting some of the most powerful Indians in the colony. The Tuscaroras had long been migrating down the Neuse River and by the 1690s Tuscarora villages dotted the river all the way to the coast. Though the English referred to them as the Neuse and Core Indians, these seemed actually to be Tuscarora towns that had moved down the Neuse River and to Core Sound, respectively. So King Taylor was a Tuscarora chief and Chattooka a Tuscarora town. Essentially, De Graffenried's three hundred settlers had invaded Tuscarora territory. And the baron's people were not the first, as English settlers had preceded them. In 1701, Furnifold Green took land near the Tuscarora town of Nonawharitsa, on the coast near present-day Oriental. William Hancock claimed land near the Tuscarora town of Haruta. These towns and others soon found themselves hemmed in by settlers and eventually forced to move.[33]

De Graffenried witnessed some of this anger in person. Wanting to make friends with the Indians and to assure them of his peaceful intentions, the baron visited a Core Indian town about twenty miles up the Neuse from Chattooka. He heard that two chiefs governed at Core Town, as it came to be called, one named Core Tom and the other Sam. Core Tom hated the English, while Sam seemed friendly and amenable. But on this visit, Sam was gone and now the baron found himself alone with Core Tom. He did not stay long as Core Tom was openly hostile and the baron's offer of friendship rebuffed.[34] Later, around the end of August 1711, De Graffenried, his valet, and some surveyors, while laying out lands, found themselves caught in the open when a storm rose up. The baron and his valet decided to head back to New Bern but became lost in the woods. Some Indians from Chattooka eventually found them and conducted the two men to their village. But De Graffenried's anxiety increased when he found Core Tom there in council with King Taylor. Core Tom glowered at the baron, and "I got off with a little fear." Nevertheless, King Taylor welcomed the two men, fed them, and gave them cider to drink and a place to sleep. Yet the baron complained that the Indians kept him awake all night with their singing and dancing. The next day, two Indians escorted him and his valet back to New Bern. As a thank-you, De Graffenried sent back two bottles of rum to King Taylor. "This was very well received as I have learned." This favor would serve De Graffenried well in the future.[35]

De Graffenried had been impressed with Core Town up the Neuse, just about a mile below the river's junction with Contentnea Creek. He found Core Town "very well situated" and the weather cooler there than down at New Bern. "If these Indians had wished to change places I should have liked very much to do so."[36] So by early September 1711, with his settlement improving, the baron's mind turned to additional lands up the Neuse. Up to this time, he had not gone any further upriver than Core Town. Now he wanted to see what lay beyond. And John Lawson was just the man to show it to him.

❖ Colonies seemed to attract enigmatic and intriguing characters and Lawson was just that. We know little about his early life and scholars dispute much of what we do know. He was born, it seems, in London around 1665. In February 1675, at the age of ten, he found himself apprenticed for eight years to John Chandler, an apothecary. But two years into it Chandler died and Lawson spent the remaining six years apprenticed to another apothecary, James Hayes. This training served him well in that he developed a curiosity about plants, herbs, and natural history. Somewhere along the way he also became rather skillful as an artist, which allowed him to accurately draw plants and animals. All this, along with his love of travel, made him an excellent explorer who could easily relate what he had seen. While we have no evidence that he attended Oxford or Cambridge, somewhere along the way he took to calling himself a "Gentleman."[37]

Around 1700, Lawson decided to see something more of the world. As he told the story, in 1700, on his way to Rome to witness the pope's jubilee, he met a man who told him stories about America. Intrigued, Lawson decided to go see for himself. On May 1, 1700, he took ship for the Americas where he was to collect plant specimens for the London apothecary James Petiver. His ship arrived soon after in New York, where he spent two weeks. He then sailed for Charles Town, South Carolina, and arrived there in August. In December, the Lords Proprietors tasked him with making a reconnaissance expedition through the Carolina Piedmont. This meshed perfectly with his search for apothecary plants. Lawson's fifty-nine-day, five hundred-fifty-mile journey gave him personal knowledge about the geography and peoples of the Carolinas. Throughout, he kept a journal and recorded his interactions with the many Indian peoples he met.[38]

Lawson left Charles Town on December 28, 1700. His party consisted of a spaniel dog, six other English travelers, and four Indian guides who changed out to other Indian peoples as they went along. They headed up the Santee-Wateree River in canoes, eventually gave them up, and then crossed into North Carolina just east of present-day Charlotte. From there Lawson jogged east to the Yadkin River and then north, crossed the Uwharrie Mountains and on to about present-day High Point. There he turned east toward the coastal plain and in March 1701 reached the plantation of Richard Smith on the Pamlico River, near present-day Washington. There he first laid eyes on Smith's daughter, Hannah. Eventually John and Hannah would fall in love and consummate a common-law marriage. They would have one daughter, Isabella.[39]

By necessity, Lawson's journey meant that he spent much time among Indians. Most of these were Siouan-speaking peoples of South Carolina and the North Carolina Piedmont, such as the Santees, Sewees, Waterees, Catawbas, Saponis, Eno-Shakories, and Keyauwees. After he turned east in North Carolina he started meeting Tuscaroras. Like De Graffenried, Lawson was fascinated by Indian culture. Also like De Graffenried, he often found it humorous and inferior. Still, he marveled at Indian hospitality and how well they fed him and his party no matter when they showed up. Indian religion intrigued him, especially the tales of a "great Deluge," their sense of right and wrong, and how Indian afterlife did not seem all that different from the Christian afterlife. He noted how Indians did not steal from each other but only from "foreigners," then complained when the Waterees pilfered small items from his baggage. He noted the Eno-Shakories' addiction to playing the game "chenco," in which a stone disk was rolled along the ground and bets placed on who could correctly guess where it would stop and throw a spear at that point. It amazed him how easygoing and stoic the Indians were, taking misfortune and disappointment in stride. How they did not accumulate wealth, but gave away much of what they had.[40]

Had Lawson taken closer note, he would have seen that all was not well in Indian country. He heard a story that the Sewees of South Carolina had become frustrated at the high prices English traders charged for goods. Thinking themselves cheated and imagining they could get a better price for their deerskins from the source of goods in England, they lashed together some canoes and set sail across the Atlantic. But a great storm blew up and drowned most of the Sewee sailors. Lawson found it funny that the Indians thought they could cross the Atlantic in canoes. But he overlooked how low prices for deer hides and high prices for European merchandise frustrated the Indians and made them attempt unusual strategies.[41] He commented on the "trading girls" he found among the Siouan villages. These specially selected young women, noted by the particular cut of their hair, bedded European visitors in exchange for gifts of merchandise for her and her family. Lawson thought it prostitution, but the trading girls were a rather recent institution among these Indians of the Carolina Piedmont. The trading girls stemmed from a mistaken idea European travelers had about Indian women. Lusty European visitors to Indian villages imagined all Indian women as highly sexual. Thinking this, European men, who would have never done such back home, often sexually assaulted respectable Indian wives and daughters. Indians were outraged by this, but beating or killing an Englishman could bring repercussions. So the trading girls" attempted to channel that European lust into a right and more profitable direction.[42] He also noticed that Seneca war parties from western New York were making powerful raids on the Piedmont peoples, killing and capturing many and forcing them to move their towns in search of safer areas.[43] He saw Virginia traders, with long horse caravans full of European merchandise, openly trading in North Carolina territory and directing Indian deerskins away from Carolina and up to Virginia.[44]

Once his journey ended in March 1701, Lawson remained in North Carolina and became a staunch supporter of the colony. He became one of the first settlers along the lower Neuse River, built a house about half a mile from Chattooka, and eventually owned 640 acres at the confluence of the Neuse and Trent Rivers. He considered himself a Proprietary man, became a friend of Thomas Pollock, and received his first colonial government position as the colony's deputy surveyor. He acquired land north of the Pamlico River and as deputy surveyor played an instrumental role in the founding of Bath in March 1706, the first town in North Carolina. In 1707–8, Lawson served as clerk of the court and public register for Pamlico (Beaufort) Precinct in Bath County, and in April 1708, he became surveyor general of North Carolina. In 1709, the Proprietors appointed him as one of the North Carolina commissioners to meet with Virginia authorities to settle the boundary between the two colonies. That would not happen in Lawson's lifetime.[45]

While in North Carolina, Lawson continued writing about the colony's flora and fauna, Indians, and natural history. Besides the journal of his 1701 expedition, he also penned several short pieces: *A Description of North Carolina*, *The Present State of North Carolina*, *The Natural History of North Carolina*, and *An Account of the Indians of North Carolina*. In all of these he portrayed North Carolina in glowing terms and played up the favorable climate, the good land, the possibilities of trade, and the friendly Indians. "Husbandmen living almost void of care, and free from those fatigues which are absolutely requisite in winter countries."[46] Life here was so good that settlers came for "profit and pleasure."[47] The settlers enjoy "large and spacious rivers, pleasant savannas, and fine meadows" and produce great harvests of corn, but also "beef, pork, tallow, hides, deer-skins, and furs; for these commodities the New England Men and Bermudians visited Carolina in their barks and sloops and carry'd out what they made, bringing them, in exchange, rum, sugar, salt, molasses, and some wearing apparel."[48] As for land, there was plenty up the navigable rivers and creeks. Life was sweet and easy in North Carolina as Lawson described it, just short of Eden. The Lords Proprietors surely appreciated Lawson's propaganda.[49]

On January 6, 1708, Lawson, Lyonell Reading, Richard Dereham, Christopher Gale, and De Graffenried's future friend Louis Michel all took passage for London to meet with the Lords Proprietors. They planned to explain to the Proprietors why settlement lagged in the colony. Additionally, Lawson hoped to get his writings published. This he quickly arranged and later that year John Stevens of London published *A New Voyage to Carolina*. His meetings with the Proprietors went well.

At a meeting at Craven House in August 1709, the Proprietors gave him £20 to make maps of North and South Carolina. While there, he and Michel met Christopher De Graffenried, sold him some land on the Neuse River, and concocted the plan for the Neuse River colony.[50] In January 1710, Lawson and Gale escorted De Graffenried's 650 Palatine colonists to North Carolina.

Back at the Neuse River, Lawson realized he had made a mistake. In the land he sold De Graffenried in London, he had inadvertently included the tract where Chattooka town sat. He knew King Taylor was not happy about this mistake, but Lawson believed he had a good rapport with Taylor and the local Indians. He once had a Neuse Indian roommate at his house on the Neuse River and had helped build a coffin for a Tuscarora killed by lightning. He truly believed the Indians actually liked the English and would not mind working for them. He even advocated that lower-class English settlers marry Indians. It would encourage Indian children to become apprentices, bring Indians into civil society and government, and make them become Christians and give up their "savage" ways. On the other hand, the English would learn the Indian language, but also acquire Indian skills in medicine and surgery, which Lawson felt superior to that of Europeans. It would also bolster the English colony against their French and Spanish enemies.[51]

But Lawson was gaining a bad reputation among the Indians as a land taker. As a surveyor, he was a visible sign of Indian land loss, as surveyor's chains always meant more settlers and less Indian land. They accused Lawson of using alcohol or shifty trade practices to get Indians to do what he wanted. And then he brought the three hundred or so Palatines to the Neuse and deposited them on lands claimed by the Tuscaroras. Indian anger at Lawson simmered that summer of 1711.[52] He might have heeded his own words when he wrote that the Indians "are really better to us, than we are to them; they always give us victuals at their quarters, and take care we are arm'd against hunger and thirst. We do not so by them (generally speaking) but let them walk by our doors hungry, and do not often relieve them. We look upon them with scorn and disdain, and think them little better than beasts in human shape. . . . We reckon them slaves in comparison to us, and intruders as oft as they enter our houses, or hunt near our dwellings."[53] However, he warned that Indians fought not for the nation's interest but to take revenge and would take the war to the enemy that injured them until they had destroyed the enemy or "make them that satisfaction which they demand." And Indians "never forget an Injury done, till they have receiv'd satisfaction."[54]

Once De Graffenried arrived with his Swiss settlers and saw his settlement's chaos, he blamed Lawson. He fumed that Lawson cheated him on the land, making him pay for it several times over. He felt the Indians and Chattooka town should not be on that point of land and that Lawson had dropped his responsibilities on getting rid of them. The baron also believed the surveyor general should have had the entire colony and town laid out before he arrived.[55] Relations were strained between Lawson and the baron. But they both needed each other. Lawson needed De Graffenried as a client who would be purchasing even more land from him, so he could not afford to anger the baron too much. And De Graffenried needed Lawson to help lay out his colony, survey the lands, and deal with the local Indians. So it was in both De Graffenried's and Lawson's interest when they decided to take a trip up the Neuse River in September 1711.

❖ Lawson had been wanting to go upriver for a while and hoped to persuade De Graffenried to come along with him. It seemed a good time to make a river trip. The second week of September meant summer was fading, the days getting shorter, nights cooler. Lawson promised they would find sweet, wild grapes upriver, and it would be a good chance to check out the upcountry. But De Graffenried refused at first.[56]

He worried about Indians. Maybe he had heard something. Maybe he just had a bad feeling that things were not right. Lawson assured him that there was no danger up the Neuse. The Tuscarora lived along Contentnea Creek, not the upper Neuse. Besides, they would bring a couple of Indian guides to smooth things over if they encountered any. Then the surveyor general dangled more inducements. The Neuse had low water and a slow current right now as there had not been rains in a while. This would give them a chance to see just exactly how far they could navigate the river by boat. Lawson then laid down his trump card. The trip would also let them search out a place to lay a new road to Virginia. These last two reasons show that this was not to be just some innocent excursion up the river to eat wild grapes. It was the first step in a land grab and the extension of settlement up the Neuse River. A road from the wilds of the Neuse River to Virginia meant nothing if no one lived there. But it would become very important if settlers moved upriver. Same with wanting to find out how far the Neuse was navigable. There was no need to know unless settlers planned to put farms and plantations up there. De Graffenried had long eyed lands up the Neuse and lusted for Core Town. So had Thomas Pollock and Governor Edward Hyde. And if these men showed interest in lands up the river, then Lawson was certainly interested as well.[57]

De Graffenried gave in. They planned a two-week trip, mainly by boat, but horses would be brought along as well. They took two black slaves to row the boat and two Indian guides to scout the riverbanks. The baron felt comfortable with the two Indians as "one of the savages knew English, and we thought, as we had those two Indians with us, we had nothing to fear from the others."[58] They also invited their old friend Christopher Gale to come with them. Gale initially agreed to go. But he received a message that his wife and brother were very sick and wanted him to come home to Bath. So Gale excused himself and headed for the Pamlico River. He later called this a "happy sickness."[59]

So on about September 9, 1711, De Graffenried, Lawson, the two black slaves, and two Indian guides, along with two horses, shoved off in a large canoe or periauger. One of the horses apparently rode in the boat, while one of the Indian guides rode the other along the riverbank. Lawson and De Graffenried adjusted their wigs and the party sailed up the Neuse, passing the newly relocated Chattooka town. At some point they sailed by Core Town on the south bank of the Neuse, passed the river's junction with Contentnea Creek, and continued left up the Neuse. At night, they camped on the water's edge. It had been a pleasant two days on the river.[60]

They started again on the third morning, but had not gone far before Lawson decided he wanted to scout the woods for a good place to lay the road to Virginia. He asked De Graffenried for the use of his two horses. The baron refused. As De Graffenried explained, one of the Indian guides was using one to scout up the riverbank ahead of the boat and he did not want to lose track of his other. Lawson pleaded and De Graffenried gave in. But unknown to them, events were moving quickly a few miles away to the north.[61]

While De Graffenried and Lawson made their way upriver that morning, the Indian scout on the horse had crossed to the north side of the Neuse and ridden toward Contentnea Creek, eventually ending up at the large Tuscarora town of Catechna, near present-day Grifton. This was King Hancock's town, about six miles up the creek from its confluence with the Neuse. De Graffenried later wondered whether the scout's appearance at Catechna was deliberate treachery or just an unhappy circumstance. Whatever the reason, the Tuscaroras were surprised to see an Indian on a horse. Indians in North Carolina did not much use horses, so seeing one was unusual. They asked the scout about it. He told what he knew, that two Englishmen and their slaves were at that moment sailing up the Neuse while he scouted the forest. The Tuscaroras may not have fully understood who the baron was, but they certainly had to know

Lawson. This alarmed Hancock and the Tuscaroras. Word spread and soon warriors poured in from the farms around Catechna. Two Englishmen, one of them the surveyor general of North Carolina, had sailed into Tuscarora territory and deliberately not called upon King Hancock at Catechna. Another insult suffered at the hands of the insolent English, and hostile diplomacy as well. Long suspicious of English motives, King Hancock and his warriors could easily see this as the first step toward a land grab in the heart of Tuscarora country. The Tuscaroras confiscated the horse and King Hancock told the Indian guide to go back to the boat and order the Englishmen not to proceed any further upriver.[62]

Lawson apparently made his road reconnaissance and returned to the boat. The party continued upriver and in the late afternoon, they heard a shot in the woods. The men took this as a signal from their Indian scout telling them to halt. The boat fired an answering shot and the scout soon appeared. He gave Lawson and De Graffenried the order from King Hancock that they should halt and go no further. As it was late, the men decided to make camp at some springs just a little further upriver, about twelve miles up the Neuse from its confluence with Contentnea Creek. When they got to the springs, they found two Indians there, both armed. This worried De Graffenried and he now suggested they return down the Neuse. Lawson laughed at him. "We had hardly turned our back, when things began to look serious, laughter, in a twinkle, expired on his lips," De Graffenried recalled.[63] Suddenly, sixty Tuscarora warriors stepped out of the bushes. Others came swimming across the Neuse. Before they could do anything, Lawson and De Graffenried found themselves in the hands of the Indians.[64]

The situation looked grim and the two men tried to talk their way out of it. They asked to be able to stay here at the springs for the night, with an Indian guard if the Tuscaroras so desired. Then the next morning they would return downriver, pay their respects to King Hancock, and ask for permission to travel through Tuscarora territory. But the warriors mistook De Graffenried for Governor Edward Hyde. They believed they had taken a great prize. So instead of releasing De Graffenried and Lawson, the warriors swarmed the boat, confiscated the baggage and supplies, and in minutes De Graffenried, Lawson, and the two slaves found themselves hustled across country. De Graffenried remembered that "we were compelled to run with them all night through the woods, across thickets and swamps, till we arrived at about 3 o'clock in the morning at Catechna or Hencocks-Towne, (that is to say: the village of Hencock), where the king, called Hencock, was sitting in state, with his council, on a kind of scaffold."[65] The situation had turned most serious.

CHAPTER TWO

King Hancock and Core Tom

The Defenders

Once De Graffenried, Lawson, and their two slaves appeared before him, King Hancock of Catechna town found himself caught in his own bad situation. He had sent his warriors only to turn them back, prevent them from venturing further into Tuscarora territory. He had no intention of taking the men captive. But the war party overstepped its orders. Thinking they had Governor Hyde in their grasp, they brought the captives back to Hancock. But the four scared men standing before Hancock exposed a serious fissure in Tuscarora politics and King Hancock knew it. He was being challenged by his young men, the warriors of Catechna and its outlying farms. The decisions King Hancock would make over the next few days had far-reaching consequences both for the Tuscaroras and for the English, Germans, and Swiss living along the Pamlico and Neuse Rivers.

❖ Some said their name meant "Hemp Gatherers." Others said "Shirt Wearers." But they called themselves Unkwa-hunwa, meaning "the Real People."[1] The Europeans in North Carolina just called them Tuscaroras and spelled it a variety of ways. Nevertheless, they were *the* Indian power in eastern North Carolina, the largest and strongest of all east of the North Carolina Appalachians and a force to be reckoned with.

The Tuscaroras were an Iroquoian people, speaking an Iroquoian dialect, and were originally from the area south of the Great Lakes in present-day New York. Around A.D. 500 they began migrating out. Tuscarora oral tradition says that Tarenhiawagen—the Master of Life and Ruler of Skyland—led the Tuscaroras west to the Mississippi River where they split, some going west across the river and some remaining east. Tarenhiawagen then took those Tuscaroras east of the Mississippi, taught them to use the bow and arrow, and led them to the Neuse River, which they called the Cautanoh, sounding very similar to "Catechna." Thinking themselves favored by Tarenhiawagen made them believe they were superior to the other peoples they encountered in the region. Certainly by A.D. 600, they had firmly settled themselves in villages atop the sandy ridges along the waterways of east-central North Carolina.[2]

Their coming to North Carolina was not without consequence to the Indian peoples already living there. As the Tuscaroras settled along the fall line, they formed a wedge, pushing the Algonquian peoples further east and the Siouan peoples further west. By 1600, the Tuscaroras were the southernmost Iroquoian people and the tip of an Iroquoian arrow pointed at the heart of North Carolina. Behind them lived other Iroquoian peoples: the Meherrins and Nottoways of Virginia, the Susquehannas of Maryland and Pennsylvania, all the way up to their original kinfolk in New York, who by this time had arranged themselves into the five-nation League of the Iroquois, which included, from west to east, the Senecas, Cayugas, Onondagas, Oneidas, and Mohawks.[3]

Like so many Indian peoples who farmed to put food in their bellies, the Tuscaroras were a matrilineal people, meaning a child was born into his or her mother's clan and children traced their kinship through their mother and her family. A person never changed clan and all members of the same clan considered themselves kinfolk, so one chose a marriage partner from a different clan. When they married, men left the homes of their parents and moved into the homes of their wives. There were at least six Tuscarora clans: Turtle, Beaver, Deer, Wolf, Bear, and Snipe. From the moments of its birth, a Tuscarora child found itself wrapped in the folds of an *ohwatcira*, an extended family from which one received love, protection, and assistance. But one owed these same obligations to the other kinfolk of the *ohwatcira* and clan. So the giving of gifts and kindnesses played an essential role in Tuscarora society, and in the societies of all North Carolina Indians.[4]

In North Carolina, the Tuscaroras and their Indian neighbors thrived through hunting, fishing, and farming. This meant that Indian peoples needed and utilized large expanses of land to provide for their families, maybe even hundreds of square miles. To limit access to these lands, something the coming of the English to North Carolina did, could threaten the very survival of the people. Indians hunted mainly in the fall and early winter, with white-tailed deer their main prey, though they took bear and smaller animals as well. During these cold months, men, women, and children left their main town and moved to hunting quarters miles away where they set up a temporary village. Older men and women remained behind to maintain the permanent town. One of the most common methods used during the hunt was to burn the woods. Fire drove the deer and other animals onto necks of land or into corrals where they became trapped and so made it easy for Indian hunters to take them. Burning the woods also cleared out the tangled undergrowth, giving the forest a parklike appearance and making travel easier. New grass attracted deer and so gave hunters another advantage. In other instances, men might go out alone or in twos or threes and stalk deer. Dogs might be used to run a deer until it became exhausted. Other times the hunters actually wore disguises complete with antlers and a flap that showed the deer's distinctive white mark on its chest. Some disguises were so good that hunters could even get among a deer herd and not spook them. Of course, there was always a danger to disguising oneself as accidental shootings by other hunters were not uncommon.[5]

During these winter hunts, the Tuscarora town came away with hundreds, if not thousands of pounds of meat. Women sliced much of this into thin strips, dried them on racks over a low fire, and cured the meat into jerky, which could last months. Animal skins proved another important by-product of the hunts. Once the deer was killed, women skinned it, soaked the hide in water, then carefully scraped off the hair using a deer hoof, seashells, or a metal knife acquired from the English. Then they worked the brains of the deer into the skin, making it soft and supple. Once cleaned and dried, the hides were turned by the women into breech cloths, shirts, skirts, moccasins, leggings, bedding, cordage, and just about anything for which leather might be used. So while men hunted, women spent much of their day tanning deer hides, making clothes, weaving baskets and mats, or creating utensils. As the English settled in North Carolina, they also saw the value of deerskins. A demand for them certainly existed back in Europe. Demand stimulated supply and by the late 1600s, Tuscaroras and their Indian neighbors found themselves hunting ever more deer and bears for their skins, which they exchanged with English traders for metal goods, guns, ammunition, beads, rum, kettles, and whatnot. So deer not only provided food, but by 1711 they also provided the means by which Indians received manufactured goods, which were already becoming necessities in their families.[6]

The watery North Carolina environment also fed Indian peoples. They took water birds such as ducks, geese, and teal. As for fish, the Algonquian and Tuscarora peoples along the coast, bays, and sounds were expert fishers, paddling dugout canoes and using nets, spears, arrows, and weirs to take huge quantities of fish. They ate large quantities of shellfish and left giant mounds of discarded shells at Harkers Island and Core Point. The Tuscaroras had an affinity for freshwater sturgeon and the herring that ran up North Carolina rivers. They also enjoyed turtle meat and visited an island in the Neuse River that had so many they called it Roquist Island, meaning "Turtle Island." Before they went on their autumn hunts, Tuscaroras and other Indians further inland headed to the coast, following well-worn trails down to the fishing beaches, where they used seines to catch fish. What fish they did not eat or keep for themselves, they salted, smoked over a fire, and then carried back to more westerly Piedmont Indians to exchange for corn and other foods. This fish-for-corn trade became especially important when drought scorched Tuscaroras crops.[7]

And crops, the huge fields of corn, beans, and squash, were really what fed Tuscarora villages. Farming was the domain of women and so women worked and controlled these fields, which gave them a tremendous amount of social clout. That explains why men left their own families and moved into their wives' homes, as it would have been foolish to break up that gang of mothers, sisters, and daughters who harvested tons of corn each year. Even then, women still went out into the forest to gather hickory nuts, berries, seeds, wild parsnips, wild turnips, and such. Gathering served as an important addition to Indian food supplies, especially when crops failed. In the woods, women also collected firewood, cut cane for making baskets, gathered silk grass that could be woven into a sort of cloth, and bloodroot used as a hair dye. So men hunted and fished, both important contributions, but calorie per calorie, it was the women who fed the Tuscaroras.[8]

Using slash-and-burn agriculture, Indians cut their fields from the forest, used them for years until the nutrients gave out, and then moved to new areas where fresh fields could be cleared. Again, this meant that Tuscaroras and other North Carolina Indians always needed access to fresh lands for survival. Women planted huge fields of corn, beans, and squash and throughout the growing season watered and weeded the plants and scared off animals that might feed on them. North Carolina Indians got two crops of corn a season. They planted the first in March or April, after the last frost, then harvested it in early June. They planted the second crop in June and harvested in early September. So in good, well-watered years, the Tuscaroras might harvest tons of crops, then supplemented this with women's forest gathering and men's hunting.[9]

Besides the big, communal village fields that might take up hundreds if not thousands of acres, each Tuscarora house had its own garden nearby tended by the women. Usually about one hundred feet by two hundred feet, the personal gardens furnished food for the house until the village fields could be harvested. North Carolina Indians produced three types of corn, often of various colors, such as red, yellow, white, and blue, which Europeans called "Indian corn." They also grew several varieties of beans, with kidney beans and lima beans the most common. Ground covers included squash, pumpkins, and gourds, though Indians rapidly took to growing watermelons once Europeans introduced them. Sweet potatoes, or yams, might also have been grown. Tobacco served as an important crop. Indian tobacco, *Nicotiana rustica*, was harsher than the *Nicotiana tobacum* cultivated by the settlers in Virginia and favored by Europeans. Nevertheless, Tuscaroras and other North Carolina Indians, both men and women, were avid tobacco smokers. They made pipes from stone or clay, which held about an ounce of tobacco. Tobacco smoking was common in rituals and ceremonies, but Indians also smoked for recreation and relaxation. An Indian at rest usually had a tobacco pipe in his mouth and a puff of smoke curling over his head.[10]

By 1700, the Tuscaroras lived in fifteen or so towns stretching in an arc from the Roanoke River in the north, down across the Tar-Pamlico River, south to Contentnea Creek and the upper reaches of the Neuse. Tuscarora towns also stretched all the way down the Neuse River to the coast as the Neuse, Cores, Weetocks, and Bear River Indians seem to have been Tuscarora peoples and the towns merely misnamed by the English. Each village, with its outlying farms, may have contained anywhere from a few score to five hundred people, maybe more in some. Language, culture, religion, clans, and history identified them as Tuscaroras, but they were not necessarily united politically. The English called them a "nation," though a single political leader did not govern all the Tuscaroras, and this often baffled the English. No Tuscaroras thought of themselves as members of a "tribe." Nor were they a confederacy or a league, the way the Five Nations in New York had created their League of the Iroquois. In North Carolina, the town served as the basic Tuscarora political unit. In 1709, John Lawson listed them, in no particular order and without providing locations, as Haruta, Waqui, Con-tah-nah, Anna Ooka, Conault-Kare-Harooka, Una Nauhan, Kentanuska, Chunangets, Kenta, Eno, Naur-hegh-ne, Oonossoora, Tosneoc, Nonawharitse, and Nursoorooka. Yet every Englishman pronounced or spelled these names as he saw fit and few the same way. Similarly, we have firm geographical locations for only a few. For example, Lawson's town of Waqui was usually called Tasqui or Tasky and sat on the Roanoke River. His town of Con-tah-nah was King Hancock's town of Catechna on Contentnea Creek.[11]

Governed by a leader called a *teethha*, every Tuscarora town was politically autonomous, independent, could make its own diplomacy, and make or break alliances as it saw fit. The *teethha* did not so much make village policy as coordinate those policies made by the village council. He rarely made a decision without first consulting this council, usually men who were or had been great warriors or men known for their clear thinking and success. And in these councils, achieving consensus was important. As for the *teethha*, whom the English often referred to as a "king," he usually inherited the position from his mother's brother and passed it to his sister's son as the rules of matrilineality prescribed. Nevertheless, the *teethha* needed to be a man of ability in his own right.[12]

Yet a closer look at the Tuscarora towns and where they sat reveals some important natural divisions and diverging interests that came to light during the war. First off, the Tuscaroras were geographically divided into three regions as their towns lay along three major east-west rivers and their tributaries. In the north, towns sat along both sides of the Roanoke River, not far from present-day Williamston. Here one found the towns of Tasqui, Resootka, Ooneroy, and others. As the northernmost Tuscarora towns, they sat closest to English settlers on the Albemarle. However, since at this time English settlement moved south rather than west, these Tuscaroras were not yet being pressed by colonists. And being so close to Virginia, these towns received regular visits from Virginia traders with whom they exchanged deerskins for guns, ammunition, and other merchandise. These towns were also closest to their ancient enemies, such as the Chowans, Yeopims, and various Algonquian peoples, as well as the once-feared Pamunkey raiders coming out of Virginia. Because of this, the Roanoke River towns clustered closer together and built palisades around each town for defense. Few outlying farms surrounded these towns and towns often hunted in the same forests. Diplomatically, they were oriented toward the north and tended to look for allies among the Nottoways and Meherrins, even the Chowan and Yeopim when needed.[13]

Twenty-five miles to the southwest on the Tar River, not far from present-day Greenville, sat the middle branch of Tuscaroras. Here lay the town of Ucohnerunt, which King Tom Blount governed in 1711. Not far away sat other towns, such as Nonawharitsa downriver, while Toisnot, the most westerly of Tuscarora towns, sat on Toisnet Creek near present-day Wilson. There were others, but we are unclear on which. However, the Tuscarora villages along the Tar-Pamlico and the Roanoke tended to ally politically.[14]

Twenty miles south-southwest from Ucohnerunt lay the largest concentration of Tuscarora villages along Contentnea Creek and its tributaries. Each town sat on hills or ridges overlooking water. Six miles up from its confluence with the Neuse River sat King Hancock's town of Catechna, where Lawson and De Graffenried had been brought as prisoners. Up the Creek in succession sat Caunookehoe, Innennits, Neoheroka, Kenta, and Torhunta. Unlike the Roanoke River towns, the Contentnea Creek towns spread far along the creek with numerous farms and hamlets in between. Outlying fields brought in tons of corn every season, while the generous spacing between towns meant that hunters rarely competed over the same tract of forest. Prior to 1711, few of these towns erected palisades as they seemed to sit far from enemies, though Siouan slave raiders out of South Carolina sometimes targeted them. In fact, these might really be towns in name only, having only a few buildings and a central plaza. Most people lived outside the town among the many farms dotting the area. As the southernmost Tuscarora towns, they did not get many visits from Virginia traders, making them rely on the Roanoke River Tuscaroras and other Indians for manufactured goods or on the settlers down on the Neuse and Trent Rivers. Diplomatically, they tended to look for allies among the Machapungas, Pamlicos, and the offshoot Tuscarora towns of the Cores, Neuse, Weetocks, and Bear River Indians.[15]

Exactly how many Tuscaroras there were in 1711 has been open for debate as firm numbers are impossible to come by. John Lawson said the fifteen towns could produce twelve hundred warriors, making the total population just under five thousand.[16] More recent estimates put the Tuscarora population at about eight thousand.[17] Whatever the number, it was far less than it had been before 1696, when a terrible smallpox epidemic swept across the American Southeast, killing thousands upon thousands of Indian people. Smallpox hit the Tuscaroras hard, killing a thousand or two. And smallpox seemed to return every few years killing off more. Disease affected all Indians in North Carolina as it returned year after year and their numbers dropped precipitously. In all, there were probably less than ten thousand Indian men, women, and children in eastern North Carolina in 1711. As former governor John Archdale saw it, "the hand of God was eminently seen in thinning the Indians to make room for the English."[18]

Though each Tuscarora town was politically and diplomatically independent, they could join in alliance and become a formidable adversary. All Indians in eastern North Carolina, as well as the English, feared provoking the Tuscaroras. As De Graffenried himself pointed out, "what I observed worst in them is their strong anger, which generally becomes wrath."[19] Almost every Indian people in North Carolina and the surrounding colonies had at one time watched in horror as a party of Tuscarora warriors carrying war clubs, bows made of black locust, and arrows of arrowwood came rushing out of the woods at them. Revenge was the most common reason for Tuscarora war. As Governor Archdale once said, they make "personal murders oftentimes national quarrels," even down to the third or fourth generation.[20] But political and economic reasons could also play a role.

Still, going to war was an important decision for a Tuscarora town. The council and older men debated it while the priests implored their deities for help and guidance. Feasts were given and dances held. New songs composed. War captains selected. Strategy and tactics worked out. Warriors underwent purification rituals, while women helped dress and paint them. Tuscarora men normally painted their face red with a white circle around one eye and a black one around the other. Then they applied dots or stripes as their individual taste dictated or how a spirit guardian told them. All this helped add a dose of terror among their enemies while making it hard for individuals to be identified. War parties usually consisted of between six and thirty warriors. And depending on the size and nature of the conflict, there might be several war parties in action at a time. Tuscarora warriors were hard men, great walkers, and large war parties often separated, traveled long distances by different routes, then reformed again on time several hundred miles away. On the attack, they usually moved through the woods in a half-moon formation, which allowed them to envelope the enemy. But surprise and ambush were the preferred methods of attack, while going up against a fortified position was considered foolhardy and avoided if possible.[21]

A successful attack meant that enemies were killed, houses and villages plundered, and captives brought home. Lawson said that a warrior who returned with a captive was "the proudest Creature on Earth, and sets such a value on himself, that he knows not how to contain himself in his senses."[22] Tuscarora families adopted some captives, especially women and children but some men as well, particularly those who had lost family members to war, disease, or mishap. They designated others to be tortured to death; in that way vengeance was taken, harmony restored, and the spirit of those Tuscaroras killed could be at peace. The tortures could be horrific. Lawson himself witnessed one. "He that is appointed to be the chief Executioner, takes a knife, and bids him [the victim] hold out his hands, which he does, and then cuts round the wrist through the skin, which is drawn off like a glove and flead [flayed] quite off at the fingers ends; then they break his joints and bones, and buffet and torment him after a very inhuman manner, till some violent blow perhaps ends his days, then they burn him to ashes, and throw them down the river. Afterwards they eat, drink and are merry."[23]

Over the centuries, the Tuscaroras battled not only their immediate neighbors in North Carolina but also the Cherokees out west in the mountains, the Creeks down in Alabama, Powhatan's chiefdom in Virginia, and especially the many Siouan peoples of the North Carolina Piedmont and South Carolina, such as the Occaneechis, Enos, Catawbas, Waterees, Cape Fears, and many others. So large and powerful had the Tuscaroras become that by 1700 most North Carolina Indians spoke Tuscarora, as the language had become the Indian lingua franca of the region.[24]

Early on, the Tuscaroras delighted in a visit by an English trader or settler to one of their towns as the English brought things the Tuscaroras wanted. Indians possessed no metal goods, nothing manufactured, nor any mills or forges to make such things. At their very first meeting with the English back in 1584 on Roanoke Island, the Indians marveled at the items the English brought and wanted them. Commonplace things of little value to the English, such as a tin plate, held great spiritual value to the Indians.[25] But Indians quickly realized the utilitarian value of these goods. Firearms, shots, and gunpowder, as well as metal knives, tomahawks, axes, and barrel hoops that could be cut into arrowheads made them better hunters and more formidable warriors. And if their enemies possessed guns, then they needed them as well. Hospitality deepened as metal kettles, much stronger than pottery jars, could sit directly on a fire, meaning food simmered throughout the day, ready for any visitor who stopped by the longhouse. Women took metal needles and glass beads, and soon beaded shirts and moccasins became works of art. But Indians could be choosy buyers. They realized that Europeans traders needed the deer hides they produced as much as they wanted the goods the traders brought. Over the years, this exchange relationship deepened. By the mid-1600s, Virginia and South Carolina traders regularly made their way to North Carolina Indian towns, leading long horse caravans loaded with guns, lead, powder, pots, mirrors, beads, glass jars and bottles, needles, tobacco pipes, brightly colored cloth, shirts, pants, and skirts.[26]

While British traders served their purpose, the Tuscaroras and other Indians of North Carolina also existed as part of a web of trade networks that stretched in all directions. Indians also served as traders, moving these same goods across the region. The Great Trading Path ran south from around present-day Petersburg, Virginia, into North Carolina and skirted west of Tuscarora territory down to about present-day Charlotte, North Carolina, and then on to Augusta, Georgia. Senecas, Nottoways, and Meherrins from north channeled goods to Roanoke River Tuscaroras who in turn moved them to the Contentnea Creek Tuscaroras, Cores, and others. And the Contentnea Creek Tuscaroras continued the exchanges to Indians in the Piedmont and further south. It is even possible that Spanish goods from Florida and French goods from Louisiana or Canada made a roundabout appearance among North Carolina Indians. And raids on Indians and European settlers also proved a source of merchandise.[27]

However, the influx of these goods saw a subtle, and sometimes not so subtle, change among North Carolina Indians. The making of clay pots and jars declined as women began using European brass kettles, glass, and stoneware. Arrow points made of metal and glass replaced those made of stone. Loincloths and hide skirts gave way to linen or woolen shirts, skirts, and pants. These kinds of changes could be expected since new and better tools usually push out the old. But more significant societal changes resulted as well. Hunters took increasing numbers of deer, and usually not for food but for their hides. Hunting became more of an individual process than a village outing. Women worked harder, constantly tanning deer hides to pay for these goods. Guns became prized possessions and Indians became very good shots with them. But there was a constant need for muskets, powder, flints, and lead that only the Europeans could supply.[28]

This Indian desire for manufactured goods gave the English authorities a trump card to play. If Indians balked at a colonial demand, then prohibiting traders from visiting their towns usually made the Indians fall into line. Often just the threat of cutting off trade was enough. Unscrupulous English traders made things worse. Many found that rum was the very best trade item. Rum in name only, it was a doctored-up alcohol that packed a punch, but many Indians took to it. Alcohol addiction followed and all the problems that come with alcoholism afflicted Indian towns. Men gave away everything they owned for a mouthful of rum, and often it was sold by the mouthful. Drunkenness ensued, brawls erupted, people injured or killed each other, or they severely injured themselves. As Lawson pointed out, the four things killing North Carolina Indians in the early 1700s were smallpox, rum, poisoning each other, and constant warfare.[29]

The colonial government of North Carolina took a dim view of Virginia or South Carolina traders entering its territory and taking control of the Indian trade. Though the North Carolina Assembly passed laws barring these outside traders, it could do little to enforce them. And without a deepwater port into which large cargoes of trade goods could be shipped, North Carolina would always lose out to well-supplied Virginia and South Carolina. Nevertheless, settlers in eastern North Carolina participated in the trade on an individual basis. Since deer hides served as a colonial currency, a wise settler always kept a packet of trade goods or a few jugs of rum on hand when Indians passed by. And hungry settlers used trade goods to purchase meat and fish when Indians returned from their hunts.[30]

So for the Tuscaroras, long the dominant power in eastern North Carolina, the coming of settlers to North Carolina did not initially create many problems. Their towns lay west of the settlements, while the colonial government was too weak and divided to stop them from trading with whomever they wanted. But after 1700, many Tuscaroras began to see threats. And if they did not see them, then the Machapungas, Bear Rivers, Neuse, Weetocks, and Core Indians were glad to tell them of their bad experiences with the English.

❖ The problem was that by the eighteenth century, two totally different peoples—Indians and Europeans—with different cultures, different ways of seeing the world, different technological abilities, lived too close to each other in eastern North Carolina. Each thought the other inferior. Each thought the other treacherous and dangerous. Each attributed to the other a history of insults, slights, and complaints that went all the way back to their first meeting in the 1580s.[31]

As the colonial government of North Carolina saw it, Indians were the subjects of the English monarch, living on lands belonging to the Lords Proprietors. They should obey the laws as established and enforced by the North Carolina governor, Council, and Assembly. Though the Proprietors always promised strict justice to the Indians, it did not always happen down at the colonial level. Officials kept promises and paid respect only as long as the Indian nation was strong enough to resist the English. Once English power trumped that of the Indians, the officials abandoned any pretense of equality and the Indians became tributary nations subject to the colonial government. But by 1711, the English colony of North Carolina was itself not that powerful and so could only make a few Indians nations into tributaries, such as the much-weakened Chowans and Yeopims who lived north of Albemarle Sound. The Tuscaroras, Machapungas, Cores, Neuse, and Bear River Indians still wielded enough power to cause problems if not properly respected.[32]

Though the average English, German, or Swiss settler in North Carolina might fear the Indians, in truth they had little respect for them. Profoundly suspicious of anyone who did not look, speak, and act like them, many Europeans believed that Indians could not be trusted and that they were going to have trouble with them. Expecting trouble, they found it. To them, a smiling, friendly Indian was just one waiting to tomahawk them in the back. As they saw it, Indians held no rights that an Englishman had to respect as far as he could get away with it. And the colonists loudly complained to the colonial government when Indians stood in their way. They felt that Indians took up too much land and so limited colonial expansion. Settlers hated how Indians burned the forests during their deer hunts and so destroyed valuable stands of timber. Colonists let their hogs and cattle run free in the forest and then complained when Indians hunted them for food. They did not like how passing Indians often stopped at their cabins to ask for food or water. Most Englishmen turned them away in annoyance, claiming the Indians pilfered things from their homes. And, of course, rumors constantly circulated of Indians killing lone hunters or attacking isolated farms, but facts were hard to come by.[33]

Indians had their own issues and often appeared before the North Carolina Council to lodge them. Complaints about being cheated or abused by rum-wielding traders were commonplace. But run-of-the-mill colonists caused their own problems. An Indian named John King complained that two settlers, John Parish and William Godfrey, "abused him and other Indians" to prevent them from hunting in their normal hunting quarters.[34] Indians caught hunting on lands claimed by settlers normally had their guns and game taken from them. Threats and a beating usually came with it. Sometimes it went further and Indians wound up dead. But Indians complained most about settlers encroaching on their lands. As the European population in eastern North Carolina grew, settlers increasingly claimed lands that Indians had long used as hunting quarters. Even lands guaranteed to the Indians by the North Carolina government, such as the Chowan, Yeopim, and Meherrin reservations in Albemarle County, soon had settlers squatting on them and refusing to leave. The Meherrins became particularly enraged when in July 1707 the wealthy planter Thomas Pollock led eighty militiamen to their village and imprisoned thirty-six Meherrin men inside their fort for two days during hot weather and without any water. Pollock wanted the Meherrin lands and this was his way of forcing them out. The Meherrins swore they were on lands granted to them by Virginia and complained to Virginia governor Alexander Spotswood about this treatment. But, as so often happened, nothing came of it.[35] So it should have come as no surprise that the Tuscaroras and other Indians south of the Pamlico River worried as De Graffenried placed several hundred German and Swiss settlers on lands long claimed by the Tuscaroras. They worried even more when they found Lawson the surveyor and De Graffenried the colonizer upriver looking over their land.

Besides land, the Tuscaroras, the Cores, and the Neuse, Bear River, and Weetock Indians worried about the Indian slave trade. England and its English colonists believed in slavery, that owning one's "inferiors" was perfectly legitimate and profitable. As plantation agriculture took hold in the American colonies—tobacco in North Carolina and Virginia, rice and indigo in South Carolina, sugar on the Caribbean islands—the demand for slaves increased. The African slave trade was only just gearing up in England's American colonies, so Indians made the most logical choice of slaves. There were more Indians available and they cost less than Africans. In North Carolina, some took advantage of this and might own one or two Indians. Pollock had at least two Indian slaves working for him: Dinah and Harry. William Thirrell owned four. William Frayly sued William Hancock for the return of an eight-year-old Indian slave boy. Indian slaves even counted toward headright claims, and a settler could get an additional fifty acres of land for every slave, black or Indian, he brought into the colony. John Lawson was all for Indian slavery. He had been amazed when he saw an Indian carve a gunstock out of a piece of wood with a dull knife. As slaves, Indians, he believed, could easily learn the same crafts and skills that would be profitable for the English.[36]

But making Indians into slaves posed problems. Some Englishmen tried kidnapping Indians and spiriting them away. That was dangerous as no Indian wanted to be made into a slave and would fight back. Lawson believed that settlers kidnapping Indian children had doomed a late-seventeenth-century English settlement on the Cape Fear River. The English soon learned that the best way to acquire Indian slaves was to get them from other Indians. Sometimes a trader allowed an Indian to buy on credit and then run up a huge debt. When big enough, the trader suggested that the debt could be cleared by handing over a slave or two. English slave traders never inquired too hard into where their client acquired the slave. But the easiest and most effective way to acquire the large numbers needed to meet planter demands was by arming Indian allies, have them attack other Indians, capture those they could, and march them back to the traders who purchased them from the captors with manufactured goods.[37]

The colony of South Carolina took the Indian slave trade to new heights, making it both highly profitable and very dangerous. South Carolina merchants began arming the nearby Westoes, Savannahs, Yamasees, Sewees, Catawbas, Waterees, and others, then turned them lose on everyone else. As the Anglican missionary Dr. Francis Le Jau in Charles Town astutely pointed out, these English traders incited the Indians "to make war amongst themselves to get slaves which they give for our European goods. I fear it is but too true and that the slaves we have for necessary service, (for our white servants in a month's time prove good for nothing at all) are the price of great many sins, I pray that they may not be imputed to us."[38] The slave trade turned Indian warfare on its ear. Prior to this, Indians had taken few captives in their raids, and a prisoner was merely a happenstance of war. But once English South Carolinians introduced a profit motive into it, Indians began making war for the purpose of taking captives, whom they then sold to the English.[39]

The twenty-five years between 1690 and 1715 were horror-filled years for the Indians of the American Southeast. No Indian town or village could count itself safe, even peoples living as far west as the Mississippi River. Who knew when Indian raiders out of South Carolina would launch a surprise attack, gun down anyone who resisted, then capture everyone else, especially women and children. In fact, women and children were the most desirable of slaves. Male captives would be killed, usually burnt to death. Women and children would be shackled, then marched the many long miles back to Charles Town. There the South Carolina merchants sponsoring the raiders purchased the captives from them. In Charles Town, local planters bought some to work their fields. Other slaves would be sent to the colonies along the Atlantic coast, such as North Carolina, Virginia, even Pennsylvania, New York, and Massachusetts. But slave merchants shipped off the vast majority to Barbados, Jamaica, or England's other sugar islands. During those twenty-five years, thousands upon thousands of Indians found themselves enslaved and sent out of the region.[40]

The slave raids devastated the Indian Southeast, shattering towns and villages. Survivors sought shelter among other towns, even other peoples. The slave trade caused a great movement of Indian peoples toward the west as they tried to put distance between themselves and South Carolina raiders. But the raids also spread disease as slave raiders marched infected Indians across the American South. This was one reason the great smallpox epidemic of 1696 affected so many people. Slavery, disease, and death went hand in hand for Indian peoples during this time.[41]

Sitting just to the north of South Carolina and its Siouan and Yamasee allies, the Tuscaroras and other Indians of eastern North Carolina became targets of slave raiders. They fought back when they could, but the very fact that they were targets angered them. They wondered why, if they were allies of English North Carolina and Virginia, they should be attacked by Indian allies of English South Carolina? Tuscarora *teeth-has* begged the North Carolina government to halt these raids. As usual, North Carolina ignored them. Yet other colonial governments worried about the situation.[42]

In 1706, the Pennsylvania Assembly prohibited any further importation and sale of Indian slaves coming from the Carolinas. The reason was that Pennsylvania's Iroquois allies had become upset and angry seeing their Tuscarora kinspeople enslaved and sold. The governors of New York heard similar complaints from the Five Nations of the Iroquois and worried they might take matters into their own hands. Governor Alexander Spotswood of Virginia also grew concerned about the consequences of enslaving the Tuscaroras. These colonial governments feared anything that might drive the Five Nations of the Iroquois and the Tuscaroras into an alliance with the French.[43] Nevertheless, the governments of North Carolina and South Carolina seemed willfully, even criminally, deaf to Tuscarora and Iroquois complaints and the slave raids continued.

But Tuscarora patience was running out. On July 8, 1710, Iwaagenst, Terrutawanaren, and Teonnottein, three chiefs representing several North Carolina Tuscarora towns, tired of the slave raids and abuse by North Carolina settlers, met at the Conestoga Indian town in Pennsylvania with representatives from Pennsylvania, a delegation from the Senecas, and Opessa, king of the Shawnees. The Tuscaroras presented eight wampum belts to the council. Each belt represented a grievance the Tuscaroras had with North Carolina or an action they wanted Pennsylvania to take. With Belt Six, they asked for a lasting peace with Pennsylvania so they could get rid of "those fearful apprehensions they have these several years felt." Belt Seven asked for a "cessation from murdering and taking them, that by the allowance thereof, they may not be afraid of a mouse, or any other thing that ruffles the leaves." And finally, Belt Eight asked the Pennsylvania government to "take them by the hand and lead them, and then they will lift up their heads in the woods without danger or fear." These chiefs were asking permission for the Tuscaroras to be allowed to relocate to Pennsylvania, where they would be protected by the Senecas and that colony.[44]

The Pennsylvania government liked the Tuscarora attitude and welcomed them wanting to make peace. They also seemed amenable to having them relocate to Pennsylvania. But to facilitate a relocation, Pennsylvania needed to confirm the Tuscaroras "past Carriage toward the English, & to raise in us a good opinion of them." To make their relocation a reality, "it would be very necessary to procure a certificate from the Govmt. they leave, to this, of their good behavior, & then they might be assured of a favourable reception." And then an interesting thing took place, which should have been a clue to Seneca thoughts on the Tuscaroras and their situation. The Seneca delegation stepped up and thanked the Pennsylvania officials for their support of the Tuscarora petition, but now directed that the eight belts of wampum be sent to the Five Nations of the Iroquois rather than be kept by the Pennsylvania government. By redirecting the wampum belts, the Senecas shifted Tuscarora subservience from Pennsylvania to the Five Nations. With that, the council ended and the Tuscaroras went home, though the "sincerity of their intentions" much impressed the Pennsylvania delegation.[45]

The North Carolina government had no intention of providing a certificate of good behavior that would allow the Tuscaroras to leave the colony. It never even addressed the topic. North Carolina did not want the Indians to leave but to be obedient. Tuscaroras and other Indians were profitable trade partners. They served as buffers to protect the settled areas from attacks by other Indians. So there was no way North Carolina was going to let the Tuscaroras relocate to Pennsylvania. Besides, the North Carolina government was quickly becoming convulsed with Cary's Rebellion. So Tuscarora complaints received little attention, which only frustrated and angered the Indians all the more.[46] Conversely, the Five Nations of the Iroquois in New York, particularly the Senecas, now took special interest in the Tuscaroras down in North Carolina. The July 1710 council at Conestoga showed them the conditions their Tuscarora kinfolk labored under. It also showed them just how weak they were. This presented ideal conditions for Five Nation meddling and possible diplomatic expansion.

One of the most phenomenal stories of seventeenth-century North America was the rise and expansion of the Five Nations of the Iroquois: the Senecas, Cayugas, Onondagas, Oneidas, and Mohawks. Long before Europeans ever arrived, each was a separate Iroquoian nation with little love between them. Murder and revenge were the order of the day. People feared to go out at night lest they be waylaid and killed. Then sometime between A.D. 1400 and 1600, the Peacemaker arrived and brought the Great Law of Peace, which ended the wars and established the League of the Longhouse or Haudenosaunee, which unified the New York Iroquois spiritually and politically into the Five Nations and a powerful confederation.[47] There was also an evangelical aspect to the Great Law, as it and league membership was not just for the Five Nations but open to all. Other nations, if they promised to obey the Great Law and put themselves under the authority of the league, would be offered peace and welcomed into the confederation. However, they would be non-voting members of the league and subservient to the wishes of the Five Nations. If other nations refused to accept the Great Law of Peace, then the Five Nations felt they had the right to subjugate them. Every nation in Europe thought they possessed the same right.[48]

This sense of purpose and expansionist outlook served the Five Nations well as the coming of Europeans to the region in the early 1600s played into their hands. As the French in Canada and the English in New York battled for empire, the Five Nations increased their own power. Backed first by Dutch and then by English guns and merchandise, the Five Nations expanded militarily. Over the course of the seventeenth century they conquered such Iroquoian neighbors and French allies as the Hurons, Neutrals, and Petuns, and made war on the Algonquians of New England. Nations as far away as the Mississippi River lived in terror of Iroquois raiders. The English courted them as allies to fight the French in Canada, while the French saw them as powerful enemies. Toward the end of the seventeenth century, the Five Nations, particularly the Senecas, had pushed south into Pennsylvania, Maryland, and Virginia. They gradually pulled such Indians as the Piscataways, Susquehannas, Conestogas, and others into their diplomatic orbit. The Five Nations called this "linking arms together," but these nations would be tributaries of the Five Nations, "props" that supported the League of the Longhouse. These tributaries recognized Iroquois authority, allowed the Five Nations to handle their diplomacy with the colonial governments, and contributed warriors when the Five Nations demanded, all in return for Five Nation peace and protection.[49]

But Five Nation success came at a steep price. War brought war and raids brought counterraids. Several times in the late 1600s, French armies or their Indian allies invaded Iroquois country and destroyed Five Nation towns and farms. French Jesuit Black Robes, offering Christian salvation with one hand and guns and merchandise with the other, caused political divisions among the peoples of the Five Nations. Many individuals and families moved to French Canada, putting themselves under the protection of the French and in effect becoming French allies. At this same time, the English, long the allies of the Five Nations, lost their luster in

Iroquois eyes, particularly with the Senecas, Cayugas, and Onondagas, the three nations that sat furthest from the trade centers of English New York and closer to those of New France. While the English never hesitated to call on the Five Nations for military assistance, they rarely supported Five Nation diplomacy or warfare. And the English made great political demands on the Five Nations, insisting they subjugate themselves to the English. Many people of the Five Nations took this as an insult and felt the English saw them as nothing but puppets and proxy warriors. This only drove more of the westernmost of the Five Nations into the French orbit. So by the early eighteenth century, English influence among the Five Nations was declining, while French influence increased. Then came the Grand Settlement of 1701, in which the Iroquois made two significant peace treaties. In the Treaty of Albany, they reaffirmed their peace with the English, but they also signed the Treaty of Montreal, in which after almost a century of continuous warfare, the Five Nations and the French signed a peace treaty. The Treaty of Montreal was the more significant and would have repercussions as far south as North Carolina.[50]

The Iroquois found the 1701 Treaty of Montreal both liberating and confining. The peace treaty secured the northern and western borders of Iroquoia and gave the Five Nations a breather from the constant attacks of the French and their Indian allies. It also meant that raiding parties from the Five Nations could now no longer attack the Indian allies of the French. And war and raiding played an integral part in Five Nation life. Politically, men gained prestige from brave conduct during battle and this often led to political power. Economically, raids brought in furs and hides, which they traded to French and English merchants for guns, ammunition, and hundreds of other useful things. Socially, raids bolstered declining Five Nation populations. Called "mourning war," Five Nation raiding parties attacked enemy villages or towns and captured men, women, and children as they could. They marched these captives back to their Five Nation towns, where some would be tortured to death to relieve the mourning of Iroquois families who had lost members. They adopted others into these same families to replace those who had died. After 1701 and at peace with Indians to their north, east, and west, Five Nation raiding parties, particularly the Senecas, looked south toward the Indian peoples living in North and South Carolina.[51]

After 1701, south really was the only place open for Five Nation raids. In a way, this bolstered French diplomatic machinations. English colonial authorities were not at all happy about the 1701 Montreal Treaty as it allowed the Five Nations a measure of independence and an ability to stand up to English demands. It also signified the ascendancy of the Senecas and the pro-French Iroquoian faction. French diplomatic goals began to be bandied about in league discussions. French officials encouraged the Senecas to strike south against the Yamasees, Catawbas, Saxapahaws, Waterees, and other allies of the English in South Carolina. Fortunately for the Senecas, their Tuscarora cousins lived in North Carolina on the Siouan frontier and so gave them an excellent base from which to make raids. Barely was the ink dry on the Montreal Treaty than Seneca raiding parties launched attacks on the "Flatheads," as they referred to their Siouan enemies.[52]

During his 1701 journey across North Carolina, John Lawson heard numerous reports of "Sinnagers (Indians from Canada)" in the area.[53] His party came across "seven heaps of Stones, being the Monuments of seven Indians, that were slain in that place by the Sinnagers, or Troquois. Our Indian Guide added a Stone to each heap."[54] Just ten days before he arrived at the Saponi town on the Yadkin River, the Saponies had captured five Seneca warriors. Lawson understood all too well the Five Nation threat, describing them as "a Sort of People that range several thousands of Miles, making all Prey they lay their Hands on. These are fear'd by all the savage Nations I ever was among, the Westward Indians dreading their approach."[55] He despaired for peace. "They cannot live without war, which they have ever been used to; and that if peace be made with the Indians they now war withal, they must find out some others to wage war against; for, for them to live in peace, is to live out of their element, War, Conquest, and Murder, being what they delight in, and value themselves for."[56]

As Seneca attacks on the Siouan nations heated up, their Tuscarora cousins in North Carolina became much more important to them. At the July 1710 council at Conestoga, the Senecas saw how weak the Tuscaroras were. Now seemed a good time for the Senecas to "link arms" with their Tuscarora kinspeople, make them a "prop" to the League of the Longhouse, and pull them into the Five Nation's diplomatic orbit. By the summer of 1711, Seneca warriors and ambassadors could be found among the Contentnea Creek Tuscaroras in North Carolina. These Senecas became enraged when they witnessed the abuses done to the Tuscaroras and urged their kinspeople to do something about it. Appealing to Tuscarora manhood and masculinity, the Senecas warned the proud Tuscaroras that they were being used by the North Carolinians and that when the English had finished using them they would "knock them on the head." They "were fools to slave & hunt" to acquire food from the Carolinians. It would be better for the Tuscaroras to kill the English and just take what they wanted. And if a war started between them and the English, then so be it as the Senecas promised to visit them twice a year, bringing more than enough ammunition to win it.[57] Besides, after two failed English military expeditions against the French in Canada in 1709 and 1711, the Senecas possessed little faith in the English ability to make war. And since they never signed a treaty of peace with the North Carolina government, settlers in that colony could be considered fair game.[58]

At least the Tuscaroras had presumptive allies with the Senecas. The smaller Indian nations of eastern North Carolina did not. And during that first decade of the 1700s they had problems of their own. Certainly strained relations existed between the Cores and the English. The Cores, sometimes called Coree Indians, seemed some of the most enigmatic of all eastern North Carolina Indians. When Lawson published his book in 1709, he listed the Indians of eastern North Carolina and neither the "Core" nor "Coree" appear. The closest are the "Connamox Indians," which Lawson said had two towns—Coranine and Raruta—and could put only twenty-five warriors into the field. Their town of Coranine sat near Cape Lookout on the North Carolina coast and the southernmost point on the Core Banks, while Raruta seemed located on the mainland south and east of the mouth of the Neuse River.[59] However, evidence indicates that the Cores were merely Tuscarora towns that had moved down the Neuse River to the coast. The Tuscarora town of Haruta, also found southeast of the mouth of the Neuse River, sounds much like Lawson's Connamox town of Raruta.[60] A few years earlier in 1697, the North Carolina Council reported that the Core Indians "are slaves to the Tuscarora Indians" and ordered Tuscarora chiefs to explain the robberies and injuries settlers around Bath blamed on the Cores. The Council demanded these Tuscarora chiefs give restitution for Core robberies and make sure they did not happen again.[61]

Even before De Graffenried brought in his four hundred or so colonists, the Cores found their situation increasingly untenable. In the 1690s, the great smallpox epidemic hit them hard, killing off many.[62] Their lands also came under pressure from English settlers. William Hancock took possession of the lands on which the town of Haruta sat. The Cores resisted this land loss and by 1703 settlers complained that the Cores were becoming insolent and aggressive. It got so bad that traders refused to provide them with guns and ammunition. The Cores reasoned the settlers wanted to make them powerless and so destroy them. They may have had a point, as in 1704 North Carolina declared war on the Core Indians.

It was not a major war, but it forced the Cores to move Haruta up the Neuse River, just below its confluence with Contentnea Creek, placing them nearer their Tuscarora kinspeople. There it became known as Core Town. It was here that De Graffenried met the affable Sam and the angry Core Tom. The other Core town of Coranine moved off Cape Lookout and onto the mainland to just north of the White Oak River. There these Cores may have been misidentified as the Weetock Indians of the White Oak River. The attacks on the Cores angered the Tuscaroras and it appeared that they might actually declare war on the English. But Governor Robert Daniel arranged a council with Tuscarora leaders and so avoided hostilities.[63] Nevertheless, by the summer of 1711, the Cores and Weetocks seethed with anger. So did many Tuscaroras proper.

The Machapunga Indians were also angry. Consisting of around two hundred people, they lived north of the Pamlico River, not far from Bath, but often ranged south of the river. Lawson said they had one town called Mattamuskeet, though he wrote it Maramiskeet. Because of this, settlers often used the names Machapunga and Mattamuskeet interchangeably for these Indians. Known as excellent boatmen and swamp warriors, they appeared to be the Algonquian remnants of the many earlier towns and villages Raleigh's explorers found north of the Pamlico back in 1585. As settlers moved in around Bath, the Machapungas also found themselves losing access to their lands. In 1705, the settler Edward Pitts claimed land on Machupunga Creek, forcing the Indians to relocate. Though they had long considered the Core Indians enemies, by the summer of 1711 the Machapungas put aside their differences and added their fifty warriors to an alliance with the Tuscaroras and Cores.[64]

The Bear River Indians also joined the anti-English alliance. Their one town—Raudauquaquank—sat on the Bay River, north of the Neuse and probably not too far from present-day Bayboro. Because they lived on the Bay River, the first English settlers in the region just called them the Bay River Indians. But somewhere along the way, due to some English dialect twang, settlers referred to them as the Bear River Indians. So the names Bay River and Bear River Indians became interchangeable. Their origins are unclear. But their location also makes them a candidate for being another offshoot Tuscarora town. In fact, many settlers in the area commented on the "more than ordinary familiarity" between the Bear River Indians and Tuscaroras.[65]

Living on the coast, the Bear River Indians gained a reputation as looters of beached ships, sometimes willing to attack stranded sailors. In 1699, the North Carolina government tried to make them into tributaries and demanded they stop their attacks and plundering. They should also pay two deerskins every July to the General Court as tribute. But old habits were hard to break and in 1701 Thomas Amy charged that the Bear River Indians, who were serving as canoe guides, had pulled guns and bows on his party and threatened their lives. The Indians told a different story: that Amy and his friends had gotten them drunk on rum and when the Indians heard the Englishmen talking about the Ashley River in South Carolina, they feared they were going to be enslaved, jumped out of the canoes, spilling three of the Englishmen's guns into the water in the process. Things only got worse. In the fall of 1704, the settler William Powell complained that King Louther and sixteen Bear River Indians looted his cabin of all his ammunition and other items. King Louther said he was doing this because he had heard the English were going to "cut them off." When Powell protested, Louther told Powell that he "might kiss his arse" and that Powell was a "son of a bitch & said they would burn my house & when it was light moon they would gather my corn & ye English men's corn." By the summer of 1711, the moon had come and Bear River patience had run out.[66]

It is safe to say that other Indians south of the Pamlico River experienced similar difficulties. De Graffenried's settlers at the confluence of the Neuse and Trent Rivers forced King Taylor's Neuse Indian town of Chattooka to relocate further up the Neuse. The Weetock Indians on White Oak River south of the Neuse, who were probably relocated Cores from Coranine Town, voiced their own complaints. So did the Pamlico Indians and those Indians living north of the Albemarle and on the Outer Banks: Chowans, Yeopims, Meherrins, Poteskeets, Pasquotanks, and Hatteras Indians. All had lost lands and hunting quarters. All suffered abuse at the hands of the English government and settlers. Diseases reappeared and made life more miserable.[67] By the summer of 1711, many Tuscaroras, as well as Cores, Machapungas, Bear River Indians, Pamlicos, and Weetocks, came to the realization that things could not go on as they had. Urged on by the Senecas among them, many now believed the best thing to do was remove the English from the equation. Or at least teach them a lesson that would make them more understanding of Indian complaints.

❖ It was three o'clock in the morning when the Tuscarora warriors deposited Baron de Graffenried, John Lawson, and their two slaves in front of King Hancock at Catechna. According to De Graffenried, Hancock awaited them, sitting in state on a scaffold surrounded by his council of elders. King Hancock has always been something of a mystery. We do not know his Indian name. Somewhere along the way, either he took the name of the English settler William Hancock who had lands on the lower Neuse River or someone gave it to him. But it is as King Hancock that he has forever been known. Other Indians, both kings and commoners, took or were given similar English names: King Sothel and King Louther of the Bear River Indians; King Taylor of Chattooka Town; King Tom Blount of the Tuscarora town of Ucohnerunt on the Tar River; King John Durant of the Yeopim Indians; and King John Hoyter of the Chowans.[68]

At this point, King Hancock had to know two things. First, that the capture of De Graffenried and Lawson was going to cause trouble with the North Carolina government. Lawson and De Graffenried would complain and there would certainly be repercussions. But the North Carolina government was weak and divided at this time, suffering the shocks of Cary's Rebellion. So Hancock and his council could not be sure how severe those repercussions would be. Second, that he was being challenged by his warriors and younger men who advocated war against the English. He had dispatched his warriors merely to turn back De Graffenried and Lawson. Instead, they had gone beyond his directive, captured the four men, and brought them to Catechna. His next moves would be critical to his own political power and to his people as a whole.[69]

Hancock listened as the leader of the capturing party made a "sharp speech." Once finished, Hancock, the council, and his first war captain approached the captives and spoke briefly and kindly with them. De Graffenried and Lawson could only understand a few words.[70] Then Hancock returned to his own house about two miles away, leaving the men guarded by seven or eight warriors. There they remained for several hours, until about ten o'clock in the morning, when many of Catechna's people gathered around them, debated their fate, and wondered whether they should be "bound as criminal or not." At about noon, King Hancock returned and brought buckwheat dumplings and venison to the four men. After they had eaten, he allowed the men to wander around the village but ordered them not to leave.[71]

While De Graffenried, Lawson, and the two slaves roamed, Hancock sent runners to nearby towns, explaining the situation and asking their *teethhas* to come to his town. At about ten o'clock that evening, De Graffenried and Lawson found themselves at the center of an Indian council. At the town's ceremonial ground, a circle of Indians formed and De Graffenried and Lawson were placed on mats at its center. They were told it was a place of honor. Hancock and about forty Tuscarora elders then took their place in front of the captives. The gravity, solemnity, and pomp of the council impressed De Graffenried. With their Indian guide serving as translator, Hancock now asked why they had made their journey up the Neuse. Shading it as best they could, the men replied they had come to gather wild grapes and see how far the river was navigable so they could have better trade with the Tuscaroras. They said nothing about looking at land for future settlement or blazing a road to Virginia. Hancock next asked why they had not notified him of their planned trip. But before De Graffenried or Lawson could answer, several Indians began complaining loudly about having "been badly abused by the inhabitants of the rivers Pamptego, News, & Trent, what could not be suffered any more. They spoke the name of the offenders, and especially of Surveyor-General Lawson, who, being present, excused himself as well as he could."⁷² Some complained "that Mr. [William] Hancock had taken a gun from an Indian, and that Mr. Price [Brice] also dealt too hard with the Indians."⁷³ Others asked King Hancock how they could "avenge themselves of the rough dealings" and what help "they could expect from their Indian neighbors."⁷⁴ Hancock seemed on the verge of losing control of the situation.

For the captives, the council must have been interminable. For hours the "pros and cons were discussed, and they consulted over the matter of these questions. After that they came to a conclusion."⁷⁵ Hancock carried the argument and informed the captives they would "be liberated and the following day was appointed for our return home."⁷⁶ The council then broke up and Hancock returned to his home a couple of miles away. De Graffenried, Lawson, and the slaves had to have been relieved. Promised their freedom, they were now allowed to sleep. The next morning the four men began to collect their belongings for the trip back to their canoe. But it took awhile before they could gather everything and that delay proved fatal.⁷⁷

That morning, in response to the message carried by Hancock's runners the day before, at least two "foreign kings" and several "great men" from nearby towns and villages now showed up at Hancock's home. Nick Major, king of the Meherrins, arrived as well as King Taylor of Chattooka town. More important, so did Core Tom of Core Town.⁷⁸ Led by Core Tom, these newly arrived kings argued with Hancock about his decision to release the captives. They wanted to know how these two Englishmen justified their actions and excused the abuses the settlers inflicted on the Indians. Hancock found himself backed into a corner. He now ordered De Graffenried, Lawson, and their two slaves be brought the two miles to his house so they could be questioned again.⁷⁹

At Hancock's house, the four men suddenly found themselves on trial for their lives, but now before a much more hostile gallery. The men were asked the same questions as the night before: Why did they come up the river and why did they not notify Hancock? They gave the same answers. But now Core Tom stepped up. He directly accused Lawson of abusing the Indians. And as surveyor general, he was to blame for the taking of Indian lands. As Core Tom berated him, Lawson's temper got the best of him. He loudly argued back, his anger and sarcasm apparent to all. Foolishly, Lawson threatened Core Tom and the Indians with violence for taking him prisoner and guaranteed they would pay for it. "This spoiled everything for us," De Graffenried said.[80] "Though I made every effort to get Lawson to quit his quarreling, I could not succeed."[81]

At some point the interrogation came to an end and the captives were allowed to get up and walk about. But De Graffenried worried about what had just happened and scolded Lawson "for his imprudence in such a delicate conjuncture."[82] Then, without warning, three or four of Hancock's principal men seized De Graffenried, Lawson, and the slaves and marched them the two miles back to Catechna. Once there, they found the council in session and awaiting them. As before, the Indians placed them in the middle of the ceremonial ground, but there were no mats or places of honor this time. "They took our hats and periwigs and threw them into the fire, after that, some young rascals plundered us anew, and searched our pockets."[83] For De Graffenried, Lawson, and their two slaves, things had suddenly gone horribly wrong.

Things had gone wrong for King Hancock as well. By all indications Hancock wanted peace and to escape from this predicament with as few problems as possible. He had sent his warriors to turn De Graffenried and Lawson back, but they captured them instead. Then he hoped to release the prisoners and send them back downriver with a stern warning about violating Tuscarora territory. Hancock won that argument and managed to get the men set free, but then Core Tom showed up. De Graffenried and Lawson still had the chance to come away free after the second interrogation, but Core Tom skillfully provoked Lawson and the surveyor general's own words worked against him. All Hancock's machinations to free the men came to naught as Core Tom swung the Indians, especially the young warriors, to his side and now pushed everyone toward war. In a society that stressed consensus, Hancock's warriors seemed to be turning against his leadership. So who was this Core Tom who so hated the English and had the power to confound an important *teethha* such as Hancock?

Unfortunately, we know little about Core Tom and most of that comes from De Graffenried. Several things make Core Tom unusual. That Core Town, which was not all that large, would have two chiefs and be so obvious about it that a European would notice it. That Core Tom was never addressed as "King Tom." And that Core Tom, one of the leaders of a small town and a minor ally, could force King Hancock's hand and get these two important Englishmen to stand trial for their lives. With all this in mind, and with a good dose of circumstantial evidence and conjecture, it seems quite possible that Core Tom was a Seneca diplomat, or at least an agent provocateur, whose job was to ensure that the Tuscaroras went to war against the English. A war that would drive the Tuscaroras firmly into the arms of the Senecas, where they would become "props" to the League of the Longhouse and "little brothers" to the Five Nations. Incorporating the Tuscaroras would strengthen the Senecas and Five Nations. And if a few North Carolina Englishmen got killed in the process, then so be it.

The Five Nations often used manipulation of this type. By 1697, the Senecas had diplomatically subdued the Susquehannas of Maryland and Virginia and now looked to force the Piscataways into their orbit. To do so, they used an Indian named Squire Tom. Squire Tom was a known associate of the Senecas and in 1697 they directed him to go to Maryland where he was to get the Piscataways involved in a war with the English. In Maryland, Squire Tom killed an English family and a black slave, but he made it look as if the Piscataway Indians did it. It worked as Maryland declared war on the Piscataways. Needing protection, the Piscataways turned to the Five Nations, where they submitted themselves as "little brothers." The war was soon over, but now the Piscataways were firm props of the League of the Longhouse. And as for Tom, soon after his murders, he was given refuge by the Iroquois. Two years later, Tom was living as a Five Nations diplomat among the Piscataways. But his days as a provocateur may not have been over. [84]

By the early 1700s, the Senecas' attention turned to making props of Virginia's Iroquoian Indians, such as the Nottoways. And they used the same tactic. In 1704, two Iroquoian diplomats, Long Tom and Qualks Hooks, along with a few others, went down to St. Mary's Parish in Virginia. There they tried the same tactic and killed some English settlers. Again, the idea was to get Virginia to attack peaceful Indians, who would turn to the Senecas for protection. But this time, Virginia authorities captured most members of the Indian party and hanged them, except for Long Tom and Qualks Hooks. Both got away, apparently with Seneca help.[85]

It would make the story amazingly complete if we could definitely connect Squire Tom, Long Tom, and Core Tom as the same person. Unfortunately, we cannot confirm it one way or the other. And "Tom" was a rather common name among both the English and the Indians. But then who knows, because besides the names, the methods in all three instances seem similar. At Catechna, Core Tom certainly provoked the situation and now had the baron and Lawson on trial again for their lives. If the Tuscaroras executed the Englishmen, then war would be a reality and the Senecas would benefit. Could it be that knowing that Tom could deliver the goods, so to speak, the Senecas sent him to the Neuse River as a *teethha* among the Iroquoian Core Indians at Core Town? Now on this day in September, Core Tom, who hated all things English, and to the cheers of the Tuscarora warriors, overcame King Hancock's reticence and forced a new trial of De Graffenried and Lawson. If things worked out the way he planned, then the North Carolina colonial government would have to retaliate, and so the Tuscaroras would find themselves in a war whether Hancock wanted one or not. If the Tuscaroras won, then it was also a victory for the Senecas. If they lost, then the Tuscaroras would have to turn to the Senecas for protection and so "link arms" with the League of the Longhouse. It was a game the Toms seemed to play exceedingly well.

Core Tom played his role to perfection. With De Graffenried, Lawson, and their two slaves sitting in the middle of Catechna's ceremonial ground, the council now informed them that they were to be executed. According to De Graffenried, they were not told why, "though I could nearly guess at it." The verdict given, the men now sat all night in the ceremonial grounds and then at daybreak the Indians led them to the execution ground. "I addressed Mr. Lawson," De Graffenried said, and "reproached him bitterly, and told him that his imprudence was the cause of our misfortune, and that we had nothing better to do than to make peace with our God, what I did with great zeal."[86] As the Indians hustled the four men into the circle where the execution was to take place, De Graffenried happened to see an Indian who was dressed like an Englishman. The baron managed to get a quick word with him and found the Indian spoke English. "I asked him if he could tell us what was the cause of our condemnation? He answered me with a very disagreeable face, why had Lawson quarreled with Core Tom and why had we threatened that we would get revenge on the Indians?" Terrified, De Graffenried promised the Indian anything if he would explain to the chiefs that he was innocent. He assured him that he was sorry that Lawson quarreled with Core Tom and that he himself had never threatened anyone. Maybe the Indians were

Trial of John Lawson and Christopher de Graffenried. Courtesy of Burgerbibliothek Bern, Switzerland, Mss. Muel 466 (1) p. 1

mistaken, having heard him or Lawson threaten his own black slaves for making too much noise, but that certainly was not directed toward the Tuscaroras. The Indian walked away.[87]

At the place of execution, De Graffenried, Lawson, and their two slaves were undressed, bound, and sat down before a great fire. It seemed a descent into hell for the baron. An Indian priest chanted prayers nearby, but De Graffenried imagined him conjuring up the Devil. Before them stood their executioner, armed with a knife and an axe. Four men with guns surrounded them, while behind stood two lines of armed men to ensure they did not escape. Not far away, drums pounded and men, women, and children sang and danced. All the while, the council members whispered and debated among themselves. The baron's mind reeled. This went on all day until the dancing stopped just before sundown and the prisoners were left under guard. "I was wholly resolved to die, and accordingly I offered up my fervent prayers during the whole day & night," De Graffenried said.[88]

That night, the council reassembled at the ceremonial ground. Knowing that some of them spoke English, De Graffenried took the chance to declare his innocence and that "the great and powerful Queen of England would avenge my blood, as I had brought that colony in those countries by her orders, not to do them any wrong but to live on good terms with them." He also promised that if freed, he would do them whatever favors he could. Then just a hint of hope sparked in De Graffenried. He recognized his neighbor, King Taylor of Chattooka, among the men of the council and he seemed to be strongly defending the baron to them. "Then it was forthwith resolved to send a few members to their neighbors, the villages of the Tuscaroras, and to a certain King Tom Blunt, in high repute among them."[89]

The Englishmen had earned a brief reprieve, but there they remained throughout the night, bound and awaiting King Blount's advice. De Graffenried spent the time praying and encouraging his black slaves. As for Lawson, the baron left him to his own prayers. At about three or four in the morning, the runners returned from Tom Blount's town on the Tar River and met with the council out of earshot. In a little bit, an Indian came to De Graffenried, untied him, and led him away. The baron, thinking he was being taken to be executed, "followed him as a poor lamb to the slaughter."[90] But the Indian whispered not to worry as De Graffenried had been spared, but Lawson would die. It seemed that King Tom Blount had recommended freeing De Graffenried, but they could deal with Lawson as they pleased. Soon a crowd of Indians surrounded De Graffenried, smiling and congratulating him on his escape from death. One of the baron's black slaves was also freed, the one smaller in stature.[91] Lawson and the larger slave were left bound in the center of the circle. "I could understand that all was over for him," De Graffenried said. "I tried to show him my compassion by a few signs." He did not have any words for the other slave, the one larger in stature, who was condemned along with Lawson. Then the Indian led the baron to a house, where he was to wait until they decided what to do with him.[92]

Shortly thereafter, Surveyor General John Lawson, the intrepid explorer who always considered himself a friend to the Indians, was executed. The smallish black slave reported the Tuscaroras cut Lawson's throat with a straight razor they found in his pocket. Other Indians said that he was hung. While others said the Indians burnt him.[93] Christopher Gale, who had planned to make the trip upriver with De Graffenried and Lawson but backed out at the last minute, claimed the Indians "stuck him full of fine small splinters of torchwood like hog bristles, and so set them gradually on fire."[94] As word leaked out about the execution, William Byrd of Virginia commented that the Tuscaroras "resented their wrongs a little too severely upon Mr. Lawson, who under colour of being Surveyor Gen'l had encroached too much upon their territories" and so "cut his throat ear to ear."[95] But no one was ever really sure, for as De Graffenried said, "The Indians kept that execution very secret."[96] The "big" slave seemed to have been executed along with Lawson.

The execution of Lawson proved that King Hancock's peaceful diplomacy had been repudiated by his warriors. In Tuscarora and most other Indian societies, when it came to political decisions such as war, consensus was the goal. Councils could be lengthy, with almost all men getting a chance to offer their opinion. As Lawson and De Graffenried witnessed, discussions might go on for hours, even days. Eventually a consensus emerged. At that point, the remaining opposition must either accept and join the majority or withdraw, possibly even leave the town if they could not stomach the decision.[97] Over the course of the past few days at Catechna, King Hancock had been overruled and now his leadership was at stake. As the need for consensus dictated and to keep his position, Hancock now gave up his drive for peace with the English and went over to those who advocated war. The day after they executed Lawson, the Catechna council explained their position to De Graffenried. It was their intention, he recalled, "to make war in North Carolina, and that they were especially embittered against the people on the Rivers Pamptego [Pamlico], New, Trent, and Cor Sound, and that they had accordingly good reasons not to let me go, till they would have ended their expeditions. What was I to do?"[98]

CHAPTER THREE

William Brice

The Fighter

The watershed in men's lives comes at different times. For Christopher de Graffenried and William Brice, two neighbors on the Neuse River, they overlapped. Brice had been living on Brice's Creek, a tributary of the Trent River just south of the mouth of the Neuse, when De Graffenried and his colonists moved in. Almost immediately the two men clashed. That was to be expected. The aristocratic Switzer was haughty and the bluff Englishman crass. But if De Graffenried was at the low point of his life, then Brice was about to enter the high point of his. Or so it seemed.

❖ The first attacks came at dawn on September 22, 1711, the autumnal equinox. Some said that was a Saturday; later calendars said it was a Tuesday.[1] The day before, scouts from the Catechna town Tuscaroras, Cores, Machapungas, Pamlicos, Weetocks, and Bear River Indians had filtered into the settled areas among the farms and plantations between the Neuse and Pamlico Rivers as well as around North Carolina's only town of Bath, nestled on the north side of the Pamlico. For the settlers, these Indians were not strangers, but almost regulars, known to them, and many had done odd jobs for them. The Indians did what they usually did, approached the cabins and houses and asked for food. Some, said Christopher Gale, "were esteemed as members of the several families . . . and that with the smiles in their countenances, when their intent was to destroy." None of the British, German, or Swiss settlers in the area suspected anything. But this was traditional Indian warfare: appear friendly and then strike suddenly from ambush when the enemy's defenses were down.[2]

That evening the scouts returned and made their report of who was where and what could be expected. Then during the night, five hundred warriors from those Indian nations and towns took up their positions in the woods and marshes, as near as feasible to the farms and plantations. It was the night before the new moon, so it was particularly dark. The Machapungas were to hit the settlers around Bath and the town itself if possible. The Pamlicos were ordered to range north of Bath and attack whatever they could. The Bear River Indians were to strike north of the Neuse River and along the coast. The Weetock Indians along the White Oak River were to hit the settlers along that southerly watercourse. The Tuscaroras from Hancock's Catechna town and nearby farms, along with the Cores, would assault the settlements around New Bern, the Trent River, Brice's Creek, all the way to the coast. The Indians were well armed and well prepared for a surprise attack. However, not all Tuscaroras took part in these attacks. Most of the Tuscarora warriors came from Hancock's Catechna town and possibly a few others from nearby farms and towns on Contentnea Creek. But the Tuscarora towns along the Roanoke River, the Tar-Pamlico River, and even some towns along the upper Contentnea Creek did not participate.[3]

At sunup, the warriors streamed out of the woods, carrying muskets, bows and arrows, war clubs, and tomahawks. Some greeted just awakening settlers as they often did and then pounced. Others bands, moving quickly in their half-moon formations and shouting the Tuscarora war cry *Go-Weh! Go-Weh!*, attacked without warning. It was a slaughter. Warriors cut down early rising settlers in their fields, laggards inside their own houses. Men, women, and children were killed, both European settlers and African slaves. Houses were burned, crops and livestock destroyed. Legend says that John Porter Jr.'s house at the head of Chocowinity Bay off the Pamlico River was the first house hit in the attacks. A band of warriors ran up to the house, where one managed to grab Porter's infant child. As he readied to dash it against a wall, Porter's wife, Sarah, snatched the child back from him and ran. In the meantime, Porter and Dr. Patrick Maule, who was visiting, grabbed their guns and managed to fend off the warriors. Then the Porter family and Dr. Maule raced for the river bank, boarded a boat and cast off into the middle of the river. From there they watched their home and everything in it go up in flames.[4]

Others did not fare as well. The Indians killed Furnifold Green Sr. at his Neuse River plantation, along with one of his sons, a white servant, and two black slaves. Another son was wounded in the shoulder. Then the warriors burned the house and destroyed all their livestock.[5] Peter Foundgill, who had a 640-acre tract on Bat's Creek off the Neuse River, was killed along with his entire family. Their house and everything in it burned.[6] Down on the White Oak River, the Quaker William Bartram was killed, but his wife and two children were taken captive by the Weetocks.[7] Edward Berry was killed, leaving a widow and four children.[8] One of De Graffenried's Palatines, John Conis, later pronounced and spelled as Koonce, survived the first day but was killed the next at Core Creek. Also killed were his wife, Alice, his fifteen-year-old son, and his one-year-old daughter. One son, seven-year-old George Conis, survived and was taken captive. The Palatine family of Kneegee, later pronounced and spelled as Kornegay, found itself under attack. Only a boy, George, survived.[9] One North Carolina official later claimed that eighty children died during the course of the war.[10]

Even as they attacked, the Indians were leaving messages for the settlers. Warriors shot dead one Mr. Neville in his own cabin, laid him out on the floor, placed a pillow under his head, turned his stockings down over his shoes, covered his body in new linen, and then placed his wife's nightcap on his head. His wife was also killed, her body placed on her knees, leaning on a chair next to the chimney, her hands together as if she was at prayer and her coat turned up over her head. They killed Neville's son out in the yard and he was stretched out, a pillow also placed under his head and a few twigs of rosemary left under his nose. One of the black slaves had been killed, and his right hand cut off. The neighboring farm to Neville's had also been attacked and the family killed. "The master of the next house was shot, and his body laid flat upon his wife's grave. Women were laid on their house floors and great stakes run through their bodies. Others big with child, the infants were ript out and hung upon trees."[11]

These were very personal insults. According to the historian Michelle LeMaster, laying out Mr. Neville and his son, both with their heads on pillows and Neville's wife's cap on his head and his son with a sprig of rosemary under his nose, said that they were soft, like women, certainly not warriors. Mrs. Neville being placed in a position of prayer mocked Christianity. As for the dead English women, it certainly was unusual for warriors to kill women, as they were not warriors and so beneath being killed. Captive women were also valued for their labor. But these were unusual times and now the Indians avenged their own women. Stakes driven through women and their unborn children ripped out, which horrified the English, struck a blow to the burgeoning English population, but also at the traders who abused and raped Indian women. It also served as a fatal slap to haughty English women who saw little good in Indian men. The English winked at men who took Indian women as bedmates or wives, but English racial and gender beliefs meant that Indian men could never be the husbands of English women. Besides, the Indians had lost too many of their own women and children to the Indian slave trade and North Carolina had done nothing. So now some English women paid the price.[12]

The attacks went on for days as roving bands of Indians terrorized the region. Some settlers hid in the woods, but many were hunted down and killed or taken captive. Along with scores of farms and plantations, the Craven Precinct courthouse went up in flames, and with it went important documents and land deeds. The loss of these records would cause confusion for years to come. New Bern was caught undefended, its craftsmen having few guns and little ammunition, and so came under siege. Though the town survived, several buildings burned. Bath on the north bank of the Pamlico River also survived, though farms and plantations on its outskirts were hit. John Lillington and Richard Swinson had their farms, storehouses, and livestock plundered and destroyed.[13]

Those who escaped the Indians took refuge wherever they could. Bath was awash in refugees. William Brice's plantation at the confluence of Brice's Creek and the Trent River withstood the attacks and now sheltered scores of terrified settlers. So did Lyonell Reading's plantation on the south side of the Pamlico River near present-day Washington and the Shackleford plantation on the North River near Core Sound. About eleven of these plantations scattered over the area managed to become places of refuge and potential garrisons.[14]

By the evening of September 24, the attacks were losing momentum. Few targets still existed. Some warriors had discovered the jugs of rum Indian traders usually kept on hand and now many were too drunk to do much of anything. Most now trudged back to their own villages, weighed down with plunder: horses, cattle, clothes, furniture, tools, anything of value. Surprise had been complete and the attacks a resounding victory, a perfect example of the Indian "cut-off" strategy. Plunder and captives had been taken while warriors gained honor, prestige, and scalps. They had inflicted high casualties among the English, and then slipped away with few losses of their own. The English had not been wiped out, but that had not been their intention. They had taught the English a lesson, a severe one, and so the colonists should now be more careful about how they treated the Indians. As the warriors saw it, the Indians were dominant once again.[15]

For the surviving colonists along the Pamlico, lower Neuse, Trent, and White Oak Rivers, life ground to a halt. For days, if not weeks, the survivors were too frightened to venture out of their refuges. Many farms, plantations, and fields were now smoking ruins. Those not destroyed had been abandoned. Carcasses of dead livestock littered the area. Dead colonists remained unburied, "so they were left for prey to the dogs and wolves and vultures whilst our care was to strengthen our garrison to secure the living."[16] The death toll shocked most. Furnifold Green Jr., who lost his father in the attacks, calculated that about 100 people had been killed and 20 to 30 taken captive. The survivors "forc'd to keep garrisons and watch and guard, day and night."[17] De Graffenried said that 70 of his Palatines and Swiss had been killed and about 15 taken captive.[18] Final tallies figured that between 130 and 140 colonists had been killed. An unknown number wounded. And between 20 and 30 taken captive, most of these women and children.[19] While horrible in the eyes of the colonists, the losses were actually less than 10 percent of Bath County's white and slave population.

Word of the attacks soon spread. "There hath by ye permission of Almighty God for our sins and disobedience been a most horrid massacre committed by ye Tuscarora Indians," wrote a group of survivors on the Neuse River to Virginia's Governor Alexander Spotswood.[20] Up in the Albemarle, which had not been touched by violence, Governor Hyde and the Council president Pollock called up the militia, ordered plantations fortified, and strongpoints manned.[21] But panic swept Albemarle County as settlers assumed they would be next. Many abandoned their homes and farms and headed to Virginia or Maryland for protection.[22] Spotswood heard that the Indians had attacked "without any previous declaration of war or show of discontent."[23] William Byrd of Virginia got word of the attacks when Governor Spotswood sent him an express, "by which I learned that 60 people had been killed by the Indians at Neuse and about as many at Pamlico in North Carolina." Spotswood ordered Byrd to meet with him to discuss Virginia's response to the attacks.[24] On November 15 the *Boston News-Letter* reported, though its facts were a little skewed, "that the Cape Fair Indians had cut off about 20 families . . . [and] that the said Indians have cut off 127 of the Palatines, and kill'd or carry'd off Baron De Gravenrodt, a Swiss nobleman."[25] Months later, on April 22, 1712, the *London Gazette* reported that "about ten weeks before, a great number of Indians came down upon the people of North Carolina, and plunder'd and ravag'd the whole country."[26]

As survivors began to creep out of their fortifications and bury their dead, North Carolinians tried to figure out what had provoked the attacks. Council President Pollock said rather disingenuously that they came "without any cause that we know of, or any complaint made unto the government."[27] In reality, many reasons could be given for the Indian attacks. De Graffenried blamed it on the rough treatment and the killing of an Indian by some "turbulent Carolinians, who cheated those Indians in trading, and would not allow them to hunt near their plantations, and under that pretense took away from them their game, arms, and ammunition. . . . These poor Indians, insulted in many ways by a few rough Carolinians, more barbarous and inhuman than the savages themselves, could not stand such treatment any longer."[28] William Byrd of Virginia agreed. He said traders, acting like "petty rulers," taught good Indians bad habits. Worse, they cheated the Indians, oppressed them, abused Indian women, and mistreated the Indian men. The Indians finally became tired of this "tyranny and injustice" and "resolved to endure the bondage no longer."[29] As one Tuscarora later explained "the beginning of the quarrel arose about an Indian that the white men had punished for a small fault committed in his drink."[30] Along with sharp trade practices and insults by settlers, one might add the Indian slave trade, which had the wholehearted support of English traders and settlers. Revenge had to be taken.[31]

Some blamed it on the taking of Indian lands, particularly by De Graffenried's new colony of Swiss and Palatines near the mouth of the Neuse and Trent Rivers. Several hundred settlers dumped into the area certainly shocked the Indians. They knew that as settler populations grew, fewer and fewer lands would be open to Indian hunting and farming. The Bear River and Machapunga Indians on the coast had already been hemmed in, while the Cores, Neuse, and Tuscaroras had towns that had been forced to move as settlers took the land. But there was no letup as men such as Lawson, Pollock, Hyde, Edward Moseley, William Maule, and others were already claiming lands ever further up the Neuse and into Tuscarora territory.[32]

De Graffenried refused to accept any blame. As he saw it, his settlement and the founding of New Bern had not been bad in themselves; rather it was his neighbors' "slanders and insinuations" against him that "made the savages believe that I had come to expel them from their lands." The baron certainly had to be pointing his finger at William Brice as the source of these insinuations. Nevertheless, De Graffenried claimed that he had convinced the Indians that he was not going to take their land, his payment to King Taylor for the site of Chattooka town proof of his good intentions.[33] In fact, he and his settlers had been friendly with the Indians and "there was not a single complaint against me."[34] That was selective memory on the baron's part.

One of the most controversial and widely believed reasons for the attacks said that supporters of former governor Thomas Cary, who had been ousted as governor by the coming of Edward Hyde, had sicced the

Indians on their political opponents. Even before the attacks, Governor Hyde had blamed John Porter Sr., a Cary supporter, of "going in person to several Indian towns and by promises of reward, to bring down the Indians to cut off man, woman, and child on the western shore of Chowan."[35] Virginia's Governor Spotswood believed that Cary supporters held "a traitorous correspondence with the Tuscarora Indians wereby they have endeavoured to incite and stir up the said Indians (by promises of reward) to cut off Her Majesties good subjects of the said province of North Carolina."[36] De Graffenried believed Cary supporters "defamed Govr. Hyde, in the opinion of the Indians, to such a degree that they held him for their declared enemy."[37]

Some of Cary's staunchest supporters had been Quakers and now they garnered their share of the blame from the Albemarle Proprietary men. Thomas Pollock claimed "our own divisions (chiefly occasioned by the Quakers and some other evil disposed persons) hath been the cause of all our troubles." And these evil persons, Pollock said, tried to undermine Governor Hyde's administration by saying it had no authority.[38] Christopher Gale believed the internal divisions among the English encouraged the Tuscaroras and Cores to attack and "cut off" two hundred settlers.[39] The Lords Proprietors in London heard that "several of H. M. subjects in North Carolina had been destroyed by the incursion of the Tusqueroro Indians, which Indians (as is suggest) have receiv'd encouragement from some of ye inhabitants of that place."[40] Even Tuscarora tradition said that during that summer of 1711, some white men in long coats and wide-brimmed hats visited them "and told them that those settlers who were on the borders of their lands and constantly encroaching and committing depredations upon the Indians, were not of the government, but merely squatters, who settled there of their own accord, and if they were cut off, there would be none to avenge them, and were advised to do so."[41]

These internal divisions between old settlers and Proprietary men, Cary supporters and Hyde supporters, Quakers and Anglicans seemingly convinced many Indians, especially the younger warriors, that the colony was weak and ripe for an attack. There would never be a better time to cut off the North Carolina settlers.[42] Pollock believed the Indians saw the Quakers disobeying the law and took that disobedience as a sign that they might as well attack.[43] Throughout the summer of 1711 there had been signs of Indian unrest, but North Carolina had not bothered to read the clues, and so forts and garrisons sat unready and unprovisioned. There were few guns and little ammunition. Militia troops had not been drilled. Smallpox reappeared among the settlements. And the colony was in the midst of a food shortage.[44] De Graffenried complained about the "general carelessness, negligence, and lack of precautions of the Carolinian residents."[45] He felt "the carelessness of the Carolinians contributed not a little to the audacity and bold actions of these Indians, because they trusted them too much, and for safety there was not a fortified place in the whole province to which one could retire; also in case of any eruption or hostility no arrangements were made and much less were there the necessary provisions of food and supplies."[46]

Others saw a Seneca hand at work. It was only as the war progressed that they would see how right they were. Carolinians later discovered that at the time of the attacks, there had been at least twelve Seneca diplomats among the Tuscaroras pressing them to go to war.[47] Even the *Boston News-Letter* reported the Tuscaroras "were put upon that bloody action by the Sinnecke Indians, one of our Five Nations."[48] Spotswood heard that the Senecas had tried to unite all the Indians in North Carolina and Virginia for a strike against those two colonies and believed the French were supplying the guns and ammunition.[49] Governor Robert Hunter of New York heard that the Five Nations were considering joining the war on the Tuscarora side, but he was working feverishly to prevent it.[50] Certainly, the Senecas and other members of the Five Nations kept in close contact with the Tuscaroras throughout the war's duration. And the North Carolina government always believed they would see Seneca warriors striking deep into the Albemarle.[51]

For whatever reason, the war was on and the first battle went to the Indians. During the next few weeks, small bands of warriors scoured the woods, looking for targets of opportunity. But for the most part, both sides stopped, took a breath, and waited. The Indians felt they had righted a host of wrongs, but they knew the colony would have to make some response. They did not know exactly what that would be. Many hoped the English would take the lesson learned and now allow things to go back to the way they were, only with the English more respectful of Indian concerns. On the other hand, the English staggered under a powerful blow. Dazed and reeling, the colony tried to regain its footing. While authorities prepared their defenses in the Albemarle and called up the militia, Governor Hyde and Council President Pollock knew it was not enough. They needed help and so now turned to Virginia and South Carolina.

❖ Back at Catechna, De Graffenried watched as the warriors went off to make their attacks. The town and its surrounding farms were almost emptied of young men, but De Graffenried insisted that most of the other important Tuscarora towns did not join Catechna's men in the attacks. The baron was astonished at the nonchalance of the Indian people. While their men were at war, the women went about their daily business, picking cherries, digging sweet potatoes, gathering foods from the forest as if they were at peace with the world. Though a prisoner, he had the run of the town, and one day he found himself alone. For a brief moment he thought about slipping into the woods and escaping back to New Bern. Then he came to his senses. He realized that if a single Indian saw him, all would be over. They would recapture him and he would face the same fate as Lawson. So he waited for his release.[52]

Nevertheless, he worried about his colonists. Hancock and his principal men assured him that no harm would come to New Bern town, so all his settlers should take refuge there. But for those who did not, these Indian leaders "could not answer for the evil which could happen." De Graffenried begged to be allowed to go warn them. Hancock refused. Then he asked them to take a message to his colonists. No one would do it. His settlers were on their own.[53]

He was also at Catechna when the warriors returned from their attacks. De Graffenried looked on in horror at the plunder they brought back. He recognized much of it as having belonged to his own people. Then came the captives, mainly women and children. The first were those taken along the Pamlico River, and they were soon followed by those from along the Neuse, Trent, and White Oak Rivers. It shocked him to see some of his own colonists among them. "The very Indian with whom I lodged happened to bring with him the young boy of one of my tenants, and much clothing and furniture which I well knew." De Graffenried asked the boy about the attack. Through great sobs the boy told him that the Indian in whose house the baron was staying was the warrior who killed his father, mother, and brother. His whole family had been wiped out and only he survived.[54]

That evening the victory ceremony began with much feasting and dancing. Warriors showed off plunder and forced captives to dance. And if they refused, De Graffenried said, then the warriors "took them under the arms, lifted them, and let them down alternatively, as a sign that these Christians had now to dance after *their* music, and had become their subjects."[55] Once again, De Graffenried asked to be freed. As a ransom, he promised them large quantities of goods. But the Indians refused and the baron spent weeks waiting at Catechna.

Unknown to De Graffenried, efforts were in the works to liberate him. Peter Poythress, a trader out of Virginia, had been at the Tuscarora town of Tasqui on the Roanoke River when De Graffenried and Lawson had been captured. While there, he learned of Lawson's execution and the attacks. In late October, Poythress returned to Virginia to report it all to Governor Spotswood. The Virginia governor leapt into action. He immediately prohibited trade of any sort, but especially of guns and ammunition, with all Tuscarora towns and any other Indians involved in the attacks. He ordered this to be widely published so that all Virginia traders would know and abide by it. He next called up the militias from Prince George, Surry, and Isle of Wright Counties and sent word to William Byrd and other planters that they should join him at the Nottoway village in southern Virginia for a council with Indian leaders on October 17. He then dispatched Poythress back to Tasqui with two messages. One to be sent to King Hancock at Catechna. The other for King Tom Blount and the *teethhas* of the other Tuscarora towns that had not participated in the attacks, summoning them to meet Spotswood in council at the Nottoway village just over a week later.[56]

At Tasqui, Poythress delivered his messages to the Tuscarora chiefs. The one for King Hancock he entrusted to an Indian, putting him on a horse and sending him to Catechna. At Catechna, Hancock and his council called on De Graffenried to read it to them. A flicker of hope sparked in De Graffenried as he read Spotswood's demand that "we intimate and command you in the name of the Queen of Great Britain, whose subject he [De Graffenried] is, that at sight of this order you liberate him and send him to our government. And we let you know by these presents that if you kill him or do him any violence or harm whatever, we shall avenge his blood, spare neither men, nor women or children." These were strong words and gave Hancock and his council pause. They decided to send De Graffenried and some of Catechna's principal men to meet with Poythress and other Tuscarora leaders at Tasqui. So De Graffenried was put on a horse, and accompanied by the Indian messenger and four Catechna "notables," he made his way northeast about thirty-five miles to Tasqui.[57]

Tasqui impressed De Graffenried, which unlike Catechna, had a strong log palisade built about it. "The houses or cabins were neatly made out of tree bark, they stood in a circle, and in the midst of them was a beautiful round place, in its center a big fire, and around it the Council was sitting on the ground, that is the leader of the Tuscarora nation."[58] Places had been made for De Graffenried and Poythress. At the council meeting, the Tasqui Tuscaroras asked those from Catechna what crime De Graffenried had committed and what would happen if they released him. But the Catechna representatives replied that they had no authority to free

De Graffenried. Besides, they explained, the baron had promised them a rich reward for his release and if they gave him up now, that ransom may not come through. Poythress offered to pay the ransom De Graffenried had promised if they released him now. The Catechna delegation again declined. Instead, they said they would take De Graffenried back to Catechna and then would release him only after Hancock and their council met. But they would keep De Graffenried's surviving slave as security.[59]

So the next day, a disheartened De Graffenried, who had imagined himself on the verge of freedom, rode back to Catechna. He and his escorts were just three or four miles from King Hancock's town when they were surprised by a large number of Tuscarora warriors running by them, warning that a force of English and Palatines were nearby. "They mimicked the Palatines in their gestures, with an angry countenance, uttering the words 'Ta, Ta.'" This news terrified De Graffenried. Throughout his captivity, the baron had promised that his colonists posed no threat to the Indians. Now he learned that they were part of an attacking force. Thinking fast, De Graffenried assured the Indians that what they had seen were only Englishmen and what they had heard was "Ja, Ja," a corruption of the English "aye, aye." When his party reached Catechna, the baron saw the Tuscarora women, children, and old men all packed and provisioned and as a precaution soon removed to a small, fortified island in the middle of Contentnea Creek.[60]

They would not have to stay there long as Tuscarora warriors ambushed the advancing party of English and Palatines and chased them back down the Neuse. It proved another great victory for the Indians. De Graffenried watched as the women of Catechna prepared a great celebratory feast, bringing food to the town's ceremonial ground where each family put up a small arbor. They kindled a fire in the middle of the ground and families gave shell necklaces as offerings of thanks. The women began to dance and the town priest chanted his prayers of thanksgiving. As the victorious warriors returned to Catechna, De Graffenried spotted one carrying a pair of half boots lined with silver that he recognized as his own. At first De Graffenried believed the Indians had plundered his house in New Bern. But he soon realized that his own settlers, thinking him dead, had taken his belongings. Now he was forced to admit to himself that despite his word, his settlers actually had taken part in the attack against the Indians.[61]

Summoned to King Hancock's house, De Graffenried tried to negotiate for his release. He offered to give to each of the chiefs of the "ten villages" a cloth jerkin. To Hancock, he promised two bottles of gunpowder, five hundred grains of small shot, and two bottles of rum. But with their victory over the English expedition, the Indians felt they had the upper hand. Hancock and his men demanded more, especially more guns, powder, lead, and shot. De Graffenried refused, explaining that North Carolina law, on pain of death, prohibited him from supplying them with weapons. Still, he would give them a canoe-load of goods and, even better, he offered to sign a peace treaty with Hancock in which he promised that he and his colonists would remain neutral in the coming war. Hancock and his principal men, in a good mood, agreed.[62]

De Graffenried worked out a six-point treaty of peace with the "Tuscaroras and their neighbors . . . Core, Wilkinson's Point, King Taylor, those of Pamptego and others from that country." First, they would put the war behind them and now be friends. Second, his colony of Germans and Swiss would be "absolutely neutral" in the war between the Indians and North Carolina. In the future, misunderstandings between the two peoples would not be avenged but come to a peaceful understanding. Third, De Graffenried promised that his colony would not expand or take any more land but remain within its current boundary. And if any additional land was needed, Hancock and the other chiefs would get "due warning." Fourth, De Graffenried would try to arrange a temporary, fifteen-day cease-fire in which an acceptable peace could be arranged between the Indians and the North Carolina government. It is not known whether this was something wanted by De Graffenried or the Indians. But if this was an Indian stipulation, it indicated that they saw the initial September 22 attacks as a onetime attack, more or less to wake up the English and teach them a lesson, rather than actual war. Fifth, the Indians would be able to hunt wherever they pleased and not be bothered by the English, though they promised to not venture onto plantation lands lest they scare the livestock. And sixth, trade goods and merchandise should be sold to the Indians at reasonable prices. Also, no harm would come to his Palatines and Swiss, who marked their houses with a certain sign on the door. De Graffenried signed the paper and the Indians made their mark.[63]

Having done all he could, De Graffenried again asked to be allowed to return home. But the baron had promised much merchandise and the Indians feared to let him go without some security. Instead, they told him to order his "little" slave to go back to New Bern, gather what the baron had promised, and then return with it to Catechna before they released him. De Graffenried explained that his slave could not do this by himself and certainly could not pull a canoe loaded with goods back upriver by himself. He needed to be accompanied by some Indians. But knowing how the frightened Germans and Swiss would react if Indians suddenly appeared on their doorsteps, no Tuscarora agreed to escort the slave. Now they were at loggerheads. They either had to let De Graffenried return to New Bern and trust that he would keep his word, or it was nothing. They let him go.[64]

Two days later, early in the morning, the Indians brought De Graffenried his horse and then a couple of Hancock's principal men escorted him the two miles back to Catechna. The little black slave remained behind at Hancock's house, as security. That was the last time De Graffenried ever saw him. At Catechna, the Indians built a fire to warm them on that cool October morning, gave the baron some Indian bread, but then took the horse away. De Graffenried begged for his horse as it was about thirty miles to New Bern. He promised to send it back once he returned home. If they did not believe him, they could escort him to New Bern. The Tuscaroras refused. They advised him that he should get moving as "foreign" Indians prowled the area and that he should "run as fast as [he] could for a couple of hours." And so the baron ran and "did so until night overtook me, and I came to that dreadful desert through which I could not go in the darkness."[65]

He spent that first night in a ditch, half filled with water, without weapons, and no way to light a fire. Cold and miserable, he feared he would be captured by other Indians or "torn to pieces by the many bears who growled all night through around me."[66] The next morning, stiff and sore, he set off again, walking as fast as he could, so much so that his legs ached. He became somewhat lame and so crafted crutches from tree limbs. It was a tough march that had him crossing streams by climbing over downed trees. He made it back to New Bern on the evening of his second day of freedom. As he approached the town, he saw that his house had been barricaded and fortified and that the town was full of people seemingly awaiting an Indian attack. When the townspeople first saw him approaching, they thought he was an Indian spy dressed in De Graffenried's clothing. He soon convinced them that he was not an Indian. "And so all came in crowds, men, women, and children, shouting and crying out, part of them weeping, others struck dumb with surprise." The relief at seeing his people, their warm welcome, and the tension of about a month or so of captivity finally caught up with De Graffenried and he broke down and cried.[67] But that warm welcome would not last.

❖ At about the time of De Graffenried's release, up at the Nottoway town in southern Virginia, Governor Spotswood, along with William Byrd and other important Virginia officials, finally had their council with King Tom

Blount and some of the other upper Tuscarora chiefs. These chiefs had not joined in the attacks against the English. Nevertheless, they depended too heavily on Virginia traders and their merchandise to not go when Spotswood summoned them. On October 17, the Virginia militia arrived at the Nottoway town. Spotswood commanded they be drawn up as if on parade to over-awe the Tuscarora headmen. There were about 730 horsemen and 900 infantry, in all, a considerable colonial force. Nevertheless, Spotswood worried as the militia carried little ammunition, possessed few reserves of powder and shot, and Virginia's defenses lay in disrepair. Though Spotswood issued orders to strengthen Virginia forts, he could not be sure what would happen if the Tuscaroras were not sufficiently impressed and decided to throw in with King Hancock's warriors.[68] The next day, October 18, Governor Spotswood and thirty horsemen traveled a few miles south to the Saponi Indian town to meet the Tuscarora delegation and escort them back to the Nottoways. Byrd, already gaining a reputation for sexual escapades, stayed behind to chase Indian women, "with which we played the wag."[69]

The next day, October 19, their commanders divided the sixteen hundred militiamen into fifty-man companies and drew them up, ready to impress the Indians. It was not long before Governor Spotswood, the trader Peter Poythress, and the thirty-man escort arrived with the delegation of Tuscarora leaders. Poythress had explained to Spotswood that De Graffenried was still alive, though Lawson "was killed because he had been so foolish as to threaten the Indian that had taken him."[70] King Tom Blount of the Tar River town of Ucohnerunt led the delegation of five Tuscarora chiefs representing about eight towns from the Tar-Pamlico and Roanoke Rivers. Spotswood drew up the militia companies, made the Tuscaroras walk along the ranks to see how impressive his own warriors could be, and then ordered the companies to wheel and parade in close-order drill. This display of Virginia military power seemed to have its affect as Byrd said the Tuscarora chiefs "seemed very much afraid lest they should be killed." Spotswood decided to let the impression sit with the chiefs overnight and so dismissed the militia. Byrd spent the night dancing and drinking, then found Jenny, "an Indian girl" who had gotten drunk "and made us good sport."[71]

The next morning, October 20, Spotswood and the Tuscarora chiefs met in council. It was rather cut and dried as Spotswood gave them a three-point ultimatum. First, these Tuscarora towns should join with Virginia and North Carolina and now "cut off" those Indian towns that had attacked the settlers in North Carolina. Second, Virginia would pay them six blankets, worth about forty shillings, for the head of every enemy Indian they brought in and "the usual price of a slave for each woman and child delivered as captives." Third, to ensure the good behavior of these Tuscarora towns, they should send one of the chief's sons from every town to serve as a hostage. These would be sent to school at Williamsburg and so educated in English ways.[72]

But Blount and his fellow chiefs were not ready to throw in with the English just yet. They knew that many of their young men supported the warriors of Catechna and pushed for war. Some had even joined in the attacks, though Blount did not admit that to Spotswood. While they were not necessarily against the treaty, they told Spotswood they did not have the authority to make the treaty the Virginia governor proposed. They needed to return to their villages where the town councils could discuss it. They asked to be able to come back to Williamsburg on November 5, with a leeway of five days, where they would give their answer as to whether they would go to war against Catechna and deliver the hostages Spotswood demanded.[73] With that, the Tuscarora chiefs headed home.

Whether he fully realized it or not, Spotswood had uncovered a dangerous schism inside the Tuscarora nation. The majority of the Tuscaroras in North Carolina had not taken part in the attacks. From the start, King Blount and the chiefs from towns in the northern part of Tuscarora territory along the Tar and Roanoke Rivers feared going to war against the English. That they actually came to Spotswood's council instead of just attacking showed their reluctance to follow Hancock's lead. The sixteen hundred militiamen Spotswood paraded before them had been impressive. And with their towns just south of Virginia and west of the Albemarle, any English counterattacks meant they would be hit first. Besides, Spotswood's prohibition of trade with all Tuscaroras hurt and would leave them short of guns and ammunition to protect themselves. On the other hand, the Virginia governor's willingness to pay bounties for scalps and captives certainly sweetened his offer. But these chiefs stood on dangerous political ground, just as Hancock had. Consensus seemed to be running against peace in these upper towns, as many of their own people supported Hancock's war. So it would take all their political and diplomatic skills for King Blount and the chiefs to navigate these troubles. If anything, most hoped they could remain neutral and steer clear of having to actually fight against their Contentnea Creek kinspeople, on the one hand, and not be attacked by the English, on the other.[74]

Had these chiefs been fully aware of the chaos that had overtaken the North Carolina government and the Albemarle as a whole, they might well have considered throwing in with King Hancock. In the Albemarle, life pretty much came to a standstill even though it had not suffered a single attack. Scared settlers packed up what they could and headed north to Virginia. The courts and just about all government offices ceased to function. Governor Hyde and Council President Pollock, from a little settlement on Queen Anne's Creek, now present-day Edenton, called up the militia, but the Quakers refused to participate. In fact, the Dissenter-dominated Assembly refused to do much of anything for the colony's defense. By mid-October, North Carolina could raise only 160 or so badly armed, terribly frightened militiamen. The only thing the colony could do was ask for help, so Hyde and Pollock dispatched Christopher Gale to South Carolina to enlist support. They also appealed to Governor Spotswood of Virginia. So while the survivors on the Pamlico, Neuse, and Trent Rivers reeled, the Albemarle held its breath, prayed the Indians would not attack them, and waited for assistance from its neighbors.[75]

Then while everyone else in North Carolina either cowered or dithered, Capt. William Brice of Brice's Creek and the Trent River made the first move.

❖ Brice was a complex man. In many ways a rascal, a scoundrel, a hard, brutal man. Nevertheless, he embodied traits found in just about every English colonist in North Carolina who tried any and every way to get ahead. We know nothing of his early life, and no picture of him has ever surfaced.

In February 1699, a William Brice served as the deputy provost marshal of Bermuda, essentially a colonial police officer. But this Brice nurtured a criminal streak and was soon involved in coin clipping, meaning he shaved gold or silver from coins to make them appear legitimate but actually worth less. Authorities also accused him of trying to extort money from some of Bermuda's wealthiest colonists. One day Deputy Provost Brice arrested a gang of pirates and jailed them. But just a few days later, someone sprung them from jail and allowed them to escape Bermuda. Island officials blamed Brice. There was an investigation and an inquest, but then in February 1700, Brice disappeared from Bermuda.[76]

About a year later, the first mention of a William Brice in North Carolina appears in early April 1701 with a fellow calling himself a butcher by trade who purchased the 300-acre Old Town Creek plantation on Blank's Neck off the Pamlico River near Bath. It was a working plantation with cherry trees, an apple nursery, some tobacco, corn and wheat fields, with the usual house and outbuildings. Brice paid Thomas Arnold £7 10s. for the plantation, a very low price even then for such a place. One wonders how Brice got it so cheap.[77] In December 1701, Brice claimed 450 acres of land at the confluence of Whitby's Creek and the Trent River where he planned to raise hogs and cattle. In April 1702, he sold his Old Town Creek plantation and moved south to his holdings on the creek. John Lawson served as witness for the sale. As Brice was one of the first settlers south of the Neuse and the first on Whitby's Creek, it was soon called Brice's Creek. It retains that name to this day.[78] Was this William Brice the same former deputy provost of Bermuda who got into legal trouble there? We cannot be sure. Bermuda was certainly an important trade partner with North Carolina. And back in 1702, his plantation on Brice's Creek was about as far south as one could be and still live in North Carolina, at the far reaches of the British Empire. A place where a man on the run, maybe someone who once ran with pirates, might find a haven.

It does not seem that Brice ever plied his trade as a butcher. But if this William Brice was the same one from Bermuda, then his provost experience served him well as he soon became "sheriff" of Bath County.[79] As sheriff, he ensured that people showed up for the general court and accepted their bonds. Brice claimed his 450 acres on Brice's Creek under the Lords Proprietors' headright system in which he received one hundred acres for transporting himself to North Carolina and then another fifty acres for every other person whose way he paid over. In this case, he received lands for transporting his wife, Ann, as well as Robert Shrieve, Elisabeth and David Dupuis, and Francis, Mary, and John Linfield. It is not known whether these were Brice's friends, relatives, or servants. Brice and Ann eventually had three children, two sons, Francis and William, and a daughter, Elizabeth. We know nothing of their birth dates, but since he did not list them on his headright claim, they must have been born after William and Ann settled in North Carolina.[80]

On the creek, Brice built a house and gradually strengthened and fortified it. He was among an early group of English settlers who arrived along the banks of the lower Neuse and Trent Rivers in 1701 and 1702. These included men such as John Lawson, Furnifold Green Sr., William Hancock, and others. It was not long before the men whom Brice claimed on his headright, Robert Shrieve and David Dupuis, were working their own lands.[81]

Trouble soon erupted between these English settlers and the local Indians. Furnifold Green claimed a tract of land on which sat the Tuscarora town of Nonawharitsa, just south of present-day Whortonsvillle. Though the Tuscaroras grumbled, they eventually relocated their town. By 1703 or 1704, a group of settlers along the lower Neuse, which included Brice, Lawson, Green, and others, protested to the North Carolina government that the Indians demanded "unreasonable prices for their land, which we are neither willing or able to give them, all which hinders the speedy and well settling so Commodius a river." They also complained about a party of Neuse Indians who had killed one of their hogs, broke two house locks, and looted it of goods valued at 250 deerskins. When the settlers confronted the Indians, the petitioners said they received "nothing but reproachful language in respect to the honorable Governor and to the rest of the English."[82]

By February 1704, these same settlers south of the Pamlico complained that the nearby Tuscarora towns had become upset with the English settlers and so allied with the Bear River Indians, becoming more familiar with them than ever before. Though off by seven years, Brice and the others felt the Tuscaroras were trying to persuade the Bear River Indians to make war on the English. If anything, they said the Indians had become more "impudent" than ever and were killing the settlers' livestock, then openly bragging about it. They wanted the governor to do something. They suggested he order the chiefs to visit him up in the Albemarle and so get it settled. They also wanted the governor to send them an Indian interpreter, and a good one, who could tell the Indians what to do. Things would not really get any better.[83]

Nevertheless, Brice soon settled in and found himself a leader in the settler community. He certainly counted himself as a Proprietors' man and forged a working relationship with Thomas Pollock up in the Albemarle. Brice prospered from it, being named sheriff and later a captain in the Bath County militia. When Cary's Rebellion broke out in 1709, he sided with Hyde and Pollock. That paid off. When Hyde took over as governor, he appointed Brice, along with Lyonell Reading, as a land commissioner for Bath's Craven Precinct, which encompassed all lands south of the Pamlico River. As commissioners, Brice and Reading examined the validity of land grants made while Thomas Cary was governor. It probably did not cause him too much difficulty, as throughout that first decade of the eighteenth century, Brice had often served as an official witness for land transactions among the settlers. And Brice was very much interested in land. He speculated in it and bought what he could and sold when it was profitable. He eventually owned lands up and down Brice's Creek, on Hanging Point, and near Cape Lookout on Core Banks.

By 1708, Brice, along with the Furnifold Green and the William Hancock families, counted himself as one of the largest landholders along the Neuse and Trent Rivers.[84]

Not everything went well for Brice. Colonial North Carolina was a highly litigious society. And though he had been one of the original petitioners to get a courthouse for the Neuse River area, Brice often found himself involved in lawsuits, sometimes as plaintiff, others times as defendant. He sued Ralph Chapman, a New England mariner, for £30 in New England "current money." In March 1705, Col. William Wilkinson of the Albemarle sued Brice for £18 10s. 10d. to be paid in deerskins, half in dressed buckskins at two shillings per skin, and the other half in dressed doeskins at 18 pence per skin. Later, in October of that year, Wilkinson sued Brice again, this time for £2. 13s. 5d. payable in pork and seven large dressed doeskins. Even as sheriff he found controversy. In 1705, colonial officials charged Brice with contempt of authority for not serving a justice of the peace's warrant. This dereliction of duty even angered Pollock and Brice was to be taken into custody. The court acquitted Brice, but ordered him to pay court costs. It would not be the last time Brice would disappoint Pollock.[85]

Though Brice wore many hats—sheriff, militia officer, planter, rancher, land speculator—he also became heavily involved in the Indian trade. So did almost every settler along the Neuse and Trent Rivers. But Brice gained a reputation among the Indians as a tough, mean man who bargained hard and never hesitated to abuse Indians. During De Graffenried's and Lawson's trial at Catechna, the Indians mentioned both Brice and William Hancock by name when they complained about the sharp dealings of the traders down on the lower Neuse.[86] Brice may well have been one of those traders Lawson was talking about when he acknowledged that Indians tried to avoid dealing with angry, passionate men, who they said "are mad wolves, and no more men."[87] Brice and the Tuscarora king Tom Blount certainly had uneasy trade dealings. Brice once rented Blount a mare for a period of three months. Blount was to return the horse by a certain date and if not, the Indian king would have to pay fifty doeskins as penalty. The deadline came and went without Blount returning the horse or paying the deerskins. Brice went to court to compel Blount to make satisfaction. It did not make for good relations between Brice and the Indians. Further angering them, Brice dabbled in the Indian slave trade. He promised to deliver an Indian slave, between the age of twenty and thirty-five, to Will Lewis on his plantation on the Pamlico River by the end of March 1711. If Brice could not meet that deadline, then he was to pay Lewis £14—half in current silver money, the other half in dressed deerskins at two shillings per pound.[88]

So when the Indians attacked on September 22, they targeted Brice's house on Brice's Creek. But Indian traders such as Brice had long learned to fortify their houses to keep intruders out of their trade goods. Now this served Brice well, and his was one of the few houses to fend off the attackers. Soon refugees from around the creek and Trent River flooded into Brice's house, including some of De Graffenried's settlers. There they awaited help from North Carolina. When that did not come, Brice and his neighbors bypassed North Carolina's Governor Hyde and appealed directly to Governor Spotswood of Virginia, telling him how every day they lost horses, cattle, and fences to Indian raiders. "If not speedily prevented, we must all likewise perish with our brethren, for we have not force, nor indeed any speedy care taken to prevent it in our country." They asked Spotswood to "send to our release some considerable force of men, arms, and ammunition to detect ye barbarous insolency of those rebellious rogues, and as for provision, we are ready to ye uttermost of our ability to assist ye army if your Excellency pleases to send them."[89]

When help did not soon arrive from either North Carolina or Virginia, it was William Brice who took matters into his own hands. The militia captain now began arming some of the men taking refuge in his house. He was soon in contact with now Maj. Gen. Thomas Pollock in the Albemarle, who directed him to round up as many of De Graffenried's Palatines and Swiss who could bear arms. By early October, Brice commanded a force of about 50 or 60 men. He and Pollock now drew up the colony's first response to the Indians. They planned to attack King Hancock's town of Catechna. Pollock would send 150 Albemarle militiamen down to Bath. Then in mid-October, they were to cross the Pamlico and march overland to Core Town, which had been abandoned by Core Tom and the Indians. Brice was to take his men up the Neuse and rendezvous with the Albemarle militia at Core Town. From there they would march up Contentnea Creek and lay waste to Catechna.

Brice managed to get his men up to the abandoned Core Town. But the 150 terrified Albemarle militiamen refused to leave Bath. Fearing the Indians, nothing could make them join Brice upriver. So sometime around October 12, while De Graffenried was at Tasqui, Capt. Brice and his troops decided to make the attack on their own and began moving up Contentnea Creek. And suddenly things began to go wrong for William Brice. The Tuscaroras had been shadowing Brice's company the entire way and had sent their women, children, and old men onto the island in the creek for safety. Then, when Brice's men were about three miles from Catechna, 300 warriors sprang an ambush.[90]

It was a disaster for Brice's men from the first shot. De Graffenried had been heading back from Tasqui to Catechna when the attack began and was informed it was made up of his Germans saying "Ta, Ta." But that force was now getting mauled by the Indians. "Nearly all were wounded and an Englishman killed. Seeing that the Indians were too strong, they took flight and went home; the Indians went after them, but without doing them much harm; they only caught some little booty. The savages returned to Catechna with some horses, victuals, hats, boots, and a few jerkins."[91] The *Boston News-Letter* certainly got it all wrong when it reported that Brice's men "have been in pursuit of them [Indians] and have kill'd and taken about 50. One of the Indians whom they took has promis'd to carry the English to the Indians head quarter, provided they do but spare his life."[92]

Brice and his beaten troops fought their way back to his house on Brice's Creek. As De Graffenried commented, the Indians, good shots that they were, "drove away that poor set of Carolinians like a gang of wolves does a herd of sheep."[93] Brice came home to total chaos. The Indians had planned very well. While Brice was leading his troops against Catechna, another party of Tuscaroras attacked his own house. While the defenders there were trying to hold off these attackers, a group of Indian captives that Brice and his men had taken earlier and planned to sell as slaves now rose up from inside and began their own attack. It was touch and go for a while and only with herculean effort did the settlers beat down the prisoners inside, killing nine in doing so, and fight off the attackers outside. Once the fight was over, Brice sold off the surviving thirty-nine captive Indian women and children as slaves.[94] These had been setbacks for Brice. And now another challenge arrived as De Graffenried returned home in late October to the tears and cheers of his New Bern colonists.

Though glad to be home, De Graffenried quickly realized that his colonists' attitude toward him had soured. While he whiled away six weeks in captivity, they had been attacked by Indians with sixty or seventy of them killed, others wounded or taken captive. Much of their property and livestock had been destroyed. At least half of his surviving colonists did not think the baron could fulfill his medieval duty to protect them. And so while he was a prisoner at Catechna, many of his German and Swiss settlers had turned to William Brice for leadership. De Graffenried fumed over this. Though "I had done much good" for the Englishman,

De Graffenried claimed that Brice "debauched and led away from me, by all kind of promises and artful tricks, my people, in order to turn them, with a few English residents, into a garrison. So I had to content myself with a crowd of women and children, having not more than 40 men able to bear arms." These he could barely feed.[95]

De Graffenried lost even more support when he announced his treaty of peace with the Catechna Tuscaroras and that he would not participate in any counterattacks against the Indians. This did not sit well with many of his own people, nor did it with his English neighbors. As Brice and most Englishmen saw it, you made peace treaties with Indians when you were weak and you broke them when you were strong. Now that De Graffenried was home, Brice felt he should renounce the treaty and go all in on a counterattack. The baron refused; he had given his word. He even refused to kill the Tuscarora messenger who appeared one day to ask about the ransom the baron had promised and had been guaranteed safe passage. Besides, De Graffenried claimed, attacking the Indians or killing the messenger would just endanger the lives of the fifteen Palatine captives held by the Indians. Nevertheless, this stand cost him the loyalty of even more of his own colonists, who now threw in with Brice.[96]

One of the most outspoken settlers against De Graffenried was a blacksmith whom the baron had once punished for some infraction by making him chop wood all day. The blacksmith wanted revenge and he teamed up with Brice to get it. De Graffenried believed that the blacksmith secretly met with some Tuscaroras and told them that the baron had fooled them back at Catechna and never intended to pay the promised ransom. De Graffenried managed to defuse this by convincing the Tuscarora messenger that he did intend to honor it.[97] The blacksmith, backed by Brice, called De Graffenried a traitor for living up to his treaty and levied twenty criminal charges against him. De Graffenried defended himself and sent letters to North Carolina's Governor Hyde and Virginia's Governor Spotswood, explaining his treaty and his actions. The treaty, De Graffenried said, gave North Carolina settlers breathing room, time for them to get their defenses ready and round up men, ammunition and supplies so they could be prepared for defense and ready to go on the offense. Spotswood wholeheartedly supported the baron's treaty, saying Carolina "receives great advantage by his neutrality," as the baron would be able to discover "all the designs of the Indians, tho' he runs the risque of paying dear for it, if they ever come to know it."[98]

North Carolina was not so ready to let the baron off the hook. De Graffenried eventually had to go to the Albemarle, where he appeared first before the North Carolina governor and Council and then later before the Assembly. He defended his actions and the treaty, angrily protesting that his honor had been impugned and his reputation blotted. Even his life was in danger, he claimed. They listened to him in silence. Later, the governor and Council apologized and complimented him on his actions. The Assembly, many members of which did not like the baron's stand against former governor Cary, refused to clear his name. His colony and reputation were in shambles.[99]

As De Graffenried's fortunes plummeted, Brice and the blacksmith made their boldest move yet. The blacksmith possessed something that both De Graffenried and Brice wanted: his blacksmith tools, particularly those he used for gunsmithing and musket repair. Hammers, tongs, files, and the like were invaluable equipment to the baron's colony, but also to his now-estranged English neighbors. Unfortunately for Brice, all that equipment was locked away with De Graffenried in New Bern, now palisaded with fortified gates. Brice and his company of about forty men, fifteen or twenty of them Palatines, planned to march on New Bern, demand De Graffenried surrender the tools in the name of colonial defense, and if he did not, they would arrest him and confiscate the tools. But a boy who overheard Brice and the smith making their plans tipped off De Graffenried. So when Brice's company approached New Bern, the baron "immediately ordered the drums to beat to arms, the gates to be shut, and my men to defensive position." Brice asked the guard why the gates were closed. "To guard against Indians and Christian savages," came the reply. Did the baron consider them enemies, Brice asked. Friends did not come armed the way Brice's men were, he was told. But if Brice wanted to come in by himself, then the baron would allow it.[100]

Brice did and met the baron face to face. Brice asked why he was being treated as an enemy. De Graffenried told him all he knew of Brice's plans to take New Bern and the blacksmith's tools. And now the baron drummed up all the noble bearing he could muster. He reminded Brice that he, De Graffenried, was deputy to the Duke of Beaufort, lieutenant governor, landgrave of Carolina, and commander of this district. Was this the way Brice treated his superiors? If anything, he should arrest Brice and haul him before the governor "as a turbulent, restless, seditious and foolhardy man." This was heady stuff and Brice had to have been somewhat cowed as the baron unleashed all his aristocratic bluster. But De Graffenried did not arrest Brice as he had no adult witness against him, only the boy who had tipped him off. So the baron demanded that Brice and his men go home, but should be ready to appear when the Governor's

Council convened next to answer for this near treason. Brice, the black-smith, and the mob went home.[101]

But Brice was enraged. De Graffenried had backed him down. He must have seen this as another defeat. Ambushed at Catechna, forced to retreat, chased downriver, his own home under attack from both inside and outside, chastened by De Graffenried, and unable to get his hands on the gunsmithing tools. These were not the makings of a good military commander. He needed a victory. So Brice roused his militia company and now attacked the Bear River Indians. This time things went better for him and he took about thirty-eight of them captive, including the Bear River king. According to De Graffenried, Brice now dealt "most barbarously" with the king, whom he "nearly roasted alive near a fire, so much so that he died."[102]

De Graffenried felt that Brice's attack on the Bear River Indians spoiled any chance at peace and evaporated all the goodwill he had established with the Indians. The Tuscaroras saw Brice's attacks on Catechna and the Bear River Indians as a violation of De Graffenried's treaty and so they began another round of attacks around New Bern. "The Indians have gone on to destroy everything, and my poor people's houses, although the doors were marked with a sign, 37 had to be burned. The rest of the household furniture, although concealed and buried, was hunted up, taken away, and the cattle in the forest shot down. From there the Indians have beset one plantation after another, plundered, slaughtered and done much harm here and there in the province." He especially felt Brice's roasting of the Bear River king "embittered the Indians that it is not to be wondered at that they also treated the Christians cruelly."[103] As the baron saw it, "there were, among Brice's gang, daring fellows and men of courage, but unprincipled and brutal. If a part of the planters or residents of other places in Carolina had behaved better or been less cowardly, the Indians could have been mastered soon, and less evil would have happened."[104] Brice certainly had not covered himself with glory, but enslaving Indians endeared him to his English neighbors.

De Graffenried, however, felt abandoned by North Carolina officials, who ignored his pleas for help while they insulted his honor. Nor had they taken advantage of his treaty to prepare the colony for war. All his good work had gone for naught. "It was useless to try to bring those Carolinians to their senses."[105] He felt the same away about his own colonists. "They were, I mean most of them, unfaithful to, and deserters from, their true sovereign, and they actually did act in the same way towards me, having left me in the greatest straits."[106] Nevertheless, he felt it was his duty, his sense of noblesse oblige, that he save what he could of his colony. He spent the winter of 1711–12 trying to secure food for what remained of his settlers. He begged for something, anything, from Governor Spotswood of Virginia. But nothing came. He became a familiar figure at the Governor's Council in the Albemarle. He berated them for doing nothing. "It is surprising, ye, scandalous to see such coldness and such lack of sympathy in the inhabitants of Albemarle County."[107] He finally wheedled a shipment of corn, powder, lead, and tobacco. But Fortune turned her back on the baron when his sloop ran aground on the way to the Albemarle and was only refloated with difficulty. On the way back, loaded with supplies, sailors smoking a pipe caught the sloop afire. The crew abandoned ship just before the fire exploded a keg of gunpowder and destroyed the entire boat.[108]

Once again, De Graffenried's colony suffered. Brice's raid on the Bear River Indians brought another spate of Indian counterattacks. Many North Carolinians along the Pamlico and Neuse Rivers who had survived the September attacks did not survive these. Up in the Albemarle, Governor Hyde, Pollock, and other members of the Council increased taxes in hopes of raising £4,000 to prosecute the war.[109] Pollock hit on another way to raise money while striking at the enemy and that was to sell as slaves any Indians that had been captured. He now authorized the sale of those Bear River Indians captured by Brice, but insisted they be sold out of the colony. Brice herded the Bear River captives to Capt. John Hecklefield's house on Little River in the Albemarle, where on December 3, 1711, they were auctioned to the highest bidder. The purchaser had to give a security of £1,000 and promise to export them out of the colony with a month.[110] In the meantime, the Council tried to reinforce those garrisons that still stood and establish others in strategic areas. They ordered the canvassing of Albemarle County to come up with sufficient supplies of guns, ammunition, corn and other food, as well as militiamen.

But the colony of North Carolina had much working against it. The shoal-dotted waterways and lack of good boats hindered moving troops and supplies. As always, the Quakers refused to join the militia, and they also would not provide corn or supplies for any expedition against the Indians. De Graffenried did not think the colony could come up with even three hundred armed men. And those they did scrape up were not "well-clothed or well armed, had no ammunition, and felt not at all inclined to go to battle."[111] In Pasquotank Precinct, a committee of Quakers visited Ephraim Overman to discuss "his forwardness in assisting the soldiers to defend himself and others with carnal weapons contrary to our known principles." After the meeting, Overman "acknowledged to be an error in him and hoped for the future to take better care and walk more circumspectly."[112] Even down in Bath County men refused to go to war. John Tanyhill, William Huston, Francis Hill, Edward Pearce, Thomas Jones, George Moy, John Haman, John Slocomb, Thomas Masters, John Sheaver, and Christopher Miller were just some of the North Carolinians who refused to be drafted into the militia. These were later taken into custody for not joining Capt. William Hancock's militia company.[113] North Carolina was finding it almost impossible to mount any type of coherent response.

Mixed news came from Virginia. Spotswood assured Hyde and Pollock that the Burgesses had appropriated £4,000 to help North Carolina and had two hundred militiamen ready to be sent south. But Spotswood insisted that North Carolina pay for the Virginia troops' supplies, salary, and upkeep. Hyde and Pollock were flabbergasted. The colony barely had enough money and food as it was and could in no way pay the Virginia troops. They suggested Spotswood support them at the Queen's expense. Spotswood found this hilarious. "Why should indeed the Queen contribute to such an extent for a province from which she drew no income?"[114] Nevertheless, Spotswood promised Virginia would do what it could to help its southern neighbor.[115]

However, Spotswood did get his treaty with the Tuscarora towns along the Tar and Roanoke Rivers. He had been very concerned that Virginia's own tributary Indians, such as the Nottoways and Saponis, might throw in with Hancock's Tuscaroras and attack plantations and farms in Virginia. Fearing the war might spill over into the Old Dominion made Spotswood hesitant about supplying North Carolina.[116] He realized that the best way to neutralize any warlike intentions on the part of Virginia's own tributary Indians was to get that peace treaty signed with the upper Tuscaroras. Though King Tom Blount and the other chiefs missed the November 20 deadline, by early December they were in Williamsburg for a council.

Blount and the upper Tuscarora chiefs found themselves in a difficult situation. They had no desire to go to war against North Carolina or Virginia, and except for a few warriors they could not control, they had not taken part in the initial attacks. But neither did they want to make war on their own kinfolk. Besides, among the upper Tuscaroras rose a tide of support for their Contentnea Creek cousins as they racked up victories. With each, one more of their young men headed south to join Hancock's forces. Every day the war dragged on increased the chances of the upper Tuscarora chiefs being forced to make a hard decision. On December 10,

Spotswood made Blount and the chiefs a rather simple offer: promise to remain at peace with the English, make war against those Indians who committed the attacks, and he would reopen trade with them. The same bounties would be paid for every enemy scalp or captive. The wily King Blount and the other chiefs readily agreed.[117] After all, they had never intended to go to war if they could help it and welcomed the idea of Peter Poythress and other Virginia traders returning to their towns with trade goods. As for making war on the Catechna Tuscaroras and the other Indians, no stipulations or timetable had been demanded, so they would get around to it whenever. It also did not appear that they brought in the child hostages that Spotswood demanded. Still, Spotswood had his peace treaty and he considered Virginia and the Albemarle safe from the upper Tuscaroras.

However, other than Brice's attack on the Bear River Indians, nothing had been done about Hancock's Tuscaroras and their Core and Machapunga allies. Raids continued across the area. The roads and rivers were still not safe for settlers. The Indians along Contentnea Creek and its tributaries used this lull during the late fall and early winter of 1711–12 to prepare their own defenses by palisading their towns and creating block-houses.[118] Brice's attacks, ill-fated as they were, had shown the Indians that the English planned to fight. And Hyde and Pollock wanted nothing more than to take that fight to them. But if North Carolinians were going make a successful attack on the Tuscaroras, they would have to rely on their neighbor to the south.

CHAPTER FOUR

Col. John Barnwell

The Opportunist

It took almost a month for news of the September 22 attacks to reach
Charles Town, South Carolina. A black slave named Fenwick began
spreading a rather sketchy account of an Indian attack in North Carolina, but no one knew how he learned of it or even exactly what he told.
Nevertheless, his story worried the citizens of that thriving town and
they wanted solid news. Then Christopher Gale arrived in Charles Town
on October 26, 1711.[1] Gale was in Bath when the Machapungas attacked.
Governor Hyde had then sent him to South Carolina to appeal to that
colony for help. Within weeks Gale was standing before South Carolina's Governor Robert Gibbes and the colonial assembly, and he laid it on
thick. He told how the Tuscaroras and Core Indians had attacked without
warning, killing 130 settlers. How they killed the Neville family, then
laid out the men's bodies with pillows under their heads and Mrs. Neville
placed in a position of prayer. How the Senecas planned to come down
this winter and join the Tuscaroras to make war not just on North Carolina but on South Carolina as well. The stunned Governor Gibbes and
assembly listened in horror. Rev. Dr. Francis Le Jau, an Anglican minister
in Charles Town, deplored the Indian attacks, but heard that the Indians
"were oppress'd and had no justice done to them when they asked for it,
some suspect they were set on by a discontented party."[2] After making
his case and coordinating plans with South Carolina, Gale sailed back to
North Carolina. And then the trouble started.[3]

❖ South Carolina was a much different colony than North Carolina in
1711. For one thing, it was prosperous. Blessed with a deepwater port,
Charles Town was already a beautiful, bustling place, the largest town

in the English colonies south of Philadelphia. It far outshone North Carolina's towns of Bath and New Bern. The Low Country surrounding Charles Town produced large quantities of rice and indigo, and South Carolina rice planters were absolutely the wealthiest men in England's North American colonies. It certainly attracted its fair share of visitors and migrants. John Lawson went there in 1701 to start his trip across the Carolinas.

South Carolina had also been settled differently than North Carolina. Most of the early migrants to North Carolina had been small farmers, traders, workers, even a good number of fugitives coming out of Virginia or Maryland. Thomas Pollock and William Brice showed that money could be made in North Carolina, but the colony's lack of a deepwater port kept wealthy numbers in check. South Carolina had been settled by migrants from England's Caribbean colony of Barbados. The small island of Barbados in the Lesser Antilles was a "sugar colony," meaning its whole economy was given over to the production of sugar. Europe and its colonies discovered they had a sweet tooth along with a taste for the rum that sugar produced, so Barbadian sugar planters also became fabulously rich. This attracted more men who wanted to make it big. By the 1660s almost all available land on Barbados had been taken up for sugar plantations. It was this that sent Sir John Colleton and others on expeditions to what would become South Carolina in hopes of finding another Barbados. It was not long before the small settlement at the mouth of the Ashley and Cooper Rivers was catching the overflow from Barbados.

However, the problem with Barbadian sugar production, besides taking up land and destroying the forests, was that it ran on slave labor. Sugar production ate up slaves at a phenomenal rate. Working in extreme heat and humidity, slaves planted and tended sugarcane, harvested it using machetes, crushed the stalks, boiled the juice into molasses, and created the valuable granulated sugar, all while underfed, overworked, and infected with disease. A slave's life did not last long on Barbados. But Barbadian planters wanted, needed slaves, and on a continuous basis. As early as the 1640s, the island planters began buying African slaves from Dutch merchants. But when a sugar plantation's army of slaves dwindled, then anyone would do.

As migrants from Barbados settled in South Carolina, they brought this Barbadian outlook on slavery with them and so affected South Carolina in several ways. First, it made the colony overwhelmingly amenable to chattel slavery in which one human being legally owned another for life. The master also owned their labor and their offspring. Other colonies, even England itself, utilized chattel slavery, but South Carolina took it to new heights. The expanding rice and indigo plantations in South Carolina needed their own slaves, and so like their planter kinfolk in Barbados, South Carolina planters threw all in on importing slaves from Africa and the Caribbean. The colony quickly passed laws to regulate the life of slaves, while making it as easy as possible for masters to own them. South Carolina imported more slaves than any other colony, even Virginia with its vast tobacco plantations. By 1700, South Carolina boasted 4,200 settlers, mainly British and a few French Huguenots. At the same time, they colony counted 3,200 black slaves and 800 Indian slaves.[4]

With their own constant need for slaves, South Carolinians now looked on the nearby Indian nations as sources of labor. Most colonies, North Carolina included, saw nothing wrong with enslaving an Indian taken captive in a justified Indian war. But South Carolina took the Indian slave trade to extremes. Not long after the founding of Charles Town in 1670, several Englishmen migrated from Barbados to South Carolina and settled on Goose Creek just north of Charles Town. These men, such as James Moore Sr., Maurice Mathews, and Arthur Middleton, became very successful in the Indian trade, exchanging guns, manufactured goods, and rum for deerskins.[5] Business proved profitable as South Carolina was hemmed in by numerous Indian nations, and some very powerful ones at that. North of Charles Town, spreading in an arc from the coast to the Carolina Piedmont, lived a host of Siouan-speaking peoples such as the Waccamaws, Cape Fears, Sewees, Santees, Waterees, Sugerees, Catawbas, and many more. To the west and southwest sat the Westoes, Savannahs, and the Muskhogean-speaking Yamasees. And beyond them were the Cherokees and the many towns of the powerful Muskogee people whom the traders called the Creeks. To the south lived the coastal Cusabos and beyond them glowered Spanish Florida with its capital at St. Augustine, barely two hundred miles from Charles Town. In eastern Florida one could find the Guales and Timucuas, while in the west lived the Apalachees, though most of these peoples lived at or near Spanish missions.[6]

It did not take long for the Goose Creek Men to take the trade a step further and begin accepting Indian slaves in exchange for trade goods. Indians found providing slaves rather lucrative as traders offered large quantities of merchandise for them, at one time even up to fifteen trade muskets per slave. With so much being offered, Indian peoples around Charles Town began to make war on their enemies with the idea of taking captives to be sold as slaves. To facilitate the process, the Goose Creek

Men armed their Westo, Savannah, Yamasee, and Siouan trade partners, then encouraged them to raid villages across the American South. They were to capture whom they could, particularly Indian women and older children. It was these raids that so angered and terrified the Tuscaroras in North Carolina. Once taken, the captives were bound, marched back to Charles Town, then sold to slave buyers, often bringing between £5 and £10 sterling, sometimes more. While some Indian slaves, usually only women, remained on South Carolina plantations, most Indians slaves found themselves shipped off to Barbados, Jamaica, and other Caribbean islands, but also to North Carolina, Virginia, Pennsylvania, New York, or wherever they could find a buyer. By 1700, the most important items shipped out of Charles Town were deer hides and Indian slaves.[7]

This highly profitable and unregulated trade in Indians made the Goose Creek Men very wealthy as well as powers in South Carolina society and politics. James Moore Sr. would become South Carolina's governor in 1700. The problem was that the Goose Creek Men were not that discriminating in whom they took as a slave. Sometimes the slave catcher himself would be taken and Indian allies of the colony often found themselves enslaved. This brought the Goose Creek Men into conflict with colonial and British Empire policy, which saw the need for Indian allies as buffers against enemy Indian raids and auxiliaries when war was declared. By the early 1700s, a counterfaction was growing south of Charles Town, in Colleton County, near Port Royal, St. Helena, and present-day Beaufort. Led by Thomas Nairne, they wanted a more regulated Indian slave trade. Nairne was not against Indian slavery; he just believed slaves should be taken from enemy Indians and not from valuable allies. South Carolina put a few slave-taking regulations on the books, for example, a trader could not buy an Indian captive from another Indian until the captive had been in that town for at least three days. Traders were not allowed to let their own slaves go to war. But officials found these hard to enforce.[8]

So now in October 1711, as Christopher Gale appealed to them for help avenging the Tuscarora attacks on North Carolina, South Carolina officials, many of them who had made their money in the slave trade, knew an opportunity when they heard one. They could earn gratitude and favor by helping a sister colony in distress, but even better, here was the chance at a legitimate slave raid. Thomas Nairne was all for it. So on October 26, 1711, Governor Robert Gibbes spoke before the South Carolina Assembly and encouraged its members to help North Carolina. "They are subjects of the Queen, tenants of the same Lords Proprietors, Christians, and Neighbors, we will speedily & willingly afford them our assistance,

& heartily entreat us to send them a number of Indians with all dispatch."
The assembly agreed and voted overwhelmingly to help the inhabitants of
North Carolina "in their present deplorable condition."[9]

This assistance would come in the form of a military expedition. Governor Gibbes demanded "that a sufficient number of warlike Indians,
such as lie most convenient for this expedition, be immediately raised &
a proper officer or officers appointed to command them. That a sufficient
quantity of armes & ammunition be provided & that all due encouragement be given to bring this necessary war to a happy conclusion." The
South Carolina Assembly immediately ordered Indian traders "to raise
levies of Indians for ye said expedition."[10] Then they asked Gale what
North Carolina could contribute to the South Carolina forces. Only fifteen hundred bushels of corn, six barrels of gunpowder, and about the
same amount of bullets and shot, he replied. That was not much. So the
Assembly appropriated £4,000 to pay for the expedition and raised the
duties on African slaves imported into the colony to fund it. Governor
Gibbes directed Col. Hugh Grange, Col. Alex Parris, Col. John Fenwick,
Capt. Thomas Nairne, and Col. George Logan to form a committee and
begin gathering supplies and helping the Indian traders get the warriors
ready.[11]

Using Indians to fight other Indians was common practice throughout England's North American colonies. Colonial officials believed that
Indians were better at it, as many Englishmen found guerrilla warfare
risky. Besides, it was cost-effective. The European way of war meant
moving heavy artillery, gathering months of supplies, then finding oxen
and horses to haul everything over often difficult roads and terrain. All
this was expensive. It was much cheaper to use Indian allies as an invasion
force where the colony's outlay was mainly in gifts of gunpowder, ammunition, clothing, blankets, and such. Indians carried their own weapons
and were thought to be able to live off the land. There was still some expense, but not nearly as much if colonial officials tried to mount a major
expedition composed of English troops and heavy artillery. And in this
instance, South Carolina had some doubts about their own Indian allies
and wondered whether or not they would suddenly throw in with the
Tuscaroras. At least getting their Indians to fight in North Carolina meant
they would not be fighting them in South Carolina.[12]

The South Carolina traders were all for these expeditions as they expected to reap a tidy profit. They would receive the slaves the Indians
brought back and then resell them at a nice return. The South Carolina government also expected these traders to provide the Indians with

ammunition, flints, powder, and gifts of merchandise, which the traders were glad to do for the right price. And the South Carolina Assembly was more or less held hostage by the traders, because if they did not get the price they wanted, the traders would just persuade the Indians to not go on the expedition.[13]

For their part, the South Carolina Indian allies jumped at the chance to be part of the expedition. It was an opportunity to take revenge and settle scores with their old Tuscarora and Core enemies. It was also a chance for a warrior to display bravery and so increase his prestige. But above all, it was a chance to enrich oneself by looting the Tuscarora towns and taking slaves, which they could sell to waiting South Carolina traders for guns and merchandise.[14]

Now South Carolina only needed someone to lead the expedition. On November 3, 1711, the assembly made its decision. "Resolved that John Barnwell Esqr. be Commander in Chief of the forces of white men & Indians to be raised to march agt ye Tusqueroras & other nations of Indians now in rebellion agt the government of North Carolina."[15]

❖ A fiery-tempered Irishman, Barnwell was born in Dublin in about 1671 into what would have been considered the upper middle class. His family descended from the Normans who settled in the area back in the 1100s. Grandfathers of both his mother and father had been Dublin aldermen and strong supporters of the English Crown. His grandfather on his father's side, a merchant, had even been Lord Mayor of Dublin and gained the Archerstown estate in County Meath. Barnwell's father, Matthew, had been a captain in King James II's Irish army but was killed at the siege of Derry in 1690. Unfortunately, Barnwell's father had supported the wrong English king, and when James was deposed in the Glorious Revolution that brought William and Mary to the English throne, the Barnwells lost Archerstown. They could at least console themselves with a coat of arms, which consisted of an ermine shield with a red border, a crest with five ostrich feathers in different colors, atop which sat a silver falcon and helmet. Inscribed on it was the family motto *Malo Mori Quam Foedari*—"I would rather die before being disgraced." Death before dishonor.[16] With his father dead and their estate gone, in 1701 at the age of thirty, John Barnwell decided to leave Ireland and head to Charles Town, South Carolina. Irish acquaintances said it was, "out of a humor to go to travel but for no other reason."[17]

Charles Town in 1701 was a place where past political misalignments proved no hindrance and a city where a bright young man could make a name for himself. And Barnwell did. Not long after arriving, he was taken under the wing of Nicholas Trott, who in 1703 became chief justice of South Carolina. Barnwell profited much from this connection. In 1703, the South Carolina government appointed Barnwell as deputy surveyor general of the colony and ordered him to map Port Royal Sound. He fell in love with the area and in 1705 received a 1,400-acre grant, which became the basis of his "Doctors Plantation." Eventually he would own 6,500 acres of land around Port Royal and two lots inside the town of Beaufort. He also participated in the Indian trade, especially with the Yamasees who lived not too from his plantation in Port Royal. He was named clerk of the Governor's Council and in 1704 became the deputy secretary of South Carolina. In 1707, he was appointed as comptroller of the province, a definite promotion. At some point before 1704, he married Anne Berners, the sister of a Charles Town merchant. They would go on to have eight children: Margaret in February 1704, Nathaniel, Anne, Mary, Bridget, Catherine, John, and Elizabeth, the last, in March 1711.[18]

However, Barnwell had principles and the grit to stand up for them. In 1709, in an amazing turn of events, Barnwell openly broke with his mentor, Nicholas Trott. At this time, South Carolina was undergoing some of the same internal turmoil between Anglicans and Dissenters that North Carolina was. Rolled into this were political and geographical rivalries. On the one hand were the Anglican Party represented by the Goose Creek Men north of Charles Town, backed by Trott, the Moores, and other families who wanted an unregulated Indian trade. The "Dissenters" were Thomas Nairne and his allies who represented the up-and-coming Port Royal area south of Charles Town and who wanted a more regulated Indian trade. Barnwell, who possessed a reformist streak, was Nairne's neighbor in Port Royal and so threw in with the Dissenters. His stand cost him all his government positions and salary. But his neighbors in Colleton County strongly backed him, and he was named a justice of the peace and in 1711 represented them in the South Carolina Assembly.[19]

While his break with Trott and the loss of his offices dismayed his family back in Ireland, it really did not do him much political harm in South Carolina. Though hotheaded, he seemed an affable fellow with many friends and strongly supported by the people of Colleton and Granville Counties. His experience as an Indian trader even gained him respect from the Goose Creek Men. He had also proven himself a capable soldier. Queen Anne's War, between England on one side and France and Spain on the other, had been hot since 1702. In 1707, a Spanish fleet from Florida tried to attack Charles Town, but was repulsed. On its way back to

Florida, one of the Spanish ships tried to raid the area around Sewee Bay. Barnwell, aboard a sloop, managed to capture the Spanish ship. He even got to announce his victory before the Assembly. In 1708, Barnwell led several raiding parties up the St. Johns River in Spanish Florida, attacking Spain's Timucua Indian allies.[20] So when the South Carolina Assembly called on the forty-one-year-old Barnwell to command the expedition to North Carolina, they were at least appointing a battle-tested commander experienced in leading Indian allies.

Throughout the rest of October, November, and December, Barnwell and South Carolina built his expedition. The Assembly allowed Barnwell to purchase £200 worth of provisions and stores. Nairne wrote the Lords Proprietors to ask if they would be willing to pay some of the costs of the expedition. Nothing came of that. Traders began raising their contingents of Indian warriors. In Charles Town, officials worried that Spain might get wind of the expedition and attack South Carolina while its Indian allies were gone. To keep word from reaching St. Augustine, two Florida Indians who had been visiting Charles Town were now prevented from returning home. God was called on as Governor Gibbes designated Friday, November 16, as a day of prayer to ensure Barnwell's success. Hoping for fresh intelligence, Barnwell sent an agent in a small boat to North Carolina. In what should have foretold of troubles to come, Barnwell instructed the unnamed agent to let the North Carolina government know that he was coming, how much South Carolina was spending on this expedition, and to try to get a promise of reimbursement.[21] But it does not appear as if Barnwell's agent ever made it to North Carolina governor Hyde and Council President Pollock.

By mid-November, Barnwell had assembled a force of seven hundred men, maybe more. About thirty-five or so of these were South Carolina officers and militiamen, the rest were Indian warriors. The total number probably changed daily as warriors came and went. Dr. Edmund Ellis petitioned the Assembly to serve as the expedition's surgeon and was told to talk to Barnwell. But Barnwell's Yamasees had complained about Ellis selling rum to them and so Barnwell turned him down. When finally assembled, Barnwell's expedition consisted of four companies and was not only a large army by colonial standards but an amazing alliance of Indians from across the lower Southeast. Barnwell himself and his second-in-command, Maj. Alexander Mackay, commanded the Yamasee Company, which consisted of Yamasees, Apalachees, Cusabos, and a Yuchi people Barnwell called the Hog Logees. These warriors tended to come from areas south of Charles Town. Capt. Robert Steel's troop consisted of thirty

English militiamen, most of them mounted on horses. They also brought war dogs to track down enemy Indians. Captain Jack, a renowned Catawba Indian warrior much respected by Barnwell and his officers, commanded the Esaw Company, which comprised the more northwesterly Piedmont Catawbas, Waterees, Sugerees, Waxhaws, Santees, and Congarees. The Esaws and Catawbas were essentially one and the same people. Capt. Burnaby Bull's Company was composed of Waterees, Pedees, Winyaws, Cape Fears, Hoopengs, Wareeres, Cheraws, and Saxapahaws, most of these from directly north of Charles Town.[22]

A complicated, ridiculously optimistic, and ultimately unfeasible plan of attack had been worked out between Barnwell and Gale. Gale was to sail back to the Albemarle and take command of the North Carolina militia or of whatever forces were available. He would gather supplies for his own men, but also have some ready for Barnwell's once they arrived in North Carolina. Incredibly, Gale was then expected to move his men and supplies up the Neuse River 120 miles, through Hancock's Tuscarora territory, and rendezvous with Barnwell and his army on the headwaters of the Neuse, west of Tuscarora country. One has to wonder what Barnwell was thinking. Had North Carolina been able to do that, they would not have needed South Carolina's help. It certainly showed how out of touch both Barnwell and Gale were about the situation in North Carolina. The colony still reeled from the attacks, with few troops, fewer supplies, and little ability to help Barnwell. Then muddling everything, Gale was captured by French privateers on his way back to North Carolina. He remained a captive on the island of Martinique for four months and so had no way to inform Hyde or Pollock of South Carolina's plans. Barnwell could not know that he was marching into enemy territory on his own, in the dark, with no real knowledge of who was friend, who was foe, and where, when, or if North Carolina troops and supplies would catch up with him.[23]

Barnwell's expedition left the Congaree towns in late December or early January. "Many wise in this province doubt of the success," Dr. Le Jau deplored from Charles Town.[24] Nevertheless, the expedition slowly headed north through the Wateree and Pedee towns to the Waxhaws. There Barnwell's troops turned due east to the Cheraw town on the Yadkin-Pedee River, then north, crossing into North Carolina not far from present-day Rockingham. From there his expedition headed northeast toward the upper Cape Fear River. He recruited as he went. The weather turned snowy and it took him eight days to go the sixty miles from the Pedee River to the upper Cape Fear River, just below where the Deep and Haw Rivers join to form it. Then it took him two more days to cross it. The bad weather caused a rash of desertions among his Indian troops, particularly among the Pedees, Winyaws, Cape Fears, and Saxapahaws of Captain Bull's Company, leaving Bull with only sixty-seven men. Barnwell worried about the affect these desertions would have on his troops' morale, so he lied to conceal them. He told his army that he had sent Captain Bull's company by another route and that they would join up later.[25]

Once across the Cape Fear, they marched east to Tuscarora territory and crossed the upper Neuse River on January 28, 1712, probably somewhere between present-day Clayton and Smithfield. At the Neuse, Barnwell seemed befuddled and angry that Gale was not there waiting for him with North Carolina troops and supplies. He sent out scouts, but they found no sign of Gale. Barnwell did learn that he was only about twenty-seven miles from the Tuscarora town of Torhunta. He also met a village of Saxapahaws on the run. They told Barnwell they had been attacked by Tuscaroras from Catechna in early January because they had refused to join in the attacks on English settlers. Sixteen of their people had been killed. Forced off their lands, the Saxapahaws said they were heading to South Carolina to pay tribute and ask for protection. Instead, Barnwell, calling them "brave men and good," persuaded them to join his expedition.[26]

He certainly wanted the Saxapahaw recruits, as by the time he got to the Neuse, desertions had whittled his army down to 528 Indians and militiamen. Despite this, the weather had cleared and Barnwell decided to attack Torhunta. On January 29, he marched his troops hard throughout the night in hopes of surprising the village with a morning assault. In fact, Barnwell's appearance on the Neuse River had taken the Tuscaroras by surprise. No one expected an English-led force to show up there in mid-winter. Then again, the Tuscaroras could not have been shocked by an army's appearance on their western flank as Torhunta and other nearby towns had been building protective forts and blockhouses for just such an occurrence. And Barnwell's night march did not achieve a surprise as Torhunta was waiting for him.[27]

Torhunta was not the westernmost Tuscarora town, but only Toisnot near present-day Wilson was further west. It was one of the older Tuscarora settlements and sat south of Nahunta Swamp on Beaver Dam Run, a tributary of Contentnea Creek in present-day Wayne County. Its name means "It Stays Overnight," indicating that Torhunta town was considered a sort of way station or oasis for Tuscarora travelers heading to or from the Piedmont. It was the westernmost of a series of towns and settlements associated with the Contentnea Creek Tuscaroras. Just east of

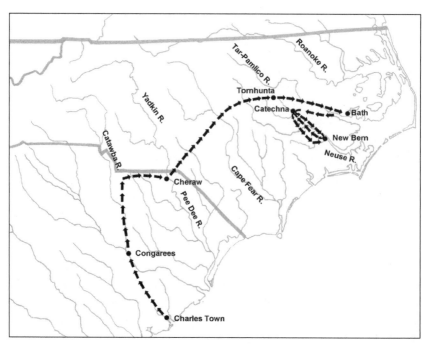

Col. Barnwell's Expedition, December 1711–July 1712. Map by David A. Norris

Torhunta sat a cluster of communities called Kenta, meaning "Prairie," on Cow Branch, also a Contentnea Creek tributary. Almost directly east several miles sat Neoheroka town on Contentnea Creek proper north of present-day Snow Hill. Called "Forked Field" because the creek bisected Neoheroka, it was connected to Torhunta by a well-worn trail. East of Neoheroka, on the north side of the Contentnea, was Innennits, meaning "Conjoined Hills," east of present-day Snow Hill on Panther Swamp. Further east down the creek sat Caunookehoe, meaning "Great Pot," near present-day Maury. Finally, down the Contentnea, about six or so miles above its confluence with the Neuse, sat King Hancock's town of Catechna, where John Lawson met his fate. Meaning "Submerged Loblolly Pine," it sat near the present-day town of Grifton.[28]

Barnwell quickly realized about Torhunta what De Graffenried had seen about Catechna, that they were not so much closely packed, nuclear towns like Tasqui, but rather "only a plantation here and there scattered about the country, no where 5 houses together . . . so it is impossible to surprise many before the alarm takes."[29] Nevertheless, the Tuscaroras of Torhunta, Kenta, and other towns along Contentnea Creek and its tributaries had prepared for the appearance of an army such as Barnwell's.

Knowing their dispersed settlements could not be defended, these Tusca-roras had recently built centralized palisaded forts, each about a mile or so from the other. Barnwell counted nine of them. But most of these had not been fully completed by the time Barnwell's army arrived at Torhunta at the end of January 1712. Even worse for the Tuscaroras was that it was the time of the hunt and most of Torhunta's young men were gone, leaving only old men and a few women to man the fort. Tipped off about Barn-well's approach, the older men of Torhunta retired to the nearest fort, ready to resist, while most, but not all of the women and children took to hiding places in the swamps and forest.[30]

That morning of January 30, Barnwell decided to attack what he con-sidered the strongest fort guarding Torhunta. He called it Fort Narhantes. He originally planned to make an orderly, European-style assault on the fort walls, but his Yamasees were hot to fight. So he immediately or-dered a headlong assault. Barnwell's South Carolina militia advanced on the walls with the Yamasees charging up behind them. It turned bloody as Tuscaroras fired from the walls. Barnwell's men eventually forced their way into the uncompleted fort. But the Tuscaroras had planned well as Barnwell's troops now found themselves facing two strongly fortified and well-defended blockhouses. Again they attacked, with a militiaman named Parence throwing the expedition's flag atop the blockhouse then calling for the men to come retake it. Barnwell, impressed with the man's bravery, immediately promoted Parence to coronet, the lowest officer's rank in the militia. The Tuscaroras fought fiercely and refused to surren-der. Some women had taken refuge in the blockhouses and they fought as hard as the men. "The enemy were so desperate, the very women shooting arrows, yet they did not yield until most of them were put to the sword," Barnwell complained. He counted ten women killed in the attacks.[31]

It took about thirty minutes for Barnwell's men to take the Torhunta fort and blockhouses. "The word was revenge," Barnwell said. "Which we made good by the execution we made of the enemy." While the South Carolina militia mopped up any resistance, his Indian allies busily looted the fort and the houses surrounding Torhunta. Barnwell complained that "while we were putting the men to the sword, our Indians got all the slaves & plunder, only one girl we got." His troops took fifty-two scalps and captured thirty slaves. The ten dead Tuscarora women distressed him as women captives were the most valuable slaves. It was unusual to have this many women killed in an Indian war. But Barnwell's men had also been bloodied. By his count, he suffered six killed, twenty-eight wounded. All were Indians. Among the dead were the Wateree king, the Peterba King, and Cusabo Tom.[32] The Virginia trader Peter Poythress soon got wind of the attack and passed it on to Governor Spotswood. But word was that Barnwell had killed only about twenty "old men and women" and taken "about 30 children prisoners when all the young men were not at home."[33]

It had been a hard fight, so that night Barnwell rested his men at what was left of Torhunta. At about dawn the next morning, warriors from the nearby town of Kenta launched a surprise attack on Barnwell's forces. Now on the defensive, Barnwell ordered two Indian detachments from Captain Jack's company to cross a swamp and come in behind the attacking Kenta warriors. Suddenly, the men of Kenta found themselves with enemy in their rear and so were beaten back, though Barnwell complained that Captain Jack's men sprang the ambush a little too early. Barnwell's men suffered only two wounded, but they lifted nine Kenta scalps and brought in two captives. And now we must wonder a little about Barnwell as he "ordered [them] immediately to be burned alive."[34] It was a brutal, sadistic war.

Then, suddenly, on the heels of these two very convincing victories, Barnwell's Indian army deserted him. They had their captives and plunder and now headed back to the merchants in South Carolina who would buy it from them. Maybe they also felt the war was over. Barnwell had taught the Tuscaroras a lesson and things had been set right. It had been a somewhat successful raid for slaves and plunder. Now every man in Captain Bull's company took off. Captain Jack's Esaw Company lost everyone except Captain Jack and twenty-three men. Barnwell was shocked to see them "loading themselves with English plunder of which these towns are full and running away from me. Nothing left for the white men but their horses tired & their wounds to comfort them."[35] Almost all the Piedmont Siouans deserted. Not only did they take English plunder, but they also made off with ten bags of valuable musket balls and many of the militia's horses. This left Barnwell with fewer than two hundred men, essentially the South Carolina officers and militia and his own Yamasee Company. And many of these were wounded. He was now short of men, ammunition, and horses. Even the Yamasees talked about returning home, but Barnwell convinced them that the best way to do that was to head for the North Carolina coast.[36]

His bad fortune continued as now the weather turned rainy and for the next four days, Barnwell and his depleted army used Torhunta and Fort Narhantes as a forward base where his sick and wounded could recover. From there, he sent out raiding parties and they destroyed five Tuscarora settlements, 374 houses, and two thousand bushels of corn. Though they could not locate the Tuscarora women and children, his men captured a few warriors. This time, instead of burning them, Barnwell interrogated them. He learned that Seneca warriors had been among the Tuscaroras, urging them to attack the North Carolina settlers and promising plenty of supplies if they would. In fact, there were still at least two Seneca diplomats among the Tuscaroras. Barnwell also learned that the flash point that set off the war was the beating of a drunken Tuscarora by an Englishman. Barnwell hoped to discover if Virginia had been supplying Hancock's warriors with weapons, but he could not confirm it.[37]

From the number of farms, plantations, and villages his men reported, Barnwell figured there should be somewhere between twelve hundred and fourteen hundred Tuscarora warriors in the area. But his scouting parties could not locate them. They reported the towns, forts, and blockhouses all deserted. The Tuscaroras, it seemed, were using an age-old strategy of giving up land and towns and moving the women and children as far away from Barnwell as possible. In this case, they were sent north toward the upper Tuscarora towns along the Tar and Roanoke Rivers. Though these upper towns had not participated in the attacks on the settlers, they were still kinfolk and Tuscaroras, and the rules of hospitality still applied. With the women and children out of harm's way, the warriors planned to avoid Barnwell's troops, except for harassment ambushes, and retreat down to Hancock's town. They, along with war parties even now being recalled from the coast, would make a stand at Catechna's heavily fortified fort. If all went according to plan, Barnwell and his army would run out of supplies long before they could take the fort and so be forced to retreat.[38]

On February 4, the rain quit and Barnwell decided to move. He originally wanted to march down Contentnea Creek and attack the Tuscaroras at Catechna. But the desertion of so many his Siouan allies, the wounded he had to carry, the reluctance of his Yamasee warriors to make the attack, and the general shortage of ammunition, horses, and guides forced Barnwell to change his mind. He did not want to be stumbling around Tuscarora country where he imagined fourteen hundred unseen warriors waiting for him and his two hundred men. Instead, they would march for Bath on the Pamlico River, where he expected to find North Carolina troops with supplies and ammunition. So now Barnwell demolished Fort Narhantes at Torhunta and set off down the trail, which bypassed Kenta, for Neoheroka. He reached Neoheroka that afternoon, but found he would have to cross over Contentnea Creek on logs. The only real incident was when "three skulking Tuscarouros shot" one of his men, "Seneca Tom" Giles. Giles died and Barnwell sent out war dogs to track down the snipers. His men returned with a captive, whom Barnwell interrogated and decided to use as a guide. Barnwell's men looted the deserted Neoheroka and surrounding farms, and stayed there that night.[39]

The next morning they left Neoheroka, moving east down Contentnea Creek, looting and destroying whatever they could find. They reached the town of Innennits by noon. It was deserted. But here Barnwell found the scalps of fourteen white people and "a world of plunder" that had been taken from the English, German, and Swiss settlements during the September attacks. His Yamasee warriors now dropped their Torhunta plunder for what they considered better spoils. Barnwell ordered his South Carolina militia to not take anything as they were already overloaded with weapons, ammunition, and provisions. His men spent two hours at Innennits, burned the town and a small fort, then continued down Contentnea Creek. They marched through many, many deserted Tuscarora farms and plantations, and spent the night in the small town of Caunookehoe.[40]

The next morning, the Tuscaroras at Catechna got a pleasant surprise. They expected Barnwell to continue marching east down the creek and attack them at Catechna's fort. Anticipating this, they had been massing their forces there and the fort contained possibly three hundred warriors. Instead, on February 6, the English expedition detached itself from Contentnea Creek, forgoing any attack on Catechna, and marched northeast cross country toward the Pamlico River and out of the lower Tuscarora country. The Tuscaroras had to see this as a great victory. Once again, they had forced an English army to retreat. Barnwell's army spent the day crossing pine barrens and streams deep enough to swim their horses. At one point, his scouts discovered five Tuscaroras returning from a raid on the English settlements, at least that was what Barnwell said. His scouts gave chase, but the men escaped, though they dropped their packs and guns. They found the packs full of "delicate parsnips & turnips with a turkey & sev'll other household goods." That evening his men returned from patrol with six Indian women taken for slaves and two Indian men. He spent the night on the south side of the Pamlico River, just five miles downriver from King Tom Blount's town of Ucohnerunt and not far from present-day Greenville.[41]

The morning of February 7, Barnwell began moving his troops across the wide Pamlico. First he swam about thirty "stout fellows" across with their weapons to a deserted Tuscarora farm, where they fanned out to protect the landing site. Next, he readied log rafts and began ferrying his men across—horses, wounded, and baggage first—then his militia and warriors. But the Tuscaroras were not willing to let them go without something to remember them by. In the middle of the crossing, when

Barnwell's forces were split, some on the north bank and some still on the south, a party of about fifty Tuscaroras attacked his rear guard. Expecting this, Barnwell's men stood firm while he dispatched about eighty Yamasees to edge around the attackers and hit their flank. But once again the Yamasees sprang the ambush too soon and the Tuscaroras managed to withdraw, leaving guns, packs and blood trails behind. The Yamasees took only two scalps. But the firefight delayed the crossing. It would not be until after nightfall that Barnwell got all his men across the Pamlico. Even then he had to chase off six Tuscarora warriors found skulking nearby.[42]

The crossing had been tough and it took Barnwell's men until noon the next day, February 8, to get moving. Making matters worse, it began to rain again, and to rain hard. Creeks flooded, streams overflowed, making progress difficult. Barnwell placed the wounded atop the remaining horses while he and the rest of his South Carolina militia walked. As Barnwell saw it, this good turn would encourage all his troops to fight well for him. They slogged east all day, down the north bank of the Pamlico River, and made camp that afternoon.[43]

The next morning, February 9, Barnwell, as usual, arose at about 4 A.M., well before dawn. He had just relieved the sentries, at about 5 A.M., and was warming himself near a fire when the Tuscaroras attacked, pouring volleys of fire into the sleeping camp. Several shots hit the tree Barnwell was leaning against, making him believe they were deliberately targeting him. Barnwell's troops roused quickly and about thirty or forty of them returned fire. Soon the Tuscarora attackers withdrew, though his men remained on guard until daybreak. He reported no casualties but neither could he see where any Tuscaroras had been hit. Barnwell soon had his troops on the move. Within a few miles, they came upon "a ruin[ed] English plantation where [we] killed beef & hogs." They spent the remainder of the day using logs to ferry his men across a broad creek. It took the entire day, so the expedition camped that night at the destroyed plantation.[44]

On February 10, Barnwell and his army continued their march toward Bath. They went three miles, passing several more destroyed English plantations, until they came to another wide creek. The colonel figured the road to Bath was nearby, so he sent a party of two Indians and a white militiaman to locate it. If they found the road, they were to go on to Bath and order the commander of that town, if it was not deserted, to send a periauger upriver to his camp to take his wounded and leave some men to guide the rest of his troops and horses to the town. The party must have made it, as at about midnight three periaugers came up the Pamlico and found Barnwell's camp. The next morning, February 11, he loaded his wounded and supplies aboard the boats while the rest of Barnwell's men marched for town. His army entered Bath later that afternoon "to ye incredible wonder and amazement of the poor distressed wretches here, who expressed such extremity of mad joy that it drew tears from most of our men."[45] When they heard of it, Pollock and the Council sent their congratulations. "Return the hearty thanks of this board to the Hon. Col. John Barnwell Esq. Genl. and Commander in chief of all the forces etc., for his great care, diligence and conduct, and to congratulate him on the success already obtained against the enemy."[46]

At Bath, Barnwell was both excited and disgusted. On the one hand, he saw himself as the savior of Bath and North Carolina. The town, he found, was full of frightened widows and orphans, all begging him to get them out of there and to any place of safety. He still had no word of Christopher Gale, not realizing he had been captured by French privateers. But Barnwell was angry to discover there was little food at Bath, certainly not what he expected to find there for his troops. The Albemarle militia sent there by Pollock in October, who refused to join Captain Brice on his expedition to Catechna, had stayed only long enough to eat up all the supplies and then abandoned the town. He was also surprised that there were no North Carolina troops waiting for him. Nevertheless, Pollock up in the Albemarle ordered five hundred bushels of corn to be sent to Barnwell. He promised North Carolina reinforcements would soon arrive as well.[47]

After spending a few days in Bath, Barnwell and his troops crossed to the south side of the Pamlico and made their headquarters about fifteen miles upriver near Lyonell Reading's fortified home. He now decided that once supplies and reinforcements arrived, he would make an attack on Hancock at Catechna. During his march, Barnwell learned from prisoners that Hancock had three hundred warriors and several large guns with plenty of powder. But he also discovered that the Tuscaroras, even those at Catechna, were not united in strategy or tactics. He believed Hancock had "wheedled" his young men into going to war, while the "old men & chiefs went bitterly and told them the ill consequences would follow." In reality, it had been the young men and Core Tom who had wheedled Hancock. Now Barnwell determined to end the war by taking Hancock's fort at Catechna. All this would shower glory on his home colony, he believed, and be an addition to the many "laurels" South Carolina armies had gathered over the years from Florida to Virginia.[48]

But the war was not yet over. And Barnwell soon found that his Irish temper and tendency to speak the truth as he saw it could make him some powerful enemies.

CHAPTER FIVE

Thomas Pollock

The Destroyer

The arrival of Barnwell's army in Bath truly was a boost for the colonists of North Carolina. Here stood visible evidence that they were not alone in this. Many believed that the tide of war had already turned and it would only be a short time before Barnwell destroyed the Tuscaroras and their allies. Barnwell's army also gave confidence to the North Carolina government. Though the Quakers of the Albemarle and in the Assembly still refused to support the war, the government was able to start rounding up supplies and militiamen. Regular communications were established between Barnwell on the Pamlico and the North Carolina government in the Albemarle. Forts were ordered to be established wherever Barnwell designated. While Governor Hyde was the face of the North Carolina government, the actual prosecution of the war fell to Thomas Pollock. It soon came to pass, as has happened so often in American military history, that the commander in chief and his general in the field did not see eye to eye. Barnwell's arrogance may have blinded him to the fact that Pollock was not a man to be taken lightly.[1]

❖ In many ways, Thomas Pollock and William Brice were North Carolinians cut from the same bolt of cloth. Both were men on the make, always looking for opportunities to increase their wealth. Only Pollock seemed much better at it than Brice. Thomas Pollock, named after his father, was born May 6, 1654, in Glasgow, Scotland, though the family was more associated with the little hamlet of Balgrey, a few miles northwest of Glasgow. Solidly upper middle class, the family had gained fame back around 1500 when a Pollock ancestor saved the Scottish king James IV from an attack by a wild boar. We know nothing of Pollock's mother, but he had an older brother, James, and two sisters, Margaret and Helen. His education seemed adequate, though spelling would not be his strong suit. Since young Thomas was not the firstborn, he was not going to inherit anything from his father, so he turned to business in Scotland, though what that business was has never been clear. At some point he decided his best chance to strike it rich was to head to America. With some money from his business dealings and a little from his family, he left Scotland. We do not know the date. He seems to have had some business dealings with Bermuda and Barbados as well as with Maryland, Boston, and Virginia. Then on June 27, 1683, the twenty-nine-year-old Pollock arrived in North Carolina. He was home.[2]

On November 6, 1683, Pollock bought a tract of land from William Bread and his wife, Lydia, on the west bank of the Chowan River, just across the river from present-day Edenton. He named his plantation Balgra in honor of his boyhood home back in Scotland. This would become the base of his business empire. On June 19, 1690, Pollock married Martha Cullen, the daughter of Thomas Cullen of Dover, England, and the widow of Robert West. This seems to have been truly a marriage for love. In North Carolina, Pollock began to experience both business success and personal tragedy. Martha gave birth to twins, two girls, Elizabeth and Martha, on March 20, 1691, but both died before the year was out. Soon Martha was again pregnant and again gave birth to twins, again named Elizabeth and Martha, but they died that same night. Then things got better. Another girl was born March 4, 1694, and they again named her Martha, but this time baby Martha lived. Pollock's first son, Thomas Jr., was born November 9, 1695. Cullen was born September 27, 1697. Then George, the baby, was born October 25, 1699. But birthing eight children, half of them dead within days or months, seemed to have worn heavily on Pollock's wife, and she died on February 17, 1702. Pollock himself would have bouts of illness that would hit him hard in 1698, 1705, and 1708.[3]

While experiencing the tragedies and happiness of home life, Pollock was on his way to becoming a highly successful merchant and North Carolina's wealthiest man. He began shipping out barrels of pickled pork, tobacco, and deerskins to Bermuda, Barbados, or other North American colonies. But colonial business was full of booms and busts. Bad debts, market downturns, and losses from various colonial wars bit into his profits. However, things improved for him in the 1690s and he never looked back. Putting him in a different class than most North Carolina merchants, Pollock owned a fleet of ships: a ketch named the *Dove*, a brigantine named *Martha*, the sloop *Speedwell*, and another sloop *Greyhound*. In

1710, he would come to own De Graffenried's sloop, the *Return*. In turn, he imported tools, shoes, rum, guns, anything that was in demand by settlers or Indians in North Carolina.[4]

As a merchant, Pollock was at home trading in deerskins, tobacco, pork, land, and colonial current money even more than he was with pounds sterling, which were rare. He not only bought from and sold to North Carolinians; he also gave credit and lent money. Pollock was also quick to sue when a client could not pay their bills. The colonial records are full of lawsuits initiated by Pollock for nonpayment: John Bursbre for £8 12s. in pork; Stephen Scott for 43s. 4d.; Thomas Hawkins for £10 4s. in skins at the Virginia rate; Capt. Richard Smith for £12 sterling. And these are just a few. In 1704, he sued the master of his brigantine *Martha*, Henry Montfort, for £700 in damages he claimed Montford negligently did to a load of 244 barrels of pork, 2,690 dressed deerskins, a considerable number of furs, some tanned leather, and other goods. Pollock received a judgment of £400, but Provost Marshal John Hecklefield allowed Montford to escape without paying. So Pollock sued Hecklefield. Pollock won that case, the court ordering Hecklefield to pay Pollock the £400 plus court costs.[5]

Pollock was also a planter. He grew tobacco and raised hogs and cattle. In the early 1700s, he began producing tar, pitch, and other naval stores. To maintain his profits, he purchased slaves in great numbers. By the end of his life he owned at least eighty, some African, some Indian. As a slave owner, Pollock found himself beset with runaways. Around 1700, two of his slaves ran away with a "mulatto" from Virginia. He asked to be excused from attending chancery court as he had learned that the three runaways were hiding out on his plantation on Salmon Creek. He now went to round them up. It was, he wrote to the court, for his own interests, his family's safety, and the peace of the community that he could not attend the court lest more of his slaves take his absence as an opportunity to run.[6]

Though it did not appear that Pollock had any legal training, in North Carolina he often did lawyer's work. Over the years, he served as an attorney for several men, including his father-in-law, Thomas Cullen. He was often called as a legal witness or to serve as an attestor, a person who authenticated witnesses. Pollock served as the executor of wills and the administrator of estates, which could be rather lucrative. His most frustrating case was when he was named executor of former governor Seth Sothel's will and estate. Sothel had been something of a criminal and North Carolinians threw him out of office in 1689. After his death around 1694, many lawsuits were filed against executor Pollock by Sothel's creditors. It would take years for Pollock and the courts to untangle Sothel's estate.[7]

Where Thomas Pollock shined was in land acquisition. As Pollock saw it, a man could never have too much land. From his original 640-acre Balgra plantation on the west side of the Chowan River, Pollock began buying, acquiring, swapping, and selling tracts of land in the Albemarle, south of the Albemarle along the Scuppernong River, along the Roanoke River to the west, as well as along the Neuse and other southerly rivers. He gained control of several tracts of land once belonging to Governor Sothel. Pollock owned 710 acres at a place called Half-Way House on the north side of the Trent River and another 640 acres on the Neuse at Wilkinson's Point. From his marriage to Esther Wilkinson he gained additional plantations, including Sandy Point on Salmon Creek, west of the Chowan. And these were just a few. By the time the Tuscarora War broke out in 1711, Pollock probably owned about 35,000 acres. This number would only increase over the years.[8]

Pollock could be a hard man and absolutely nothing would stand in his way of advancing his personal interests. He had no hesitation in sending the North Carolina militia to imprison thirty-six Meherrin Indian men to force them off lands Pollock wanted. His greed could even be seen with the treatment of his second wife, Esther. If he married Martha Cullen West for love, he married Esther for money. In fact, it does not appear they even lived together; she stayed on her Sandy Point plantation and he on nearby Balgra. Esther Sweetman was from Maryland. Her first husband was John Harris, but he died soon after. She next married Col. William Wilkinson of North Carolina. In a strange twist, in March 1695, Pollock was a member of the Governor's Council who ordered the arrest of Col. Wilkinson and Esther for various crimes and offenses. While the outcome of this is not known, it certainly could not have made for a rosy relationship between the future married couple. Then Col. Wilkinson died around 1706 or 1707.[9]

Like so many colonial Southern women who outlived their husbands, Esther gained considerable property and wealth from her marriages and so became a target of fortune hunters, men who saw rich widows as a way to prosperity. Once married, these women, and often their property, came under the control of their husbands who could squander it as they pleased. How Pollock managed it and why Esther agreed to his proposal is not clear, but the two married around 1707. Esther imagined she had protected herself and her assets with a prenuptial agreement, but Pollock managed to get his hands on much of her property. She kept her valuable plantation Sandy Point on Salmon Creek, but by January 1708 Pollock was selling off twenty African slaves belonging to Esther, as well as Sandy Point's livestock, tools, and household goods. It must have been a scheme to get everything legally in his name, as within days the buyer, Capt. David Henderson, sold it all back to Pollock. He also gained access to the twenty-five-ton sloop *Susana* and the fifteen-ton sloop *Reserve*, both partially owned by Esther's deceased husband.[10]

In May 1712, Esther made out her will. She named Maj. Thomas Lutten and Thomas Lutten Jr. as her executors. Her plantations in Maryland went to a cousin there. Major Lutten received all her lands and plantations in North Carolina that she received from her previous marriage. Sandy Point plantation, where Esther lived, was to go to Lutten Jr. Other properties and money went to other people. She even bequeathed Governor Hyde a slave woman named Cuttoe. But she willed not a single property or penny to her husband Thomas Pollock. Pollock took this as a slap in the face. When Esther died childless in 1716, Pollock initiated legal proceedings to cut out the Luttens and get his hands on it all. Eventually her will was overturned and Pollock received everything of Esther's, helping make Pollock the wealthiest man in North Carolina. It had been a good, profitable marriage for Pollock. Less so, it seems, for Esther. Pollock would not remarry.[11]

That hardness, that single-mindedness had become evident as Pollock became more involved in colonial politics. It was not enough for his enemies to be defeated; they had to be destroyed. Opposition must be cut down; compromise was not tolerated. As a Proprietary man and a deputy of the Lords Proprietors, he soon became a force in North Carolina politics. By 1689 he was a member of the North Carolina Assembly and in that year played a role in the ouster of Governor Sothel, who once jailed Pollock for opposing his illegal land acquisitions.[12]

After this, Pollock began holding important positions within the colonial government. By 1694, he was sitting on the chancery court, the general court, and was also named harbor master and coroner. In that same year, Pollock replaced Col. William Wilkinson as colonel of the Albemarle militia. He seemed to take great pride in that rank of "colonel" and often referred to himself as such until he was promoted to major general during the Tuscarora War. On February 21, 1696, the Lords Proprietors officially named Pollock as one of their deputies for North Carolina, which allowed him to sit on the Governor's Council. He would, except for periodic reasons of bad health and during Cary's Rebellion from 1708 to 1711, remain on the council for the rest of his life. And he would for much of that time be president of the council, who served as the acting North Carolina governor between official appointments by the Lords Proprietors.[13]

The Sothel case shows another curious insight into the mind of Thomas Pollock. He was a Proprietary man, a law-and-order man through and through, supporting the Crown, the Lords Proprietors, and the Anglican Church. Still, he was no extremist. In reality, Pollock wanted colonial stability and was against anything that would disrupt that stability, which he certainly equated with his own interests. He turned on Governor Sothel only when Sothel usurped the laws and North Carolina's Fundamental Constitutions. He was not against Quakers and Dissenters because of their religious beliefs. But their refusal to take the necessary oaths or support the wars with men or provisions showed them to be scofflaws whose actions made for a dysfunctional colony. He supported the establishment of the Anglican Church in North Carolina, was a vestryman, and believed settlers should pay their tithes not so much because he was a religious man, as he declined to be named a church warden and soon found ways to skip meetings of the vestry. Rather he supported it because it was the official Church of England and her colonies. Even on the Governor's Council he appeared rather lackadaisical, often ceding leadership to others, until the biggest threat to colonial stability came in 1708 with the ascension of Thomas Cary to the governorship.[14]

Pollock was a major player in Cary's Rebellion. He backed William Glover as governor and never accepted the idea that Cary was the legal governor of North Carolina. In 1708, he withdrew from the Governor's Council and even left North Carolina altogether to live in self-imposed exile on a plantation in southern Virginia near the York River. He explained that he was "unwilling to live under a government I knew was altogether illegal, and to avoid occasion of difference."[15] He managed his businesses, ships, and plantations from there and kept abreast of what was happing in North Carolina through couriers such as John Lawson and William Maule. To foil prying eyes, he sometimes wrote his letters and journals in a code, apparently of his own devising, which consisted of numerals mixed with the English and Greek alphabet.[16] His revenge on Cary came in 1710 when the Lords Proprietors appointed Edward Hyde to be the first governor of a fully separate North Carolina. From his Virginia plantation, Pollock threw his support behind Hyde and soon had the new governor's ear. Within weeks, Pollock ended his exile and returned to Balgra with Governor Hyde in tow. From there, they forced Cary out and Hyde took over as governor. Pollock returned as president of the Governor's Council. From that point, he and Hyde were close political allies pursuing like policies.[17]

Cary's Rebellion had barely ended that summer of 1711 when the Tuscaroras and their allies attacked. For the next several months, the North

Carolina government was powerless to respond in any way, either to the appeals from help by survivors along the Pamlico and Neuse Rivers or to mount a coherent counterattack. Pollock's one undertaking, Brice's expedition against Catechna in October, had been a dismal failure. Governor Hyde, known more as a jolly, hale fellow, had never developed a coherent plan to end the war other than ask other colonies for help. So Barnwell's arrival at Bath gave Hyde, Pollock, and their government a tremendous boost. In February 1712, Hyde and the Council issued a statement blaming the Tuscaroras for the war. Pollock saw it as a war of extermination. In March 1712, the North Carolina Assembly, over the objections of its Quaker members, finally appropriated £4,000 to fight the war and narrowly passed laws giving the government full power to "impress men, horses, or canoes, or whatsoever else may be needful" to fight the Indians. De Graffenried found his two sloops, the *Return* and the *Dolphin,* impressed into government service. Refugees were now prevented from leaving the colony. A fort was built on Core Sound and other strongpoints as well. Lyonell Reading's fortified home on the south bank of the upper Pamlico River was garrisoned with ten men. Nevertheless, problems with rounding up men, provisions, and especially ammunition, remained.[18]

Down on the Pamlico, Barnwell grew impatient. Where were the supplies? Where were the reinforcements Hyde and Pollock had promised? He spent much of February 1712 fretting and then his temper got the better of him. He began to openly criticize Governor Hyde, calling him "pusillanimous." Council President Pollock and the Assembly also received their share of Barnwell's ire. He blamed them for not supplying his army. He just could not accept the difficulties and internal divisions that prevented North Carolina from doing much at all. Finally, on February 26, 1712, Pollock was able to send Barnwell a force of sixty-seven North Carolina militiamen. About fifty of these were Palatines led by De Graffenried's old business partner Capt. Louis Michel. The overall commander of the North Carolina troops was none other than now Lt. Col. William Brice, with Capt. Thomas Boyd as second in command. Barnwell's temper exploded when he discovered they brought no food, no supplies, and no ammunition. He would have to take both food and ammunition from his own scant reserve to supply the North Carolinians. North Carolina, he said, had made him "a great many promises to supply me day after day with more men, provisions and ammunition. I waited so long for bread until half of my men fell sick and willing to preserve the health of the rest, I proceeded to get that of the enemy, which was delayed by my friends."[19]

While Pollock and many North Carolinians certainly thanked the South Carolina colonel for coming to their rescue, many settlers held a grudge toward Barnwell for allowing his Indian allies to take off with their property that had been looted by the Tuscaroras. Then Barnwell began to dabble, perhaps unknowingly, in North Carolina politics. While at his camp, Barnwell had been visited by Edward Moseley, one of former governor Cary's staunchest supporters and a firm enemy of Pollock. Moseley and Barnwell became good friends and Moseley never lost an opportunity to demean Governor Hyde and Pollock. At the same time, Moseley planted the idea in Barnwell's head that the colonel might eventually replace Hyde as governor of North Carolina. Moseley assured Barnwell that he would have the support of the Quakers in this. Pollock was enraged when this got back to him.[20]

Nevertheless, Hyde and Pollock encouraged Barnwell to make his assault on Catechna. However, Pollock instructed Barnwell in no uncertain terms that he should not accept any peace treaty, any treaty of neutrality, or any treaty of commerce with Tuscaroras until they handed over King Hancock. Neither should he make peace with any of the allied towns who participated in the attacks. Rather, Barnwell should "extirpate them according to the laudable custom of South Carolina." In turn, Pollock promised that North Carolina would raise two hundred men within four months to assist Barnwell and that magazines would be erected on the Neuse and Pamlico Rivers to support his expedition.[21]

Barnwell, short on food and encouraged by Hyde and Pollock, finally decided to march on Catechna. At least he knew there was plenty of food there.

❖ Barnwell's army, much smaller than the one he had left South Carolina with, moved out of its camp on the Pamlico River on February 27. It consisted of 27 South Carolina officers and men; 68 North Carolina militia commanded by Lt. Col. William Brice, and 148 Indians, mostly Yamasees. Barnwell provided scant information on the march, but it seems his expedition moved cross-country, almost in a direct line from his base on the Pamlico to Contentnea Creek. Recent rains had bogged the roads and swollen the rivers, making progress difficult. At some places, the men marched in water above their waists.

On March 2, the army arrived at Catechna. They found it deserted. However, Barnwell's scouts told him there was a large force of Tuscaroras upstream across the creek. These Tuscaroras had fired at his scouts, but had done no damage. Now they seemed to be keeping their distance. At

Catechna, as had Barnwell predicted, they found plenty of stored corn. The only thing lacking now, he said, was "Pamplico beef." It had been a hard march through rough country, so Barnwell rested his troops in the abandoned town that night.[22]

No one could accuse Barnwell of not being offensive-minded. He immediately made plans to attack the mass of Tuscarora warriors camped on the south side of the Contentnea. The next day, March 3, he marched his army up and down the creek in search of a ford. But heavy rains had raised the water level and they could not find a suitable place to cross. The Indians, knowing what Barnwell wanted, had taken all the canoes in the area and scuttled them. Making matters worse, the warriors on the other side of the creek shadowed his troops and periodically fired on them, forcing his men to stop and take cover. Eventually he found a place to make some rafts and decided to force a crossing the next day. That evening, his scouts returned with a captured Tuscarora warrior. Barnwell tortured him for information and learned that about 130 Tuscaroras warriors awaited him in a strong fort on the south side of the creek. A call had gone out for raiding parties to return to the fort and the Indians expected reinforcements to arrive at any time. The women and children had returned from the safety of the upper Tuscarora towns once Barnwell's army made for Bath back in February, but now they had taken refuge in a swamp along with their English captives. Barnwell also learned that the Indians in the fort were well-armed, having used the gold and plunder looted from the English plantations and farms to pay for weapons and ammunition. Most of this probably came from other Indians, such as the upper Tuscaroras or the Meherrins and Nottoways, but Barnwell always believed it came directly from Virginia traders.[23]

On the morning of March 4, Barnwell called his officers together to plan strategy. He ordered Lt. Col. Brice to take about seventy men, mostly his North Carolinians, and march about three or four miles upstream. They were to make lots of noise, shout "Huzza" and give cheers, even take axes to trees to make it appear they were preparing to cross. This would create a diversion, drawing the Indians to him while allowing Barnwell to quickly raft his men across the creek.[24]

Brice and his troops moved off, while Barnwell's men began building a raft that could hold five men. At this point, Brice's military deficiencies became apparent. He did not march the three miles Barnwell ordered nor did he stay out as long as needed. His men did draw the Indians on the opposite bank along with them, but this spooked the North Carolina troops, who grew more nervous the farther they went from Barnwell. Way too soon Brice returned downstream and essentially led the shadowing Tuscaroras directly to Barnwell, who was only beginning his crossing. The Tuscaroras put up a heavy fire on the men making the first crossing of the creek, wounding two. Under fire, Barnwell managed to get a few more men across. Then the fortunes of war smiled on him. Instead of digging in and making a protective perimeter, those first few men charged up the riverbank, surprising the Tuscaroras who, Barnwell said, ran "like deer, upon which our Indians took ye river one & all." Barnwell now crossed the rest of his troops while his Indians chased the retreating Tuscaroras. Once all were on the south side of Contentnea Creek, the army moved upstream about a mile and made camp. Barnwell gleefully reported that "the enemy did not expect us to pay them a visit on that side of the river." However, he began to have his doubts about Brice and the North Carolina troops, complaining that he had difficulty getting them to raft across the creek, "for I could not prevail with one of this cowardly crew to venture, w'ch was a presage of what followed." Nevertheless, Barnwell figured that since he had all the Tuscaroras penned up in one place, he might as well attack the fort the next day.[25]

Before dawn on March 5, Barnwell divided his forces and laid out a plan of attack. Barnwell himself would take a hundred men and quietly creep around behind the fort. Brice would take the remainder of his North Carolina troops and at daylight position them directly in front of the fort for an attack. Both Barnwell and Brice got their units into place without incident. From his position Barnwell inspected Hancock's fort with a spyglass. What he saw surprised him. It was a strong, well-built, European-style fort, something that up until this point was unheard of among North American Indians. It sat on a high bluff along the creek bank, close to a swamp, and was protected by a large trench. The dirt excavated from the trench formed an embankment, the front of which bristled with sharpened river cane to prevent attackers from scaling it. Atop the embankment ran a log palisade that formed the fort's walls. These towered over the flat ground in front of them. The palisades had two sets of firing ports, a lower and an upper, with the lower able to be plugged if needed. Bastions at the fort's corners allowed for a cross fire. In front of the trench and along the ground in front of the fort, the Indians had strewn large tree limbs as obstacles to hinder any attack that might charge the walls. Barnwell was impressed.[26]

Hancock's fort was truly unique among Indians and showed a mix of Indian and European fortification styles. Southeastern Indians had long used fortifications and the English found palisaded villages along the

North Carolina coast back in the 1580s, just as De Graffenried had seen them among the upper Tuscaroras at Tasqui. But the Contentnea Creek Tuscaroras had taken Hancock's fort to new heights. The log palisade and the sharpened river cane were pure Indian, but the firing ports and corner bastions were all European. Barnwell later learned that the fort had been designed by Harry, a black slave who had apparently once worked on forts in South Carolina. Harry had later been sold to Virginia and then had run away to the Tuscaroras. Runaway slaves often received mixed receptions from Indians. Sometimes they were returned to their masters for the reward; other times they found refuge. In Harry's case, the Tuscaroras recognized his ability. Using his memory and some pretty good engineering skills of his own, the black man constructed a very intimidating fort. One wonders if Harry was the same "little slave" De Graffenried left at Catechna as security for the ransom he promised. Nevertheless, Harry's work also showed a change in Indian strategy. Hancock's fort had not been built to protect a town or even provide protection for women and children, who were still hidden away in the forest. Rather, it was to be a fortress full of well-armed warriors. Their plan was to force Barnwell to attack and so inflict high casualties on his attacking South Carolinians. At the same time, the drawn-out battle would strain Barnwell's resources and supply lines. If the Indians could hold out long enough, Barnwell would be forced to retreat. It was not a bad plan.[27]

Barnwell thought he had figured out a way to attack it. The night before, he ordered the Palatines among Brice's troops to make two hundred fascines, which were long sticks tied into large bundles. These would be carried by the attacking troops rushing the fort walls and serve as shields from arrows and musket balls. At the foot of the walls, the bundles would be thrown into the trench, filling it up to allow the attackers to cross it. Now, as dawn broke on the morning of March 5, Barnwell prepared to order the attack. But Brice and his men jumped the gun and attacked before Barnwell was ready. The North Carolina troops, their fascines in front of them, charged toward the fort and got within ten yards when the palisade walls erupted with heavy fire. Musket balls and arrows crashed into the fascines and stopped Brice's charge in its tracks. The sound of the musket balls smashing into the bundles of sticks unnerved Brice's North Carolina troops and now they panicked, dropping everything, including their fascines and guns, and raced for the rear. Many were shot in the back as they scurried for safety. Barnwell's South Carolinians stood firm, as did at least twenty-three North Carolinians, but most of Brice's men ran. Barnwell tried to rally them, "but all my endeavour was in vain, tho' I mauled sev'll with my cutlass, and as soon as they saw me running towards them, they would scamper into the swamp that was hard by."[28]

With this, Barnwell's attack on Hancock's fort fizzled. All was confusion and Barnwell knew he did not have enough men to face the heavy fire coming from the fort. Reluctantly, he ordered a retreat, which he said was "bravely managed, for every man got his faschine on his back, and of my own number, I had but one wounded." But they left their dead on the field. The fascines had done a good job of providing protection, and in camp that evening Barnwell found that just about every bundle had been hit ten times or more. As for casualties, his South Carolinians had one man wounded, while the twenty-three North Carolina troops who stood firm with his men had three killed and two wounded. Brice's runaways suffered one killed and eighteen wounded. Barnwell's Indians did not appear to have taken any casualties. In all, he calculated four killed, twenty-one wounded. Now he needed to retrieve his dead. Then it began to rain. He ordered his Indians to make a feint attack on the rear of the fort while his militiamen crept back to locate the bodies of their comrades. In the dark, only three bodies could be found. Not wanting to go to bed with a loss, Barnwell contemplated a night attack, but he found morale was dropping. Only sixteen of his South Carolinians would agree to a night action. The North Carolina troops and the Yamasees absolutely refused. So he canceled the assault. It had not been a good day for colonial forces.[29]

As a soldier's soldier, Barnwell was very concerned about his wounded. The four dead and twenty-one wounded was a large number for such a small force. Come morning, March 6, Barnwell took thirty men and marched the six miles downstream to the confluence of Contentnea Creek and the Neuse River. Nearby sat the now abandoned Core Town, but Barnwell saw where the Indians had been building new houses and clearing new fields. That could certainly be interpreted as Indian confidence that they would win this war. From here, Barnwell hoped to send a message down the Neuse to New Bern and have canoes come up to take away his wounded. But a party of Tuscarora warriors soon showed up and began firing at his men. Barnwell determined that it was too dangerous to send a messenger downstream and so marched back to his army near Hancock's fort. His wounded would have to suffer along with the rest of them. Still, the march had given him time to think. That evening, after a personal reconnaissance of the fort, he ordered his men to build a breastwork near the creek that overlooked the fort's access to water and canoes. The Indians in the fort periodically fired at them and he lost two more wounded. But by morning, Barnwell had fifty men positioned inside the breastworks.[30]

On the morning of March 7, the Indians in the fort woke up to see Barnwell's new position. A few warriors tried to get to their canoes, but Barnwell's men drove them back into the fort. When men tried to get water, they were also driven back. The Indians suddenly realized they were trapped inside their own fort. But they still had a good card to play. Inside the fort were twelve English captives that the Indians had kept as a bargaining chip and now they used them. They sent some of the women captives to the creek to get drinking water, knowing Barnwell would not fire on them. Barnwell and his men yelled to these captives, telling them to be patient, that they would be rescued by the next morning at the latest. According to Barnwell, the Indians in the fort heard this and began torturing some of the captives. Barnwell claimed they even killed an eight-year-old girl of the Taylor family. The captives cried out to Barnwell, "begging of me to have compassion on the innocents, w'ch was renewed by crys & lamentations of the captives being about 35 or 40 yards of there." The screams of the captives had a devastating effect on Barnwell and his troops and he yelled to the Indians for a parley. They sent out a captive named Mrs. Pearce, who had five children inside the fort. Barnwell insisted all the captives be released. The Tuscaroras must have laughed at him. They would release no one as long has Barnwell besieged their fort, they told him. And if he did not lift his siege, then they would kill all their captives and fight to the last man.[31]

Barnwell knew he was playing with a weak hand. He asked for another parley. He and two of his officers went to the fort's gate and asked to speak to Hancock, who refused to come out. Barnwell then asked if one of his men could come inside. Again the Indians refused. Nevertheless, Barnwell managed to get a glimpse inside the fort and what he saw disturbed him. Inside were two blockhouses and a great many Indians, possibly even some Senecas. Back at his camp, Barnwell weighed the pros and cons of another attack, and decided he could not take the fort with the forces he had. There were too many Indians, "desperate villains who would do all the mischief they could before their death." He knew his Indians would not assault the walls and he could only count on about thirty of his colonial troops to actually fight. Even then, they were sure to take a good number of wounded if they did. The North Carolina troops did not even have four shots per man. Anyway, Barnwell figured they would run and "leave me in the lurch." If he attacked and was forced to retreat, he would probably have to leave the wounded "to the mercy of ye most barbarous enemy." If he did attack, it would take him at least two days to take the fort, mainly digging approach trenches to get close enough to it. During that time the Indians would kill their captives. Indian strategy was working. With all this in mind, Barnwell now asked for another parley, this time to offer a treaty.[32]

Barnwell laid it out for the Indians. He would lift the siege and they would release the twelve captives they had inside the fort. They would also provide him with two canoes to move the captives and his wounded downriver to New Bern. They should send a couple of men to tell the warriors downstream of their truce and so not attack the canoes. He and his men would then withdraw to New Bern. Then, in twelve days, on March 19, he and the Tuscarora headmen would meet at the head of Batchelor's Creek, about six miles upriver from New Bern. There he expected them to deliver up an additional twenty-two captives he heard the Indians had. In turn he promised to arrange a firm peace between them and the government of North Carolina, something Thomas Pollock had expressly forbidden. The Tuscaroras' hand was not as strong as they had originally thought. That Barnwell could trap them inside the fort by covering the water access had shaken them. So they accepted this truce, released the twelve captives, provided the canoes, and warned those downriver not to fire on them. In fact, the colonials in the canoes met several Tuscaroras "who spoke kindly to them, and told them they hoped before long to be good friends."[33] The Indians had won another great victory.

The next morning, March 8, Barnwell and his troops lifted the siege and withdrew down Contentnea Creek to its confluence with the Neuse River. There they used the two canoes to move his forces across the Neuse. It took most of the day and so he camped that night at nearby Core Town. He was impressed with Core Town, but complained that the Core had taken all their corn and hidden it in a swamp. Badly needing food, Barnwell sent out search parties to look for the corn, but they did not find any. The next day, March 9, his ragged army marched the twenty miles downriver, through country Barnwell called "the most lively, pleasantest, richest piece of land in either Carolina upon a navigable river." He and his troops arrived later that day at New Bern.[34] The *Boston News-Letter* would get it wrong again, claiming that South Carolina forces had destroyed about three hundred Tuscaroras and other Indians and many more taken prisoners, who were delivered to the governor of Virginia.[35]

In New Bern, Barnwell licked his wounds and awaited the March 19 council with the Tuscaroras. The expedition certainly had not come off as he expected. As he saw it, he could only blame North Carolina for his failure. Other than Capt. Louis Michel, whom Barnwell commended for his valor and presence of mind, Brice and his North Carolina troops had been useless. It was their cowardice, he believed, that had prevented him from taking the fort. From there he blamed Governor Hyde, whom he said the people of North Carolina regard as "no more than a broom staff. They pay much more deference to my cutlass which I now & then send some of their toping [drunken] dons."[36] Diplomacy was never Barnwell's strong suit and once he began criticizing the North Carolina government he could not stop. As he saw it, while his brave South Carolinians did their fighting for them, "I found that 2 or 3 of ye Assembly supplied ye rest of their wise brethren with such plenty of punch that they voted, acted, signed, & strip'd naked & boxt it fairly two & two, all the same day, Gov'r Hyde, Collo. Boyd, a member of ye Council, the only ragged gown parson with Mr. Speaker, the Provost Marshal with another hon'ble member and so round it went." So while the North Carolina government danced and drank punch, he complained that all he had was cold water to drink and bread to eat. What he should have done, Barnwell grumbled, was have returned to Charles Town with his slaves instead of putting South Carolina to the expense of another £4,000.[37] Up in the Albemarle, Pollock fumed when he heard this.

Still, Hyde and Pollock did what they could. Pollock dispatched the sloop *Core Sound Merchant* to the Pasquotank River on the north bank of Albemarle Sound where it was to take on as much corn as it could carry. From there, it should "embrace the first fair wind and weather to go to Bath County," deliver the corn to Barnwell, and follow whatever instructions the colonel gave.[38] Hyde and Pollock again appealed to Virginia for two hundred militiamen to help. Once again, Governor Spotswood and his council dithered, then did nothing. Hyde sent out another call for North Carolina troops to support Barnwell but got the same feeble response. Once again the Quaker-dominated Assembly refused to purchase ammunition or supplies, nor would they appropriate money to feed or clothe their soldiers in the field. Men refused to be called up for military service. David Wharton, when he was called up, hired Edmund Ennett as a substitute, paying him a cow and a calf. The Quakers themselves refused to provide men or corn. Other settlers, seeing the Quakers thumb their noses at the government's demands, did the same and refused to pay taxes. Some tax collectors were beaten for their efforts.[39]

Barnwell in New Bern was in no mood for excuses and things got worse as sickness hit his troops. He claimed it was due to the bad diet his men were forced to endure, another dig at the North Carolina government.

It was unclear what illness hit them, but Barnwell, Capt. Burnaby Bull, Maj. Alexander Mackay, some of his South Carolina militiamen, and several Yamasee Indians all got sick, with about four or five of the Indians dying. When March 19 arrived, the day appointed for the Tuscarora hostage release, Barnwell was too sick to go. Instead, he sent Capt. Michel to Batchelor's Creek in his place. Michel waited, but the Tuscaroras never showed and no captives were freed. Barnwell was enraged. To try to force the issue, he sent out some of his Yamasee warriors and they returned with three scalps, presumably enemy Indians. But the meeting Barnwell had been depending on never materialized.[40]

Barnwell and others saw the Tuscaroras' nonappearance as proof of Indian treachery. "Ye enemy were worse than their words," he said.[41] However, there may have been more to this than Barnwell realized. King Hancock of Catechna had already given up all his captives to Barnwell after the battle on March 7. And since each Tuscarora town was autonomous, Hancock had no power or authority to compel other towns to give up their captives. Nor could he compel the kings of other Tuscarora towns or his allies to meet with Barnwell. Besides, the Indians may have seen no reason to deal with Barnwell. Up to this point, they had been victorious. And while it had been touch and go at Hancock's fort, they had made Barnwell back down. White captives had served an important purpose there and it stood to reason that other towns did not want to give up so valuable a bargaining chip. For Barnwell, the only thing to do was march his army back to Hancock's fort and this time take it. In the meantime, he unleashed his Yamasee warriors and they attacked Core Town, which had been reoccupied after Barnwell's retreat. Barnwell's Yamasees "drove out the king and his forces, and carried the day with such fury, that after they had killed a great many, in order to stimulate themselves still more, they cooked the flesh of an Indian 'in good condition' and ate it." No word if the king was Sam or Core Tom, but the surviving Cores took refuge at Hancock's fort.[42]

On March 25, Barnwell ordered a garrison to be created at "Durhams," just across the Pamlico River from Bath to facilitate communications between that town and his army on the Neuse. A few days later, he ordered all his army's horses and baggage to be sent to New Bern, so all would be ready for his victorious troops to return to South Carolina immediately after they took the fort. By this time, Barnwell wanted out of North Carolina. On March 29, Barnwell, with fifteen South Carolina militiamen and thirty Indians, these being all he could feed, marched up the Neuse. He met no resistance and found Catechna deserted, though his men did surprise a party of Indians moving corn into Hancock's fort. Barnwell said he marched to within three hundred yards of Hancock's fort, spent about fifteen minutes scouting it, found some corn, and then returned down Contentnea Creek to Core Town. There Barnwell found another hundred bushels of corn. At Core Town, on a bluff thirty feet above the Neuse, the colonel began building a forward operating base he christened Fort Barnwell. He reinforced its natural defensive advantages with breastworks and soon had a strong position in which he said fifty men could hold off five thousand. From here, he sent out his Yamasee scouts who over the next few days returned with a scalp or two.[43]

Now Barnwell gathered his forces at Fort Barnwell. He called up his remaining troops at New Bern and the few garrisons he maintained on the lower Neuse. On April 1, he received a letter from Governor Hyde informing him that seventy North Carolina troops were on their way. This seems to have been the end of Lt. Col. William Brice's less than illustrious military career as Col. Thomas Boyd now commanded the North Carolina reinforcements. Also, two sloops with provisions were on their way. Everyone's mood improved that night when a boat delivered a shipment of ten gallons of rum, two casks of cider, and a cask of wine. But Barnwell's good mood evaporated the next day when the promised supply ships arrived. Instead of the 115 bushels of corn expected, he received only 52. Then he heard that a sloop from South Carolina carrying corn to his army had been stopped by North Carolina officials in Bath and the corn unloaded so the sloop could be used to transport rum out of the colony. That may have just been a rumor. In reality, Hyde and Pollock felt they were doing all they could to get supplies to the colonel. Commissioners again scoured the Albemarle with authority to impress all corn and ammunition above what a family needed to survive.[44]

Over the next few days, reinforcements trickled into Fort Barnwell. Col. Boyd showed up with the seventy North Carolina troops and a small party of Chowan Indian warriors. Once again Barnwell was disappointed as they brought no food or ammunition. Instead, they began to eat up Barnwell's small store of corn and then "began to grumble for better victuals." This just stoked Barnwell's hot temper. He ordered one of the North Carolina officers, an unnamed major, "to be tied neck & heels & kept him so, and whenever I heard a saucy word from any of them, I immediately cut him, for without this they are the most impertinent, imperious, cowardly blockheads that ever God created & must be used like negroes if you expect any good of them." Nevertheless, by April 6, Barnwell had a force of 153 white militiamen and 128 Indians. He also acquired a small battery of artillery: two three-pounders, two "patterarors," seven granardo shells, which were a type of hand grenade, and twenty-two cannonballs, though he had only enough powder for ten discharges. The artillery had been De Graffenried's idea. Despite the powder shortage, Barnwell was hopeful as Capt. Michel of the Palatines had devised some "ingenious fireworks & a mortar to throw them into the fort."[45]

In the early morning hours of April 7, 1712, Barnwell and his army marched to Hancock's fort and surrounded it before those inside even knew they were there. The Indians awoke to find themselves besieged. But this was not going to be easy for Barnwell. During the month since his failed attack, the Indians had strengthened the fort's defenses. A second palisade had been moved further outward and was protected by a wide ditch. They had put up a cover to protect anyone going down to the creek for water or canoes. He also found the Indians very well armed and supplied with powder. Barnwell believed that Virginia had sold them four hundred buckskins worth of ammunition. Virginia strongly denied this. In reality, guns and ammunition may well have come from Virginia in a roundabout way as some traders, along with Virginia's own tributary Indians, continued doing business with the upper Tuscaroras, many of whom supported their Contentnea Creek kinspeople.[46]

Barnwell now began the difficult task of taking Hancock's fort. Rather than a full frontal assault, which had not worked last time, he started his troops digging approach trenches to get them close to the palisades. As the trench crept closer, parties of Tuscarora warriors sallied out of the fort and attacked those in the trench, panicking English troops and forcing them to retreat. It was only with "extreme difficulty" that Barnwell compelled them to go back to work. Though the Tuscaroras took casualties during these sallies, the South Carolina commander was amazed at the Indians' stiff defense. He had never experienced Indian fighting such as this. Even the few rounds of artillery had done nothing. In a truly astonishing turn of events, the Indians began digging their own counter tunnel to try to thwart Barnwell's trench. This forced Barnwell to waste time and energy in building false trenches to decoy the Indian tunnel away from his men. Eventually Barnwell's troops reached the ditch protecting the palisades. He again ordered fascines made so his troops could attack across it. But "ye enemy had a hollow way under their palisade that as fast as we filled ye ditch, they would carry away the faschines." His men tried to set fire to the palisades, but the Indians quickly extinguished them. Nor could he get his men to make an assault on the walls. He called them "cowardly." And even if they did capture this outer palisade, he realized it would not have done anything toward taking the fort itself.[47]

Barnwell now considered tunneling under the ditch to reach the palisades, but realized this would take way too much time. Already he had taken some serious casualties: six white men and one Indian killed and thirty-five white men and one Indian wounded. He was also running out of food. On April 17, the tenth day of the siege, Barnwell finally had to admit defeat, though he would not call it such. "I was thro' extreme famine obliged to hearken to a capitulation for the surrend'ng thereof upon articles, which leaves above 100 murderers unpunished besides the women & children of those villains killed & executed." As Barnwell saw it, had North Carolina sent him supplies for just four more days, he could have "made a glorious end of the war." Now he called for a parley and offered to make a treaty.[48]

Once again, the Tuscaroras and their allies had fought Barnwell's army to a standstill. But the siege had scared them. There had been under a hundred able-bodied men in the fort and they had taken heavy casualties in their sallies against the trenches. Not realizing just how weak Barnwell's army actually was, the Tuscaroras leaped at the chance to end the battle. Barnwell, as if he had won a great victory, now dictated ten points the Indians would have to follow. The Indians were immediately to turn over all captives within their fort, both white and black. They had ten days to bring any others to Fort Barnwell. King Hancock and his three principal men were to be given up to Governor Hyde. He demanded three hostages be turned over to him immediately, two of these being Hancock's brother and the brother of the Core King.[49] They were to give Barnwell all the corn inside the fort. Then they had ten days to gather all horses and plunder taken from the settlers and deliver it to Fort Barnwell. From now on, they were to pay an annual tribute to the North Carolina government and have the courts decide any conflict between them and the settlers. The Tuscaroras would abandon claims to all territory between the Neuse River and the Cape Fear River, including all fishing, planting, and hunting, as that land would now belong to South Carolina's tributary Indians. And finally, Barnwell's troops were to be allowed to march victoriously through Hancock's fort with flags flying. Then within two days they were to demolish the fort and not build any more. In return, Barnwell promised that within twenty days, the North Carolina governor would accept and formalize these treaty articles and the war between them and the English would be over. With peace guaranteed, the Tuscaroras agreed.[50]

But the Core Indians did not agree. In fact, a serious quarrel broke out between the Cores and the Tuscaroras. Core Tom had helped spark the war and wanted it carried on, though it did not appear that Core Tom was inside the fort. As the Cores saw it, they had been victorious up to this point so why make a treaty? Besides, this treaty would just about obliterate Core territory, which lay on the south bank of the Neuse. But the Cores did not have the manpower to stand up to the Catechna Tuscaroras. They grumbled, but reluctantly agreed to the treaty. As Barnwell saw it, if he had just a few more days of provisions, "I could oblige the Tuscaroras to have delivered all the Cores for slaves." Barnwell also found himself pressured by some North Carolinians to forget his cease-fire now that he had the Indians in the open. As they saw it, he should kill or enslave them now that he could. Barnwell refused. "If our Indians found that there could be no dependence in our promises, it might prove of ill consequence."[51] The *Boston News-Letter* almost got it right when it reported that "Col Barnwell had defeated all the Tuscarora Indians except 150 or 200 which surrender'd themselves, and all to be pardon'd except one Hancock and 3 or 4 more of the most notorious of them."[52]

The Tuscaroras were as good as their word. However, Hancock and his principal men were not in the fort, having gone to Tom Blount on the Roanoke River, so that point could not be carried out. But the Tuscaroras promised to hand him over later. They did give up twenty-four captive children as well as two black slaves. One of these was the runaway, Harry, who had designed Hancock's fort. Barnwell immediately had him "cut to pieces." They also gave up two sons of King Hancock and "a brother of the Core King." There was not much English plunder left, but what little there was they returned to Barnwell. Nor was there much corn. The Tuscaroras agreed to pay tribute, go to court, and give up their land south of the Neuse. They broke down the fort bastions and Barnwell and his troops made their victory march through what remained. In a fit of pique, Barnwell refused to let the North Carolina troops, other than Col. Boyd, march through with them. He was again amazed as the fort's sophistication. "I never saw such subtill contrivance for defense, but I found a good fire would have made greater havoc than I expected." After a speech and the firing of a salute, Barnwell and his army retired downstream to Fort Barnwell. He spent the next ten days there as the Indians met the treaty demands. Then around May 1, 1712, he and his troops moved back to New Bern. As Barnwell saw it, he had won a great victory.[53]

Barnwell spent the next two months in New Bern, allowing his wounded and sick to heal and getting his army prepared for the march home. Then one of the haziest and most controversial incidents of the entire war took place. Sometime during these two months of May and June, the date is unclear, a council was called with the Core, Bear River Indians,

Neuse River Indians, and Machapungas to meet with the English at Core Town. The Indians imagined this was to be a peace council where a treaty would be worked out with the remaining Indians. Thinking themselves safe, the Indians brought whole families with them. Then, when all the Indians had assembled, and in spite of Barnwell's treaty of peace, they were suddenly attacked. About forty or fifty Indians were killed outright and at least two hundred women and children taken as captives and enslaved. The number may actually have been as high as four hundred. Who committed this bit of treachery has forever been debated. De Graffenried, Thomas Pollock, and Governor Spotswood of Virginia all blamed Barnwell. As De Graffenried saw it, Barnwell was angry at his treatment by North Carolina officials, believing that they had not honored him as he felt they should, nor had his men received the provisions they needed. "For these reasons, he thought of a means of going back to South Carolina with profit." And Barnwell's Yamasees were all for it "as they hoped to get a considerable sum from each prisoner."[54]

Others believed that it was actually done by North Carolinians. It does sound similar to William Brice's attack on the Bear River Indians in October 1711. But Barnwell was the perfect scapegoat. The colonel had gone out of his way to insult Governor Hyde and Pollock. He had become friends with their political enemies and seemed to be conspiring behind their back for the governorship. So blaming Barnwell was their chance at revenge. His treaty with the Tuscaroras, against their explicit instructions, only made hard feelings worse. As Pollock saw it, Barnwell had made a sham peace with the Tuscaroras, then called off his attack when he was on the verge of a great victory. As for De Graffenried and Spotswood, they may have just been repeating the story North Carolina officials told them.[55] Maybe it was North Carolinians instead of Barnwell, as on May 30, 1712, Governor Hyde wrote "I have cut off and took prisoners betwixt 3 or 400 Indian enemies and am in hopes in a little time to have matters so ripe as to have a treaty of general peace set on foot."[56]

While the full details will never be known, circumstantial evidence can go either way. Though Barnwell talked of his honor and how he would not attack the Tuscaroras after the treaty, he was very interested in acquiring slaves. He had often complained about losing out on slaves to his Indian allies. The Cores and other Indians had been enemies, only reluctantly accepting the treaty, and so fell into Barnwell's concept of legally taken slaves. He had spent a lot of his own money on the expedition and certainly did not feel appreciated by North Carolina. While Pollock and Hyde may have had an axe to grind and De Graffenried may have just repeated what he heard, Governor Spotswood had access to highly effective traders who had long done business with the Tuscaroras and probably would have ferreted out the truth. Spotswood bore no real animosity to Barnwell and the governor had often criticized North Carolina officials in rather scathing terms. So his saying that it was Barnwell has a ring of truth.[57] One the other hand, Barnwell considered himself a man of honor and breaking a truce so soon after making it was certainly dishonorable. But where did Governor Hyde get those three to four hundred slaves if not from the Core Town attacks? And in a later appeal for assistance to South Carolina, neither Pollock nor Hyde blamed Barnwell at that time. So who did the attacking has never yet been resolved. In the end, it did not matter, except to the Indians.

Around the last week of June, probably no later than July 1, Barnwell and his army left for South Carolina. Though South Carolina sent a sloop to bring him and his militia back to Charles Town, he and his troops marched overland for home. If Barnwell did have more than two hundred Indian slaves taken at Core Town, then marching them overland was the only logical way of getting them and his troops back to South Carolina as sloops were not that big. According to a map Barnwell later drew, he marched south out of New Bern to the White Oak River, turned west and crossed the Northeast Cape Fear River just above present-day Wilmington. On July 5, while on the Cape Fear, Barnwell was shot in his thigh and severely wounded. The first word was that he had been shot by some Winyaw Indians, but it turned out that it was one of his own men. Details were sketchy and the perpetrator never revealed. The whole issue seemed to be hushed up. The South Carolina sloop now met Barnwell on the Cape Fear River and the wounded Barnwell was back in Charles Town on July 8. The rest of the troops and slaves continued overland, arriving in Charles Town several days later.[58]

Back in South Carolina, Barnwell was hailed as a hero. He was given a month to recover from his wound, then on August 8, the South Carolina assembly ordered Col. John Fenwick, Capt. Peter Slarim, and Mr. Benjamin Godin to visit Col. Barnwell and "return him the thanks of this House for his great services performed in heading our forces in the late expedition against the Tusqueroras for the relief of the government of North Carolina." The next day, they awarded him £60 sterling from the Public Treasury. The hero of Catechna also received a new nickname: "Tuscarora Jack." He would wear it proudly for the rest of his life.[59]

CHAPTER SIX

King Tom Blount

The Negotiator

Barnwell thought he had achieved a great victory. In reality, he had left the Tuscaroras as strong as ever, though their Indian allies had certainly been hit hard by the surprise attack on Core Town. As for the Tuscaroras, Thomas Pollock calculated that Barnwell had only killed about thirty of them. They were, if anything, he believed, more confident, even to the point of raiding their old enemies the Waxhaws and Catawbas in South Carolina and hitting the Nottoway villages in Virginia. Other than being defeated at Torhunta and having some of their villages looted, they had protected their women and children while beating back Brice's expedition and then forcing Barnwell to give up his attack not once but twice. The treaty they signed was not that onerous as it essentially brought things back to the way they had been before the war. They would continue to interact with the North Carolina government and settlers, only now these would be a little more respectful of Indian land and complaints. Had Hyde and Pollock wanted, Barnwell's treaty could have brought peace to the region. But the treaty would not have taken revenge on the Indians or broken their power, something Pollock demanded.[1]

Then the attack and enslavement of the Cores, Neuse, Machapungas, and Bear River Indians upset everything. Now the Tuscaroras and their surviving allies learned some important lessons. That the English were a treacherous people who would not abide by a treaty even of their own making. They could never be trusted. They treated all Indians alike no matter if they were friends or enemies and would abuse Indians, take their lands, and enslave them whenever they could. They also learned that fortifications worked. So now, during the summer and fall of 1712, the Tuscaroras and what was left of their allies went back on the attack.

Though Barnwell had kept a contingent of about twenty Yamasees under the command of Maj. Alexander Mackay garrisoned along the Neuse River, the colony was still well-nigh defenseless. With its own militia seemingly incompetent, North Carolina would again turn to its neighbors. Even more, and as much as he hated to do it, Council President Pollock realized he was going to have to turn to King Tom Blount of the upper Tuscaroras for assistance as well.

❖ Governor Edward Hyde and Council President Thomas Pollock were outraged at "Tuscarora Jack." Barnwell's earlier ravings had alienated both of them. Then against their explicit orders he had made a treaty with the Tuscaroras and their allies, which essentially let them off the hook. If that were not bad enough, as they saw it, he had then violated his own treaty by attacking and enslaving the Cores and their allies. That had only started the Indian attacks all over again. Hyde and Pollock were not so much angry at his enslaving the Indians; rather they blamed him for not having utterly destroyed the Indians in the first place. Now North Carolina was paying for Barnwell's actions.[2]

The enslavement of the Indians at Core Town had galvanized the Contentnea Creek Tuscaroras and their allies. As De Graffenried saw it, the Indians gave "no more confidence to the Christians. They accordingly fortified themselves still better, and made terrible raids along both rivers, News and Pamptego, and the last troubles were worse than the first."[3] Settlers and slaves living along those rivers who had survived the September 22 attacks were now hit again. Parties of warriors skulked the woods, striking when and where they could, forcing most settlers to remain close to their farms and plantations. As Rev. Giles Rainsford said about the settlers, "when they lie down in their beds (they are so often invaded) that they can't say they shall rise [come] morning." In July, North Carolina's top commander in the field, Col. Thomas Boyd, was shot in the head while leading a party of militia against the Indians. "Few of his men came home but what shared in his fate and fell sacrifices to the same common misfortune," wrote Rainsford.[4] Though initially reported dead, Boyd lived, but he never led troops again. In the early fall, about two hundred Indians attacked Reading's fort on the Pamlico, but they were beaten back, with about five of the attackers killed. One Englishman was killed and the Indians managed to burn a sloop. At about the same time, warriors burned five more plantations near the mouth of the Pamlico River, but with no loss of life to the settlers.[5] Even the *Boston News-Letter*, not always the most accurate of newspapers, reported that in June about sixteen Indians surprised a party of twenty-two Englishmen at work, killing all but one woman and child, who escaped.[6]

North Carolina officials did what they could. By September, Hyde and Pollock had about 130 to 140 militiamen under arms, as well as the 20 Yamasees left by Barnwell. That was not nearly enough to destroy the Indians. The Assembly just barely, and over much objection, passed a law calling up for militia service every man between sixteen and sixty years of age who could carry a gun. If they refused, then they would be fined £5. Nevertheless, so many men in the Albemarle refused to serve that Governor Hyde finally resorted to press gangs. Even then many would not serve or quickly deserted. As usual, the Quakers refused to support the war in any form. Making matters worse was that some Dissenters, such as Thomas Cox Sr. and William Stafford Sr., both of Currituck Precinct, "did in a mutinous manner seduce & draw aside divers men who had enlisted in ye service of this government to ye great detriment of ye present expedition agt. the Indian enemy."[7]

Economically, the war crippled North Carolina. The colony was already a thousand pounds in debt and that hole was growing by the day. It could not pay its troops, nor did it have the funds to buy weapons, ammunition, supplies, or hire the ships to move them. And this situation was not going to be alleviated anytime soon as the war so disrupted trade that custom duties were falling rapidly. A severe food shortage now hit Bath County and emergency supplies of corn were sent to the area. More settlers deserted the colony. Finally, officials resorted to confiscating food, salt, ships, supplies and whatever the colony needed to fight the war. Making the summer of 1712 even more miserable was that North Carolina was hit with a severe outbreak of yellow fever. Governor Hyde was stricken and died on September 8, 1712. Exhaustion may have played a role as well. In one of his last letters, Hyde complained that he had "been under the sharpest tryalls of any person in the world, and I hope I have acquitted myself with duty to my Queen and fidelity to my masters. I am really (my Lord) almost worn out, having had continual trouble without any allowance hitherto."[8]

Pollock said that Hyde's death "left us in a most deplorable condition; a barbarous enemy to deal with; a scarcity of provisions, being scarce able to supply our garrisons and what small forces have out; and, the worst of all, a divided ungovernable people." The Council first offered the governorship to De Graffenried as he was a landgrave and the highest-ranking noble in the colony. De Graffenried wisely turned down the position. Instead, Pollock became acting governor and commander in chief of North

Carolina and its forces until the Lords Proprietors could send an official replacement.[9] Albemarle Proprietary Men cheered his selection. Reverend Urmston told the Bishop of London that "Colonel Pollock . . . is prudent, is a gentleman, hath labour'd heartily to preserve the Church and State from being ruin'd by intestine as well as a foreign enemy . . . hath been at a vast expense and even hazarded his life for the common safety and wellfare of us all."[10]

Hyde's death may have been the last straw for De Graffenried. After years of work and putting himself into heavy debt, he now threw up his hands and abandoned his colony. All had looked so promising just a year ago. But cracks had appeared early in his happy medieval fiefdom as most settlers did not see themselves as serfs. Then the Indian attacks killed many and destroyed much, including his colonists' faith in him. Others lost patience when De Graffenried insisted on upholding his own treaty with the Indians. It had not sat well with his neighbors either. William Brice had used that against him. All his efforts to rescue his people since the attacks had fallen flat. His ships had been impressed or wrecked, and he had no more money to purchase food or supplies even if he could get these to his settlers.

By December 1712, his New Bern colony lay in shambles. "Our poor colonists were not in the best plight, but scattered here and there among the English & Carolina planters; some returned to New Bern where they could farm some little." He even allowed many to leave their own lands and work as laborers for English planters. During the summer, De Graffenried had visited Governor Spotswood in Virginia and discussed relocating his colony there. Spotswood was all for it. But in the end, it never happened. De Graffenried had mortgaged all his colony's land around New Bern to Pollock and so had no resources to do anything. Finally, in early 1713, he left North Carolina permanently, going to Virginia. He stayed there about a year and then returned to Switzerland. "I was more sorry to leave such a beautiful and good country than such wicked people," he wrote as a parting shot.[11]

With Hyde dead and De Graffenried withdrawing, Pollock worked feverishly for the remainder of 1712 to create or expand garrisons along the Pamlico and Neuse. He manned them as best he could. Fort Barnwell near the confluence of the Neuse and Contentnea Creek was renamed Fort Hyde and garrisoned with thirty men. Smaller garrisons were manned along the Neuse under the command of Col. Louis Michel and South Carolina Maj. Alexander Mackay. Lyonell Reading's fort on the Pamlico River kept its ten men. The garrison at Shackleford Plantation was reinforced. Rangers were put into the field. The Council ordered twenty men in two canoes to patrol the Pamlico and Core Sounds "to suppress a party of Indians which we are informed doe harbor in and about those Sounds."[12] North Carolina even tried to acquire its own Indian allies. The Council sent emissaries to the Saponi Indians to see if they would actively support North Carolina. The Saponis did not want to get involved.[13]

Especially worrisome to North Carolina officials was the rumor that the Senecas and possibly the entire Five Nations in New York were going to throw in with the Tuscaroras and make war on North Carolina and Virginia. Word was that the Tuscaroras had actually sent emissaries to the Five Nations and asked for their active support. Virginia's Governor Spotswood had intelligence that the Senecas were supposed to join the Tuscaroras by late August or early September, spurred on by the French, who had been urging them to make war on North Carolina. Up in New York, Governor Robert Hunter heard the same stories and worked hard to prevent it. "I have sent some men of interest with them to dissuade them from this fatal design with presents and promises," Hunter wrote. He hoped to not only prevent the Senecas from joining the Tuscaroras but get the Five Nations to act as peacemakers to end the conflict in North Carolina. If the war did not end soon, Hunter feared it would spread to other colonies. But North Carolina worried about Five Nation peacemaking, fearing that the Senecas might defeat the Tuscaroras and then settle on their land. North Carolina would then have a worse and more powerful neighbor than the Tuscaroras. Besides, Pollock had no interest in making peace with the Indians. He wanted them destroyed. Nevertheless, Pollock and other officials believed it was just a matter of time before Seneca warriors descended on the helpless colony.[14]

With this in mind, back on June 2, 1712, even before Barnwell had left for home, Hyde and Pollock sent the diplomat John Foster to South Carolina to ask for additional help. They gave him rather detailed instructions. Foster should explain to South Carolina officials that despite Barnwell's assault and treaty at Catechna, war with the Tuscaroras and their allies continued. It even looked as if the Senecas would soon be joining with them. So North Carolina again needed the help of South Carolina. Foster was to try to repair the image of the North Carolina government that Barnwell had so tarnished in his letters back to South Carolina. He should also explain that Cary's Rebellion and Barnwell's sudden appearance in North Carolina, something North Carolina officials were unprepared for, was what had prevented them from having men ready to serve with Barnwell's expedition. Also, explain that Barnwell's forces had been on the

Pamlico and Neuse Rivers, which were very difficult to supply by land or sea. Even then, there had been few ships available to deliver what little supplies North Carolina had. What was needed, and Foster was to stress this, was about a thousand South Carolina tributary Indians led by a few competent white commanders, but this time they did not want Col. Barnwell to be part of any future expedition. His actions at Catechna, by not destroying the Tuscaroras when he had a chance, had left the colony in an extremely precarious situation. And as a final inducement, they told Foster, "you must lay before them the great advantage may be made of slaves, there being many hundreds of (them) women & children may we believe 3 or 4 thousand." For immediate needs, Foster should ask for about ten or twelve barrels of gunpowder, the shot that goes with it, and two to three thousand gunflints to be sent to North Carolina as soon as possible.[15]

It is unclear what caused the delay, but Foster did not appear before Governor Charles Craven and the South Carolina Assembly until August 6, more than two months after receiving his diplomatic instructions. South Carolina officials listened gravely as Foster outlined North Carolina's needs. Governor Craven and the House instantly agreed to send a second expedition. In the meantime, Craven ordered twenty guns and some ammunition to be sent immediately to Governor Hyde in North Carolina. By the time they arrived, Hyde was dead. His widow, Catha Hyde, turned the guns over to Pollock, who sent them to the garrison at Fort Hyde.[16]

Once home in South Carolina, Barnwell finally realized his mistake in antagonizing Thomas Pollock. In North Carolina, Barnwell had often made incendiary remarks about Hyde, Pollock, and the North Carolina Assembly. He also had to know they were incensed about his treaty with the Tuscaroras. In May, even before Barnwell had returned to South Carolina, Pollock and the Council wanted to investigate his conduct during the war and if found wanting, considered prosecuting him before the South Carolina government.[17] But North Carolina needed South Carolina's assistance and dropped the idea. Instead, they demanded that any new South Carolina expedition be commanded by someone, anyone other than Barnwell. Despite these bad feelings, Barnwell decided to press the idea that North Carolina should pay his expenses. On August 18, Barnwell wrote to Governor Hyde to make his case.

It was a letter Barnwell would regret. In it, he called himself a "faithful friend" of Governor Hyde but was concerned that his old friend Col. Louis Michel was now trying to cast him in a bad light. Nevertheless, Barnwell told Hyde that it was only through his own efforts and influence that the South Carolina Assembly even agreed to send a second expedition to fight the Tuscaroras. To further ingratiate himself, Barnwell said that he was soon going to England and if North Carolina paid him, he would strongly recommend that Governor Hyde be made the governor of the much more prosperous South Carolina. Now, as for his losses in North Carolina, Barnwell claimed he lost five horses worth £84. He distributed £50 of his own money for several work projects and had a voucher of £39 for the building of Fort Barnwell. He also spent a few smaller sums to take care of the sick and wounded. He reminded Hyde that he had been promised twenty shillings—one pound—for every day he was in North Carolina. He calculated he spent 156 days, from January 28 when he crossed the Neuse River to when he was wounded on the Cape Fear on July 3, though he earlier said it was on July 5. He knew South Carolina could and would have paid all these expenses, but felt North Carolina should do so as South Carolina could use the money for the second expedition.[18]

Hyde was dead when Barnwell's letter arrived in North Carolina and it was instead delivered to Thomas Pollock. Pollock was a skillful politician and realized he possessed the means to take revenge on Col. Barnwell. Pollock now sent the letter to Governor Craven in South Carolina where he knew Barnwell's words would work against him. They did. Craven was strongly offended that Barnwell schemed behind his back to get him replaced as governor. He also knew that while Barnwell had supported sending a second expedition to help North Carolina, Craven and the entire South Carolina Assembly had readily agreed and so it was not just to Barnwell's influence. Besides, Craven was no fan of Barnwell, as the governor aligned himself with the Goose Creek Men. Craven had Barnwell's letter read before the entire assembly and its members were just as insulted as Craven had been. The South Carolina Assembly publicly resolved that Barnwell's letter was "false, scandalous, highly reflecting upon and derogatory to the Right Honorable Charles Craven Esqr., and our present Governor, and this present General Assembly."[19] Pollock always relished how Tuscarora Jack, because of his "foolish reflections," found himself discredited not in one but in both Carolinas.[20]

While Barnwell's tongue and temper often got in his way, in reality he had probably done as well as he could. And North Carolina was not nearly as incompetent as Barnwell had made the colony out to be. The capture of Maj. Christopher Gale by privateers had been a real loss and fouled communications from the start. Once in North Carolina, Barnwell just did not appreciate the desperate situation facing Governor Hyde and President Pollock. The southern half of the colony lay in ruins while the

Albemarle was beset with Dissenters who refused to support the war effort in any way. Corn, men, ammunition, and shipping were in short supply. And the destruction of De Graffenried's brigantine was proof of just how treacherous North Carolina waters could be.

In turn, Pollock expected more than Barnwell could deliver. The desertion of his Siouan allies after the attack on Torhunta cut his army from five hundred men to less than two hundred. Then North Carolina had saddled him with unreliable troops who ran when the battle got hot. Then there was the Tuscarora fort. Barnwell's men could assault fortified positions; their victory at Torhunta was evidence of that. But no one had ever seen Indians build anything like Hancock's fort. As Barnwell himself later testified, "our Indians will never of themselves attempt the taking of any fort, without they be led on by a considerable number of white men." Pollock could never appreciate that this was not a typical Indian stronghold and Barnwell just did not have the troops and supplies to take it. And Pollock had not been there to hear the cries of tortured captives and the begging of North Carolina troops to call off the attack to spare the prisoners inside. Instead, Barnwell advised that North Carolina make the best peace it could with the Indians. "It's morally impossible to totally destroy the enemy in a considerable time, but that the Government there may take this opportunity while our forces are there of making a firm & lasting peace, which will be much for their interest."[21] Pollock strongly disagreed.

While Hyde and Pollock were again asking South Carolina for help, they were also working Virginia. The response of the two colonies to North Carolina's pleas could not have been more different. Where South Carolina readily sent one expedition to North Carolina and now prepared to send a second, Virginia merely talked about sending support. According to Virginia's Governor Spotswood, there was just no working with the "unaccountably irregular" North Carolina government. From the first appeal, Virginia voted to send a force of two hundred militiamen and tributary Indians but North Carolina refused to pay for their provisions. In fact, North Carolina levied a 10 percent tax on all provisions brought into the colony, so, Spotswood complained, Virginia troops would have to "pay a duty for the victuals they eat while they were employed in the defence of that country." By the time all this got worked out, Barnwell had made his treaty with the Tuscaroras and so there seemed no need for a Virginia expedition.[22]

Besides, Spotswood felt he had already done much to assist the hapless colony. He had immediately cut trade with the Tuscaroras, then made a truce with Tom Blount and other Tuscaroras and urged them to take the war to Hancock. He even wrung promises from some that they would bring Hancock in to him. He interrogated his own tributary Indians to find out what had been behind the attacks. His rangers scooped up any Tuscarora refugees who tried to make their way into Virginia. Young men of warrior age were held in jail and interrogated until Spotswood was sure they had not taken part in the attacks. He had even offered to send in the Virginia militia, but only if North Carolina promised to pay and feed them. As Spotswood saw it, he alone had managed to keep the upper Tuscaroras out of the war.[23] Nevertheless, once the attack on Core Town sparked hostilities again, Pollock again called on Virginia for assistance. Again Virginia quibbled.

By November 1712, Pollock realized that no immediate assistance was going to come from Virginia and that it would take some time before South Carolina's second expedition could do its work. As Tuscaroras, Machapungas, Cores, and other Indians continued their attacks, Pollock was finally going to have to turn to King Tom Blount for assistance.

❖ We know just slightly more about Tom Blount than we do about King Hancock. Tradition has it that Blount was born into the Tuscarora Bear clan about 1675. His home was the town of Ucohnerunt on the Tar River just before it turns into the Pamlico. We do not know his Tuscarora name as the English who dealt with him always referred to him as Tom Blount, though they sometimes spelled it as Blunt. As for his English name, several legends have been passed down. There was a Capt. Thomas Blount who lived in the Chowan Precinct of Albemarle County. Some have said that Capt. Blount was Tom Blount's father. Others said that Tom Blount of the Tuscarora had been orphaned and raised by Captain Blount of the Chowan. Neither of these stories carries much weight. More likely, his name came from a Tom Blount who served as Virginia's interpreter to the Indian towns south of the James River between 1691 and 1703. Since Virginia traders and interpreters spent a good deal of time in these upper Tuscarora towns, it seems more likely his name came as a show of favor to the Virginian. Somewhere along the way, maybe through working with this interpreter, Tom Blount learned to speak and understand passable English. Nevertheless, he would always rely on the North Carolina interpreter William Charleton whenever he met with colonial officials. For his good services, Blount would later give Charleton six hundred acres in Tuscarora country west of the Chowan River.[24]

His childhood was probably much like any Tuscarora boy's: listening to stories, learning to hunt, becoming a warrior, and doing the things men were expected to do. From his later life we might infer that he had been born into a rather high-status family that was expected to produce town and clan leaders. He was involved in trading with English settlers and had even been sued by William Brice. At some point in his life he was injured, as several people commented on him being lame.[25] Though each Tuscarora town was autonomous and had its own council and king, or *teethha*, by 1711 Tom Blount possessed a high standing throughout the Tuscarora nation. Even King Hancock of Catechna had sent messengers to Blount asking what they should do about Lawson and De Graffenried. One wonders what Blount was thinking when he told Hancock's men that they should free De Graffenried, but do whatever they wanted with Lawson. Surely he knew this would condemn Lawson to death. Did he imagine that North Carolina would let something like that pass? Or maybe that North Carolina was too weak to do anything about it? He must have had some indication from his own warriors that Hancock's young men were agitating for war. And why did Blount and the upper Tuscaroras not throw in with Hancock once they saw the success of the September 22 attacks?

While the Contentnea Creek Tuscaroras provided the bulk of the warriors, in some ways it was a war of the small Indian nations, many of them offshoot Tuscarora towns, and King Hancock found himself pulled into it. Certainly many Tuscarora warriors agitated for war, and the Senecas were pressing hard for one, but it had been the small nations, the Cores, Machapungas, and Bear River Indians, who seemed most eager for it, especially if they could be backed by the powerful Tuscaroras. Up to 1710, a quirk of geography had spared the Tuscaroras from too much land loss and too much abuse. English settlement in the Albemarle had reached west to the Chowan River by the 1670s, but only a few settlers, such as Thomas Pollock, had actually moved west of the river. Most settlers wanted land on a navigable waterway where they could ship out their goods. So instead of moving further west onto Tuscarora territory, settlement moved south, to the southern bank of Albemarle Sound, then to the Pamlico River, down to the Neuse and Trent Rivers, and along the coast. It had been the Machapungas, Cores, Pamlicos, and Bear River Indians who suffered most, been abused most by settlers, and had lost the most land, not the Tuscaroras proper. But those Tuscarora towns along Contentnea Creek now became nervous as they knew Lawson, Pollock, and De Graffenried had eyes on lands they claimed as their own. But in the summer of 1711, it was the smaller nations who were the angriest. It was Core Tom who stood up to Lawson. It had been Core Tom, backed by Catechna's warriors and the Seneca diplomats, who forced Hancock to give in. Like Pontius Pilate, Hancock had made a feeble attempt to save Lawson, but finally washed his hands of the situation, allowing Lawson to be executed and the September 22 attacks to take place. But it would be Hancock who would be blamed by the English and so have to take responsibility for the war.

Up on the Tar River, Tom Blount of Ucohnerunt and the kings of the other towns on the Roanoke River had even less reason to make war on the English. Their land was not under assault and they were in regular contact with Virginia traders. They had more to lose than to gain, so these towns had refused to join in the September 22 attacks, though some young men had gone to fight alongside their Contentnea Creek kinfolk. Surely in those first heady weeks of the war, when the Contentnea Creek Tuscaroras and their allies were plundering farms and turning back Brice's expedition, Tom Blount and the other kings must have secretly cheered on the warriors and laughed at the plight of the English. Then Virginia's Governor Spotswood stopped all trade with the upper Tuscaroras, summoned Blount and the other chiefs to Virginia, awed them with his militiamen, and demanded they sign a treaty of peace. Blount and the other chiefs hesitated, but eventually signed the treaty in which they were supposed to make war on Hancock's Tuscaroras and the smaller nations. But Blount had no wish to alienate his own young men who wanted war. Nor did he wish to make war on Tuscarora kinfolk. So for an entire year while Hancock's warriors romped and fought Barnwell to a standstill, Blount and the upper Tuscaroras remained neutral, not fighting against the English, but neither fighting for them.

But by September 1712, things had changed. Spotswood's trade embargo was making itself felt among the upper Tuscaroras and merchandise was becoming scarce. The Senecas had not joined the war as their diplomats had promised. With Governor Hyde dead and Pollock in charge, it was apparent that North Carolina was not going to accept the peace treaty forged by Barnwell, but had asked South Carolina for a second expedition. Word was that South Carolina had agreed and was in the process of organizing the second expedition. Even Virginia had been asked for troops and supplies and Governor Spotswood and his Council were considering it. Possibly Blount saw the future and realized the Tuscaroras could not win this war. That Pollock was never going to accept anything short of breaking Tuscarora power and turning them into tributary Indians, if any survived. Adding to this was that King Hancock and many of his principal men had come north to the upper Tuscaroras. The English blamed

Hancock for the war and harboring him was dangerous for Blount. At the same time, Blount may well have seen Hancock as a political rival trying to lure his young men away from him and into war. So now King Tom Blount made a momentous decision.

During the war, Blount had always tried to show North Carolina that his people were no threat. In June 1712, Blount personally returned two horses that had been taken from John Lillington. Even then, Pollock had never trusted Blount and always believed that he would eventually throw in with Hancock. Nevertheless, in early October 1712, with the South Carolina forces not yet appearing, Pollock sent word to Blount to come visit him for a council. During the council, Blount had asked about receiving trade goods. Pollock told him in no uncertain terms that he would not receive anything from North Carolina or from Virginia until he had captured King Hancock and brought in the scalps of those who had any hand in the killing of settlers. Blount replied that there was no way his warriors could do that without ammunition. Pollock offered a deal. If Blount would bring in twelve hostages from each upper Tuscarora town or fort, excluding Blount's own town, then Pollock would give him ammunition. Blount considered this and told Pollock that he had four towns that might give hostages. But he had to present this idea to his people. He would return on October 17 to give his answer.[26]

Blount and sixteen of his principal men returned to Pollock at his Balgra plantation a few days after October 17. He explained they were late because they had spotted several Catechna Indians roaming north of the Pamlico River and had followed them for several days. But Blount had brought no hostages for Pollock. Once again he asked about receiving trade goods. Pollock now scaled down his demands and only insisted that Blount and his warriors bring in Hancock. Blount now agreed. He told Pollock that he would go hunting with Hancock and his men and then, all while feigning friendship with him, would capture Hancock and his men and return within eight days. Pollock insisted that Hancock be brought in alive. But Pollock was also shocked by Blount's offer. "His own words make it clear there is no dependence on his promises, who will act so treacherously to those of his own nation and his near relation." Still, Pollock was heartened that Blount and the upper Tuscaroras would join the war on North Carolina's side.[27]

At some point before November 25, Blount was as good as his word. It seemed to work out as Blount said. Blount and some of his men went hunting with Hancock. At a signal, Hancock was taken prisoner. From there it gets hazy. Soon after, word was that Hancock and another Tuscarora named James Cohery had been executed. The problem is that there are no records that actually detail it. The most we have is Pollock writing that Blount "brought him in here" and Hancock received "his deserved punishment." When Governor Spotswood in Virginia heard that Hancock was dead, he angrily wrote to Pollock, insisting that Hancock should have been turned over to him. He felt this would have been proper as Spotswood had made the earlier treaty with Blount and had sent James Cohery back to North Carolina. This surprised Pollock, who replied that Hancock's attacks had been against North Carolina and it had never entered into Pollock's head that Spotswood wanted Hancock. But he would have sent Hancock to Spotswood had he known, but now it was too late.[28] One wonders how the execution was carried out. Firing squad? Hanging? Cutting his throat? There are no records of a trial or execution, or at least none yet found. And so ended in relative obscurity the life of King Hancock of Catechna, a tragic figure who could not prevent a war he had not wanted and then paid the ultimate price for it.

Hancock's death did nothing to stop the war, though Pollock now had more faith in King Blount and the upper Tuscaroras. At the same time, Hancock's death and the direction the war seemed to be taking now showed that even some Contentnea Creek towns wanted peace. On November 25, 1712, Tom Blount and four other Tuscarora kings—Sarooka, Hoonnkhanohnoh, Chaunkhorunthoo, and Noroorksookrosy—met with Governor Pollock and agreed to a nine-point treaty. These five Tuscarora kings represented nine Tuscarora towns, including Blount's own town of Ucohnerunt on the Pamlico River; Resootka and Ooneroy on the Roanoke River; Toisnot on Toisnot Creek; and most interestingly Torhunta, Kenta, Neoheroka, Innennits, and Caunookehoe on Contentnea Creek. Of these last five, Barnwell had in February successfully assaulted the fort at Torhunta, defeated a force of warriors sent by Kenta, and then plundered the deserted towns of Neoheroka, Innennits, and Caunookehoe. It seems that with this treaty, Catechna town, whose warriors had started the war, along with the remaining Cores, Machapungas, Bear River Indians, Weetocks, and Pamlicos were being isolated, allowed to face the English on their own. The other lower Tuscarora towns, already victims of South Carolina attacks, did not want to face another. In truth, they may not have wanted to take part in the war in the first place.[29]

In the treaty, Pollock dictated terms. First, these kings were now to make war on "all Indyans belonging to ye towns or nations of Catechney, Core, Neuse, and Bare River and Pamptico and that they shall not nor will not give any quarter to any male Indyans of those towns or nation above the age of fourteen." All males under fourteen were to be sold as slaves to North Carolina. After destroying those Indian towns, these Tuscaroras were to join with the English and "destroy and cut off" the Machapunga Indians. Second, any slaves, presumably both Indian and African, who had been captured during the course of the war would be returned to their rightful masters. Similarly, any English captives they found still held by the Indians would now be delivered up to North Carolina.[30]

More than just a treaty of alliance, Pollock's demands now made the Tuscaroras into tributary Indians. From now on, those towns along Contentnea Creek, Toisnot Creek, and the Pamlico River should not go among the English plantations at all. Nor should any Indian parties consisting of more than three men go south of the Neuse River or below Contentnea Creek at its confluence with the Neuse, nor on the north bank of the Pamlico River below Nostaterhanrough on Bear Creek. From this point on, any injuries caused by either party should be brought to the attention of North Carolina officials and a council called to adjudicate them. Once a general peace was made, these principal men would pay a yearly tribute to North Carolina. By the next full moon, if they had not yet destroyed all the enemy towns, these principal men from Resootka, Toisnot, Torhunta, Kenta, Neoheroka, Innennits, and Caunookehoe were to deliver to Pollock six children of their chief warriors from each town as hostages to their good behavior. Finally, Pollock now pointed out specific enemy warriors he wanted brought in alive that he had heard were in their towns. These included "Caurinotkguorhkerion, Enrighrionghau, Corsnonkin, Nonrontisgnotkau called John Pagett, Ekohosgsier called Henry Lawson, Corornion called Barbar, Colsora called Henry Lytle, Ounskininorese called Squire Hooks, Toreghinanth, Erentantyse called Goring Tylor." Once the Indians had captured these men, they were to send two emissaries to Reading's Fort on the Pamlico to inform the government. To ensure that that they would not be mistaken for enemy Indians by the garrison there, they should give three whoops and wave a white flag. Then a boat and pilot would bring them over. With that, Tom Blount and the four kings made their mark on the treaty, their names written beside it.[31]

With Hancock dead, Blount and most other towns allied with the English, and another South Carolina expedition on the way, the war appeared to have turned in favor of North Carolina. All Pollock had to do was await the arrival of South Carolina forces.

❖ The September 22, 1711, attacks had devastated that southern part of North Carolina. The area stretching from the Pamlico River down to the

White Oak River had been a battleground. Hundreds of people had been killed or wounded, hundreds of farms and plantations destroyed, court-houses and public records burned, property worth thousands of pounds sterling plundered. De Graffenried's colony of Palatine and Swiss colonists had been particularly hard hit. The Albemarle, terrified it would be next, fortified as best it could, but was not at all united in what it should do. Proprietary men in both Albemarle County and Bath County supported strong counterattacks and the destruction, if not extermination, of the enemy Indians. Quakers and old settlers, far enough away as to not be threatened by Indians, gave moral or economic reasons for not supporting the war.

The Lords Proprietors in London took almost no interest. They knew about the attacks as Pollock had written several letters, so had Governor Spotswood, and the *London Gazette* had announced the war it its pages almost a year earlier. The Proprietors' first letter mentioning anything about the war did not arrive until January 1713. Even then, the Proprietors were more concerned with North Carolina's impressment of a brigantine owned by Emanuel Low, something they deemed illegal, than they were with the war. Instead of support, Pollock was informed that the Proprietors were sending Col. Francis Nicholson to investigate the problems and disorder coming out of their colony. Pollock was also to stop any further prosecutions of former governor Thomas Cary's supporters until Nicholson arrived.[32] The Proprietors, it seemed, were several years behind events. By the time their letter arrived, things seemed at a standstill in North Carolina. Indians still attacked periodically, and the North Carolina government was powerless to do much to prevent them. So during 1712 and in the years afterward, North Carolinians learned to live with a state of war and the constant threat of Indian attack.

Despite the conflict, Anglican ministers still took up their assignments in the colony and many tended their stricken flocks as best they could. Rev. Giles Rainsford arrived in Chowan Precinct on June 5, 1712, and was heartily welcomed by Pollock. Rainsford was shocked at the state of the colony and the "Indian cruelty" that made people afraid to leave their homes to hear his sermons. But he was also the recipient of Indian kindness. During one of his travels around the colony, Rainsford was captured by Indians, but after a talk they let him go. Two Indians even escorted him to safety. Other Anglican ministers, such as the always sour Rev. John Urmston, feared that the town of Bath and its library would be burned by the Indians.[33] They were not.

Despite the hostilities, colonial business slowly picked up. Farms and plantations in the Albemarle were still worked, as were those that had survived in Bath County. Ships once again arrived in North Carolina waters, bringing in the usual goods. At the same time, ships from North Carolina carrying tobacco, naval stores, anything except corn and food, sailed to Philadelphia, New York, Boston, and other ports.[34] Up in the Albemarle, the Assembly again began meeting regularly. In every election of 1712, the Quakers and old settlers gained clout. When Governor Hyde and Pollock refused to allow Cary supporters to be seated in the Assembly, it became gridlocked and would not appropriate further money for colonial defense. Nevertheless, the government was functioning again, if in name only.[35]

The courts, even in Bath County, were soon again in session. The destruction from the war caused a legal boom. The wills and estates of the dead now had to be adjudicated. In September 1712, Hannah Smith, the mistress of John Lawson and the mother of his children, petitioned the colonial government to appraise Lawson's estate so his will could go into effect. Several times William Brice requested to serve as the administrator of estates of men killed in the war. Brice went before the Council and asked to be named as the administrator of Peter Worden's estate as Worden owed him £40. The Council granted him his petition. He asked for the same with Samuel Slocum's estate, but Slocum's brother challenged it and Brice was turned down. At other times, Brice served on a team of appraisers appointed by the courts. Even then, Brice did not hesitate to sue the heirs and estates of men who had been killed while still owing him money.[36]

Besides wills and estates, orphaned children also had to be cared for. Most of these were apprenticed out to surviving settlers. Palatine children, such as seven-year-old George Conis, the only survivor of his family, and George Kneegee, the only survivor of his, both became wards of Capt. Jacob Miller. William Brice became the guardian of three orphaned children, two boys and a girl: thirteen-year-old Hodman Richman, his eleven-year-old sister Lees Richman, and eight-year-old James Castage. The two boys were bound over to Brice until they reached the age of twenty-one. The girl, Lees, only had to wait until she was eighteen.[37]

The war, with its destruction and disruption and the need to prosecute it, created opportunities for profit. No one used those opportunities more than Thomas Pollock. With Hyde's death promoting him to acting governor and the Dissenters in the assembly thwarting his war efforts, Pollock began concentrating power in his own hands. Pollock would, in fact, become one of the most powerful governors in the history of North Carolina. When the Council was not in session, Pollock, as council president, could be both judge and jury to any Indian accused of a crime or misdemeanor. He was "fully empowered to inflict such immediate punishment on them as he shall think ye crime requires."[38] As governor and major general, the Council granted him full authority to "negotiate any affair relating to ye war," and he had the right to spend government funds as he saw fit.[39] When the Meherrin Indians asked to make a treaty, the Council said Pollock could negotiate whatever articles "he shall think fit."[40] Even the Lords Proprietors appointed him as the North Carolina deputy to the Duke of Beaufort. And he shared the wealth with his family. With Lawson dead, Pollock appointed his son, Thomas Pollock Jr., as surveyor general of North Carolina.[41]

As for his personal wealth, Pollock claimed that he lost about £2,500 during the war, much of it going to provide food and equipment for the army. That did not include the debts De Graffenried owed him when the baron abandoned his colony. As Pollock detailed it, De Graffenried owed him £612 for supplies he provided when the Palatines arrived destitute in 1710. Pollock had also bought a £56 debt De Graffenried owed to Thomas West. Add on £91 4s. interest and that came to almost £770. The total would only continue to rise as long as De Graffenried did not pay. Pollock had also paid De Graffenried's taxes owed on his land in Bath County. All together, Pollock figured the baron owed him close to £1,000 sterling. Of this, De Graffenried had only paid back £312 in North Carolina current money, worth much less than pounds sterling. Pollock was now prepared to take De Graffenried's lands in Bath County, totaling more than fifteen thousand acres, if De Graffenried did not pay £700 sterling by the end of 1715.[42]

But Pollock knew the baron would never pay. He grumbled that De Graffenried "did withdraw himself secretly out of this government into places remote and unknown to them without taking any other or further care, for the paying, securing or otherwise satisfying their said debts."[43] Pollock summed it up, "I took him for a man of honor . . . but have found this contrary, to my great loss."[44] The Palatines would agree. They complained that soon after De Graffenried returned from his Tuscarora captivity, he did not stay long in New Bern, but "carried off from our settlements all that he could conveniently come at, promising to return with provisions and necessarys for the war, but never returned." Just as bad was "that as soon as our Trustee departed the said Colonel Thomas Pollock came to our settlements and took everything, even the mill stones, and left us without any assistance entirely, naked to the mercy of the Indians."[45] Once De Graffenried left North Carolina for good, never paying his debts, all the Palatine and Swiss lands down on the Neuse fell into Pollock's hands, as did most of the town lots inside New Bern itself. These settlers would file suit to retain their lands and the case would last well into the middle of the eighteenth century, long after most of the principals involved were dead.[46]

One could never have too much good land, and Pollock always kept an eye open for choice pieces. One particular piece Pollock wanted was Core Town and its cornfields. So did Governor Hyde and Col. Barnwell. Core Town's lands stretched for about three miles along the Neuse and had already been cleared by the Cores for farming. But then someone attacked and enslaved the Cores and the area around their now-abandoned village was ready to be planted. It was a splendid piece of land. Then Hyde died in September 1712. Barnwell imagined Core Town would be given to him in appreciation of his services to North Carolina. But with Pollock now acting governor, Tuscarora Jack would never get his hands on it. So Pollock pressed his claim for Core Town and the Council backed him, seeing it as some compensation for all the money Pollock had personally expended on the war. But there were other claimants and the Lords Proprietors would have to weigh in on this. That meant waiting. Never one to rest when it came to land, Pollock also pointed out to the Council that the grant to 640 acres at Wilkinson Point on the north bank of the Neuse River, near present-day Minnesott Beach, had lapsed as the grantee had never settled or improved it. Pollock asked for the land patent to Wilkinson Point and received it.[47]

While he enriched himself, Pollock also knew the war was not yet over. That would only come with the destruction of Tuscaroras and their Core, Machapunga, and Bear River allies. But North Carolina was not strong enough to do this on its own. It still needed help.

CHAPTER SEVEN

Col. James Moore

The Soldier

It would have been easy for South Carolina to wash its hands of North Carolina. Officials had already appropriated £4,000 pounds to prosecute the war, sent an expedition commanded by the experienced Col. Barnwell, forced a peace treaty with the Tuscaroras, and still North Carolina wanted more. Once again, South Carolina did not hesitate. On August 6, 1712, no sooner had North Carolina's emissary, Robert Foster, finished making his plea, Governor Craven and the South Carolina Assembly decided to help. Craven said the colony did it out of its "nobler principles" and confessed "the secret pleasure of doing good is inexpressible, to succour our distressed brethren, to save our sister colony from a barbarous enemy, are actions truly Christian & heroic & stands recorded to all posterity." He pointed out that not all of the £4,000 appropriated for the Barnwell expedition had been spent, so the remainder should be used to "extirpate a savage people with whom no peace can be made."[1] Of course, there was the lure of numerous Indian slaves there for the taking.[2]

❖ The South Carolina Assembly met the next day, August 7, and wholeheartedly supported another expedition to North Carolina. Barnwell had to have felt insulted by North Carolina's demand that the army be led by anyone other than him, but even he supported a second expedition. South Carolina traders should encourage the Indians to volunteer for the expedition, he said, and asked that special attention be given to the Waccamaws and Cape Fear Indians. But Indians were not enough, Barnwell advised, as they would never attack a fort. To take such strongholds as the ones the Tuscaroras had prepared, a force of colonial militia would be needed.[3]

On August 8, the South Carolina Assembly first offered command to Col. Robert Daniel. But Daniel wanted "very large & extravagant" compensation, and the Assembly refused him. Next they voted to give it to Capt. Robert Lorey. Governor Craven vetoed him. "We have no exception against Capt. Lorey either, as to his courage or conduct," Craven explained. "But not being a person acquainted with the way & manner of Indian war, we believe a more proper officer may be thought of for this occasion." As Craven saw it, command should go to one of two men: Col. John Fenwick or Col. James Moore Jr. The Assembly chose Moore.[4]

James Moore Jr. was born in South Carolina around 1682 into a well-connected and rather remarkable Goose Creek family. His father was James Moore Sr. and his mother Margaret Berringer, the stepdaughter of the influential early governor Sir John Yeamans. James Jr. was the oldest of ten children: James, Jehu, Roger, Maurice, John, Nathaniel, Anne, Mary, Rebecca, and Margaret. James and his brothers were close and many of his brothers would make names for themselves. As Goose Creek Men, they had no problems with Indian slavery. They certainly encouraged it and profited from it. And the Moores learned it at their father's knee, James Moore Sr., a bigger-than-life South Carolinian who even there had a rather notorious reputation as an Indian slaver.[5]

James Moore Sr. had migrated to South Carolina from Barbados around 1675 and became a founding member of the Goose Creek Men. By 1683 he owned a 2,400-acre plantation there and was fast accumulating more. A true opportunist, he did everything he could to increase his fortunes. He was a planter, a merchant, a part owner of several ships, and known to do business with pirates. He was involved in the Indian trade and made several illegal slave raids. Even the Lords Proprietors condemned him in 1683 for "sending away of Indians & have contrived most unjust wars upon ye Indian in order to ye getting slaves."[6] Nevertheless, he began holding important positions in South Carolina government, eventually becoming secretary of the province in 1698, receiver general in 1699–1700, chief justice during that same time, and finally governor of South Carolina in 1700. One of his most infamous ventures came in the early 1700s, after Queen Anne's War began. In October 1702, Moore Sr. led a company of South Carolina militia and allied Indians in an attack on Spanish Florida's capital at St. Augustine and burned the city. After being replaced as governor in 1703, Moore Sr. the next year led an expedition against the Apalachee Indians who lived in Spanish missions in western Florida. It was an overwhelming victory for Moore, but in reality it was nothing more than a slave raid. He and his Indian allies marched thousands of Appalache captives back to South Carolina. His son, James Moore Jr., accompanied his father on these raids and so early on learned how to fight Indians and take slaves.[7]

When Moore Sr. died in 1706, James Jr. took over as head of the family. At some point, James married Elizabeth Beresford and they had six children: James, Jehu, John, Margaret, Mary, and Elizabeth. In 1706, he was elected to the South Carolina Assembly by voters in Berkeley and Craven Counties. He was a strong Anglican, a member of the vestry of St. James Goose Creek Parish, and even had a pew given to him in recognition for his piety and industriousness. He proved a good friend to Rev. Dr. Francis Le Jau, giving him money when the reverend's salary was late. In 1707, Moore was named as a captain in the South Carolina militia. In June of that year, the Savannah Indians, normally allies of South Carolina, "revolted" by leaving their towns along the Savannah River and headed north to live in Pennsylvania and Maryland. South Carolinians hated seeing their Indian buffer deserting them, believing they had been lured away by Virginia traders. So the Assembly sent Capt. James Moore and twenty men to confiscate the goods of any Virginia traders they found among the Savannahs and to persuade the Savannahs to return. When the Savannahs refused, the Assembly sent Moore and his Catawba allies to attack them. It was good training for Moore, who was promoted to colonel.[8]

Where Col. John Barnwell had been passionate and hot-tempered, Col. James Moore seemed more thoughtful and deliberate. He had performed well against the Savannahs, but it was yet to be known how he would fare against the Tuscaroras. Still, South Carolina was going to give the thirty-one-year-old colonel as much support as it could. Almost immediately, in August 1712, Governor Craven informed Pollock in North Carolina that Col. Moore and his army were being readied. The North Carolina Council again gave Pollock full authority to make any agreements and treaties he needed with Moore or with the Indians to bring about victory. South Carolina also sent word to its Indian allies, asking them to volunteer. South Carolina traders were again ordered to encourage their Indian trade partners to go along. There was some worry about the Indian desertions that had hamstrung Barnwell, and officials interviewed some of Barnwell's early deserters. The Sewees, Winyaws, and Saxapahaws claimed they had no weapons or ammunition, so they left Barnwell. But Governor Craven felt their account was very "dark."[9]

The expedition was supposed to depart in mid-September 1712, but things moved slowly. As late as November 20, Governor Craven was visiting the Congaree Indian towns far up the Santee River, the jumping-off point for the expedition. He deplored the lack of Indian volunteers and blamed it on the traders for "the discouragement they gave the Indians contrary to my orders, prevailed on several to stay at home and others to go to war where they thought fit."[10] By late November, Col. Moore had an army of 33 white officers and militiamen and more than 900 Indian allies. Moore himself commanded the Esaw, or Catawba, Company. His brother, Capt. Maurice Moore, led a company of 50 Yamasees from Barnwell's old company. Unfortunately, Col. Moore did not leave the same records of his expedition that Barnwell did, so much is bare bones. For his officers he listed a Capt. Pierce, Capt. Canty, Capt. Harford, Capt. Thurston, Capt. Theophilus Hastings, and Capt. Stone, all men who had served with Barnwell, except for Stone and Moore's own brother, Maurice. Many of his 900 Indian allies had gone along on Barnwell's expedition. Moore had also managed to attract about 310 Cherokee warriors to his army. By mid-November, the army was ready to move against the Tuscaroras. As Reverend Le Jau said, Moore's army was "to bring those murderers to due punishment, we think to destroy the whole nation, that is kill the men and make the women and children slaves, this is the way of our wars."[11]

Moore and his army left the Congaree towns and headed straight north to the Catawbas and crossed into North Carolina at about present-day Charlotte. From there, his army marched directly northeast, crossing the Yadkin River, the upper Cape Fear River, the upper Neuse River, and was on Contentnea Creek by late November 1712. At Contentnea Creek, Moore found the Tuscaroras practicing their usual strategy, abandoning their towns with most withdrawn to a huge fort that had been built at the town of Neoheroka. It had not been there the year before when Barnwell had looted the town. One wonders what was happening among the Neoheroka leadership as the town was at that same moment signing Pollock's peace treaty. This time Moore deliberately did not allow the towns to be pillaged lest his Indians desert him as they had Barnwell. Instead, he and his army merely spent a few days scouting Fort Neoheroka, as it came to be called.[12]

While the fort appeared formidable, Moore believed he had the Indians just where he wanted them. Word from Tom Blount was that the Tuscaroras were low on food and ammunition and so would have to leave the safety of their forts to find it. If they did, then Moore's Indians could attack and force them back into the fort. Penned in there, they would not be able to hold out long "for want of provisions, ammunition, firewood, and everything else."[13] All Moore had to do was hold out longer than the Tuscaroras in the fort. But this was dicey strategy. Moore's army was

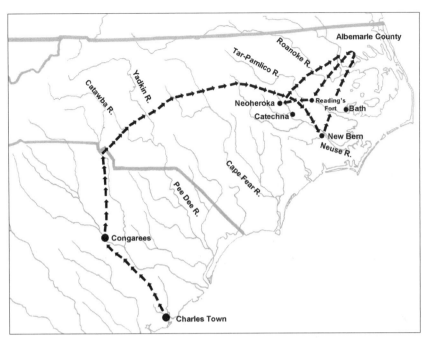

Col. James Moore's Expedition, December 1712–August 1713. Map by David A. Norris

dangerously short on provisions. If his Indians would desert if they got plunder, he also worried that they might desert him if provisions got too low. With a strong fort in front of him, low provisions, and worried about the reliability of his Indian allies, Moore felt the best plan would be to retreat down the Neuse River to New Bern. There his army would resupply. He believed he could bring the Tuscaroras to "a low condition by the middle of Febry next."[14]

No battle was offered at Neoheroka, though Moore's Indians did attack a band of what they thought were Tuscaroras, killing eight and capturing one, who was instantly enslaved. Moore soon learned that his Indians had actually attacked a party of Five Nation Iroquois from New York. This was a dangerous mistake with potentially fatal repercussions. So far the Five Nations had not joined with the Tuscaroras, but this attack had the prospect of actively bringing them, or at least the Senecas, into the war on the side of the Tuscaroras. It was also learned that this band of Iroquois, rather than being a war party, was actually a party of Five Nation ambassadors going to the Tuscaroras to advise them to make peace with the English. At least that was the story. When Pollock and the North Carolina Council heard of this, they immediately purchased the surviving captive from the South Carolina Indians, a Seneca named Anethae, freed him, and sent him back to his home in New York. As an indemnity and hoping to defuse any trouble, North Carolina also gave him four slaves for his own: three Tuscaroras and one Machapunga. Pollock sent with Anethae a letter to the Five Nations, reiterating to them that it had been the Tuscaroras who had started the war by killing between 130 and 140 settlers, not the English. Then, as Pollock saw it, the Tuscaroras had made a sham peace with Col. Barnwell, then broke it within days.[15]

Pollock had good reason to appease the Five Nations as by early 1713 he and others thought the Senecas, maybe even the entire Five Nations, were about to enter the war. Of course, they had been hearing this rumor for many months. Nevertheless, Pollock, as well as Spotswood in Virginia, believed the Tuscaroras were already receiving some kind of aid from the Senecas. Unless something could be done, especially by New York's Governor Robert Hunter, then it would be only a matter of time before they were fighting Senecas in North Carolina, possibly even Virginia. Spotswood certainly believed this as he kept getting information from refugees and his own tributary Indians that the Senecas were on their way. The Virginia governor received word that a strong caravan of Virginia traders had been attacked by Indians. He at first thought it had been Tuscaroras, but later learned that the attackers had been a party of Senecas. Pollock heard that some Seneca warriors were already with the Tuscaroras holed up at the fort at Neoheroka. Even the *Boston News-Letter* reported that Col. Moore had captured a few Tuscarora spies who before being put to death "confess'd they were set on by the French Indians who promised to assist them."[16]

Down on Contentnea Creek, Moore and his troops were low on food and so retreated down the creek to Fort Hyde, about a mile below its confluence with the Neuse. But North Carolina troops garrisoned there had already eaten everything. Disappointed, Moore's army marched to New Bern, but found no food there either. Much the same had happened the previous year with Barnwell. But that year, the North Carolina government could justly claim that it had no knowledge of Barnwell's coming and so had not prepared supplies for him. This time, Pollock and the North Carolina government had long known Moore's army was on its way and even then they did not have supplies or reinforcements ready. It could again be blamed on the divisions within North Carolina society.

As in the year before, Quakers and Dissenters in the Assembly refused to support the war with corn or men. Maj. James Cole complained that Thomas Bayly, Arthur Winchester, John Winsloe, James Fitch, John

Newby, Benjamin Munday, William Ellat, and Jonathan Sherwood "in a most mutinous manner did condemn and resist the lawful authority of this government being imprest on an expedition agt. Indyan enemy." The Council ordered their arrest.[17] Others did the same. Daniel Gutheree, the deputy provost marshal for Pasquotank Precinct, complained that Robert Morgan, John Sawyer Sr., John Sawyer Jr., Robert Sawyer, Edward Williams, and Richard Hastins not only refused to go on the Indian expedition but also refused to pay the £5 fine for refusing to go. The men then forcibly took from Gutheree various items that he had collected for the war effort. The Council also ordered these men to be taken into custody.[18] While many along the Albemarle flat out refused to serve, down along the Pamlico and Neuse, settlers were just too afraid of the Indians to do much. Men with business before the courts refused to make the trip to the Albemarle. "We are forced to keep in close garrisons for fear of ye Indians and darest not leave our families to come to court."[19] Despite Pollock's efforts, North Carolina again seemed to be at a standstill.

The previous year, this kind of delay had sent Barnwell into explosive rages where he berated Pollock, Hyde, and the North Carolina government. This only antagonized North Carolina officials and did nothing to help the war effort. But Col. Moore was a clever man. He refused to get involved in North Carolina political divisions. His next move was brilliant, worthy of a Washington or a Sherman. There was no food in the New Bern area and the only place there was food was in the Albemarle. So in late December 1712, Moore marched his entire army, South Carolina militia and "Ashley River Indians" as they were called, north into Chowan Precinct of Albemarle County. It was as if Moore had kicked over a nest of yellow jackets. The war had suddenly come to the Albemarle and its people were shocked and abuzz.[20]

Moore's Indians were allies, come to help North Carolina, but to the farmers of the Albemarle, it was as if they had been invaded. Hungry Indians scavenged the Albemarle, bringing in thousands of bushels of corn and hundreds of head of cattle. Quakers and Dissenters who had come through the earlier attacks unscathed now had their own supplies of corn plundered. Arguments and fights broke out between the settlers and the Ashley River Indians. As Pollock described it, "the Indians having destroyed all the stocks where they were ordered to be, begun to spread themselves further without orders, which put several people into such a ferment that they were more ready to fall upon the South Carolina Indians than march out against the enemy."[21] Soon, the Albemarle was, as Pollock said, in a "miserable state."[22]

But Moore's Indians had also done something that had been impossible for decades: they had unified the settlers of the Albemarle. Col. Moore had a certain force of personality that drew the Indians to him, and many in the Albemarle believed that if Moore was killed, then the Ashley River Indians, far from home, would attack North Carolina. Now most settlers in the Albemarle, Dissenters and Proprietary men alike, figured that the sooner the Indians left the area the better. Pollock and the Council again levied taxes on corn, £5 on every six bushels of tithable corn, and a quarter of all wheat. This time settlers paid them. Quakers now provided supplies, religious beliefs notwithstanding. Even Edward Moseley and John Porter, two of Pollock's worst enemies and the strongest supporters of Governor Cary during his rebellion, contributed several bushels of corn. And one may recall that it was the Porters who had been accused of stirring up the Indians to attack in the first place. Albemarle men also began showing up for militia duty and by mid-January 1713, North Carolina added eighty-five troops under the command of Capt. William Maule to Moore's army. Maule had long been a friend of Pollock's and looked to him as something of a mentor. With him now came Col. Louis Michel, De Graffenried's old business partner who had served so well with Barnwell the year before.[23]

Finally, as enough supplies came in, and probably through some diplomacy by acting governor Pollock, on January 17, 1713, Moore's army moved out of the Albemarle and marched southwest to Reading's Fort on the Pamlico River. However, snow and bad weather set in and the army found itself stuck at Reading's for the next two months. Moore spent the downtime gathering more supplies. Almost three thousand bushels of corn and a hundred barrels of pork came in, as did six hundred pounds of gunpowder and fifteen hundred pounds of shot. He was also joined by Col. Alexander Mackay and his Yamasee troops whom Barnwell had left in North Carolina. Several times Pollock visited Moore at Reading's Fort. But it would not be until March 1713 that Moore and his army moved on the fort at Neoheroka. As Rev. Le Jau back in Charles Town wrote, "Our forces have done but little yet that we can hear against the Tuscarora Indians, that war is not to be concluded without much trouble and cost."[24]

❖ If the coming of Col. Moore and his Ashley River Indians to the Albemarle frightened the English, it absolutely terrified King Tom Blount and the upper Tuscaroras. Up to this point, Blount had managed to more or less appease Pollock and Governor Spotswood in Virginia while doing very little to live up to the treaties he had been pressured to sign. Yes, he had captured King Hancock and some of his principal men and turned them over to North Carolina for execution. But Hancock had been a troublemaker, a wanted man, and Blount probably hoped that that sacrifice would placate the English. He still had not made war on the Catechna Tuscaroras and their allies, nor provided the hostages demanded by Pollock and Spotswood. He even threw away messages Spotswood sent by him to other Tuscaroras, saying he refused to be an English letter carrier. As for Spotswood's early ban on trade with him and his Tuscaroras, Blount and his people got around it with the help of the Meherrin Indians, who supplied them with guns, merchandise, and information. Even then, the embargo had been lifted soon after his treaty with Spotswood.[25]

The coming of Moore's Ashley River Indians changed all that as the upper Tuscaroras feared they would be enslaved and marched back to Charles Town. Blount now approached Pollock. Both men had complaints against the other. Pollock accused Blount of giving nothing but words when it came to fulfilling his treaty obligations. Blount complained that he had received nothing from Pollock, no supplies or ammunition. In fact, his own brother had been taken prisoner in Virginia and was languishing in jail there. Even worse, the coming of Col. Moore's Ashley River Indians to the area posed a grave threat. Both Pollock and Moore tried to assure Blount that his people would be safe from Moore's Indian army. In turn, Blount could tell Pollock that four of his own principal men had returned from a diplomatic mission to the Five Nations in New York. He now assured Pollock that the Senecas were not planning to join with the Catechna Tuscaroras. That was good news to Pollock and he was slowly coming around to the idea that he might be able to trust King Tom Blount after all.[26]

While Blount fretted, other upper Tuscaroras took actions of their own. Almost immediately after Moore's Indians arrived in Chowan Precinct, several Tuscarora towns from the Roanoke River, along with some refugees from Contentnea Creek, headed northwest for the safety of the Virginia mountain frontier. They soon found themselves in bad shape, living illegally in Virginia, with no permanent town or houses, no fields to plant, and very little food or supplies. Governor Spotswood heard rumor they had attacked some Virginia settlers. To get the facts, he sent a party of about fifty of his tributary Indians and a couple of Virginia traders to investigate. They learned that these Tuscaroras had not attacked any settlements and were in desperate straits. As they told Spotswood's emissaries, they did not know what to do. Should they return to their homes in North Carolina and so risk being "knock'd in the head by the English and South Carolina Indians?" Or should they submit to the Senecas, who had offered them abundant assistance to take revenge on the English, but on the condition that they become tributaries to the Five Nations?[27] Seizing an opportunity, Spotswood moved these refugee Tuscaroras further away from North Carolina and placed some of his tributary Indians between them and the North Carolina border. To ensure their protection and good behavior, he placed a guard of white men in each of their towns. Any Tuscaroras who had participated in attacks on North Carolina were to be ferreted out "to do justice on those rogues."[28]

Other upper Tuscaroras approached Spotswood himself. Haweesaris, known as Basket, and Naroniackkos, known as George, were sent by their Tuscarora town, which Spotswood called Tervanihow. They explained that they represented only one town and about a hundred men and many more women and children, but that there were five towns scattered nearby very interested in what the two men would report. They had been instructed to meet with Spotswood and inquire into the possibilities of making a treaty with Virginia and moving to that colony. Spotswood quizzed them. Why were they in Virginia? Had they participated in attacks on North Carolina? Did they know anything about the Meherrin Indians attacking Virginia settlements? Haweesaris and Naroniackkos assured him that none of them had been involved in the war nor wanted to become involved. They knew nothing about Meherrin attacks and no Meherrins lived among them. As for why they were in Virginia, their people feared the English in North Carolina and wanted to hear what provisions and supplies Spotswood would offer for a treaty. Still, the two men stressed that they did not have the power to sign a treaty, only bring back Spotswood's offer to their town council.[29]

Spotswood countered, saying that other Tuscaroras had come to him and made treaties, but never lived up to them. This was a dig at King Tom Blount. Haweesaris and Naroniackkos declared that their people would like to live in Virginia right now as they feared the Ashley River Indians prowling their country. They would remain in Virginia under any provisions Spotswood stipulated. If possible, they would like to live on the Roanoke River in Virginia, near the Great Trading Path they called "Weecacana." But they would live wherever Spotswood ordered. Did they plan to return to North Carolina, Spotswood wanted to know. Maybe, they answered, but it would be up to their people. And they were not sure their people would ever be willing to return to North Carolina. Why did they not go see Governor Thomas Pollock in North Carolina? Spotswood asked. Only Tom Blount goes to see Pollock, they explained, and Blount did not speak for them. Nor did Blount ask them to make peace with

Virginia as that had been their own idea. Spotswood seemed satisfied at the two emissaries' words and prepared to offer treaty stipulations.[30]

Virginia governor Alexander Spotswood was certainly one of the more remarkable figures in the colonial Southeast. In later years, he would become a close friend of Benjamin Franklin of Philadelphia. Born around 1676, he had been appointed as lieutenant governor of Virginia in 1710. The actual Virginia governor was George Hamilton, but he never came to the colony. Spotswood lived in Williamsburg and so ran the government. Where other colonial governors in English colonies often gained reputations as incompetents, Spotswood, a military man with the rank of colonel, appeared deliberate, imaginative, competent, and had little affection for those who were not. When it came to relations with the colony south of Virginia, he saw himself as the superior older brother to childlike North Carolina. His letters drip with condescension toward the colony. As he saw it, North Carolina brought the Tuscarora War on itself with its bad treatment of the Indians. The Quakers and other colonial divisions prevented it from successfully prosecuting it. Then just when North Carolina had a peace treaty with the Tuscaroras, Barnwell had started the war again when he attacked the Indians gathered at Core Town. North Carolina was again divided and seemingly powerless. They could not even help themselves. Knowing of Col. Moore's impending arrival, North Carolina had not gathered food and supplies for his army. Spotswood often wondered if this incompetent colony was worth saving.[31]

Despite the friction between Virginia and North Carolina, when the Indian attacks began again in the summer of 1712, Pollock a second time turned to Spotswood for help. Pollock and the North Carolina Council thanked Spotswood for the assistance he had already provided, such as preventing his tributary Indians from joining the war and stopping trade with the Tuscaroras. Still, Pollock complained that the Meherrin Indians, tributaries of Virginia, had been coming south of the Meherrin River and shooting up plantations and livestock. Nevertheless, North Carolina was in "the most miserable condition that ever people groaned." As Pollock wrote, "we have exerted our utmost endeavours as well by arms as by treaties to maintain the honor of the British and Christian character; but what with the greatest poverty, the repeated slaughters of our men and the disability of our few remaining by wounds and continual fatigues and marches, we are rendered not only incapable of carrying on an offensive, but even a defensive war." Now Pollock and the Council begged Spotswood with "all the ties of Christianity and all the ties of Humanity and fellow Subjects to afford us some assistance without which the destruction of many unfortunate families will follow." The North Carolina government asked for a loan of £1000 sterling. This would be used to pay troops. And if Virginia would provide some troops, then North Carolina would provide them with provisions and the expenses to transport them to the colony. If Spotswood agreed to this, then it would add to his "illustrious character," show his compassion, and confirm to her Majesty's subjects that Spotswood was really "the Protector of the Distressed."[32]

Up in Virginia, Spotswood and his Council again went into penny-pinching mode. As Spotswood explained to Pollock, even if Virginia offered to lend North Carolina a thousand pounds sterling, that sum would not cover the cost of sending Virginia troops into North Carolina. Nor could North Carolina pay for their upkeep or have enough provisions if Spotswood did send them. Then the Virginia governor made a bold suggestion. If North Carolina really needed a loan of £1000 to pay for the upkeep of Virginia troops, then it should consider mortgaging to Virginia all its lands north of the Roanoke River.[33]

Pollock was apoplectic at Spotswood's offer. He angrily replied that North Carolina did not have the authority to mortgage lands belonging to the Lords Proprietors and such a thing had never been found in the laws or the Fundamental Constitutions. Pollock did not have to point out that his own plantation of Balgra and his wife's plantation at Salmon Creek were on those lands Spotswood wanted mortgaged. Nothing came of that but hard feelings. As for Spotswood's worries about sufficient supplies, Pollock believed provisions would hold out. And £1000 loan, had Spotswood given it, was to have been used to pay Virginia forces. But now, Pollock said, Virginia troops were not needed as South Carolina had sent Col. Moore and his army. Besides, if Virginia troops mixed with South Carolina troops, then quarrels and arguments might break out and so upend the expedition.[34]

In truth, Spotswood did want to do something tangible to help North Carolina, but he was hamstrung by his own Council and Assembly, which did not want to spend the money. In the end, no Virginia money would be lent nor would Virginia troops be sent. The best Spotswood could do was supply nine hundred yards of coarse cloth. He also managed to scare up three hundred suits of clothes to be sent to North Carolina troops, but Spotswood scathingly noted that North Carolina could only come up with one hundred men. Again, Spotswood blamed North Carolina for the lack of help from Virginia. "There reigns such stupidity and dissent in the Government of North Carolina, that it can neither concert any measure, nor perform any engagement for its own security."[35] Of course, Virginia was willing to send back to North Carolina any enemy Indian prisoners taken.[36] Better to let North Carolina feed them.

In the end, while Virginia did do valuable work for North Carolina by cutting off trade with the Tuscaroras and trying to keep the upper Tuscaroras neutral, it did not take much of an active role in the war. That was left to South Carolina.

❖ By mid-March 1713, Col. Moore and his army of about 113 Carolina militiamen and officers and 760 Indians were ready. From Reading's Fort on the Pamlico River, the army marched overland directly southwest to Contentnea Creek and the Tuscarora fort at their town of Neoheroka. Called "Fork Field" by the Tuscaroras, Neoheroka was located near present-day Snow Hill about fifteen miles up the creek from Hancock's town of Catechna. It sat astride the main trail leading west to Torhunta while the creek itself ran through the middle of town. The Tuscaroras had briefly abandoned the town the previous year as Barnwell approached. His army plundered the empty town, but since then the Tuscaroras and their allies had returned. The fort sat in a small horseshoe bend in Contentnea Creek and so was protected by water and steep banks on three sides.[37]

The fort at Neoheroka was a marvel of Native American engineering, even more so than Hancock's fort, covering an acre and a half of ground. Its walls were a palisade of logs atop a berm, with the borrow pit forming a trench around the fort. Firing platforms and loopholes ran around the inside of the walls. The fort itself was somewhat square on its north, west, and south sides, which faced the creek. An elevated blockhouse crowned these three corners. The northwestern blockhouse, which faced the creek, was roofed to protect its occupants from artillery. These blockhouses also provided the Indians with excellent fields of fire. A covered trench ran from the middle of the western, or back, wall down to the creek, which provided protected access to water, something Hancock's fort initially lacked. The eastern or front wall, the only side not facing water, rather than a straight line of palisades, was built in a large outward-facing bend or bulge. Two large blockhouses or redoubts dominated this wall. The fort gate was at the northeast part of the wall and from it ran a protected trench that would allow warriors to sally out of the fort and attack Moore's troops. Behind the bulging eastern wall ran a second wall and breastworks that served as a fallback position. And then to show that the Tuscaroras planned to make this a last-ditch defense, two underground bunkers had been built and connected to each other by a tunnel. These underground rooms were used for storage, a haven for women and children, and a defensive position.[38]

The Neoheroka fort was much stronger than the one at Catechna, and more formidable, even by European standards. It had defenses in depth and showed the Indians had learned lessons from Barnwell's two unsuccessful assaults the year before: raised and covered blockhouses with good fields of fire and protected from artillery; covered access to water and canoes; protected sally ports; and underground bunkers. All these tried to remedy weaknesses that had been exposed by Barnwell while also trying to anticipate the type of attack Moore and his army might make. Neoheroka also showed a change in Tuscarora strategic thinking. Rather than planning ambushes and running battles in the forest, the Tuscaroras were betting all that their fort would be able to withstand another colonial assault. Where women, children, and provisions had previously been hidden in the forest, now they were brought into the fort and hidden in the bunkers. And rather than retreat to fight another day if things went badly, it was to be a fight to the death. As Moore's army approached that March of 1713, the Tuscaroras knew that the war would be won or lost at Neoheroka.[39]

A few days before March 20, Moore and his army arrived before the fort and quickly surrounded it. But Moore was much more methodical than Barnwell and took time to carefully arrange his forces. Directly to the east or front of the fort sat Yamasee Battery protected by breastworks. Here he stationed Col. Alexander Mackay, Capt. Maurice Moore, 10 white militiamen, and 50 Indians, mostly Yamasees. A hundred yards or so southeast of Yamasee Battery was Col. Moore's headquarters. It was far enough from the fort to not have to construct defensive breastworks. Along with Moore were Col. Louis Michel; Capt. William Maule, who commanded the North Carolina militia; Capt. Canty, Capt. Theophilus Hasting, 88 white militiamen, and 400 Indians of various nations. West of Moore's headquarters and below the fort's southern wall sat Mulberry Battery, protected by a breastwork. No troops were stationed here, but Mulberry was to be used as a foray point come the day of battle. Across Contentnea Creek in the woods northwest of the fort sat the Cherokee Battery, with Captains Harford and Thurston, 10 white militiamen, and 310 Cherokees.[40]

The fort was impressive and Moore believed the best way to take it was to knock a large hole in its walls and then rush his men inside. To do this, he decided to use a mine. His men would dig under the fort walls and place a large charge of black powder, which he would explode and so blast away some of the eastern palisades. Moore ordered approach trenches to be dug from the Yamasee Battery toward the fort's eastern wall. These

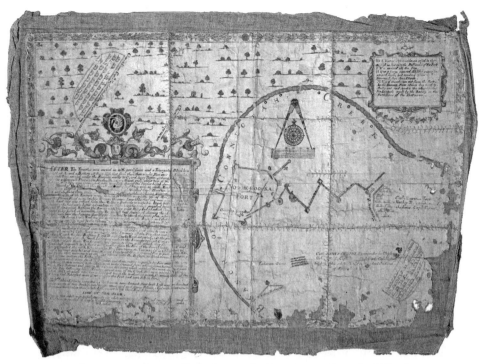

Col. James Moore's map of Noo-hee-roo-ka Fort, c. 1713. From the Collections of the South Carolina Historical Society

slowly zigzagged forward, while the Tuscaroras shot down on them from the raised blockhouses. But the trenches were well protected and Moore took few casualties. Eventually the trenches came close enough to the walls that Moore could build a blockhouse and bring up some artillery to fire over the fort's walls. It is not clear how much artillery Moore had with him, but it did not seem to be any significant amount. Once close enough to the bulging wall, Moore ordered his men to tunnel under it and place barrels of gunpowder to create a mine. The Tuscaroras realized what was happening and dug countertrenches in hopes of driving off Moore's men, but with little success.[41]

By the morning of March 20, Moore was ready to attack. His plan was to blow the mine, collapse some of the fort's eastern walls, and in the smoke and confusion have his men attack from several sides. Captain Maule and his North Carolina troops were moved to Mulberry Battery to prepare for the attack. The men from the other batteries were put in place. Then at ten o'clock in the morning, Col. Moore gave the order to blow the mine. Everyone waited for a huge explosion, but instead got only a fizzle. Nothing happened. Not even a pop. All that work had been for nothing as the mine did not explode, "the powder being damnified," Moore wrote. This was an unexpected failure and Moore took the rest of the day to decide whether to call off the attack, try the mine again, or make the attack anyway.[42]

The next morning, on March 21, Moore made his decision. From his position in the battery closest to the bulging wall, Moore ordered his trumpets to sound the attack and the Carolina army charged from all directions. And so began a day of hard fighting. Capt. Stone with twelve militiamen stormed out of the trench blockhouse and attacked the Indian blockhouse guarding the northern part of the bulging wall. Capt. Moore and his men attacked from Yamasee Battery. Capt. Hastings led his men from Moore's headquarters. Captains Harford and Thurston attacked the northwestern-most blockhouse. "The enemy fired very briskly through some loopholes that our men attacked them at," Moore wrote. And within three hours his militiamen had broken through the northern part of the bulging wall "with very little loss of men." However, North Carolina troops once again did not achieve the glory they hoped for. According to Moore, Capt. Maule and his North Carolina militia were supposed to foray out of Mulberry Battery and attack the southern half of the bulging eastern wall. Instead, Maule, "imagining he had some better advantage or mistaking his orders," actually attacked the more fortified southern wall and was instantly hit by heavy fire. Of his company only "20 escaped being killed or wounded, being the greatest loss sustained during the attack." Caught in a heavy cross fire, Maule and his men found themselves pinned down. Col. Moore, seeing Maule's predicament, ordered his artillery to put all the fire they could on the two southernmost blockhouses. This they did and Maule and what remained of his command managed to retreat.[43]

In all fairness, North Carolina troops were not the only ones who got confused in the fog of battle. Capt. Maurice Moore and Captain Canty were both ordered to attack the northern part of the bulging wall, but Capt. Moore went to the wrong side of the blockhouse, while Canty's Indians refused to come up quickly to support them. Eventually Capt. Moore's troops broke through the bulging wall and fought their way inside the fort. But then they ran up against the Tuscarora's secondary inner wall. Even worse, they began taking heavy fire from other Indian blockhouses. Now the only protection for Capt. Moore's troops was that secondary breastwork. To help get more men inside the bulging wall, Col. Moore ordered the northern blockhouse to be set afire. By the end of the first day of battle, the fort was on fire in some places, Moore's men were crouched in front of the inner breastwork, while most Tuscaroras had withdrawn to houses and the bunkers where they put up a hard defensive fight.[44]

The second actual day of fighting, March 22, began with Moore and his men trying to expand out from their toehold behind the fort's inner breastwork. It proved hard, house-to-house fighting as Moore's men slowly pushed the Tuscaroras back. Some Tuscaroras refused to retreat and stood their ground in the fort's blockhouses. They put up heavy fire until Moore's men could set the blockhouses aflame and so "chose rather to perish by fire with'n the bastion than to retreat in the caves made under ground." Others did retreat to the underground bunkers and "did very much mischief." By the end of the second day, Moore's men controlled most of the burning fort. The defending Tuscaroras were concentrated in two places: the two underground bunkers and in the protected trench at the back of the fort that led down to the creek.[45]

By ten o'clock on the morning of the third day, March 23, Moore's troops had managed to push the Indians out of the trench at the back of the fort. Hard fighting was still going on around the two bunkers. Even wounded Indians continued fighting. Rather than forcing their way into the bunkers, in which his men would take horrendous casualties, Moore decided to set them afire. Soon the two bunkers were in flames and eventually collapsed. Inside them died hundreds of Indians who refused to surrender and so become slaves. By the end of the day, Indian defense had crumbled and Moore claimed victory over the Tuscaroras. He counted his casualties at twenty-two white men killed and twenty-four wounded. Capt. Maule's North Carolina troops had twelve killed and fifteen wounded. Moore's Indian allies suffered thirty-five killed and fifty-eight wounded. As Moore saw it, most of his casualties came after they had forced their way inside the fort. As for losses of the Tuscaroras and their allies, Moore calculated that he had taken 392 as prisoners who would become slaves; his Indians had collected 192 scalps; at least another 200 had been burned alive inside the bunkers and blockhouses; and 166 had been killed outside the fort. In all, this totaled 558 Tuscaroras and their Indian allies killed and 392 enslaved in this battle alone. Moore figured the Tuscaroras lost 270 of "their briskett [briskest] men besides others aged and young fellows. And with what prisoners were taken their whole loss cannot be less than eight hundred." It had been a great victory for Moore, but a crushing defeat for the Tuscaroras and the Indians of eastern North Carolina.[46]

Word of Moore's victory soon spread across colonial America. Governor Pollock was ecstatic. While admitting that it had been a very hard battle, he wanted another quick follow-up blow to the Indians, but felt men, provisions, and ammunition were still in short supply. Still, Pollock worried that the Tuscaroras might regain their confidence and prevail on the Five Nations to join them in the war.[47] Up in Virginia, Governor Spotswood believed it an overwhelming victory as Moore had destroyed the Tuscarora's only important fort. But rather than another strike on the Indians, Spotswood felt that the Tuscaroras had been frightened by Moore's victory and so it would be best to engage the Indians "in a peace, since the government of Carolina is utterly unable to reduce them by prosecuting the war." And making peace would prevent the Five Nations from entering the war.[48] Word reached Charles Town, South Carolina, which rejoiced over Moore's victory. "I may now presume to say that we look upon that business as ended," Rev. Dr. Le Jau wrote.[49] Even the *Boston News-Letter* hoped that "the heart of the Tuskeraro war is broken; the Indians have got a great many slaves, but the white men none."[50]

Almost immediately, while the remains of the Neoheroka fort still smoldered, most of Col. Moore's Indian allies took their captives and plunder and headed back to South Carolina. Like Barnwell's the year before, Moore's army suddenly vanished. Only about eighty of his allied Indians remained with him, though Col. Mackay's twenty Yamasee warriors again stayed behind to help with mopping-up operations. And there were Indian holdouts. Worried that Moore's army was seriously undermanned, Pollock sent a letter to Governor Craven of South Carolina asking for reinforcements. Moore agreed with Pollock's worries and dispatched his brother, Capt. Maurice Moore, back to South Carolina to bring up any Indian allies who would make the trip. They were to return as quickly as they could. In the meantime, the remnants of Moore's army returned to Albemarle County to be closer to food supplies and begin cleaning out the last enemy holdouts.[51]

Though the battle at the Neoheroka fort was a terrible defeat for the Indians, the Machapungas, Cores, and Catechna town Tuscaroras who had not been at Neoheroka still wanted to fight. A good number of Tuscaroras had garrisoned themselves at a fort southwest of Neoheroka, then abandoned it after Moore's victory. Even at this late date, some upper Tuscarora warriors, ignoring Tom Blount's instructions, joined the survivors and threatened attacks. Capt. Maurice Moore, back in Charles Town, told friends that there were still "above 500 stout men of that desperate nation that are resolved to fight to the last man and that they are well fortified."[52]

Not long after Neoheroka, a band of about fifty Machapungas, Cores, and Catechna Tuscaroras attacked settlements along the Alligator River just south of Albemarle Sound and killed about twenty settlers. Soon other areas were hit, with the Machapungas raiding near Lake Mattamuskeet, while the Cores hit near Mackay's garrison on the Neuse River. It now became a low-level guerrilla war and Pollock was receiving reports of attacks from across eastern North Carolina. The Machapungas have "killed or carried away about twenty persons at Roanoke Island and at Croatan, and two Tuscaroras have killed a man upon this shore [Chowan River], about twelve miles distant from where I live," the governor reported.[53] Col. Moore dispatched all hundred of his remaining Indians to try to the clear the Machapungas out of the swamps around Lake Mattamuskeet. Pollock was not hopeful. Machapunga country was a large area full of all "manner lakes, quagmires, and cane swamps, and is, I believe, one of the greatest deserts in the world, where it is almost impossible for white men to follow them, they have got likewise boats and canoes, being expert watermen, where they can transport themselves where they please." Despite a good effort, Moore's Indians could not defeat the Machapungas on their own ground.[54] At the same time, some Tuscaroras who had taken refuge in Virginia, for the next year or so periodically raided down into North Carolina. Virginia Rangers tried to halt this but with little success.[55]

Probably no one was more surprised at Moore's victory than Tom Blount. While he had captured King Hancock and some of his principal men, Blount and his warriors had not been active in fighting the Contentnea Creek Tuscaroras and their allies. As Moore's depleted but victorious army returned to the Albemarle, Blount could not straddle the fence any longer. Governor Spotswood advised Pollock to make a treaty with Blount. "Talk high to Blunt," Spotswood suggested, and "make him king of all those Indians under the protection of North Carolina. This proposal will stir his ambition; and no doubt oblige him to be faithful to the English for the future." Then Pollock could prevail upon Blount to turn over all those Tuscaroras implicated in attacks on the settlers. Blount would also be a useful source of information on what was going on among the Indians. Pollock could use that knowledge to stave off any future attacks. Once North Carolina recognized Blount as king of the tributary Indians, Spotswood said, Virginia would recognize him as well.[56]

Pollock considered this good advice and ordered Tom Blount to council with him on April 25, 1713. There Pollock and Blount hammered out another treaty. Tom Blount would be named "King and Commander in

Chief [of] all the Indians on the south side of the Pamptico [Pamlico] River under the protection of this government." In return, there would be peace between North Carolina and Blount and all the Indians who acknowledged him as king. Blount was also required to hand over twenty of the Indians most involved in carrying out the recent war, including those who tortured to death John Lawson. In fact, Blount was ordered to hand over any Indian he could lay hands on who had been involved in killing settlers. Blount and his Tuscaroras were also to return all property they possessed that had belonged to the settlers, including "captives, horses, arms, goods, and cattle." Now that Blount was an ally of North Carolina, he and his warriors must "pursue, kill, and take as enemies, the Catchneys, Mattamuskeets, and all other Indians, enemies to the English." Finally, Blount was to provide two hostages from each of his upper Tuscarora towns until he had accomplished all this.[57]

But Pollock could now feel a little empathy with the Tuscarora king as he soon learned just how much pressure Blount had been under to make war on North Carolina and just how close the Senecas had come to entering the war. Blount told Pollock that a Seneca named Canaguanee and about a hundred warriors from New York had visited Blount at his town not long ago. Canaguanee tried to persuade Blount to abandon his friendship with Pollock, explaining that the English "only amused him with fair words to keep him from doing them mischief, but when they had destroyed the rest of his nation, he might be sure to be destroyed likewise." If Blount would give up his alliance with North Carolina, then Canaguanee would move Blount and his people out of the range of the English. Blount refused and ordered Canaguanee to mind his own business and leave his village.[58]

Spotswood felt Pollock's treaty with Blount was a bit harsh. Asking for twenty chiefs involved in the attacks was too much, as was Pollock's demand that Blount turn over every person involved in the attacks. It could easily make the Tuscaroras feel the peace was too costly and so start the war again. Spotswood suggested that Pollock demand only three or four of those involved, men specifically named, and be done with it. After all, Moore had already inflicted a major defeat on the Tuscaroras by killing or enslaving so many of them. Gentleness might get more Indians behind the treaty and so result in a better peace. Then he took Pollock to task for not having consulted him before making the treaty, which did not mention Virginia at all. Nor did it insist that Blount make peace with Virginia. He seemed to have forgotten that Blount had made peace with Virginia back in the fall of 1711.[59]

Now, Blount lived up to his word and throughout the summer and fall of 1713, he and his warriors went to work against North Carolina's enemies. Rev. Giles Rainsford crowed that King Blount "has obliged himself to clear the west shore of the Chowan River, [in] which he seems to be indefatigable." Since then, Rainsford said, the enemy had made only a few scattered attacks.[60] Pollock himself admitted that Blount and his upper Tuscaroras had "suffered much," but remained friendly to the English and had been cutting off "what stragglers may be left of the Cores or Cotechnees, and be a great help to us in destroying the Mattamuskeets that are left." The Pamlico Indians, who had lived on an island in the Pamlico River, were pretty much destroyed or enslaved by Blount's Tuscaroras.[61] Once, though Blount himself was lame and had been recently sick, his warriors brought in about thirty scalps. Another time, Blount personally delivered eight Indian captives to Pollock. The governor asked for and received permission from the Council to buy the captives for £10 each, sell them as slaves in the West Indies at a much higher price, and then return the profits to the North Carolina treasury.[62]

In fact, things looked so good that Pollock felt they did not need the reinforcements coming from South Carolina. He dispatched a quick message to Capt. Maurice Moore, who was already en route to North Carolina with a party of sixty militiamen and sixty allied Indians. On receiving Pollock's message, Moore released his Indians, sent the militia home, then joined his brother in Chowan Precinct. For once Governor Craven of South Carolina took offense at Pollock's actions. Pollock smoothed things over, explaining that Col. Moore had the war in hand and North Carolina just did not have the supplies to feed the reinforcements. Besides, he explained, with just the Machapungas as the main enemy right now, there was not going to be much chance of taking more Indian slaves.[63]

Despite Pollock's assertion, slaves were still being taken. During May 1713, some of Moore's Ashley River Indians captured King Blount's wife, two of his children, and his sister's son. When Pollock heard this, he "redeemed" all four of them and returned them to Blount in care of Capt. Maurice Moore and the shipmaster Charles Glover. Moore and Glover were assigned to help guard against any further Indian attacks on Blount's people, but also to keep an eye on Blount and his loyalty. Glover wound up spending four months at Blount's town and received £25 for his service.[64] In January 1714, Blount again complained that the Meherrin Indians, supposed tributaries of North Carolina and allies of Virginia, had taken two Tuscarora children, "the parents of which are good friends of the English." By now, Pollock considered Blount a firm friend and demanded the

Meherrins return the children or "answer the contrary at their peril." If they did not give up the children, Pollock warned, then he would "take such further measures as he shall think fit to compel them thereto." Along with this, Pollock sent 150 bushels of corn to Blount's Tuscaroras. The Meherrin, not wanting trouble, returned the children.[65]

By September 1713, though the Cores and Machapungas not been totally defeated, things were well enough in hand for Col. Moore and his army to return to South Carolina. Pollock directed Capt. Edward Bellenger of the packet boat *Yamasee Galley* to take aboard Col. Moore and whatever he needed, then carry him to Charles Town. Once he had delivered Moore, Bellenger could consider his duty done and so discharged from North Carolina service. Pollock also took this opportunity to thank Col. Moore, Governor Craven, and all South Carolina for their assistance. He considered Moore a guardian angel. "I am incapable of expressing our obligations to Col. Moore, who ever since his first arrival hath behaved himself as a valiant, wise and prudent commander ought to do." Moore's great deeds included "delivering of innocent captives, of widows and fatherless, of aged and impotent from their cruel and barbarous enemies, and the revenging innocent Christian blood shed by them." As for Craven and the South Carolina government, the people of North Carolina could never be thankful enough to those "who have been instrumental in our deliverance; yet I doubt not Heaven will pour down its chiefest blessings upon you for such virtuous, noble deeds, which shall be earnestly wished for." Pollock assured Craven that his government would try to reimburse South Carolina for the arms and ammunition it expended during Moore's expedition and for use of the *Yamasee Galley* packet boat. But to keep things peaceful, he also asked Craven to prevent any more of his South Carolina Indians from coming north to attack Tom Blount and his upper Tuscaroras.[66]

Col. James Moore returned a hero to South Carolina. In December 1713, the South Carolina Assembly gave him its official thanks. They ordered that his journal be read before the House along with the letter of thanks from North Carolina's Governor Pollock. He was to be awarded £100 in South Carolina current money from the Public Treasury. Col. Robert Daniel and Maj. George Evans were ordered to call on Col. Moore and give him the thanks of the South Carolina House for "his great services in the late expedition against the Indian enemies of North Carolina."[67] The Assembly acknowledged that he had "fully answered their expectation and acquitted yourself of the trust reposed in you (both as a soldier and General) with the utmost discretion & bravery." Daniel and

Evans delivered the House's declaration and reported back that Moore was "highly satisfied with the honor & favor done him by this House, to whom he returned Thanks for the same."[68]

Up in Virginia, Governor Spotswood began wrapping up his colony's role in the war by signing a peace treaty with those Tuscaroras who had taken refuge in his colony. Naccoueaighwha, Nyasauckhee, and Naroniackkos, representing the towns of Rarocaithee (?), Kintha (Kenta), Junonitz (Innennits), and Tahoghkee (Toisnot), met with Spotswood in late February 1714. On the twenty-second they signed a treaty that made them tributary Indians of Virginia. Blount's Tuscaroras remained tributaries to North Carolina. These new Virginia allies had seven months to remove all their people from North Carolina and settle on a six-square-mile reservation Spotswood laid out for them between the James and Rappahannock Rivers. As tribute, they were to give Spotswood and future Virginia governors three arrowheads every year in Williamsburg on St. George's Day, April 23. This was to be a firm treaty of peace and the Tuscaroras promised to hand over any Indians who committed any crimes so they could be punished by Virginia authorities. Soldiers would be stationed nearby to ensure Tuscarora peace and protect them from marauding Indians. They were allowed to sell produce at nearby markets. Also, dear to Spotswood's heart and something he always pressed for, was that these Tuscaroras would sent their children to school in Williamsburg where they would be instructed by an English teacher.[69] While the peace lasted, Spotswood did not get the new allies and tributaries he wanted. In July 1714, as violence declined, Naccoueaighwha, Nyasauckhee, and Naroniackkos, and their Tuscarora towns left Virginia and moved back to the Roanoke River in North Carolina. They were, as Spotswood said disgustedly, "induced thereto (as they say) by the people of Carolina, [and] have departed from the agreement with this government, and gone to settle once more in that Province."[70]

In North Carolina, 1714 was overall a peaceful one when compared to the previous three years. Most Carolinians thought the war was over, having ended with Moore's victory at Neoheroka. But every now and again Machapunga or Core warriors filtered out of the swamp and hit an isolated farm or plantation. Rev. John Urmston heard that "a handful of Indians who would not come into the treaty with the rest of them have spilt more innocent blood. . . . They rove from place to place, cut off 2 or 3 families today & within 2 or 3 days do the like a hundred miles off from the former. They are like deer—there is no finding them. We have men out after them to sue for peace."[71] Always the pessimist, Urmston believed it was just a matter of time before the Senecas joined with these holdouts and that will "complete the ruin of this wretched country."[72] Even down in South Carolina, Rev. Dr. Le Jau heard that some of the Indians had "escaped in the woods and marshes" and killed more than twenty people.[73] The attacks kept North Carolina on a war footing with garrisons continually manned, while expeditions by Blount's Tuscaroras waded into the swamps, but without much success. All the while, corn and food needed to be supplied to these garrisons and Pollock continued to prohibit corn from being sold out of the colony. Corn exports would not legally begin again until 1717.[74]

While the Machapungas might be safe in the swamps around Lake Mattamuskeet and the Cores in the marshes near the mouth of the Neuse River, the garrisons, rangers, and Blount's warriors were slowly curtailing their movements. They would always be hunted and on the run. In May 1714, the Hatteras Indians of the Outer Banks, whom the Machapungas may have considered allies, deserted them. The Hatteras showed up at Col. Thomas Boyd's house, claiming they had been taken captive by the Machapungas and had only just managed to escape. The Council ordered Boyd to feed the Hatteras until they could return home to the Outer Banks.[75]

But North Carolina was growing weary of chasing through the swamps for a few Machapunga and Core ghosts. Pollock, who had always advocated the destruction of enemy Indians, now began thinking it might be better to make a peace treaty rather than continuing to spend money trying to exterminate them. North Carolina's new governor, Charles Eden, supported the idea of a peace. Appointed by the Lords Proprietors and approved by Queen Anne, one of her last before she died in August, Eden arrived in North Carolina in May 1714. He was made a landgrave, received £300 a year salary, and a thousand acres of land, from which the Proprietors would receive a ten-shilling quitrent. Pollock now returned to his position as president of the Governor's Council, receiving £131 9s. 11d. as a salary.[76] By August 1714, North Carolina was reaching out to the Machapungas and Cores to make peace. The Council dispatched Capt. William Vaughan and nine white men to Sandy Banks to meet with the Cores, now led by Nonrontisgnotkau but called John Pagett. Vaughan took "Fisher the Indian," a Poteskeet Indian from north of the Albemarle, as a translator.[77] Though a few raids continued, by mid-December 1714, peace in North Carolina seemed close at hand as the rough outlines of a treaty with Pagett's Cores and Squire Hook's Machapungas was hammered out.

On February 11, 1715, the North Carolina government and the Cores and Machapungas, the last Indians fighting in the Tuscarora War, made peace. All would be forgotten and there was to be no more raiding. A recognized reservation would be created for the Cores and Machapungas, who would now live together on it south of Lake Mattamuskeet in present-day Hyde County. The governor appointed a commissioner to live among them to ensure their good behavior.[78] Pollock must have relented somewhat on executing all Indians involved in the war as Squire Hooks of the Machapungas and John Pagett of the Cores, both men Pollock had demanded be turned over to him for execution, were still alive and now served as headmen on the reservation. Apparently, bygones actually would be bygones. And so what began with the execution of a colonial official and the devastating Indian attacks of September 22, 1711, by the winter of 1715, as the surviving Machapungas and Cores withdrew onto their swampy reservation, the Tuscarora War came to a rather anticlimactic end. Moore's great victory at Neoheroka was the bang; the February 1715 treaty the whimper.

CHAPTER EIGHT

Aftermath

For North Carolina, it had been a tough, costly victory. But a victory nonetheless. As Thomas Pollock saw it, the colony had survived in the face of extreme dangers. But now it was a new day and he saw a new North Carolina coming. "The fire of difference and division amongst the people being in a manner extinguished, most of our Indian enemies killed, taken, submitted or fled, so that there is but about forty or fifty enemies left that we can hear of. The Quakers, though very refractory and ungovernable in Mr. Glover's and Mr. Hyde's administration, yet since I have concerned, must needs acknowledge they have been as ready (especially in supplying provisions for the forces) as any others in the government."[1] While Pollock may have been overly optimistic about the unity among North Carolinians, he was correct in that the North Carolina that emerged from the Tuscarora War in February 1715 would be far different from the one that went into it back in September 1711. And so would the lives of the men who played such important roles in it.

❖ Down in South Carolina, both Col. John "Tuscarora Jack" Barnwell and Col. James Moore Jr. returned as heroes. Capt. Maurice Moore, the brother of Col. Moore, liked the opportunities he saw in North Carolina and so remained there, planning to make it his home. In fact, while he and his brother were in North Carolina, both invested in real estate, with Capt. Moore purchasing three town lots in the newly built town of Beaufort on Core Sound, one waterfront lot and two back lots. Col. Moore purchased four waterfront lots. They paid £1 current money per lot.[2] In a very short period of time, Maurice Moore was at home in North Carolina and diving headlong into North Carolina politics. But once again, war would interrupt the three men's careers.

On Good Friday, April 15, 1715, a confederacy of Indians made a surprise attack on South Carolina. These included Yamasees, Guales, Apalachees, Savannahs, Cheraws, Catawbas, Waterees and most of the Siouan nations, Waccamaws, Cape Fears, and to the west the Lower Creeks, Yuchis, and Cherokees. All had been allies of South Carolina and many of their warriors had fought alongside Barnwell and Moore in North Carolina. Scores of South Carolina traders and officials then visiting Indian towns were killed instantly. Down near St. Helena and Port Royal where Barnwell lived, his old friends, the Yamasees, struck early that morning. A wounded soldier managed to swim to Barnwell's Doctors Plantation and raise the alarm. Fortunately for Barnwell and other settlers nearby, a ship carrying contraband had been seized and was in port. Now four hundred settlers crowded onto the boat and so escaped the quickly advancing Yamasee army. The Port Royal settlement was destroyed. Other plantations across South Carolina were also hit, more settlers killed. And so began what was called the Yamasee War.[3]

Like the Tuscarora War, the Yamasee War was partially a result of the many abuses suffered by these Indians as the hands of South Carolina traders and settlers. The Indians had finally had enough and now struck back. But lessons the warriors had learned in the Tuscarora War now bore fruit. One thing they all had seen was that colonial forces were not going to accept any peace or abide by any treaty until their Indian enemies were broken and enslaved. There could never be a peace among equals as Carolinians were too invested in the Indian slave trade. But now, after the Tuscarora War, the supply of enemy Indians available for enslavement had dwindled dramatically. Since the turn of the eighteenth century, South Carolina slave traders and their Indian allies had destroyed and enslaved many of Spanish Florida's mission Indians, pushed back the French-allied Indians of the American Southeast, and now the Tuscaroras, Cores, Bear River Indians, and others had been taken. Nevertheless, South Carolina's thirst for Indian slaves remained unquenchable. The Yamasees and others realized it was only a matter of time before South Carolina would turn on them. Better to stand together as Indians, hit the colony now before it became any stronger, kill the traders, destroy the plantations, burn Charles Town, and put an end to the slave buyers. And by the end of that bad Good Friday, it looked as if their plan was working. South Carolina was on its heels and the Indians closing in on Charles Town.[4]

Poor coordination by the Indians gave South Carolina a chance to get on its feet. The militia was called up and now Lt. Gen. James Moore raised three regiments and built a chain of fortifications around Charles Town.

He dispatched some militiamen against the Yamasees south of Charles Town, who were at that time making most of the attacks. In a sharp skirmish, the Yamasees lost some of their leaders. By June, the Yamasee attacks had stopped. Charles Town's southern front seemed quiet when the Cheraws, Waterees, Santees, Catawbas, and other Siouan peoples along the Santee River to the north now made their own attacks. Again settlers were killed, farms and plantations burned; refugees poured into Charles Town. South Carolina needed help and so sent out calls for assistance to other colonies.[5]

In North Carolina, Governor Eden and Council President Pollock saw this as an opportunity to return a favor to South Carolina. Eden immediately called up the colonial militia. He ordered two regiments be created, one of about thirty men to be commanded by a former South Carolinian, Col. Theophilus Hastings, who had also remained in North Carolina. This was to be outfitted and sent by ship to Charles Town. The second regiment was to be commanded by now Col. Maurice Moore, who was to raise a regiment of fifty men, but also recruit from North Carolina's Indian allies. They were to march overland to South Carolina. Eventually Moore would have a force about fifty militiamen and seventy Tuscarora and Core warriors who saw this as an opportunity to strike back at the Indians who had done them so much damage. In the meantime, militiamen would patrol between the Pamlico and Neuse Rivers on the lookout for any hostile Indians coming North Carolina's way. This time Virginia also helped and sent about two hundred men to Charles Town.[6]

The two North Carolina companies left for Charles Town that summer. Rather than the roundabout western route he and his brother had used to enter North Carolina, Maurice Moore's company marched south along the coast in a more direct line toward Charles Town. At the Cape Fear River, Moore's scouts discovered the Cape Fear Indians and the Waccamaws planning an ambush. Moore struck first, catching them by surprise. His troops took eighty captives, which they later sold as slaves in Charles Town, and seized a large cache of weapons that the Cape Fears said had come from the Cheraw Indians further west. By the time Moore's and Hastings's companies arrived in Charles Town, South Carolina's situation had changed. Some attacks on the Cheraws and Santees had quieted that front while Yamasee fighting in the south briefly flared up again. But South Carolina officials realized that the linchpin to the Indian alliance and the key to the war were the Cherokees. A combined attack by Cherokees and Lower Creeks could devastate the colony, perhaps fatally. The Cherokees had to be persuaded to change sides or at least remain neutral.

For this risky diplomatic mission, South Carolina chose Col. Maurice Moore.[7]

In early January 1716, Moore led an expedition of five hundred men to Cherokee territory out west in the Appalachian Mountains. Both North Carolina companies and Col. Hastings were part of the army. Their job was not to attack the Cherokees but to impress them and convince them to abandon the Indian alliance. Moore must have been very skillful in his diplomacy as he convinced the Cherokees to do just that. Although the reasons are not entirely clear, the Cherokees killed all the Creek ambassadors then in their towns trying to convince them to make war on South Carolina. With the Cherokees changing sides, the Yamasee War essentially came to an end. The historian Lawrence Lee called Maurice Moore's diplomatic victory "the single most important accomplishment of the Yamasee War." Now the Creeks moved further west. The Yamasees withdrew into Spanish Florida. The Catawbas and the smaller Siouan nations made peace. The last holdouts were the Cheraws, and many of them moved into North Carolina and occupied some of the abandoned Tuscarora forts along Contentnea Creek.[8]

By 1717, South Carolina was at peace. But the war had taught it a hard lesson. Abuses by traders and the unregulated Indian slave trade had been some of the reasons for both the Tuscarora and Yamasee Wars. Now South Carolina actually began regulating its traders. But times were changing. While Indian slaves could be found on North Carolina and South Carolina farms and plantations for years to come, the Indian slave trade was on its last legs. There were fewer Indians available for enslavement. And as both colonies discovered, taking Indian allies as slaves was a recipe for war. Besides, as the competition for North American empire heated up between England and France, the colonies needed Indian allies far more than they needed Indian slaves. The increasing influx of African and African American slaves soon took their place as the colonial laborers of choice.[9]

For Barnwell, the Yamasee War was personally devastating. His plantation had been plundered and burned and ten of his own slaves were taken by Indians and sold to the Spanish in St. Augustine. But just as bad was the breaking of that bond of trust and affection between him and the Yamasees. He loved them and believed they loved him back. They had stuck by him after the battle at Torhunta in February 1712, when all the other Indians had deserted. They fought beside him throughout his Tuscarora campaign; they were the only Indians he knew he could rely on. But somewhere along the way, something had gone wrong in the relationship and they had burned his plantation. Now the Yamasees were gone, resettled further south in Florida. For years Barnwell tried to arrange a peace between them and South Carolina and have them return to the colony where they would take their old place on the frontier to serve as buffers against enemy Indians. He was even appointed as one of the five Indian commissioners whose job it was to oversee the Indian trade and prevent abuses by white traders. But the Yamasees would never return to Barnwell and South Carolina.[10]

Nevertheless, Barnwell was an important man in South Carolina and he gained a reputation later in life as a designer of forts and a maker of maps. He served as the commissioner and inspector of the South Carolina militia in 1712. He represented St. Helena in the South Carolina Assembly from 1717 to 1720. Barnwell could see firsthand that the Yamasee War had exacerbated tensions between South Carolina and the Lords Proprietors. In 1719, South Carolina essentially revolted against the Proprietors and declared itself a royal colony. The next year, 1720, Barnwell was sent to England to negotiate the transfer of South Carolina from the Proprietors to the Crown. He pleaded with London to provide for better colonial defense, especially on the frontiers. He talked up his "township system," which would create communities of European immigrants who would serve as the buffers once provided by the Indians. He appeared before the Board of Trade and made a favorable impression with his plan for a continent-wide defense against the French. He also supported the creation of a colony below South Carolina, which would eventually materialize as the colony of Georgia.[11]

On his return from London, Barnwell went back into public service. He was immediately appointed to the South Carolina Governor's Council, but he resigned to serve in the South Carolina Assembly. From 1721 to 1724, he again represented Port Royal in South Carolina's first Royal Assembly. In 1721 alone he served as justice of the peace of Granville County, commissioner of the High Roads for St. Helena, and commander of the Granville County militia. Also in that year, South Carolina commissioned him to oversee the building of Fort King George on the Altamaha River near present-day Darien, Georgia. Sometime between May 4 and June 9, 1724, Barnwell died, either at his plantation near Port Royal or in the town of Beaufort. He left thousands of acres of land to his children and desired they all receive a good education. Legend says he was buried beneath the apse in Beaufort, South Carolina's St. Helena Anglican Church. But just outside the east end of the church is an iron-fenced enclosure with a metal plaque that reads: "Col. John Barnwell—Tuscarora—1724." His is considered the oldest grave in the churchyard.[12]

Honored by a grateful South Carolina, Col. Maurice Moore returned to North Carolina. By that time, settlement was beginning along the lower Cape Fear River. Now Maurice and his brothers Roger and Nathaniel purchased land along that river and built their plantations. Soon, North Carolina friends, such as Edward Moseley and Eleazar Allen, joined them and became connected by marriage. From this emerged a strong clan along the Lower Cape Fear River of rice planters, traders, merchants, and land speculators led by the Moores and called "The Family." The Moore family would eventually own more than forty-eight thousand acres of land in the area. The Family dominated the region politically and economically for years and served as a political counterweight to the Albemarle. In 1726, Maurice Moore was credited with the founding of Brunswick Town on the west side of the Cape Fear. He later served on the North Carolina council and died a well-respected North Carolinian in 1743.[13]

In a strange turn of events, the sixty or seventy Tuscarora warriors Col. Maurice Moore had led to fight in the Yamasee War never returned to North Carolina. As the Yamasees withdrew into Florida, South Carolina had no Indian allies on that southwestern frontier to protect it from Spain and its Indian friends. Colonial officials asked these Tuscaroras to remain in South Carolina and patrol the lower Savannah River. This put them near Barnwell and Port Royal. These Tuscaroras served well and were well respected by the South Carolina government. For every Tuscarora killed in the line of duty, South Carolina pledged to return at the colony's expense a Tuscarora slave taken in either Barnwell's or Moore's expedition. And for every enemy Indian they captured, they could exchange him or her for an enslaved Tuscarora. They stayed in South Carolina so long that they were eventually granted lands that once belonged to the Yamasees. It seemed somehow fitting that Barnwell would more or less take them under his wing and befriend them.

The last we hear of these South Carolina Tuscaroras is in March 1718, when they complained that the settler Daniel Callihaun had stolen one of their canoes and threatened their chief, King Forster. According to King Forster, Callihaun told him that since the Tuscaroras were no longer needed in South Carolina, the settlers should be allowed to "knock some of them in the head and enslave the rest." Forster wanted Callihaun reprimanded and demanded twenty shillings for the canoe. South Carolina supported the Tuscaroras, ordered Barnwell to give them a packet of trade goods, and demanded Callihaun appear in court. King Forster was so happy with the verdict that he offered to go back to North Carolina and bring more of his Tuscarora people to South Carolina if the government would give him a pass. South Carolina heartily agreed, wrote out the pass, but no more word ever showed up in the records about these transplanted Tuscaroras.[14]

Just as he had during the Tuscarora War, Lt. Gen. James Moore Jr. proved himself an able commander in chief during the Yamasee War. After the war, though hailed as the savior of South Carolina, Gen. Moore declined to be elected to the South Carolina Assembly and refused to take a position as one of the commissioners of the Indian trade. His refusals did not appear to be reluctance for public office, but because he now threw all his efforts into taking South Carolina out of the hands of the Lords Proprietors. He became one of the leading figures in South Carolina's 1719 "revolution" that made it into a royal colony. When the sitting governor, Robert Johnson, refused the request of the South Carolina Assembly to remain as a caretaker governor, the Assembly turned to Gen. Moore. Moore served as governor for two years, until 1721, and seemed to be a thoughtful official who used restraint during a heated political climate. His anti-Proprietor allies encouraged him to use the South Carolina militia against those who supported the Proprietors, but Moore refused. After King George I appointed Francis Nicholson as the first royal governor of South Carolina, Moore allowed himself to be elected to South Carolina's first Royal Assembly and was chosen to be Speaker of the House. During this time, he also served as justice of the peace for Berkeley County and in 1724 was named as the sole commissioner of the Indian trade. But he would not serve long as James Moore Jr. died on March 23, 1724, just months before Barnwell. The conqueror of Neoheroka left land, money, and forty-three slaves to his six children. With Moore and Barnwell dying within months of each other, one might say it was the passing of a generation.[15]

❖ Up in North Carolina, the Tuscarora War had been utterly devastating. In 1715, the North Carolina Assembly declared the "22nd of September being the anniversary of the late barbarous massacre committed by the Indians on the inhabitants of Bath County in the year 1711, are & shall be hereby appointed to be kept and solemnized, annually as Days of Humiliation with fasting & prayer." The day continued to be officially observed until 1741.[16]

Property destruction in Bath County and the impressment of Albemarle County corn and supplies impoverished many. Burned farms, houses, outbuildings, boats, and equipment; dead horses and cattle; plundered goods and destroyed crops; the loss of slaves and indentured servants cost thousands upon thousands of pounds sterling. Agriculture in the colony was set back several years. It plunged the colony into heavy debt. Pollock calculated that the war had cost North Carolina £16,000 and there were only about two thousand taxable people left in the entire colony. He tried concocting ways for the colony to pay it down. He figured that if he could get the settlers to pay a thirty-shilling poll tax, then he could raise £9,000 in three years. Since North Carolina had one million acres of land, and if it could be sold at forty shillings per thousand acres, then in three years that would be £6,000. The colony might also raise an additional £1,000 by taxing strong liquor imported into the colony from the West Indies. "And it is very evident that the importing of so much strong liquor into the country greatly impovereth the people." Still, he was hopeful that the colony would be able to fund its war debt in a short time and pay its bills. In reality, the debt was much larger and would take much longer to pay off.[17]

The human cost of the war was equally great. While no official accounting has ever been made, and accurate numbers are impossible to come by, it would be safe to say that about two hundred North Carolina settlers, slaves, and militiamen were killed, possibly more. South Carolina may have had fewer than thirty militiamen and about a hundred Indian allies killed, though this number could be too low. As for the Tuscaroras, Cores, Machapungas, Pamlicos, Neuse, Weetocks, and Bear River Indians, there is no way to say. It would not be far fetched to say that somewhere between two thousand and three thousand were killed, enslaved, or died during the war, and that number could easily be higher.[18]

The death of one or both parents, whether settler or Indian, could wreck a family. For years, the North Carolina courts were filled with orphans needing guardians or being apprenticed to other settlers. Many of these went on to very successful lives. George Conis, later Koonce, had been placed under the guardianship of Capt. Jacob Miller of New Bern. Conis eventually married a member of the Miller household and settled his own plantation on the east side of Chinquapin Creek north of the Trent River. He lived to the age of seventy-three, dying on January 28, 1778, the father of seven sons, all who settled their own plantations. Down on the White Oak River, the Quaker William Bartram, who had moved to North Carolina from Pennsylvania, was killed in the war. His wife, Elizabeth, and his two children were taken captive. Later released, they returned to Philadelphia. But one of the children, William, returned to North Carolina and settled in the White Lake area of Bladen County. But not all William's children had gone with them to North Carolina. The oldest son, John Bartram, had remained in Philadelphia with his grand-mother and so avoided being killed or captured. In Philadelphia, John Bartram educated himself and eventually became one of the most accom-plished scientists in colonial America, becoming known as the father of American botany. In one of those strange coincidences of history, he died on September 22, 1777, sixty-six years after the attacks that claimed his father's life. John Bartram's son, William, would go on to become the most renowned naturalist in colonial North America.[19]

Dead settlers and burned records frustrated the courts for years. Thomas Roper epitomized the problems. Roper had lent John Toby £7 13d., but Toby had been killed in the war, still owing the money. At the same time, Roper's indentured servant, Anthony Morrall, had been impressed into militia service and had also been killed. Roper sued the colony for Toby's debt and Morrall's militia wages.[20] Then there was the issue of plundered property. What was to be done when a person had a horse taken by Indians during the war, then a second settler acquired this horse somewhere along the way? And then if the original settler found his horse, who did it belong to? These claims wound up in court.[21]

As in any war, returning soldiers had issues of their own. John Whitby had been impressed into militia service and while on duty creditors had confiscated two of his horses for a £10 debt. Back home, Whitby success-fully sued for the return of his horses, saying they were worth far more than £10.[22] John Debt had been impressed into the North Carolina militia, as had one of his handsaws, worth about five shillings. Debt had to sue to get his saw returned to him.[23] Similarly, other impressed goods now had to be returned to their owners. Thomas Peterson had twenty guns taken for war service. The Council ordered the provost marshal to find them and hand them over to Peterson. No word on whether he finally got them.[24] When David Wharton was called up for militia service, he offered Edmund Ennett a cow and a calf if Ennett would go in his place. Ennett agreed, fought in the war, and returned home to find Wharton had died before he could pay. Now in early 1714 Ennett sued Thomas and Mary Harris, the executors of Wharton's estate, for the livestock. He won his case and the court ordered the Harrises to pay Ennett "one good cow and calfe."[25]

For many settlers, it became difficult to prove their land claims or show evidence they had paid quitrents or taxes. In April 1714, the settlers of Bath County, "by reason of ye continual outrages & hostilities commit-ted by the Indians . . . cannot so readily comply with the paymt of the purchase money for the land."[26] These people often wound up in court.

North Carolina officials were not unsympathetic to their problems and usually tried to work out something with them, even offering to reorder surveys.[27] On the other hand, lands that had been abandoned or where the owners were deceased provided opportunities for others. Much of this was cleared land, but as they had not been improved in the years since the war, settlers could make a claim for them on the basis of a "lapsed patent." A particularly choice piece of land might garner several lapsed patent claims and so the courts would have to sort it out.[28] Lost records meant fraud was not uncommon and Governor Eden and the Council tried to prevent it, even ordering lands to be forfeited when they caught it.[29] The Lords Proprietors became concerned with so many settlers being turned out of their homes for inability to pay quitrents or taxes. They instructed Governor Eden to try to prevent people from abusing the system, but for people actually affected by the war, Eden should pay their back taxes out of the Public Treasury. They would have three years to repay the loan. The Proprietors' intention, they reiterated, was that the original purchasers of the land should not be defrauded.[30]

Down along the Neuse, Trent, and White Oak Rivers, the remnants of De Graffenried's Palatine and Swiss settlers certainly thought they had been defrauded. Their promise of 250 acres of land, orchards, livestock, and a perfect life under the benevolent guidance of Landgrave de Graffenried had never panned out. The war ruined any chance of success. Though De Graffenried begged for help, neither the Lords Proprietors nor Georg Ritter and Company lifted a finger to provide for them. De Graffenried's colony continued to disintegrate. Some survivors relocated to Virginia or South Carolina. Those who remained in North Carolina found themselves in bad shape, the ownership of lands they thought as their own being questioned. The Indian attacks meant that De Graffenried had been unable to pay his debts to Pollock. Once the repayment deadline passed, Council President Pollock stepped in and as the now rightful owner, took control of the land belonging to the settlement, including much of the town of New Bern. As late as the 1740s, the remaining Palatines were petitioning the Council for relief. Some, such as Jacob Sheets, would take their case to court to fight Pollock's heirs over ownership of their land. They would lose and the land remained in the Pollock family.[31]

For Christopher de Graffenried, the high point of his life had to have been that morning in mid-September 1711 when he, John Lawson, two black slaves, and a couple of Indian guides decided to travel up the Neuse River in search of wild grapes and land for an expanding colony. Things had looked so bright back then. But within days it had all collapsed. He had been captured, Lawson executed, his settlers killed, and much of the colony destroyed. His neighbor, William Brice, turned many of his own people against him, and then when he could not pay his debts, he lost his colony's lands to Thomas Pollock. Unable to help his people, he abandoned them and the colony in the summer of 1713 and moved to Williamsburg, Virginia. He stayed there for about year and in 1714 returned to Switzerland.

The partners in Georg Ritter and Company wanted nothing to do with the disgraced De Graffenried. Not much is known about how he and his family made a living over the next fifteen years. Probably he again turned to his father for help, though he was elected as a representative from the town of Yverdon. In 1730, after the death of his brother, De Graffenried inherited the estate at Worb. It seems his last years were comfortable ones. He died in November 1743 and was buried beneath the choir in the family chapel in Worb. His son, also named Christopher, must have listened to his father tell stories of his North Carolina adventure. When he was old enough, young Christopher migrated to Charles Town, South Carolina. There he met and married Barbara Tempest Needham, originally from Hertfordshire, England. Later, they moved to Williamsburg, Virginia. America once again claimed a De Graffenried.[32]

When De Graffenried deserted his colony in 1713, his neighbor, William Brice, thought it good riddance. The two men never liked each other as both vied for the leadership of the people living along the lower Neuse. The aristocratic De Graffenried, as landgrave and personally appointed by the Lords Proprietors, felt that people should naturally turn to him. But he was no match for the rough-and-tumble Brice and vicious colonial politics. Brice's defeat at the hands of the Tuscaroras and the apparently less than sterling performance by him and his North Carolina troops did not seem to prevent him from remaining a community leader. He had also successfully attacked the Bear River Indians and enslaved many, so he was not necessarily seen as incompetent by his neighbors. By 1713, he had been appointed as a justice of the peace for Craven Precinct of Bath County. He would later become precinct treasurer, an Anglican vestryman, and was appointed as surveyor of the roads in his area, ensuring they were cleared of brush. He was often called on to serve as an attorney and frequently served as a court assistant and an appraiser of orphans' property. In an interesting turn, Col. Louis Michel, De Graffenried's old business partner, gave power of attorney to Brice, whom Michel called "my well beloved & trusty friend." Even Col. Theophilus Hastings used

Brice as a lawyer. He must have been rather successful as many people of the Craven Precinct turned to him when they needed an attorney.[33]

Like so many middling men during colonial times, Brice was more than just a lawyer and an officer of the court; he was also a planter. And a planter might double as a merchant or trader. They all might speculate in land, buying and selling with hopes of making a profit. Brice tried his hand at all of it. He purchased a lot in the new town of Beaufort on Core Sound, Number 22, between Turner and Orange Streets. He sold two hundred acres of his land on the west side of Brice's Creek to John Doss for £20. Later he purchased seven thousand acres from John Porter between Drum Inlet and Topsail Inlet in Beaufort Precinct for £260 current money. In all, Brice, his wife Ann, sons Francis and William, and daughter Elizabeth had done well as a family.[34]

But there was always something a little unsavory about William Brice. He was never averse to crossing that line between moral and immoral, legal and illegal. He certainly had a good dose of scoundrel in him, but that did not set him too far apart from his fellow North Carolinians. If this William Brice was the same who had been deputy provost marshal in Bermuda, then he was a known associate of pirates. His murder and enslavement of the Bear River Indians certainly bodes ill for his historical legacy. And one would not be surprised had he been the instigator for the attack on the Indians at Core Town after Barnwell's treaty. So despite being a community leader, after the war Brice often found himself in court, usually as a defendant or witness. After the departure of De Graffenried, Brice appropriated some lumber that actually belonged to the Palatines. He might have gotten away with it, but Thomas Pollock claimed all the land, property, and planks and so demanded Brice be investigated. Brice was accused of marking hogs that were not his. And on at least one occasion, Brice used the land belonging to his orphaned ward, James Castage, as collateral for a land deal of his own. He then later sold Castage's land. He was also able to use cattle belonging to another orphaned ward of his, Jasper Trumpra, to increase his own herd.[35]

Probably the best example of Brice's crooked character might be his attempt to start an Indian war for profit. Back during the Yamasee War in 1715, after an attack by South Carolina forces, many Cheraw Indians sought refuge among the deserted Tuscarora forts along Contentnea Creek. North Carolinians, having just rid themselves of the powerful Tuscaroras, did not want to see the somewhat powerful Cheraws take their place. Many settlers feared it would not be long before Cheraw raiders would be striking across eastern North Carolina. Then in the summer of 1716, their war fears seemed to come true. In late August, the North Carolina Council received a letter from Brice reporting that a party of Cheraws had attacked a settlement near his plantation, killing a white man and one of Brice's Indian slaves. He reported the Cheraws to be well armed, which he said came from Virginia traders. With Brice's letter in hand, Governor Eden declared war on the Cheraws. Brice then suggested that he and Maj. William Hancock and their militiamen would gladly lead an expedition against the Cheraws if the North Carolina government would pay them for it. Instead, Governor Eden sent some of King Tom Blount's warriors down to the Trent River to help Brice. Rather than welcoming them, Brice and his men were cool and insulting to Blount's warriors. Suspicious of Brice's actions, Pollock and Virginia's Governor Spotswood did some investigating of their own and discovered that it was Brice and his men who had first attacked the Indians. The whole thing had been a scheme cooked up by Brice and Hancock to get paid to hunt down Indians. As Pollock later declared, the whole war had been a sham and Brice's offer to attack would have "instead of ending our war, they may be the occasion of beginning another greater and worse."[36]

Brice would not have to face any kind of inquiry on this as he died sometime soon after November 16, 1718, when he made his last will and testament. He ordered his wife, Ann, to sell off his seven thousand–acre island called Point Look Out on the Outer Banks, as well as a second piece of land to settle his debts. After that, his wife and children got an equal share of his estate. Ann got the three hundred–acre Brice plantation on Brice's Creek as well as all his cattle. Son Francis received the land next to that all the way to Holster's Creek. Son William got another piece of land from Holster's Creek to Martine Frank's place. Elizabeth got 320 acres on the opposite side of the creek. This was to be Ann's and the children's and their heirs' forever. However, should Ann remarry, then on the day of her wedding the three Brice children would be declared adults and free to do with their property as they saw fit, unless they wanted to continue living with their mother.[37]

It seems that William Brice Jr. remained on Brice's Creek, while Francis Brice moved to the Beaufort area of the new Carteret Precinct. Brice's wife, Ann, remarried in July 1723, taking as a husband William Wilson. Brice's daughter, Elizabeth, married John Fonvielle. His sons became respected members of the community, William in Craven Precinct near New Bern and Francis in Carteret Precinct near Beaufort. In 1740, William Brice Jr. served as a Craven County representative to the North Carolina Assembly in the same session with Maurice Moore Jr., a representative from New Hanover County and the son of the famed Capt. Maurice Moore.[38] And so William Brice was the first of our European players to depart the stage. His life summed up the complexity that was England's North American colonies, where a man could be a hero, a rogue, and an upstanding member of the community at the same time. And so was William Brice: family man, planter, lawyer, speculator, Indian killer, slave-taker, scoundrel, and North Carolinian.

❖ As the war came to an end, it fell to Governor Charles Eden and Council President Thomas Pollock to end the chaos and get the colony operating normally. As a loyal Proprietary man, Pollock instantly stepped down as acting governor when Eden arrived in May 1714 and took up his position as president of the council. As he had with Governor Hyde, Pollock quickly gained the confidence of Eden and served as one of his most trusted advisors. Cementing their friendship was that Pollock sold Eden the plantation at Sandy Point on the west side of the Chowan River near Pollock's own Balgra.[39]

Up in the Albemarle, Pollock and other elites, now in their moment of victory, wanted to ensure the political dominance of the Albemarle Proprietary men. One of the first things Eden, Pollock, and the Council did was revamp the rules for electing the assembly. This took place every two years. They partially addressed the representative inequality between Albemarle and Bath Counties, which had been a root cause of Cary's Rebellion. Previously, each of Albemarle's four precincts received five representatives in the Assembly while Bath's three precincts received only two each. Under the new rules, there would still be two counties: Albemarle and Bath. Each precinct in both counties would now elect five representatives to the Assembly. But the Albemarle Proprietary men made sure their county remained dominant. Albemarle County would still have its four precincts: Currituck, Pasquotank, Perquimmons, and Chowan precincts, while Bath County would still only have three: Beaufort, Hyde, and Craven Precincts, so it continued to be outvoted. Voters had to be twenty-one years old, born in a British territory, been a resident of North Carolina for a year, and had paid one year's taxes. Specifically denied the right to vote was anyone who was not free, as well as any "Negro, Mullatto or Indians." While women were not specifically denied the right to vote, it seems to be taken for granted that only men would vote.[40]

Neither were the elections going to be open and democratic. During the war Pollock and the Council had been hamstrung by Dissenter-dominated assemblies and it had almost cost them the war. Now victory boosted the power of the Albemarle Proprietary men and they were not about to let it go. Anyone wanting to vote had to bring a list of who they wanted to vote for to the marshal or his deputy and sign their name to the list. The marshal would determine if they were qualified to vote. If they were, then the marshal would administer an oath to them. If the marshal allowed someone to vote who was unqualified, then he could be fined £20, which would be applied to the building of a courthouse or Anglican church. Once a man was elected to the Assembly, he also had to take the Oath of Allegiance and Supremacy to the King, the Abjuration Oath, and any other oaths required by Parliament in Britain. But the refusal of Quakers to take an oath or swear on anything was a major part of their beliefs. So once again, the Quakers were to be denied their political rights as much as possible. Now the Albemarle Proprietary men were in control and had the power to exclude them.[41]

The war had not only been a victory for North Carolina; it had been a victory for the Albemarle Proprietary men. Under their leadership, and despite Dissenter heel-dragging, they had beaten a tough and resourceful enemy. But the war also shattered the old settler-Bath County-Quaker alliance. Many old settlers and Bath County men had been angered by the Quakers refusal to help fight the war. So with the new 1715 election laws in place, the Albemarle Proprietary men dominated the Council and, for a while, the Assembly.[42] For Pollock, this was the stability that he had always craved. But even this was fleeting as the lower house Assembly soon slipped from Albemarle Proprietary men's' control and began battling the upper house Council over appointments and perquisites. By 1729, even the Lords Proprietors would be gone from North Carolina, as it now became a royal colony with governors appointed by the king. And that political contrariness, so much a characteristic of colonial North Carolina, remained strong throughout the rest of the eighteenth century.

In the end, Albemarle dominance of North Carolina government was also a victim of the Tuscarora War. With the Indians defeated, lands were opened and now an influx of settlers pushed North Carolina boundaries westward toward the Piedmont and south to the lower Cape Fear River. These were men cut from the same mold as Pollock and Brice, men who wanted lands, farms, and plantations, and were fully willing to use slaves, now African rather than Indians, to increase their wealth. It was not long before there were significant populations of settlers near New Bern and down on the lower Cape Fear River. Maurice Moore's Cape Fear settlements proved a particularly effective counter to the Albemarle, and many men on the outs with the Albemarle relocated there. By the 1730s, the lower Cape Fear River settlements, with the colony's only deepwater port, had undercut the political power of the Albemarle elites. Legislatures were now meeting in various places in the southern parts of the colony.[43]

For Pollock, this was a future beyond him. But in 1715, he was the master of North Carolina politics. Even the gods seemed to be smiling on him as in that year, Pollock's wife, Esther, died and he began his long quest to overturn her will into his favor. Probably the lengthy court action made Pollock give up his seat on the Council for a year. He would not return until August 1716.[44]

When Pollock did return, he was sixty-two years old and beginning to feel his age. Unknown ailments slowed him. But his appetite for land and wealth was as voracious as ever. Up into the 1720s he was still filing claims on lapsed patents. He applied for additional land grants, including 580 acres on Chowan Sound, 2,560 acres at the confluence of Raquis Creek and the Chowan River, and another 2,560 acres on the Roanoke River. And there were probably others. He tried to purchase the lands belonging to the late Governor Edward Hyde at old Core Town near the confluence of the Neuse River and Contentnea Creek. He even approached Lord Carteret personally about granting them to him. But it appeared that the settler John Lovich had gotten to Hyde's widow first and she had sold Core Town to him. Nevertheless, Pollock was making money from his town lots in New Bern and was smart enough to purchase a couple of lots in the new town being created across the Chowan River from his Balgra Plantation. Originally called Queen Anne's Town, it would soon be renamed Edenton.[45]

Pollock also never forgot a debt. In July 1720, he sent a friend to collect £3 from a widow Stone for the last fall's rent she owed him for Crany Island. He even reminded the friend he sent on this errand that the friend's own father owed Pollock 57 shillings for nine quarts of rum he had sold him during the Tuscarora War seven years earlier. He demanded that one Dr. Thomas, who lived in a house on Pollock's property in New Bern and who had maintained an orchard for him, now pay him some back rent. Pollock even wrote to a friend in Scotland, wanting him to try to collect a £33 debt owed him back before he left Scotland for North Carolina, sometime before 1683.[46]

Then on March 26, 1722, Governor Charles Eden died of yellow fever at the age of forty-eight. The Council immediately and unanimously appointed Pollock as acting governor of the colony. Taking into account that extra burden on the old man, the Council ordered him to be paid a yearly salary of £300 issued in quarterly installments. To ensure his sons' careers,

Pollock resigned as the deputy to the Duke of Beaufort and had his son, Thomas Pollock Jr., named as deputy in his place. Young Thomas Jr. now took his seat on the Council.[47]

Once again, at almost sixty-eight years of age, Pollock had been asked to take over the governorship of North Carolina. He had done this before and so the job did not seem onerous. As the acting governor, he did some official business out of his Balgra Plantation on the west side of the Chowan River. But he also found himself spending ever more time with the Council and Assembly who were increasingly meeting at Queen Anne's Town on the east side of the Chowan. He even took lodgings there. Then on the night of Saturday, August 4, 1722, a strange occurrence took place. That night, John Cope, a Tuscarora Indian from King Blount's town broke into Pollock's lodgings and apparently stole some items. Cope was apprehended, Pollock pressed charges, and the prisoner was handed over for trial to the Special Court of Oyer and Terminer. A jury of twelve men was impanelled and King Blount and some of his men were called in to serve as witnesses. Just a few days later, on August 8, the trial was held. Amazingly, Cope was found not guilty and discharged, though he had to pay the cost of the prosecution. While ideally justice is blind, one must wonder how the respected acting governor Thomas Pollock lost his case to John Cope, a Tuscarora Indian.[48]

Maybe that loss in court did something to him. Maybe not. But on August 30, 1722, Pollock died at the age of sixty-eight. William Reed was elected to take his place as president of the council and acting governor of North Carolina. Maybe it was yellow fever that took him, as seems likely. Supposedly he died in his sleep after a short illness.[49] He was buried at his Balgra Plantation, next to his first wife, Martha. In 1888 and 1889, the bones of Pollock and Martha, as well as the bones of Governor Eden and his wife Penelope, were exhumed from the west side of the Chowan River and reburied in the churchyard of St. Paul's Episcopal Church in Edenton.

Pollock had certainly died as the wealthiest man in North Carolina, and the Pollock family as the largest landholders with more than eighty-eight thousand acres on properties scattered across the colony. He left it all to his adult sons: Thomas Jr., Cullen, and George. His daughter, Martha, who had married Thomas Bray of Virginia in February 1714, did not seem to receive much if anything in the will. Pollock set up his sons well and they did well. Thomas Jr. was appointed as a justice of the peace, then in 1724 served as chief justice of North Carolina. By 1725 he was again a member of the Governor's Council and then served in the Assembly in

Thomas Pollock's grave, St. Paul's Episcopal Church, Edenton, N.C. Pollock's grave is the one in the foreground with moss on it (second from left). The one to his right (third from left) is that of his first wife, Martha Cullen. Photo by Kip Shaw

1727. He died in February 12, 1733. Cullen also did well, serving as an assistant to Chief Justice Christopher Gale on the North Carolina Supreme Court and then in the Assembly. He lived long and died on February 9, 1750. The youngest son, George, also served in the Assembly and died on October 27, 1736. Their heirs would continue to hold large swaths of North Carolina land. Though it would be too late for Thomas Pollock or the Palatines, in 1765 grandson George Pollock would lose control of nine hundred acres of formerly Palatine land around New Bern to one William Dry for a debt of £2,000. But the Pollock family, like the Moore family, would remain a force in North Carolina for years to come.[50]

So what are we to make of this Thomas Pollock, planter, merchant, land speculator, commander in chief, governor? As acting governor he probably wielded more actual power than any of the governors appointed by the Lords Proprietors. Once he got heavily involved in politics during Cary's Rebellion in 1710, he remained at the forefront of North Carolina government and politics for the rest of his life. For a while he directed the colony's war effort almost alone, having to deal with powerful Indian enemies, reluctant Dissenters, incompetent military subordinates, skillful political opponents, hot-tempered generals, and scheming colonial governors. He brought about his vision of a stable North Carolina in which the Albemarle was in charge, men swore oaths of allegiance to the English king, and supported the Anglican Church. A place where commerce took place, settlers took up land and slaves in hopes of becoming rich planters, and the Indians were either dead, gone, or submissive tributaries. To do this meant breaking the Indians, the old settlers, and the Quakers to the will of North Carolina and the British Empire. Rightly or wrongly, for good or ill, but in spectacular fashion, Thomas Pollock had done that.

The war brought tremendous losses to the Indians of eastern North Carolina. King Hancock was dead. Core Tom had either been spirited away by the Senecas or was dead. His name did not show up among the list of Indians Pollock wanted turned over to him. By the end of the war, Nonrontisgnotkau, called John Pagett by the English, was king of the Cores, who had been placed with the Machapungas on a reservation near Lake Mattamuskeet. For years afterward, the leaders on that reservation included John Pagett, but also King Squire Hooks and later one King Squires, assisted by one Long Tom, the names eerily similar to those agents provocateurs—Squire Tom, Qualks Hooks, and Long Tom—used by the Senecas years earlier to stir up trouble in Maryland and Virginia.[51]

For Tom Blount, his refusal to take part in the attacks and his late alliance with the English earned him the title of "king" of all the remaining North Carolina Tuscaroras. But there were not all that many Tuscaroras remaining in North Carolina. Hundreds had been killed and hundreds more captured, enslaved, and removed from the colony. The Tuscarora towns and villages along Contentnea Creek and the Pamlico River had been destroyed or abandoned. Even while the war raged, many Tuscarora survivors deserted the area and sought refuge among their Five Nation cousins in New York. New York's Governor Robert Hunter worried about the influx of these refugees into his colony. But the Five Nations insisted on welcoming and protecting them. Onondaga chief Teganissorens informed Hunter that the Tuscaroras had "gotten themselves into a war, and are dispersed and have abandoned their castles." Hunter should mediate a peace between them and North Carolina so the Tuscaroras "may no longer be hunted down . . . for they are no longer a Nation with a name, being once dispersed." Over Hunter's wishes, the Five Nations accepted the Tuscarora refugees. "They were of us and went from us long ago and are now returned and promise to live peaceably among us, and since there is peace now every where we have received them. . . . We desire you to look upon the Tuscaroras that are come to live among us as our children who shall obey your commands & live peaceably and orderly."[52]

By 1722, about fifteen hundred Tuscaroras, along with a few Virginia Nottoways, had moved to New York, where they were seen as kinspeople and not merely "props" or allies who had "linked arms" with the Five Nations. In that year, the Tuscaroras were officially incorporated as the Sixth Nation of the Iroquois League and more or less entrusted to the Cayugas and Oneidas as "younger brothers." The Tuscaroras added their manpower to the Six Nations while receiving all the protections, gifts, and privileges as full members of the League of the Longhouse. In dribs and drabs for the remainder of the eighteenth century, Tuscaroras in North Carolina who became unhappy with the rule of Tom Blount or the actions of North Carolina settlers would move north to join their Tuscarora kinfolk in New York.[53] Stories say the Tuscaroras saw their defeat and ouster from North Carolina as punishment for ignoring the teachings of the Great Peacemaker Deganawida who said they should not disagree among themselves, as Hancock and Blount had; should not give in to anger as Core Tom had with John Lawson; and should stand strong for what is right, something they believed Tom Blount had not done. Poverty and loss were the punishment for these violations.[54]

One of the last questions to answer is why the Five Nations, especially the Senecas, did not join the war, after provoking the Tuscaroras and promising so much. Even New York's Governor Hunter reported that the Five Nations were "in a great ferment" about the plight of the Tuscaroras after their defeat at Neoheroka.[55] But Hunter's efforts at peace had paid off. The more pro-English Mohawks and Oneidas exerted some restraint on the Senecas. And the Senecas may have been scared off from joining when they saw just how many Siouan-speaking and Yamasee warriors from South Carolina were willing to go to war, about five hundred in each of the Barnwell and Moore expeditions. Then again, a darker motive could come into play and that was that the Senecas wanted the Tuscaroras to start a war as it would be a win-win opportunity. If the Tuscaroras won the war, then it would be a victory over the English, a good turn for the Seneca's French allies, and plunder for all. If the Tuscaroras lost, the surviving remnants would flee north and so add their manpower to the Five Nations, almost a thousand potential warriors, making them stronger and more able to stand up to the English. And up through the American Revolution, the now Six Nations of the Iroquois would play a major role in the colonial affairs of the American northeast. So if the League of the Longhouse hoped to draw the Tuscaroras into their political orbit, then the war did just that.[56]

Down in eastern North Carolina, Indian power had been shattered. The Pamlico Indians, Bear River Indians, Neuse Indians, and Weetock Indians disappeared from the historical record. These may have been killed off, enslaved, or the few survivors joining with other peoples. By 1716, North Carolina officials listed only seven Indian nations living in the eastern part of the colony: Tuscaroras, Machapungas, Cores, Chowans, Hatteras, Meherrins, and Poteskeets, likely another name for the Yeopim. Eight if we count a few last Cape Fear Indians down on that river who were already tributaries to South Carolina.[57] As officials such as Pollock saw it, there were essentially three types of Indians left in eastern North Carolina: a few lone holdouts who lived in the swamps and might attack an isolated farm or traveler if the circumstances were right; Indian slaves, servants, or workers living on the margins of white society; and tributary Indian nations, such as Blount's upper Tuscaroras, who recognized North Carolina's dominion over them.

Despite the February 1715 treaty, it seems the Cores constituted most of the last holdouts. Pagett's Cores apparently did not stay long on the Machapunga reservation as differences between the two peoples could not be reconciled. This would not be unusual as the Machapungas were Algonquian peoples and the Cores were Iroquoian. In September 1715, the North Carolina government accused the Cores of having attacked and wounded Robert Shrieve, a close friend of William Brice. Though the Council admitted that the Cores had been badly treated, they called this a "revolt" and recommended that the entire Core nation be destroyed as if a peace had never been made with them. Then in July 1718, the town of Bath became alarmed when Indians were reported to have taken captive the son and daughter of Thomas Worsley, as well as a white servant and a black servant. This concerned the government enough to put forty rangers to patrolling the area along the Neuse River and Core Sound. This later turned out to be a hoax concocted by Worsley's son and daughter to protect an Indian slave named Pompey from being punished for some offense. Nevertheless, the rangers seemed to work as even the holdouts and the Cores disappeared from notice.[58] Every now and again someone might complain that Blount's Tuscaroras were raiding, but this never proved true. Blount and North Carolina chalked it up to the continuing raids taking place between the Senecas and the Siouan-speaking Catawbas, who often crossed paths inside North Carolina. These raids and counter-raids by Senecas and Catawbas would continue up through the American Revolution.[59]

For years to come, Indian slaves would be a constant, though dwindling, presence in North Carolina and other English colonies. As many as two thousand Tuscaroras, Cores, Bear River, and other North Carolina Indians had been captured and enslaved during the Tuscarora War. Most of these had been shipped out to the British West Indies, while some had been sent to other North American colonies. A few had also been retained by North Carolinians. Pollock wound up owning an Indian slave or two. The existence of Indian slaves in North Carolina mainly comes from a few court records in which friendly Indians who had been wrongly enslaved made appeals for freedom or where English slave owners sued each other for payment or demanded the return of slaves. Settlers often accused Tom Blount of harboring runaway Indian slaves at his Tuscarora town. But Indian slavery in North Carolina was a declining institution. As these slaves died out, the pool of available Indians to be enslaved diminished, and the number of African and African American slaves increased. On the other hand, since slavery followed the mother and most Indian slaves tended to be women, slaves carrying Indian genes would remain in bondage until that institution was finally abolished.[60] And for years, small groups of detribalized Indians, most not connected to any Indian town or people, lived on the margins of colonial white society, doing odd jobs and selling produce, baskets, and pottery.

At least tributary Indians had a measure of autonomy. By the end of the war, the Tuscaroras, Machapungas, Cores, Chowans, Hatteras, and Poteskeets and Yeopims were tributaries of North Carolina. The Meherrin were as good as tributaries. Once or twice a year, the tributary chief delivered a few dressed deerskins to the North Carolina governor in a symbolic show of the colony's authority over them. While they could handle their own minor internal issues, tributaries deferred to the colonial authorities when it came to politics, diplomacy, and justice. They were expected to be allies of North Carolina, serve as buffers protecting the settlements from enemy Indian raids, and be trade partners. As such, they could be relocated by the government on a whim. Though they might select their own chief, that person had to be approved, if not actually chosen, by the North Carolina governor. When one of their Indians committed a crime against a white settler, they were tried and punished according to English law. They were fair game for Anglican missionaries who wanted to convert them and take their children from them to send to school. However, as tributaries, the Indians had certain rights and expectations. They expected to be protected from attacks either by Indians or whites. They could appeal to the Governor's Council for relief, whether that meant asking for food when supplies were short or to complain about abuse. They could and often did sue in court. Perhaps the greatest benefit to tributary Indian nations was that they were given a large piece of land with recognized boundaries, a reservation, to call their own.

In some ways, a reservation was the most obvious example of tributary status. Where once an Indian people had moved their towns at will and roamed hunting quarters far from their homes, they were now confined to several square miles of land. But in land-hungry North Carolina, having surveyed and recognized boundaries was essential. This process of making tributaries and assigning them bounded tracts of land began

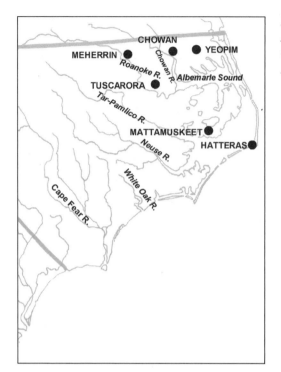

North Carolina Indian Reservations, Eighteenth Century. Map by David A. Norris

well before the Tuscarora War and continued long after it. In 1685, the Chowan Indians became tributaries of North Carolina and received a 144-square-mile reservation on the east side of the Chowan River. In 1697, the Yeopim became tributaries and received a 4-square-mile reservation on the North River in Currituck Precinct. It was expanded to 16 square miles—10,240 acres—in 1704. After the war, the Machapungas, along with the Cores, received a 4-square-mile reserve at the southeastern tip of Lake Mattamuskeet. In 1726 the Meherrin Indians officially became North Carolina tributaries and in 1729 received a 7-square-mile reserve between the Chowan and Meherrin Rivers in present-day Hertford County. The Hatteras Indians, who lived on the Outer Banks, became tributaries during the Tuscarora War when they turned to North Carolina for protection. But it was not until 1759 that they actually received a 200-acre reservation on the south end of Hatteras Island near Cape Hatteras. The largest and most problematic reservation was that of King Tom Blount's Tuscaroras.[61]

In their treaty of April 25, 1713, Pollock had anointed Tom Blount as king of all the North Carolina Tuscaroras, at least those not at war with the colony. In turn Blount and his Tuscaroras became tributaries of the North Carolina government. As the war wound down, Blount's Tuscaroras were instructed to settle on "Onion Quits-Tah Creek," between the Pamlico and Neuse Rivers. But when the Yamasee War broke out in South Carolina in 1715 and the Cheraw Indians intruded into the old Tuscarora villages along Contentnea Creek, Blount appealed to the Council. He feared that his towns might be attacked and pleaded that he and his people be allowed to move to the north bank of the Roanoke River. Though the Cheraws would eventually move back south, in June 1717, the Council agreed, saying that Blount and his Tuscaroras "have been very serviceable to this government and still continue to be. And as a particular mark of favor from the government, they do hereby give unto him, the said Blount, [the] land." On the north bank of the Roanoke River, the Council authorized the creation of a sixty-four-square-mile reserve—41,113 acres—about five miles southwest of present-day Windsor in Bertie County. It would soon earn the name "Indian Woods." Within it were two Tuscarora towns: Resootska, where Blount made his home, and Ooneroy. Blount and his Tuscaroras were warned not to disturb their English neighbors, avoid killing their cattle during their hunts, and be careful about claiming any land outside the bounds of their reserve.[62]

With the end of the war, King Tom Blount, since his Tuscaroras were still the most numerous Indians in eastern North Carolina, numbering more than a thousand men, women, and children, was the most important of North Carolina's tributary kings. He, along with King John Hoyter of the Chowan Indians and King John Durant of the Yeopim Indians, comprised the three main tributary chiefs. They often made appearances before the Council to press their complaints and in turn were called on to answer for and explain colonial Indian concerns. The naturalist John Brickell had dinner with Blount, Hoyter, and Durant and found all three kings spoke and understood English "tolerably well." As befitting the importance of the dinner, the three kings wore ceremonial dress: shirts, stockings, waistcoats, hats, cravats, and shoes. Blount wore a suit of English broadcloth, a pair of blue women's stockings with white clocks on them, and a "tolerable good shirt, cravat, shoes, hat, etc . . . after the English manner." Once the meal was over, Brickell noted, the clothes would be stored away until the next ceremonial occasion and the men would go back to wearing more traditional Indian clothing. The dinner ended with drinks and toasts to the North Carolina governor, whom Blount and the others always referred to as "brother." But Brickell also noted that alcohol was increasingly becoming a problem among the remaining North Carolina Indians. The kings and their entourage, Brickell pointed out, often bought whiskey from the traders and then got roaring drunk.[63]

Though the North Carolina government might view King Tom Blount as chief of all the Tuscaroras, he was a polarizing figure among his own people. Even before the war, many Tuscaroras distrusted him and did not want him to speak for them. After the war, resentment against him came to a boil as others felt he should have supported the war against the English and resented his involvement in the killing of King Hancock. Some saw him as a pawn of the English and disliked his personal ambition to be king of the Tuscaroras. In the days before the coming of the English, unpopular chiefs such as Blount would have lost followers to rival chiefs. He and his directives would have been ignored and so he would have lost power. By 1725, Blount found his authority under threat and so turned to the English for support. In October, he appeared before the Council, informing them that "some of his people are disorderly and are throwing off their obedience to him as their Ruler and [he is] praying the protection of this government." The Council was happy with Blount as king and did not welcome a change in leadership. In recognition of his "faithfulness & fidelity," the Council again proclaimed Blount as king of the Tuscaroras and commanded "all the Tuscaroras to render the said Blount obedience, otherwise they will be looked upon as enemies to the government."[64]

Unable to depose the unpopular Blount, and as the rules of consensus demanded, many Tuscaroras now decided to leave Indian Woods and make their way north to the Tuscarora Nation in New York, not far from Niagara Falls. Major exoduses had taken place in 1717 when the reservation had moved north of the Roanoke River; now in the mid-1720s more of those left who had had become disenchanted with Blount's leadership. For the remainder of the eighteenth century, small parties of Indian Wood Tuscaroras would leave and head north to New York. In 1731, the North Carolina government counted two hundred warriors of Blount's Tuscaroras, which would make the total population somewhere around eight hundred people. By 1754, the Indian Woods population of Tuscaroras was down to about three hundred. And these, the Moravian Bishop Auguste Spangenburg would say, "are treated with great contempt & will probably soon be entirely exterminated."[65]

Contempt and extermination were real problems facing the Indians of eastern North Carolina during the remainder of the eighteenth century. While leaders such as Blount, Hoyter, and Durant might be disliked and claim more authority than the Indians were used to, they were nevertheless facing tough challenges. Many of the same issues that had sparked the Tuscarora War arose again after the war. Now limited to reservations, game was quickly hunted out and Indian hunters who ventured off the reservation might be beaten by irate settlers. Settlers again complained about Indians killing their cattle or burning the woods. As North Carolina filled with immigrants, the Tuscaroras, Chowans, Yeopims, and others found their reservation boundaries under pressure. For decades, Blount and the other chiefs would make their way before the Council to complain about settlers squatting on their lands. Once again the deer hide trade was encouraged and once again Tuscarora and Catawba hunting parties clashed in the forests and Piedmont of North Carolina. Traders increasingly used rum as a trade commodity and soon alcoholism and all its demoralizing effects were found among Indian families. And as it always had, disease made its periodic appearance. In 1728, William Byrd of Virginia declared that the two biggest things killing off the North Carolina Tuscaroras were disease and rum. Rum "they have used so immoderately, that, what with the distempers, and what with the quarrels it begat amongst them, it has proved a doublet destruction." He chalked it up to punishment from God because the Catechna Tuscaroras had once killed a holy man. Byrd did not say who.[66]

While war, rum, and disease took their hefty toll on the Indians, one of the worst problems was the North Carolina government's unwillingness, and the Indian's unwillingness, to protect their land base. The Indians still wanted and needed the guns, powder, kettles, cloth, clothing, rum, and other merchandise the traders brought. But with the loss of their hunting quarters and as the deer hide trade dried up, the Indians found the only thing they had of value that the traders wanted was their reservation lands. The government might step in every once in a while to stop some land sale, especially if too many Indians complained about it. But for the most part, and for much of the eighteenth century, North Carolina allowed the Indians to sell off their reservation lands piece by piece.[67]

By the end of 1715, the Poteskeet Indians up north of the Albemarle, though they did not have an official reservation, sold off the last tracts of their land to Capt. Richard Sanderson and others. They would soon join with the Yeopim Indians. In 1724, the Yeopims began selling off parcels of their 10,240-acre reservation until all of it had been sold by the mid-1700s. In 1720, the North Carolina Council ordered a new survey of the Chowan Indians' 144-square-mile reservation, which resulted in a reduction to about 17 square miles due to the decimated Chowan population. In 1733, the Chowan king began selling off reservation tracts to nearby settlers. This continued for the rest of the century. On April 12, 1790, the few remaining Chowans sold off the last bit of reservation land and North Carolina declared the reservation extinguished. The Hatteras Indians, who only received a reservation in 1759, sold the last tract of the original 200 acres in 1788. The Meherrin reservation was gone by 1768. The last tract of the Mattamuskeet reservation was sold in 1792.[68]

The Tuscaroras managed to hang onto their Indian Woods reservation the longest, but in the end it was still extinguished. King Tom Blount died sometime in the first months of 1739, at least before March 5, 1739. Of all our players, only De Graffenried outlived him. The Tuscaroras now asked the North Carolina Council to allow them to elect a new chief. Though the succession is unclear, it seems Blount's son, James Blount, became the new chief and served until 1748. We know nothing of when he died or who came after him. But in November 1766, Thomas Basket was the king of the Tuscaroras. In that year, another large group of Indian Woods Tuscaroras decided to migrate to New York and sold off 21,712 acres to three nearby settlers for £1,500 to finance their move. A few years later, the remaining Tuscaroras sold off or leased more large chunks of the reservation until in 1803 only 3,000 acres remained in Tuscarora hands. In that year, the last Tuscaroras in North Carolina sold what remained of their lands to the North Carolina government and most moved north to New York. In 1831, the North Carolina government made final payments to the Tuscaroras in New York and the Indian Woods reservation was officially declared extinguished. So by the turn of the nineteenth century, except for maybe a few individuals living on the margins of white society, the Tuscaroras were gone from North Carolina.[69]

The extinguishing of Indian reservations in eastern North Carolina mirrored the disappearance of Indians from sight. By January 1755, North Carolina's Governor Arthur Dobbs counted fewer than 380 Indians living in eastern North Carolina. At Indian Woods in Bertie County, only 301 Tuscaroras remained—100 men, 201 women and children. The Chowans in Chowan County were down to 5—2 men and 3 women and children—and "ill used by their neighbors." The Meherrins in Northampton County had 8 men, which extrapolated to a total population of about 32 people. The Mattamuskeets were down to 8 or 10, while the Hatteras on the Outer Banks were also down to about 10 people. There was a rather newly arrived nation of Indians who had moved south out of Virginia, the Saponis, who lived in Granville County and numbered about 8 men, which meant a total population somewhere around 32. Conversely, farther west, the Catawbas in Anson County in the Piedmont could boast over 240 warriors and a population just under 1,000. The Cherokees in the western North Carolina mountains had close to 10,000 people if not more. But by the end of the eighteenth century, Indian people in eastern

North Carolina would disappear from sight. But that did not mean they were gone.[70]

Certainly much of this disappearance could be chalked up to death or enslavement. Thousands of Indians had died in the war, died from starvation, from disease, and thousands more were enslaved and marched out of North Carolina. After the war, death from disease, ill health, and Indian raids still stalked the eastern Indians. Their much smaller populations made it more difficult for them to recover. Others, such as the Tuscaroras, voluntarily left the colony. But not all Indians died or left, and in reality there were more Indians living in eastern North Carolina than officials or settlers realized. Indian slaves were facts of life on North Carolina plantations for decades. And what of those Hatteras or Mattamuskeet men and women who sold off the last bit of their reservation land and walked away with a few pounds sterling or new American dollars in their pocket? They were no less Indian, but now they belonged to no recognized nation, and so they took their place on the margins of white society, barely noticed by the settlers around them who may or may not have seen them as Indians.

In other instances, survivors from shattered villages and towns took refuge in the swamps and forests of eastern North Carolina, on marginal lands that were then of little interest to white settlers. There these Indian people joined with other refugees and created thriving Indian communities, but out of sight of the North Carolina government and most settlers. Eastern North Carolina Indians learned how to lay low, become invisible, being seen by the surrounding white population only when they wanted to be seen. Time and again over the next two centuries, North Carolinians would be surprised to discover communities of Indians across the eastern part of the state. In the northern counties of Halifax, Warren, Northampton, and even as far west as Alamance, descendants of the Meherrins, Saponis, and Occaneechis remained. Further south in Columbus, Bladen, Robeson, and Sampson Counties lived the survivors of many of the shattered Siouan nations, such as the Cheraws, Waccamaws, and others.[71]

What caused the surprise was that for white North Carolinians, these Indians did not look like what they thought Indians should be. As they saw it, Indians had to be part of a "tribe," and after 1803 there were no recognized "tribes" in eastern North Carolina. Indians were supposed to wear clothes made of animal skins, live in thatch-covered longhouses, paint their faces, make pottery, hunt deer with bows and arrows, cook their food over a campfire, and give a war whoop every now and again. But even before the Tuscarora War, North Carolina Indians had been changing and this process sped up afterward. Increasingly, even among those lying low in the swamps, Indians began wearing cloth shirts, pants, and skirts; living in log cabins; plowing their fields; converting to Christianity; and speaking English. Churches replaced clan houses. Men joined the Patriot forces during the American Revolution and voted in elections afterward. Some married white neighbors, some married black neighbors. In many ways, it would be hard to distinguish them from white farmers except by physical appearance.

White North Carolinians in the first decades of the nineteenth century just did not know what to make of these Indian people. But by then, North Carolina and the South, as African American slavery became entrenched, had become very race conscious. And these people who called themselves Indians did not fit into that new Southern society. They were not white. They were not black. They were not slaves. So in 1835, North Carolina rewrote its constitution, labeled these Indian peoples as Free People of Color, and took away their right to vote and carry weapons. Essentially, they stripped eastern North Carolina Indians of almost all their civil rights. The dream of Thomas Pollock and William Brice had come true. But Indian survival in eastern North Carolina is also a story for another day.

❖ So what lessons or conclusions can we make about the Tuscarora War? The old arguments are not wrong. The war broke the power of the Tuscaroras and other eastern Indians and allowed the colony to expand west and south at a phenomenal rate. By the 1730s and 1740s, the Catawbas of the Piedmont had become tributary Indians and by the 1750s the Cherokees in the mountains would begin having their own troubles with encroaching settlers. The Tuscarora War only briefly united the factions dividing the colony. But in the end, it was a victory for Proprietary Men such as Pollock and Brice as North Carolina took its place inside the expanding British Empire. The power of the Dissenters and old settlers waned after this, though other factions would soon arise. North Carolinians always had a reputation as a contrary people. Even the Lords Proprietors' days were numbered. The Proprietors had proved useless during the Tuscarora War and the confidence the colonists gained from the war allowed them to assert their independence. In 1729, North Carolina was taken from the Proprietors and made into a royal colony. Population increased. By 1729 there were thirty-six thousand white colonists and black slaves, and in 1749 there were forty-five thousand. Conversely, by 1755, there were fewer than four hundred Indians living in eastern North Carolina. The war certainly shifted the balance of power.[72]

Maybe it would be better to look more closely at the Indians. The war exposed fatal divisions within Tuscarora society. It is impossible to say if the outcome would have been any different had Tom Blount and the upper Tuscaroras thrown in with Hancock and Core Tom. But having half the Tuscarora nation sit out the war and then have Blount join the English did not help them. Similarly, the weakness of Tuscarora leadership was brought to the front. Traditionally, Tuscarora town chiefs did not have much actual power. Their success and personality drew followers to them, but the council of elders and the will of the people as a whole meant that chiefs such as Hancock had little coercive authority. So when it came to the trial of John Lawson and Christopher de Graffenried, despite Hancock's desire to free them, his warriors insisted on war and there was nothing he could do to stop it. Even Core Tom, a king from another town, managed to upend Hancock's plan. In the end, Hancock, to keep his position, had to go against his instincts and so begin the suicidal war that his young men wanted. That fatal choice would bring about the destruction of the Tuscaroras and other Indians in eastern North Carolina.

And so what actually caused this war? Abuse by settlers, victimization by Yamasee and Siouan-speaking slave raiders, loss of land, a spillover from Cary's Rebellion? These all caused anger and anxiety among the Tuscaroras, Cores, Machapungas, Pamlicos, Weetocks, and Bear River Indians and opened them to the idea of war. But the Senecas must also share some of the blame. Did the Senecas actually have some dark plan to coerce the Tuscaroras into war and then leave them hanging? Was Core Tom a Seneca plant and agent provocateur? Maybe. Maybe not. But things seemed to work out that way. Those Seneca warriors and diplomats among the Contentnea Creek Tuscaroras and Cores certainly stirred up the warriors by playing on their masculinity and pride. Maybe they promised more than they could actually deliver. Nevertheless, the promises of support and ammunition from the most powerful Indian nation in the eastern part of North America carried weight and made it easier for the young men to ignore King Hancock. And then, just when Hancock had cooled the situation and arranged to get Lawson and De Graffenried released, in stepped Core Tom. He provoked Lawson to anger in front of the Indians, and so swung everyone in favor of executing the sarcastic English official. There, at that crucial moment, when war and peace hung in the balance, Hancock and Tuscarora leadership could not stop Core Tom and the Seneca ambassadors from goading the Tuscaroras into war.

But before we write off the Senecas as fickle friends and King Hancock as a dupe of Core Tom, the Tuscarora War also showed the quest for

Indian unity. Already at this early date, Indians throughout the English colonies understood that their best chance to stand up to the English was by coming together and forming powerful alliances. Just as in the Tuscarora War, over the remainder of the eighteenth century and well into the nineteenth, some Indian leaders would try their hands at building coalitions or even creating an Indian confederation or state. But achieving Indian unity proved difficult as different Indian nations had their own agendas, often at odds with others, and it proved rather easy for colonial powers to play Indian nations against each other and so divide and conquer. The Tuscarora War was not the first and certainly not the last attempt by Indian powers to unify to stand up to colonial governments and then fail as the English, and later the Americans, responded with war.[73]

Probably one of the most remarkable things about the war was the use of forts, such as the one at Catechna and even more so the fort at Neoheroka. One of the greatest criticisms of American Indian warfare has been that it was too tradition bound. That over the course of four centuries of warfare with Europeans and Americans, Indians rarely changed their strategy or developed innovative tactics. But the European-style forts at Catechna and Neoheroka were unique in the history of American Indian warfare. They showed not just tactical innovation but that the Tuscaroras had learned from watching and fighting European colonial troops. Though it was close, the Catechna fort's ability to hold out against Barnwell and force him to give up his siege only reinforced the Tuscarora idea that these forts were the key to victory. And so the fort at Neoheroka had been strengthened and the deficiencies uncovered at Catechna addressed.

Unfortunately for the Tuscaroras, the lessons came too late. While the forts at Catechna and Neoheroka were formidable, by this time even European colonials had developed ways to deal with such fortifications through approach trenches, entrenched artillery batteries, tunnels and mines, and the use of fire on log palisades and blockhouses. Only if the attackers ran out of food or supplies, as in the case of Barnwell, could the forts have a chance of survival. But against a well-supplied, artillery-supported attack, as in the case of Moore, the fortifications were doomed, especially if the Indians did not have artillery of their own. If the Tuscaroras and their allies had had another large force outside the forts that could attack the rear of besiegers and raid their supplies, then a victory might have been possible. But the Tuscaroras did not have such a force as most of their warriors had been brought inside the forts and the upper Tuscaroras were not going to come to their aid. If anything, the Tuscaroras relied too much on these forts. Most Indian warfare used surprise attacks and ambushes, but other than in the initial attacks, none of these tactics were used in force against either Barnwell or Moore. The South Carolina Indian allies provided security against this. So the Tuscaroras, thinking their forts invulnerable, waited in them and then were finally defeated at Neoheroka.

Other Indians learned from this folly. The historian Wayne E. Lee has pointed out that Cherokee warriors who fought alongside Moore at Neoheroka now realized that forts, no matter how well built, could not stand up to European sieges. Instead, they noticed that the weak link for a European army was its supply train. So the Cherokees understood they could do much more damage by attacking supply trains than by holing up in forts. The Cherokees had seen the Tuscaroras "cut off," and so later in the eighteenth century, when European warfare came to Cherokee territory, they resisted fortifications in favor of surprise attacks. It worked for a while.[74]

The Tuscaroras, Yamasees, and other Indians also learned that they would never be seen or respected as equals by the English. There would never be a firm truce or a lasting peace as the English would never stop until Indian power was broken. Though the Tuscaroras and their allies had inflicted heavy losses on the settlers, they had never meant to wipe them out. The attacks were to be a correction, a lesson to the English to change their ways, listen to Indian complaints, and treat them better. The war was to bring back a measure of equality. During the initial attacks, unsuspecting farms and targets of opportunity were attacked, but there was little effort made against fortified houses. Brice's panicky force, far outnumbered and ambushed by Tuscarora warriors, was allowed to retreat back down the Neuse to their homes. And with the upper Tuscaroras refusal to fight, the Albemarle was not under any threat of attack.

So at any point after this, Pollock and the North Carolina government could have made peace. Especially after Barnwell's truce in April 1712. But Pollock would have none of it. His desire for the destruction of his enemies prevailed and he would not stop until Hancock and just about every Indian who had taken part in the attacks had paid with their lives, until all possible Indian threats against the colony had been destroyed. The only options open to the Indians were enslavement, extermination, or tributary status. Tom Blount learned it. So did the Yamasees in 1715, who realized they had to strike South Carolina first before the same thing happened to them. Maybe it rippled out further as Senecas, Shawnees, Choctaws, and others began turning to the French to counter the ever-expanding English. But in the long run that would not save them. It is possible to connect the dots and say that what began at Neoheroka in 1713 ended in 1890 at Wounded Knee, South Dakota, the last of the Indian wars, when the Seventh Cavalry shot down so many Lakota men, women, and children.

Nevertheless, and no matter the official counts, the report of the demise of Indians in North Carolina was greatly exaggerated. Despite warfare, destruction, enslavement, horrific disease, and mass exoduses, Indians did not disappear from North Carolina. That is an amazing point in itself. In spite of all the attempts at the physical and cultural destruction of North Carolina Indians they remained. Small enclaves of Indian people lived on across eastern North Carolina, preserving their Indian identity through oral tradition and separate schools, churches, and governing bodies. During the nineteenth and twentieth centuries these Indian enclaves would arise again as such North Carolina nations as the Lumbees, Waccamaw Siouans, Occaneechees, Meherrins, and Saponies. And we should not forget the Eastern Band of Cherokees in the mountains, a few of whom in 1838 managed to resist being forced along the Trail of Tears. By 2010, North Carolina would be surprised to learn that it had more than 122,000 Indian citizens, the most of any state east of the Mississippi River. So Hancock, Tom Blount, Core Tom, Sam of Core Town, King Taylor of Chattooka Town, John Hoyter of the Chowans, John Durant of the Yeopims, Basket, and all the others would be proud of the tenacity of their descendants. And who knows what the future of Indians in North Carolina will be. After all, history is long and not yet over.

A Note from the Author

This was the first time biography played a major role in my historical writing. So as I got closer to these eight men—Christopher de Graffenried, King Hancock, Core Tom, William Brice, Col. John Barnwell, Thomas Pollock, King Tom Blount, and Col. James Moore—the more my preconceived notions about them changed.

Of course, the most mysterious of all of them are the Indians—King Hancock, Core Tom, and Tom Blount. The problem is one facing all historians writing Indian history in that the Indians left few written records, and what is written about them was by Europeans, who were often their enemies. The little information we have on Hancock and Core Tom mainly comes from De Graffenried. Fortunately, he was an eyewitness to the events. Even then, his memoirs and reports seem to have been written later in his life. The only information on Blount comes from the official records written on the spot by Pollock or Spotswood. But rarely do these officials delve deep into the man's psyche. So I have tried to read between the lines and call on the many studies done by ethnohistorians, anthropologists, and archaeologists about Indian life and culture. After all, this is as much an Indian story as it is a North Carolina colonial story.

The more I read, the more I came to see King Hancock as a conflicted leader, a man trying to keep both the peace and his standing, but eventually unable to do either. Core Tom, the most puzzling of them all, bound by his hatred of the English, was ready to fight, even if it brought destruction to his people. Though the evidence is circumstantial, I am ready to believe he was performing Seneca diplomatic manipulation at the trial of Lawson. Blount faced the dilemma that almost every Indian leader up to 1890 faced: war or accommodation? Hancock, Core Tom, Tecumseh, Sitting Bull, Geronimo all went with war—and look where it got them. Blount, John Ridge, Red Cloud, Spotted Tail all went with accommodation, essentially tributary status. Their people survived, but just barely and often in poverty and ill health. Who made the better choice is up for interpretation. Maybe it was like the Old Man's response in *Catch-22* when Lt. Nately asked him if he had ever heard the saying "better to die on one's feet than live on one's knees." Nately had it backward, the Old Man chided, "it is better to live on one's feet than die on one's knees."

De Graffenried's own writings reveal him as a sour man who did not work well with others. Failures were never his fault. Still, he led his Palatines and Swiss to North Carolina, suffered all the same privations they did, tried to fight for them, lived through a terrifying Indian captivity, sacrificed his reputation to help his colony, and even then found he could not protect his charges. Despite his best efforts and absolutely no support, he eventually gave up and went home. Abandoning his colony does not endear him to us. But by that time his colonists and North Carolina were glad to be rid of him, and he of them. That his last years were peaceful ones and he died at home in Switzerland among his family is a tribute to him.

Col. John "Tuscarora Jack" Barnwell was an intriguing person. It is mainly through the letters he wrote during his Tuscarora campaign that we get to know him and how that part of the war played out. On one hand, he is friendly and often softhearted. On the other, he is hot-tempered, a slave-taker, given to violence and murder. His burning alive the Kenta captives and dismembering Harry the runaway black slave seems sadistic. Of course, the biggest question about Barnwell is whether he was the one who attacked and enslaved the Indians at Core Town after he had made a truce with them. Historians differ. That the Indians at Core Town were attacked after the truce is beyond dispute. I went into my research willing to believe it was Barnwell. But now I think it was done by North Carolinians, and probably William Brice had a hand in it. I just have to think that those four hundred Indian captives Governor Hyde crowed about in late May 1712 had to come from the Core Town attack. Had Barnwell done it, those slaves would have been his, not Hyde's. But I could be wrong. Governor Spotswood, who had a pretty good Indian intelligence service, believed it was Barnwell, and the colonel certainly had the motive and ability.

For all the Europeans involved in the war, the least is known about Col. Moore. This seems incredible when we consider he was a successful Indian fighter, a militia general in two wars, and a later governor of South Carolina. While a little of his writing about his campaign, and about life in general, survives, it was not nearly as detailed as Barnwell's letters about his own campaign. Of course, we sometimes forget that the early 1700s was a long time ago and it takes effort to protect records for three hundred years. Documents get lost or stolen, eaten by insects, rot away, and who knows what records went up in smoke when Columbia, South Carolina, burned during the Civil War. But we do see a competent, efficient commander who thoroughly prepared his forces to take on and defeat the Tuscaroras at Neoheroka. His willingness to take his Indians into Albemarle County where the food was stored was a brilliant maneuver. Had there been more information available on him, Moore might have taken his place as one of the best and most successful military men in colonial North America.

I was most conflicted when it came to William Brice. I both loved him and hated him. He is not listed in Powell's *Dictionary of North Carolina Biography*, but he should be. Brice turns up a lot in De Graffenried's journal and in the colonial records. He was a major player in the Tuscarora War and deserves acknowledgment. His house held out when so many others were destroyed. He was the first North Carolinian to recover from the attacks and go on the offensive. He commanded the North Carolina troops in Barnwell's first attack on the Catechna fort. That he was unsuccessful as a commander of troops or as an Indian fighter should not diminish our recognition of his bravery or his willingness to take on a formidable enemy. Many others were unsuccessful as well. On the other hand, it is hard to get by his attack and enslavement of the Bear River Indians and his roasting alive of their king. He was a slave trader and so dealt in human flesh. Then again, I hope I am not judging him too much by present-day standards, as I do see him as the epitome of the North Carolina settler in the early 1700s. I believe that just about every other Englishman, save a Quaker, would have done the same as Brice given the opportunity. He was not unusual in North Carolina: a man on the make willing to do whatever it took to survive and prosper. Both hero and scoundrel, William Brice, I think, brought me the most enjoyment.

It was with Thomas Pollock that my preconceptions changed the most. As a high North Carolina official, he had many of his writings preserved in the North Carolina colonial records. So we know more about him than about any of our other players. By 1711, he was the richest man in North Carolina, and by his death in 1722, the largest land owner. He was certainly a skilled political fighter. Because of this, my first inclination was to see him as a scheming politician who sought power for his own enrichment. The historian Noeleen McIlvenna, in her book *A Very Mutinous People*, described him as a sort of law-and-order fascist who believed it was his job to take on the Dissenters, the Indians, and all those other mutinous folks to bring North Carolina in line with the British Empire, all while instituting a slave-based plantation system. Maybe he was that. He was certainly never averse to enriching himself. However, he seemed to be personally honest, as I never saw corruption with Pollock, not like with the earlier Governor Seth Sothel. Of course, maybe he was just better at hiding it and skilled enough to not get caught. Still, when crises arose, such as Cary's Rebellion and the Tuscarora War, Pollock stood firm. He would not back down and would work and scheme until he won. No matter where one's sympathies lie, his ability to keep North Carolina going during these times and win victories over very tough opponents while facing virtual civil war at home is a testament to his character and abilities. So I find myself caught between McIlvenna's negative characterization and the historian Louis Towles's assessment of Pollock in his article "Cary's Rebellion and the Emergence of Thomas Pollock," who portrayed him as a dedicated public servant and selfless colonial leader prizing stability in North Carolina above all else. Pollock certainly had his faults, but he also deserves to be considered in the top tier of all North Carolina governors.

Finally, there is the war itself. The casual violence is shocking today. Torturing of prisoners, scalping, burning people alive, cutting down enemies, fighting to the death, plantations and forts in flames, towns pillaged. And numbers camouflage so much. When we say that 558 Indians were killed in Moore's attack on Neoheroka or that 140 settlers were killed in the initial September 22 attack, we often forget that each of those was an individual tragedy. Someone was killed, a mother cried for a dead child, a tortured captive begged for mercy, a slave was led away to a life of bondage. Both Indians and Europeans watched hopes and dreams go up in flames. Still, it is an amazing story. Just ask the people who live around New Bern, Ft. Barnwell, Chocowinity, Washington, Bath, Grifton, Beaufort, and other towns between the Pamlico and the Neuse who still remember the stories of when North Carolina burned.

Notes

INTRODUCTION

1. Barlowe, "Captain Arthur Barlowe's Narrative," 235, 237; Camp, *Influence of Geography*, 1–3; Bennett and Patton, *Geography of the Carolinas*, 16–20, fig. 2.3; Moody, "Massachusetts Trade with Carolina," 45; Franklin, "Agriculture in Colonial North Carolina," 544–45.

2. Letter from Mr. Francis Yeardley to John Farrar, May 8, 1654, *CRNC*, 1:18; Kilcocanen, Mar. 1, 1661, *CRNC* 1:19; Deposition of Caleb Callaway, July 16, 1693, *CRNC2*, 3:503; A Letter to Sir William Berkeley, Sept. 8, 1663, *CRNC*, 1:53; The Port Royall Discovery, 14 June 1660, *CRNC*, 1:137; John Vassal to Sir John Colleton,

Oct. 6, 1667, *CRNC*, 1:160; Grimes, "Notes," 109; Camp, *Influence of Geography*, 4; Watson, Latham, and Samford, *Bath*, 4; Powell, *Proprietors of Carolina*, 2; Lefler and Powell, *Colonial North Carolina*, 31–32; Lawson, *New Voyage*, 79–80.

3. McIlvenna, *Very Mutinous People*, 14; Powell, *Proprietors of Carolina*, 3, 4, 10; Lefler and Powell, *Colonial North Carolina*, 32–33.

4. Lefler and Powell, *Colonial North Carolina*, 36–38, 44; Camp, *Influence of Geography*, 14–15; Watson, Latham, and Samford, *Bath*, 4.

5. "Albemarle County," *NCHGR*, 3:304–10; Franklin, "Agriculture in Colonial North Carolina," 541–43, 549; Wolf, "Patents and Tithables," 264, 267–68; Lefler and Powell, *Colonial North Carolina*, 33–35.

6. McIlvenna, *Very Mutinous People*, 32–35.

7. Lefler and Powell, *Colonial North Carolina*, 46–47; Towles, "Cary's Rebellion," 37–38.

8. Moody, "Massachusetts Trade with Carolina," 44.

9. Urmston's Letter, July 7, 1711, *CRNC*, 1:767.

10. Gordon to the Secretary, May 13, 1709, *CRNC*, 1: 711; Fischer, *Suspect Relations*, 42–54; Lefler and Powell, *Colonial North Carolina*, 33; Towles, "Cary's Rebellion," 37–38.

11. Urmston's Letter, July 7, 1711, *CRNC*, 1:765–66.

12. Towles, "Cary's Rebellion," 37–38.

13. Ibid., 38; Lefler and Powell, *Colonial North Carolina*, 46–47; McIlvenna, *Very Mutinous People*, 1–5.

14. Watson, Latham, and Samford, *Bath*, 6–9; Camp, *Influence of Geography*, 7–11; Lee, *Indian Wars*, 17; Gordon to the Secretary, 13 May 1709, *CRNC*, 1:713–14; McIlvenna, *Very Mutinous People*, 22; Franklin, "Agriculture in Colonial North Carolina," 547, 571; *NCHGR* 1 (Oct. 1900): 613; *NCHGR* 3 (Jan. 1903): 148; BCLDR.

15. Franklin, "Agriculture in Colonial North Carolina," 550–51.

16. Hyde to Mr. Rainsford, May 30, 1712, *CRNC*, 1:850.

17. Lawson, *New Voyage*, 122; *NCHGR* 3 (Jan. 1903): 56–58, 145, 147; Examinations of William Lees, Examination of John Spellman, Aug. 24, 1697, *CRNC2*, 3:126–27. One should also read Kirsten Fischer's excellent *Suspect Relations: Sex, Race, and Resistance in Colonial North Carolina*.

18. Urmston's Letter, July 7, 1711, *CRNC*, 1:765.

19. Examinations of William Lees, Examination of John Spellman, Aug. 24, 1697, *CRNC2*, 3:126–27; Fischer, *Suspect Relations*, 13–14; Lawson, *New Voyage*, 90–91; Franklin, "Agriculture in Colonial North Carolina," 550–51; McIlvenna, *Very Mutinous People*, 43; Ludwell and Harrison, "Boundary Line Proceedings, 1710," 9–10.

20. Lawson, *New Voyage*, 91.

21. Bently Importation, Feb. 1694, *CRNC2*, 2:404; Estate of Seth Sothel, 1697, *CRNC2*, 3:38–39; General Court, May 4, 1698, *CRNC2*, 3:216–17; Thomas Norcom petition, Mar. 1699, *CRNC2*, 3:295–96; Estate of Col. Lear, Mar. 1701, *CRNC2*, 3:435; Introduction, *CRNC2*, 5:x; Sale of goods by William Duckenfield, Oct. 20, 1705, *CRNC2*, 4:204; Higher-Court Records, c. 1700, *CRNC2*, 3:513–14; Wright, *Only Land*, 148–50; Fischer, *Suspect Relations*, 131–58.

22. Representation to the Lords Proprietor, c. 1679, *CRNC*, 1:260; Introduction, *CRNC2*, 5:x; Grimes, "Notes," 101.

23. Watson, Latham, and Samford, *Bath*, 3; Lee, *Indian Wars*, 17; Clark, *Indian Massacre*, 6.

24. Council Meeting, Dec. 3,1705, *CRNC*, 1:629; Gordon to Secretary, May 13, 1709, *CRNC*, 1:714; Lawson, *New Voyage*, 90, 119–20; Dill, "Eighteenth Century New Bern," 22 (Jan. 1945): 2–6, 11–12, 14; Watson, Latham, and Samford, *Bath*, 3, 5, 7–8, 14; Lefler and Powell, *Colonial North Carolina*, 56, 59; Klingberg, *Le Jau*, 118 n. 160.

25. Lefler and Powell, *Colonial North Carolina*, 56–57.

26. Pollock's Letter Book, Oct. 11, 1708, *CRNC*, 1:699; Gordon to Secretary, May 13, 1709, *CRNC*, 1:708–11; Petition of Sundry Persons Relating to Electing Officers, *NCHGR* 3 (Apr. 1903): 258–59; Towles, "Cary's Rebellion," 38–43, 39 n. 6; Watson, Latham, and Samford, *Bath*, 14–16.

27. Pollock's Letter Book, Oct. 11, 1708, *CRNC*, 1:696–99; Gordon to Secretary, May 13, 1709, *CRNC*, 1:708–11; Watson, Latham, and Samford, *Bath*, 14–16; Towles, "Cary's Rebellion," 46.

28. Lords Proprietor of Carolina to the Council and Assembly of North Carolina, Craven House, Feb. 12, 1712, *CSPCAWI*, 26:211–31 (#306); A Proclamation, Jan. 24, 1712, *CRNC2*, 7:17; Watson, Latham, and Samford, *Bath*, 16–18; Towles, "Cary's Rebellion," 47–50.

29. Hyde to Your Lordships, Aug. 22, 1711, *CRNC*, 1:802; *CVGA*, 231–32; Watson, Latham, and Samford, *Bath*, 16–18; Towles, "Cary's Rebellion," 47–51.

30. Lawson, *New Voyage*, 232–33, 242–43; Lee, *Indian Wars*, 3–5; Introduction, *CRNC2*, 5:x. Censuses of Indians by historians have given widely divergent numbers and so actual counts are impossible to come by.

31. Lee, *Indian Wars*, 16; Stevenson, "Indian Reservations in North Carolina," 27–28.

32. Lawson, *New Voyage*, 242–43; Lee, *Indian Wars*, 3–5.

33. Lee, *Indian Wars*, 3–5; Lawson, *New Voyage*, 242–43; Boyce, "Iroquoian Tribes," 15:282–83.

34. Letter from Wm. Duckenfield Relating to Indian Depredations, c. 1696, *NCHGR* 3 (Jan. 1903): 64; Petition of Inhabitants of Matchapungo, c. 1703, *NCHGR* 2 (Apr. 1901): 193; *NCHGR* 2 (Jan 1901): 152; John Fulford Complaint, Oct 20, 1704, *NCHGR* 1 (July 1900): 437–38; Petition of Certain Persons to the Honb. Grand Court, Sept. 1707, *NCHGR* 2 (Jan. 1901): 111–12; Letter of Henderson Walker, Nov. 18, 1699, *CRNC*, 1:517; War Declared Against the Core & Nynee Indians, 1703, *NCHGR* 2 (Apr. 1901): 204; Lawson, *New Voyage*, 215–17, 223–25.

35. Petition of Benjamin Blanchard and Others Relating to Chowan Indian Lands, Mar. 28, 1702, *NCHGR* 3 (Apr. 1903): 242; Relating to the Indians, 1703, *NCHGR* 2 (Apr. 1901): 193–94; Journal of the Virginia Council, Sept. 2, 1707, *CRNC*, 1: 667–71; Lawson, *New Voyage*, 239–46; Lee, *Indian Wars*, 19.

36. Gordon to the Secretary, May 13, 1709, *CRNC*, 1:715.

CHAPTER 1

1. Recent historians have mistakenly referred to De Graffenried as *Von* Graffenried. In the North Carolina colonial records, he is always referred to as De Graffenried, or just Graffenried. He signed his own name as De Graffenried. Even

today, in the early twenty-first century, his descendants in the United States insist that he be referred to as De Graffenried, not Von Graffenried.

2. Dill, "Eighteenth Century New Bern," 22 (Apr. 1945): 154–57; Powell, *Dictionary*, 2:328.

3. Quote from Powell, *Dictionary*, 2:328; Dill, "Eighteenth Century New Bern," 22 (Apr. 1945): 160–61.

4. Otterness, *Becoming German*, 7–77; Dill, "Eighteenth Century New Bern," 157–58; Robert J. Cain, *CRNC2*, 10:89 n. 1.

5. Lawson, *New Voyage*, xxiv–xxvi; Powell, *Dictionary*, 2:328; Lefler and Powell, *Colonial North Carolina*, 59–61; Dill, "Eighteenth Century New Bern," 22 (Apr. 1945): 153–54, 160–63.

6. *CVGA*, 43, 47, 362–63; Proposal, Sept. 3, 1709, *CRNC*, 1:718; Agreement, Apr. 6, 1710, *CRNC*, 1:723; Warrant for Land, Sept. 8, 1709, *CRNC2*, 7:435; Lawson, *New Voyage*, xxvi; Dill, "Eighteenth Century New Bern," 22 (Apr. 1945): 157–64; Powell, *Dictionary*, 2:328.

7. Proposal, Sept. 3, 1709, *CRNC*, 1:718; De Graffenried's Contract for the Palatines, Oct. 10, 1709, *CRNC*, 1:986–89.

8. Dill, "Eighteenth Century New Bern," 22 (Apr. 1945): 162–63.

9. *CVGA*, 45–46, 362–63; Dill, "Eighteenth Century New Bern," 22 (Apr. 1945): 161–63, 171–72; *NCHGR* 1 (Oct. 1900): 585–86; Powell, *Dictionary*, 2:328; Lefler and Powell, *Colonial North Carolina*, 60–61; De Graffenried to Bishop of London, Apr. 20, 1711, *CRNC*, 1:756; Bishop of London to the Secretary, Jan. 12, 1712, *CRNC*, 1:831.

10. *CVGA*, 45–46, 298; De Graffenried's Contract for the Palatines, Oct. 10, 1709, *CRNC*, 1:986–89; Lefler and Powell, *Colonial North Carolina*, 61–63; Lawson, *New Voyage*, xxvi.

11. Dill, "Eighteenth Century New Bern," 22 (Apr. 1945): 163; *CVGA*, 364.

12. DGM, 905–10; *CVGA*, 51, 307; Lefler and Powell, *Colonial North Carolina*, 62–65; Holloman, "Palatines and Tuscaroras," 21–22.

13. DGM, 905–10; *CVGA*, 308–9; Lefler and Powell, *Colonial North Carolina*, 61–65, 68; Holloman, "Palatines and Tuscaroras," 21–22; Dill, "Eighteenth Century New Bern," 22 (Apr. 1945): 165–67.

14. Allred and Dill, "Founding of New Bern"; *CVGA*, 298, 366; Dill, "Eighteenth Century New Bern," 22 (Apr. 1945): 164–65.

15. Allred and Dill, "Founding of New Bern"; Dill, "Eighteenth Century New Bern," 22 (Apr. 1945): 165–67, 22 (July 1945): 296–98.

16. Dill, "Eighteenth Century New Bern," 22 (Apr. 1945): 164–67; DGM, 905–10, 978; *CVGA*, 59, 226; Seaman, "John Lawson," 24–26.

17. Lord Craven to Christopher Gale, Sept. 22, 1709, *CRNC2*, 7:12; De Graffenried Papers, 1711–1712, Folder 1, Miscellaneous Papers, TPP; *CVGA*, 287; Dill, "Eighteenth Century New Bern," 22 (Apr. 1945): 165–67.

18. Lawson, *New Voyage*, xxviii; *CVGA*, 63, 111, 287, 377; Dill, "Eighteenth Century New Bern," 22 (Apr. 1945): 170–71, 173–75; Lefler and Powell, *Colonial North Carolina*, 68.

19. Dill, "Eighteenth Century New Bern," 22 (July 1945): 173–75, 297–98; *CVGA*, 297–98, 306, 311, 313–14, 372–73.

20. *CVGA*, 310–11.

21. Quote from *CVGA*, 256; Dill, "Eighteenth Century New Bern," 22 (July 1945): 197.

22. Holloman, "Palatines and Tuscaroras," 21–22; Lefler and Powell, *Colonial North Carolina*, 64–68; Dill, "Eighteenth Century New Bern," 22 (Apr. 1945): 170–71; *CVGA*, 72–73, 287, 314–16, 316–20.

23. *CVGA*, 312.

24. Ibid., 313.

25. Ibid., 301.

26. Towles, "Cary's Rebellion," 49–50; Dill, "Eighteenth Century New Bern," 22 (Apr. 1945): 296–97.

27. *CVGA*, 74–75; Dill, "Eighteenth Century New Bern," 22 (Apr. 1945): 296–98; Letter from President and Council to Governor of Virginia, June 29, 1711, *CRNC2*, 7:438–39.

28. DGM, 982–84.

29. *CVGA*, 374.

30. Ibid., 374–75.

31. DGM, 981–82.

32. Ibid., 984.

33. Dill, "Eighteenth Century New Bern," 22 (Jan. 1945): 7–9; 22 (July 1945): 301, 301 n. 44; Smallwood, "Three Cultures," 70; Holloman, "Tuscarora Towns," 30.

34. *CVGA*, 376–77.

35. Ibid., 380–81; DGM, 922–23.

36. *CVGA*, 376–77.

37. Lawson, *New Voyage*, xv–xviii.

38. Ibid., xviii, 15–67; Seaman, "John Lawson," 10.

39. Lawson, *New Voyage*, 13, 15–67, 67 n. 80, Map "Lawson's Long Trail," x; Watson, Latham, and Samford, *Bath*, 12–13.

40. Lawson, *New Voyage*, 23–24, 38–39, 45, 62, 66–67, 206–7; Hudson, *Southeastern Indians*, 421–25; Rights, "Trading Path to the Indians," 413–17.

41. Lawson, *New Voyage*, 18–19.

42. Ibid., 46–47, 189–92, 194–95; Fischer, *Suspect Relations*, 71–74.

43. Lawson, *New Voyage*, 49–50, 53, 55.

44. Ibid., 49–50; Rights, "Trading Path to the Indians," 413.

45. Lawson, *New Voyage*, xx–xxiv, 132–33; From John Lawson to Mr. Tobias Knight, Secretary, Aug. 7, 1705, *NCHGR* 3 (Apr. 1903): 266; Haun, *CPCNC*, 4; Watson, Latham, and Samford, *Bath*, 9–12; Ludwell and Harrison, "Boundary Line Proceedings," 6–7.

46. Lawson, *New Voyage*, 69.

47. Ibid., 70.

48. Ibid.

49. Ibid., 170.

50. Ibid., xliv, 214–15; Colonial Records, Aug. 4, 1709, *CRNC*, 1:717; Seaman, "John Lawson," 10–11.

51. Lawson, *New Voyage,* 87, 92–93, 132–33, 221, 243, 245–46.

52. Seaman, "John Lawson," 18, 24–25.

53. Lawson, *New Voyage,* 243–44.

54. Ibid., 208–9.

55. *CVGA,* 226; Dill, "Eighteenth Century New Bern," 22 (Apr. 1945): 164.

56. DGM, 925.

57. Ibid., 925–26; Lawson, *New Voyage,* xxxi.

58. DGM, 926.

59. Letter of Major Christopher Gale, Nov. 2, 1711, Miscellaneous Folder, HP.

60. DGM, 925; Lawson, *New Voyage,* xxxi; McDowell, "John Barnwell and the Tuscaroras," 4; Holloman, "Tuscarora Towns," 16; Lee, *Indian Wars,* 23.

61. DGM, 926; *CVGA,* 264.

62. *CVGA,* 264; McDowell, "John Barnwell," 6.

63. DGM, 926.

64. Extract of a Letter from Baron de Graffenried to Edward Hyde, Esq. Governor of North Carolina, c. Oct. 1711, *CRNC,* 1:990–91; *CVGA,* 264; DGM, 926.

65. Quote from DGM, 927; *CVGA,* 265.

CHAPTER 2

1. Johnson, *Tuscaroras,* 1:41, 2:23; Milling, *Red Carolinians,* 113.

2. Johnson, *Tuscaroras,* 1:9, 50–51, 58; Byrd and Heath, "The Country," 99–100.

3. Boyce, "Iroquoian Tribes," 282–83; Lee, "Fortify, Fight, or Flee," 724–26.

4. Lawson, *New Voyage,* 192–95, 240; Johnson, *Tuscaroras,* 1:227; Smallwood, "Three Cultures," 21, 53–54.

5. Lawson, *New Voyage,* 29, 124, 215–17; Boyce, "Iroquoian Tribes," 283–84; Byrd, *William Byrd's Histories,* 286; Lee, *Indian Wars,* 8–9; Hudson, *Southeastern Indians,* 275–77.

6. Lawson, *New Voyage,* 217; Hudson, *Southeastern Indians,* 261–67; Archdale, *New Description,* 7.

7. Archdale, *New Description,* 7; Cecelski, *Waterman's Song,* 9–10; Lawson, *New Voyage,* 218–19; Johnson, *Tuscaroras,* 2:10; Boyce, "Iroquoian Tribes," 283–84; Byrd and Heath, "The Country," 101.

8. Boyce, "Iroquoian Tribes," 284; Perdue and Oakley, *Native Carolinians,* 16, 20; Perdue, *Cherokee Women*; Rountree, *Pocahontas, Powhatan, Opechancanough,* 12–15; Lee, *Indian Wars,* 8–9; Hudson, *Southeastern Indians,* 258–316.

9. Boyce, "Iroquoian Tribes," 285; Herndon, "Indian Agriculture," 284–88, 291–96; Hudson, *Southeastern Indians,* 258–316.

10. Lawson, *New Voyage,* 36, 176, 216; Herndon, "Indian Agriculture," 294–96, 294–97.

11. Lawson, *New Voyage,* 242; Boyce, "Iroquoian Tribes," 282–83; Lee, "Fortify, Fight, or Flee," 725–26; Boyce, "Tuscarora Confederacy," 30, 38; Dill, "Eighteenth Century New Bern," 22 (Jan. 1945): 7–9; 22 (July 1945): 301, 301 n. 44; Smallwood, "Three Cultures," 70.

12. Boyce, "Iroquoian Tribes," 283; Lee, *Indian Wars*, 9; Lawson, *New Voyage*, 204–6; Johnson, *Tuscaroras*, 1:228, 230; Boyce, "Tuscarora Confederacy," 35; Perdue and Oakley, *Native Carolinians*, 22–24.

13. Byrd and Heath, "The Country," 104–7, 124–25; Boyce, "Iroquoian Tribes," 283; Smallwood, "Three Cultures," 63; Lawson, *New Voyage*, 242.

14. Parramore, "With Tuscarora Jack," 120–22, 120 n. 15, 121 n. 22.

15. Byrd and Heath, "The Country," 114, 121–25; Boyce, "Iroquoian Tribes," 283; Byrd and Heath, "Rediscovery," 45–48.

16. Lawson, *New Voyage*, 242.

17. Byrd and Heath, "The Country," 102; Smallwood, "Three Cultures," 31–32, 32 n. 52.

18. Archdale, *New Description*, 2, 29; Lawson, *New Voyage*, 232–33, 242–43; Watson, Latham, and Samford, *Bath*, 5; Silver, *New Face*, 92.

19. DGM, 979.

20. Quote from Archdale, *New Description*, 21; Lawson, *New Voyage*, 107; Johnson, *Tuscaroras*, 1:96, 221.

21. Lawson, *New Voyage*, 201, 231; Johnson, *Tuscaroras*, 1:233–34; Boyce, "Iroquoian Tribes," 285; Eid, "'A Kind of Running Fight.'"

22. Lawson, *New Voyage*, 207.

23. Ibid., 205.

24. Ibid., 233–40; Johnson, *Tuscaroras*, 1:6–7, 2:9, 61; Silver, *New Face*, 72; Yeardley, "Francis Yeardley's Narrative," 27–28.

25. Harriot, "Briefe and True Report," 371; Oberg, "Gods and Men."

26. Rights, "Trading Path," 417; Boyce, "Tuscarora Confederacy," 31; Smallwood, "Three Cultures," 66; Johnson, *Tuscaroras*, 2:45, 47; Wright, *Only Land*, 105, 107.

27. Rights, "Trading Path to the Indians," 406; Lawson, *New Voyage*, 64; Seaman, "John Lawson," 13–14, 19–20; Boyce, "Tuscarora Confederacy," 37–38.

28. Lawson, *New Voyage*, 33, 63; Lee, *Indian Wars*, 10–13.

29. Lawson, *New Voyage*, 211–12, 232–33; Archdale, *New Description*, 8.

30. Virginia Council, Oct. 19, 1708, *CRNC*, 1:691; Representation to the Lords Proprietors, c. 1709, *CRNC*, 1:259; Archdale, *New Description*, 7–8; Lee, *Indian Wars*, 18; Seaman, "John Lawson," 20.

31. Silver, *New Face*, 190; Kupperman, "English Perception of Treachery," 263–87.

32. Instructions given by us the Lords Proprietor of Carolina, Nov. 21, 1676, *CRNC*, 1:230–31; Lawson, *New Voyage*, 220; Lee, *Indian Wars*, 16.

33. Letter of Henderson Walker, Nov. 8, 1699, *CRNC*, 1:515; Nov. 18, 1699, *CRNC*, 1:517; Minutes of the Council of Virginia, Apr. 24, 1703, *CRNC*, 1:570; Letter from Col. Hyde, Jan. 21, 1711, *CRNC*, 1:751; Diary of Bishop Spangenburg, Nov. 12, 1752, *CRNC*, 5:6; Stannard, "Letters of William Byrd, First," 281; Kupperman, "English Perception of Treachery," 264–68.

34. Complaint of John King, an Indian, Oct. 1, 1695, *CRNC2*, 2:178; Nov. 27, 1695, *CRNC2*, 2:207.

35. Council Minutes, Nov. 28, 1694, *CRNC*, 1:432; Complaint of Chowan Indians, Nov. 28, 1694, *CRNC2*, 2:95; General Court, Oct. 6, 1697, *CRNC2*, 3:80; Order to Lay Out the Reservation for the Yawpim Indians, Apr. 12, 1704, *NCHGR* 3 (Jan. 1903):

73–74; Petition of Chowan Indians Relating to Their Reservation, c. 1705, *NCHGR* 3 (Jan. 1903): 75–76; Journal of the Virginia Council. Sept. 2, 1707, *CRNC*, 1:667–71; *CVGA*, 78–79; Lawson, *New Voyage*, 64; Stannard, "Letters of William Byrd, First," 28; Byrd, *Secret Diary*, 400, 405; Towles, "Cary's Rebellion," 52; Johnson, *Tuscaroras*, 2:48–49; Stevenson, "Indian Reservations," 28–30; LeMaster, "Into the 'Scolding Houses.'"

36. Lawson, *New Voyage*, 175; General Court, Apr.–June 1697, *CRNC2*, 3:40; Lear Estate, Apr.–Jun. 1697, *CRNC2*, 3:62; Estate of Colonel Lear, Mar. 1701, *CRNC2*, 3:435; William Thirrell's Estate, General Court, Oct.–Nov. 1697, *CRNC2*, 3:91–92; Sale of Goods by William Duckenfield, Oct. 20, 1705, *CRNC2*, 4:204; William Frayly v. William Hancock, Apr. 15, 1702, *CRNC2*, 4:36; Court Records, Feb. 1694, *CRNC*, 1:393–94; Council Minutes, Oct. 10, 1704, *CRNC*, 1:613; Council Minutes, Jan. 6, 1706, *CRNC*, 1:650; Gallay, *Indian Slave Trade*, 311–14.

37. Lawson, *New Voyage*, 79–80; Seaman, "John Lawson," 27–28; Gallay, *Indian Slave Trade*, 60–63.

38. Klingberg, *Le Jau*, 41.

39. Perdue, *Slavery*, 23.

40. The best work on this topic is Gallay's award-winning *Indian Slave Trade*. See Table 2, 299; *Boston News-Letter*, no. 395, Nov. 5 to Nov. 12, 1711; Klingberg, *Le Jau*, 116.

41. Kelton, *Epidemics and Enslavement*.

42. Oakley, "Indian Slave Trade."

43. Council Held at Philadelphia, Nov. 20, 1705, Jan. 12, 1705/06, *MPCP*, 2:212, 231; Seaman, "John Lawson," 17–18; Smallwood, "Three Cultures," 67.

44. Report of John French and Henry Worley, July 8, 1710, *MPCP*, 2:511–12.

45. Ibid.

46. Seaman, "John Lawson," 22–23.

47. Saraydar, "No Longer Shall You Kill," 20–21; Richter, *Ordeal of the Longhouse*, 1, 3, 32.

48. Jennings, *Ambiguous Iroquois Empire*, 94; Saraydar, "No Longer Shall You Kill," 25–26.

49. Shannon, *Iroquois Diplomacy*, 43, 68–69; Jennings, *Ambiguous Iroquois Empire*, 101–2, 114–15, 170, 175.

50. Shannon, *Iroquois Diplomacy*, 50–53, 66, 70–71; Jennings, *Ambiguous Iroquois Empire*, 176–77, 195–203, 210; Richter, *Ordeal of the Longhouse*, 106–29, 162–77, 189, 190–204.

51. Richter, *Ordeal of the Longhouse*, 31–35; Aquila, "Down the Warrior's Path."

52. Aquila, "Down the Warrior's Path," 212–13; Shannon, *Iroquois Diplomacy*, 50–53; Lawson, *New Voyage*, 174.

53. Lawson, *New Voyage*, 49.

54. Ibid., 50.

55. Ibid., 53.

56. Ibid., 207–8.

57. Barnwell, "Tuscarora Expedition," 35.

58. Fenton, *Great Law*, 378; Shannon, *Iroquois Diplomacy*, 64; Seaman, "John Lawson," 20–21; Milling, *Red Carolinians*, 114.

59. Lawson, *New Voyage*, 63–64, 174, 242–43; Holloman, "Tuscarora Towns," 30.

60. Lawson, *New Voyage*, 242; Dill, "Eighteenth Century New Bern," 22 (July 1945): 301, 301 n. 44.

61. Chancery Court, c. 1697, *CRNC2*, 3:511–12.

62. Archdale, *New Description*, 3–4.

63. Lee, *Indian Wars*, 19–20, 23; Johnson, *Tuscaroras*, 2:56; Holloman, "Tuscarora Towns," 16, 30; Dill, "Eighteenth Century New Bern," 22 (July 1945): 301, 301 n. 44.

64. Le Jau to Secretary, Mar. 19, 1716, *CRNC2*, 10:216; Lawson to Mr. Tobias Knight, *NCHGR* 3 (Apr. 1903): 266; Lawson, *New Voyage*, 209, 219, 242–43; Garrow, *Mattamuskeet Documents*, 4–5, 14–18; Holloman, "Tuscarora Towns," 30.

65. Quote from Petition of Lyonell Reading et al., Feb. 29, 1704, *NCHGR* 2 (Apr. 1901): 194; Lawson, *New Voyage*, 211, 242–43.

66. Quote from Miscellaneous Records, 1678–1737, C.002–10001, ACP, 1:114; Henderson Walker, May 14, 1701, *NCHGR* 1 (Oct. 1900): 597; Articles of Agreement with the Bay River Indians, Sept. 23, 1699, *NCHGR* 1 (Oct. 1900): 598–99; John Lawson to Governor Henderson Walker, June 23, 1701, *NCHGR* 1 (Oct. 1900): 598; Petition of Lyonell Reading et al., Feb. 29, 1704, *NCHGR* 2 (Apr. 1901): 194.

67. Lawson, *New Voyage*, 220, 242–43; Seaman, "John Lawson," 16–17, 24; Garrow, *Mattamuskeet Documents*, 16–18; Bath, NC, c. 1693, *NCHGR* 3 (Jan. 1903): 21; Gallay, *Indian Slave Trade*, 213; Lee, *Indian Wars*, 21; Dill, "Eighteenth Century New Bern," 22 (Jan. 1945): 5; Smallwood, "Three Cultures," 73.

68. DGM, 927; *NCHGR* 1 (July 1900): 442, 510; Land Records, Mar. 5, 1697, BCLDR, 1.

69. Spotswood to Lord Dartmouth, July 28, 1711, *CRNC*, 1:796–97.

70. *CVGA*, 265.

71. DGM, 927.

72. Ibid., 928.

73. Ibid., 991.

74. Ibid., 927.

75. Ibid., 928.

76. Ibid.

77. Ibid., 929.

78. Quote from ibid., 928; *CVGA*, 266, 269; Council Journal, Oct. 27, 1726, *CRNC*, 2:644.

79. DGM, 928.

80. *CVGA*, 266.

81. DGM, 929.

82. Ibid.

83. Ibid.

84. Capt. Brents ltr to His Excellency abt Indians, Jun. 29, 1697, PCM, 23:187–88; Whitford, "On the Trail of Tom."

85. Whitford, "On the Trail of Tom."

86. DGM, 929.

87. *CVGA*, 267; DGM, 929–30.

88. DGM, 931.

89. Ibid., 931–32.

90. Ibid., 932.

91. Ibid., 932–33.

92. Ibid., 933.

93. Ibid.

94. Letter of Major Christopher Gale, Nov. 2, 1711, HP.

95. Byrd, *Histories of the Dividing Line*, 290.

96. DGM, 933.

97. Hudson, *Southeastern Indians*, 224.

98. DGM, 933.

CHAPTER 3

1. Letter of Major Christopher Gale, Nov. 2, 1711, HP.

2. Memorial of Christopher Gale, Nov. 2, 1711, *CRNC*, 1:828; Clark, *Indian Massacre*, 3; Rountree, *Pocahontas, Powhatan, Opechancanough*, 214; Edwards, "Indians Massacre."

3. Johnson, *Tuscaroras*, 2:5–6; Clark, *Indian Massacre*, 6–7; Dill, "Eighteenth Century New Bern," 22 (July 1945): 311; Kupperman, "English Perception of Treachery," 272; DGM, 933.

4. Johnson, *Tuscaroras*, 2:89–90; Grimes, "Notes," 101.

5. Petition of Furnifold Green, Mar. 15, 1756, *CRNC2*, 9:21.

6. Council Journal, July 31, 1712, *CRNC*, 1:864.

7. Earnest, *John and William Bartram*, 6.

8. Council Journal, Aug. 1, 1717, *CRNC*, 1:289–90, 303.

9. Edwards, "Indians Massacre"; Dew, "Descendant of Koonce Family."

10. Charles Eden to the SPG, Oct. 8, 1714, *CRNC2*, 10:186–87.

11. Letter of Major Christopher Gale, Nov. 2, 1711, HP.

12. LeMaster, "Tuscarora Massacre Revisited."

13. Johnson, *Tuscaroras*, 2:90; Council Minutes, Mar. 10, 1715, *CRNC2*, 7:52; Watson, Latham, and Samford, *Bath*, 19–20; Dill, "Eighteenth Century New Bern," 22 (July 1945): 317; Holloman, "Palatines and Tuscaroras," 28.

14. Watson, Latham, and Samford, *Bath*, 19–20; Johnson, *Tuscaroras*, 2:90–91; McIlvenna, *Very Mutinous People*, 149.

15. Johnson, *Tuscaroras*, 2:5–7, 90; Lee, "Fortify, Fight, or Flee," 717–23, 731–33.

16. Letter of Major Christopher Gale, Nov. 2, 1711, HP.

17. Ffarnifull Green to Friend, Oct. 26, 1711, *CRNC*, 1:815.

18. DGM, 941; *CVGA*, 235, 240.

19. To Council of Trade, Oct. 15, 1711, ASP, Letterbook, 26–28; Johnson, *Tuscaroras*, 2:90; Byrd and Heath, "The Country," 102–3.

20. To ye Right Honorable Alexander Spotswood, c. Oct. 1711, *CRNC*, 1:819.

21. To Council of Trade, Oct. 15, 1711, ASP, 26–28; Memorial of Christopher Gale, Nov. 2, 1711, *CRNC*, 1:828.

22. Spotswood to the Council of Trade, Virginia, Feb. 8, 1712, *CSPCAWI*, 26:211–30 (#301).

23. To Council of Trade, Oct. 15, 1711, ASP, 26–28.

24. Byrd, *Secret Diary*, 417.

25. *Boston News-Letter*, no. 397, Nov. 19 to Nov. 26, 1711.

26. *London Gazette*, no. 4995, Apr. 22, 1712.

27. Thomas Pollock Letter, Mar. 6, 1712/13, *CRNC*, 2:24.

28. DGM, 922.

29. Quotes from Lefler and Powell, *Colonial North Carolina*, 67.

30. Barnwell, "Tuscarora Expedition," 35.

31. Watson, Latham, and Samford, *Bath*, 18–19; Lefler and Powell, *Colonial North Carolina*, 67; Seaman, "John Lawson," 11, 27–28; Smallwood, "Three Cultures," 69; Perdue and Oakley, *Native Carolinians*, 24–26; Lawson, *New Voyage*, 209; Oakley, "Indian Slave Trade."

32. Lefler and Powell, *Colonial North Carolina*, 68; Towles, "Cary's Rebellion," 51–52; Clark, *Indian Massacre*, 4; Smallwood, "Three Cultures," 69.

33. DGM, 922.

34. Ibid., 978.

35. Edward Hyde to Your Lordships, Aug. 22, 1711, *CRNC*, 1:802.

36. Virginia Proclamation, July 24, 1711, *CRNC*, 1:776–77.

37. DGM, 920.

38. Letter of Tho. Pollock, Apr. 30, 1713, *CRNC*, 2:40.

39. Rev. Miles Gale to Archbishop of York, Aug. 26, 1712, *CRNC2*, 10:146.

40. Lords Proprietor to the Council of Trade, St. James Square, Dec. 4, 1711, *CSPCAWI*, 26:171–85 (#202).

41. Quote from Johnson, *Tuscaroras*, 2:60.

42. *CVGA*, 81, 228; Seaman, "John Lawson," 23; McIlvenna, *Very Mutinous People*, 144, 150, 189–90; Milling, *Red Carolinians*, 114–15; Clark, *Indian Massacre*, 4; Towles, "Cary's Rebellion," 52; Kupperman, "English Perception of Treachery," 283–84.

43. Letter of Tho. Pollock, Apr. 30, 1713, *CRNC*, 2:41.

44. Lee, *Indian Wars*, 24.

45. DGM, 922.

46. *CVGA*, 239.

47. Barnwell, "Tuscarora Expedition," 35; Milling, *Red Carolinians*, 115.

48. Quoted from Gallay, *Indian Slave Trade*, 265, from *Boston News-Letter*, no. 415, Mar. 24 to Mar. 31, 1712.

49. To Council of Trade, Feb. 8, 1712, ASP, 32–33.

50. Hunter to the Council of Trade, New York, June 23, 1712, *CSPCAWI*, 26:293–310 (#454).

51. Fenton, *Great Law*, 382–83; Watson, Latham, and Samford, *Bath*, 19; Council Minutes, July 31, 1712, *CRNC*, 1:866.

52. DGM, 933–34.

53. Ibid., 933.

54. Ibid., 934.

55. Ibid., 980; emphasis in the original.

56. Journal of the Virginia Council, Oct. 8, 1711, *CRNC*, 1:808; Spotswood to the Council of Trade, Virginia, Oct. 15, 1711, *CSPCAWI*, 26:110–33 (#120); Byrd, *Secret Diary*, 418.

57. Quote from DGM, 936; Byrd, *Secret Diary*, 417–18.

58. DGM, 937.

59. Ibid., 938–39.

60. Ibid.

61. Ibid., 940, 980.

62. Ibid., 935; Gallay, *Indian Slave Trade*, 264.

63. DGM, 935–36.

64. Ibid., 936.

65. Ibid., 940.

66. Ibid., 923.

67. Ibid., 923–24.

68. Spotswood to Council of Trade, Virginia, Oct. 15, 1711, *CSPCAWI*, 26:110–33 (#120); Byrd, *Secret Diary*, 422–23.

69. Byrd, *Secret Diary*, 423.

70. Ibid., 424.

71. Ibid.

72. Quote from Virginia Council Oct. 24, 1711, *CRNC*, 1:815; Spotswood to the Board of Trade, Nov. 7, 1711, *CRNC*, 1:817; Byrd, *Secret Diary*, 425; Boyce, "Tuscarora Confederacy," 33.

73. Virginia Council, Oct. 24, 1711, *CRNC*, 1:815.

74. Seaman, "John Lawson," 13–14, 18; Boyce, "Tuscarora Confederacy," 36–37.

75. General Court, Nov. 1, 1711; *CRNC2*, 5:17; Letter of Major Christopher Gale, Nov. 2, 1711, HP; Clark, *Indian Massacre*, 6, 9; Byrd, *Secret Diary*, 441; Dill, "Eighteenth Century New Bern," 22 (July 1945): 312.

76. Deposition of William Brice, London, Feb. 1, 1700, *CSPCAWI*, 18:46–59 (#71iv); Petition of Daniel Smith, Whitehall, Aug. 22, 1700, *CSPCAWI*, 18:489–94 (#730i); Affidavit of Samuel Day, Bermuda, Apr. 4, 1699, *CSPCAWI*, 17:124–30 (#235); Charge of Mr. Brice, London, Feb. 28, 1700, *CSPCAWI*, 18:83–99 (#164).

77. Apr. 1, 1701, BCLDR, 2; Watson, Latham, and Samford, *Bath*, 6.

78. Dec. 1, 1701, BCLDR, 8; Apr. 14, 1702, BCLDR, 16; Jun. 22, 1702, BCLDR, 34; Oct. 1, 1702, BCLDR, 24; Dill, "Eighteenth Century New Bern," 22 (Jan. 1945): 10–11.

79. Higher-Court Records, Apr.15, 1702, *CRNC2*, 4:35. That the document actually used the term "sheriff" is unusual and unaccountable as the proprietors abolished the office of county sheriff in 1694 and replaced it with provost marshal. It would not be until 1739 that the office of sheriff was revived. See McCain, *County Court in North Carolina*, 12.

80. Dec. 29, 1702, BCLDR, 34; Grimes, *Abstract*, 46.

81. Dill, "Eighteenth Century New Bern," 22 (Jan. 1945): 7–9; Apr. 4, 1704, BCLDR, 35.

82. Quotes from Petition to Deputy Governor and Council, ca. 1703–5, *CRNC2*, 7:396–97; Dill, "Eighteenth Century New Bern," 22 (Jan. 1945): 7–9.

83. Address to the Governor and Council, Feb. 29, 1704, *CRNC2*, 7:401–2.

84. Acts Passed in North Carolina, 1711, CR, 1:791–94; Dill, "Eighteenth Century New Bern," 22 (July 1945): 317; 22 (Jan. 1945): 16–17; Reed, *Beaufort County*, 61; Grimes, "Notes," 101; July 7, 1702, BCLDR, 12, 26; Jan. 5, 1704, BCLDR, 26; c. Jan. 23, 1710, CPCNC, 4; Higher-Court Records, Feb. 16, 1706, *CRNC2*, 4:365; Jan. 20, 1708, CPCNC, 6–7.

85. Petition of ye Inhabitants of Nuse River for a Court, c. 1706, *NCHGR* 1 (July 1900): 442; Higher-Court Records, Aug. 9, 1711, *CRNC2*, 5:14; Higher-Court Records, Mar. 28, 1705, *CRNC2*, 4:146; Higher-Court Records, Oct. 10, 1705, *CRNC2*, 4:174; Higher-Court Records, Nov. 3, 1705, *CRNC2*, 4:201–2; Higher-Court Records, May 8, 1706, *CRNC2*, 4:225; Higher-Court Records, Mar. 27, 1707, *CRNC2*, 4:337.

86. Lefler and Powell, *Colonial North Carolina*, 66; Dill, "Eighteenth Century New Bern," 22 (July 1945): 302–4; DGM, 991.

87. Lawson, *New Voyage*, 210.

88. Executive Council Papers, ca. 1695–1705, *CRNC2*, 7:372; Petition of William Brice Relating to Thomas Blount, an Indian, no date, *NCHGR* 3 (Jan. 1903): 81–82; Sale of an Indian by William Brice, Mar. 5, 1711, *NCHGR* 3 (Apr. 1903): 270.

89. To ye Right Honorable Alexander Spotswood, c. Sept.-Oct. 1711, *CRNC*, 1:820.

90. Petition of the Palatines, July 13, 1747, *CRNC*, 4:956; DGM, 938–39; *CRNC*, 1:949; Holloman, "Expeditionary Forces," 15; Watson, Latham, and Samford, *Bath*, 20; Lee, "Fortify, Fight, or Flee," 734.

91. DGM, 939.

92. *Boston News-Letter*, no. 397, Nov. 19 to Nov. 26, 1711.

93. DGM, 949.

94. Johnson, *Tuscaroras*, 2:95–96.

95. Quote from DGM, 925; *CVGA*, 262.

96. Executive Council Minutes, Mar. 12, 1712, *CRNC2*, 7:10–11; DGM, 941.

97. DGM, 942.

98. Ibid., 949; Spotswood to the Board of Trade, Feb. 8, 1712, *CRNC*, 1:834–35.

99. DGM, 947–48; Dill, "Eighteenth Century New Bern," 22 (July 1945): 311.

100. DGM, 942–43.

101. Ibid., 944; Dill, "Eighteenth Century New Bern," 22 (July 1945): 311.

102. Quote in DGM, 946; *CVGA*, 238; Johnson, *Tuscaroras*, 2:96; Lefler and Powell, *Colonial North Carolina*, 71–72.

103. *CVGA*, 238.

104. DGM, 946.

105. Ibid., 949.

106. Ibid., 971.

107. Ibid., 925.

108. Ibid., 952; Dill, "Eighteenth Century New Bern," 22 (July 1945): 313; Byrd and Heath, "The Country," 102–3.

109. An Act for the Raising the Sum of Four Thousand Pounds, Nov. 10, 1711, *CRNC*, 2:883.

110. Council Minutes, Nov. 1711, HP.

111. DGM, 953; McIlvenna, *Very Mutinous People*, 150.

112. Records of the Friends Month Meeting in Pasquotank Precinct, Oct. 9, 1711, *CRNC*, 1:813.

113. Council Minutes, Apr. 7, 1714, *CRNC*, 2:125.

114. DGM, 953.

115. To the Honble Alexander Spotswood, c. Feb. 1712, *CRNC*, 1:837–38; Lefler and Powell, *Colonial North Carolina*, 72.

116. Byrd, *Secret Diary*, 455; Council of Trade and Plantations to the Earl of Dartmouth, Whitehall, Dec. 6, 1711, *CSPCAWI*, 26:171–85 (#204).

117. Byrd, *Secret Diary*, 450–52, 478; To Council of Trade, Dec. 28, 1711, ASP, 31–32.

118. Lee, "Fortify, Fight, or Flee," 735; Byrd, *Secret Diary*, 482.

CHAPTER 4

1. Johnson, *Tuscaroras*, 2:101; Ashe, *Biographical History*, 1:292.

2. Klingberg, *Le Jau*, 104.

3. Memorial of Christopher Gale, Nov. 3, 1711, *CRNC*, 1:827–29; Ashe, *Biographical History*, 1:292; Parramore, "With Tuscarora Jack," 118.

4. Barnwell, *American Family*, 1–2.

5. Wright, *Only Land*, 108–9; Roper, *Conceiving Carolina*, 51–67.

6. Wright, *Only Land*, 108–11.

7. Gallay, *Indian Slave Trade*, 311–12; Wright, *Only Land*, 110–11; Silver, *New Face*, 92; Roper, *Conceiving Carolina*, 51–67; *JCIT*, x; *PRSC*, 1:26.

8. Aug. 3, 1711, *JCIT*, viii, 13–16; Wright, *Only Land*, 115–17; Gallay, *Indian Slave Trade*, 213–34, 242; Oatis, *Colonial Complex*, 35, 54–56.

9. Journal of South Carolina Assembly, Oct. 26, 1711, *CRNC*, 1:821; Gallay, *Indian Slave Trade*, 213–34.

10. House Minutes, Oct. 27, 1711, Book Oct. 10, 1712–June 7, 1712, SCCHJ.

11. Journal of South Carolina House Assembly, Nov. 2, 1711, *CRNC*, 1:822; House Minutes, Nov. 2, 1711, Book Oct. 10, 1712–June 7, 1712, SCCHJ; Gallay, *Indian Slave Trade*, 260; McDowell, "John Barnwell," BDC, 5, 7; Wright, *Only Land*, 119; Klingberg, *Carolina Chronicle*, 103.

12. Lee, *Indian Wars*, 26; Gallay, *Indian Slave Trade*, 197; Milling, *Red Carolinians*, 118.

13. Gallay, *Indian Slave Trade*, 287, 291.

14. Wright, *Only Land*, 119.

15. House Minutes, Nov. 3, 1711, SSCHJ.

16. Heraldry Coat of Arms Folder, Barnwell File, 30–04, SCHS; Eilers, "Barnwell Coat-of-Arms," 146; Heyward, *Genealogical Chart*.

17. Quote from Barnwell, *American Family*, 1; Edgar and Bailey, *Biographical Directory*, 2:52–54.

18. Edgar and Bailey, *Biographical Directory*, 2:52–54; Barnwell, *American Family*, 1–3; Salley, "Barnwell," 46–51; Eilers, "Barnwell Coat-of-Arms," 146; McDowell, "John Barnwell," BDC, 3.

19. Edgar and Bailey, *Biographical Directory*, 2:52–54; Barnwell, *American Family*, 3–5; "Extracts from 'Sketch of John Barnwell' written by Joseph W. Barnwell, 1898," Letterbook 1708–1860, 25-186-4, Barnwell Family Papers, SCHS, 9.

20. Barnwell, *American Family*, 5; Eilers, "Barnwell Coat-of-Arms," 146; Gallay, *Indian Slave Trade*, 260–61.

21. Journal of South Carolina House of Assembly, Nov. 3, 1711, *CRNC*, 1:823; House Minutes, Nov. 8, 1711, SCCHJ; House Minutes, Nov. 9, 1711, SCCHJ; Milling, *Red Carolinians*, 118.

22. Barnwell, "Tuscarora Expedition," 30–31, 36–37; Journal of South Carolina House of Assembly, Nov. 7, 1711, *CRNC*, 1:824; *CVGA*, 383; Gallay, *Indian Slave Trade*, 251, 267–68.

23. Parramore, "With Tuscarora Jack," 117–18.

24. Klingberg, *Le Jau*, 109.

25. Barnwell, "Tuscarora Expedition," 30; Gallay, *Indian Slave Trade*, 267–68; Barnwell, *American Family*, 5–7.

26. Quote from Barnwell, "Tuscarora Expedition," 31–32; Lee, *Indian Wars*, 27.

27. Barnwell, "Tuscarora Expedition," 32; Lee, "Fortify, Fight, or Flee," 735; Byrd and Heath, "Rediscovery," 40–42; Gallay, *Indian Slave Trade*, 267–68.

28. Byrd and Heath, "The Country," 114–24; Byrd and Heath, "Rediscovery," 40–42, 47.

29. Barnwell, "Tuscarora Expedition," 32.

30. Ibid.; Lee, "Fortify, Fight, or Flee," 735–36; Parramore, "With Tuscarora Jack," 118–20.

31. Barnwell, "Tuscarora Expedition," 32–33.

32. Ibid.; Parramore, "With Tuscarora Jack," 118–20; Gallay, *Indian Slave Trade*, 269–70.

33. Byrd, *Secret Diary*, 499.

34. Barnwell, "Tuscarora Expedition," 33–34.

35. Ibid., 33.

36. Ibid., 36–37; Gallay, *Indian Slave Trade*, 269–70; Milling, *Red Carolinians*, 119–21.

37. Barnwell, "Tuscarora Expedition," 35; Parramore, "With Tuscarora Jack," 119–20.

38. Barnwell, "Tuscarora Expedition," 34, 35, 37–38; Parramore, "With Tuscarora Jack," 119–20; Byrd and Heath, "Rediscovery," 40–42; Lee, "Fortify, Fight, or Flee," 735–36.

39. Barnwell, "Tuscarora Expedition," 35–38; Lefler and Powell, *Colonial North Carolina*, 74.

40. Barnwell, "Tuscarora Expedition," 38; Byrd and Heath, "Rediscovery," 42–43.

41. Barnwell, "Tuscarora Expedition," 35, 38–39.

42. Ibid., 39–40.

43. Ibid., 40.

44. Ibid.

45. Ibid., 40–41.

46. Council Minutes, Feb. 1712, *CRNC2*, 7:9.

47. Barnwell, "Tuscarora Expedition," 41; Council Minutes, Feb. 1712, *CRNC2*, 7:9; Parramore, "With Tuscarora Jack," 120–22.

48. Quotes from Barnwell, "Tuscarora Expedition," 35–36.

CHAPTER 5

1. Parramore, "With Tuscarora Jack," 129.

2. Pollock Genealogy, Nov. 28, 1733, Folder 2, Miscellaneous Papers, TPP; Copy of a letter sent to Sir Robert Pollock by Capt. Henderson's kinsman, Apr. 3, 1717, *CRNC*, 2:276–78; Towles, "Cary's Rebellion," 43; Ashe, *Biographical History*, 1:411; Powell, *Dictionary*, 5:116–17.

3. Pollock Genealogy, Nov. 28, 1733, Folder 2, Miscellaneous Papers, TPP; Copy of a letter from Deputy Governor, July 10, 1698, *NCHGR* 3 (Jan. 1903): 38; Copy of a letter to Mr. John Lawson, May 27, 1710, *CRNC*, 1:727–28; *NCHGR* 3 (Apr. 1903): 204, 283; Powell, *Dictionary*, 5:117; Towles, "Cary's Rebellion," 45.

4. Higher-Court Records, June 19, 1694, *CRNC2*, 2:103; Higher-Court Records, Sept. 19, 1694, *CRNC2*, 2:192; Court Meeting, Feb. 26, 1695, *CRNC*, 1:448; Higher-Court Records, June 24, 1695, *CRNC2*, 2:313; Higher-Court Records, Jan. 30, 1700, *CRNC2*, 3:394–95; Thomas Evens to Col. Pollock, July 15, 1701, *NCHGR* 1 (Oct. 1900): 557; Moody, "Massachusetts Trade, " 47–51; Towles, "Cary's Rebellion," 43–44, 44 n. 16.

5. Pollock v. John Bursbre, Jan. 19, 1687, *CRNC2*, 2:424; Pollock v. Stephen Scott, Dec. 14, 1687, *CRNC2*, 2:379; Pollock v. Capt. Richard Smith, Oct. 7, 1696, *CRNC2*, 2:321; Court Meeting, Mar. 1, 1695, *CRNC*, 1:452; Moody, "Massachusetts Trade," 52–53; Higher-Court Records, Nov. 1, 1704, *CRNC2*, 4:127–29; Higher-Court Records, Aug. 30, 1706, *CRNC2*, 4:281; Higher-Court Records, Oct. 30, 1706, *CRNC2*, 4:300; *NCHGR*, 3 (Apr. 1903): 244.

6. Higher-Court Records, May 28, 1697, *CRNC2*, 3:490; Grimes, "Notes," 139–40; Higher-Court Records, c. 1700, *CRNC2*, 3:513–14; Petition of Thomas Pollock, *NCHGR* 3 (Jan. 1903): 70–71.

7. Higher-Court Records, May 1697, *CRNC2*, 3:31; Higher-Court Records, Mar. 31, 1702, *CRNC2*, 4:7; Higher-Court Records, May 26, 1697, *CRNC2*, 3:10, 32; Higher-Court Records, Feb. 26, 1694, *CRNC2*, 2:133–34; Higher-Court Records, Mar. 11, 1695, *CRNC2*, 3:151, 438–40; July 1, 1702, BCLDR, 15; Higher-Court Records, June 26, 1707, *CRNC2*, 4:376–76; July 31, 1707, *CRNC2*, 4:357; Higher-Court Records, Dec. 3, 1696, *CRNC2*, 2:302; *NCHGR* 3 (Jan. 1903): 144; Higher-Court Records, May 25, 1697, *CRNC2*, 3:7.

8. Will of Col. Thomas Pollock, Aug. 8, 1721, *CRNC*, 22:290–94; Higher-Court Records, July 3, 1695, *CRNC2*, 2:171; Higher-Court Records, Jan. 8, 1704, *CRNC2*, 4:279; Grimes, "Notes," 139–40, 143, 146; Wolf, "Patents and Tithables," 267–68, 270.

9. Journal of the Virginia Council. Sept. 2, 1707, *CRNC*, 1:667–71; Towles, "Cary's Rebellion," 52; *CVGA*, 78–79; Warrant of Arrest, Mar. 7, 1695, *CRNC2*, 7:370; Letter from [Council] to [Governor], Sept. 6, 1694, *CRNC2*, 7:369.

10. Bill of Sale and Assignment, Jan. 12, 1708, *CRNC2*, 7:425–26; Moody, "Massachusetts Trade," 49.

11. Higher-Court Records, Mar. 1723, *CRNC2*, 5:359–60; Council Minutes, Dec. 31, 1718, *CRNC2*, 7:81; Council Journal, Aug. 3, 1716, *CRNC*, 2:240–41; Council Journal, Dec. 30, 1718, *CRNC*, 2:323.

12. Lords Proprietor to Governor Sothel, May 12, 1691, *CRNC*, 1:367–70; McIlvenna, *Very Mutinous People*, 80–82.

13. Chancery Court, 1694, *CRNC2*, 2:34, 270; Letter from [Council] to [Governor], Sept. 6, 1694, *CRNC2*, 7:369; General Court Records, Nov. 30, 1694, *CRNC*, 1:438; *NCHGR* 3 (Apr. 1903): 263; Ashe, *Biographical History*, 1:411–12; Towles, "Cary's Rebellion," 45.

14. Vestry Book, Nov. 12, 1701, *CRNC*, 1:543–45; Vestry Minutes, Nov. 29, 1701, *CRNC2*, 10:432; Vestry Minutes, Jan. 3, 1705, *CRNC2*, 10:439–40; Vestry Book, Sept. 9, 1705, *CRNC*, 1:615–17; Vestry Book, Jan. 3, 1706, *CRNC*, 1:630; Vestry Book, Apr. 18, 1706, *CRNC*, 1:679; Vestry Book, May 5, 1708, *CRNC*, 1:680; *NCHGR*, 1 (Apr. 1900): 256–67; Towles, "Cary's Rebellion," 44; Powell, *Dictionary*, 5:117.

15. Copy of a Letter to Mr. John Lawson, May 27, 1710, *CRNC*, 1:727.

16. A Copy of a Letter Sent to President Glover, Apr. 16, 1701, *CRNC*, 1:725–26; Towles, "Cary's Rebellion," 47–48; Pollock Letter Book, TPP.

17. A Copy of a Letter Sent to President Glover, Apr. 16, 1710, *CRNC*, 1:725–26; A Copy of a Letter Sent by Mr. Maule, Aug. 29, 1710, *CRNC*, 1:731; Letter from the President, June 29, 1711, *CRNC*, 1:760–61; Mr. Dennis to the Secretary, Sept. 3, 1711, *CRNC*, 1:803–4; Council Journal, May 9, 1712, *CRNC*, 1:841; Ashe, *Biographical History*, 1:411–12.

18. Quote from Council Minutes, Mar. 12, 1712, *CRNC2*, 7:11–12; Council Minutes, Feb. 1711, *CRNC2*, 7:9–10; Council Journal, Aug. 9, 1712, *CRNC*, 1:867; Clark, *Indian Massacre*, 12, 14; Lee, *Indian Wars*, 30; Towles, "Cary's Rebellion," 54; Clonts, "Travel and Transportation," 29.

19. Quote from Barnwell, "Tuscarora Expedition," 42; Council Minutes, Feb. 1712, *CRNC2*, 7:9; DGM, 954; Lee, *Indian Wars*, 28–29.

20. Pollock to Governor Craven, Feb. 20, 1713, *CRNC*, 2:20; Gallay, *Indian Slave Trade*, 271.

21. Council Minutes, Feb. 1712, *CRNC2*, 7:9–10.

22. Quote from Barnwell, "Tuscarora Expedition," 42; Parramore, "With Tuscarora Jack," 129.

23. Barnwell, "Tuscarora Expedition," 42.

24. Ibid.

25. Ibid., 43.

26. Ibid.; Byrd and Heath, "Tuscarora Homeland," 43–45.

27. Lee, "Fortify, Fight, or Flee," 728–31, 735–36, 739; Gallay, *Indian Slave Trade*, 272; Parramore, "With Tuscarora Jack," 129; Perdue, *Slavery*, 38–39.

28. Barnwell, "Tuscarora Expedition," 44; DGM, 955.

29. Barnwell, "Tuscarora Expedition," 44.

30. Ibid., 45.

31. Ibid.

32. Quotes from ibid., 46; Lee, "Fortify, Fight, or Flee," 736–37; Lefler and Powell, *Colonial North Carolina*, 75.

33. Quotes from Barnwell, "Tuscarora Expedition," 46; Parramore, "With Tuscarora Jack," 129–30.

34. Quote from Barnwell, "Tuscarora Expedition,"46–47; Milling, *Red Carolinians*, 123.

35. *Boston News-Letter*, no. 418, Apr. 14 to Apr. 21, 1712.

36. Barnwell, "Tuscarora Expedition," 47.

37. Ibid., 48.

38. Council Minutes, Mar. 12, 1712, *CRNC2*, 7:11.

39. Barnwell, "Tuscarora Expedition," 50; Spotswood to Council of Trade, Virginia, July 26, 1712, *CSPCAWI*, 27:1–20 (#25); Dill, "Eighteenth Century New Bern," 22 (July 1945): 311 n. 104; Towles, "Cary's Rebellion," 52–54.

40. Barnwell, "Tuscarora Expedition," 47; Milling, *Red Carolinians*, 123–24.

41. Barnwell, "Tuscarora Expedition," 47.

42. DGM, 954; Parramore, "With Tuscarora Jack," 131; Smallwood, "Three Cultures," 78.

43. Barnwell, "Tuscarora Expedition," 49.

44. Ibid., 49–51; Council Minutes, Apr. 12, 1712, *CRNC2*, 7:16.

45. Quotes from Barnwell, "Tuscarora Expedition," 50–51; DGM, 955; Milling, *Red Carolinians*, 124–25; Parramore, "With Tuscarora Jack," 131; Lee, *Indian Wars*, 29–30; Lefler and Powell, *Colonial North Carolina*, 76–77.

46. Barnwell, "Tuscarora Expedition," 49, 51; Spotswood to the Council, Virginia, July 26, 1712, *CSPCAWI*, 27:1–20 (#25); Byrd, *Secret Diary*, 521; Byrd and Heath, "The Country," 104.

47. Barnwell, "Tuscarora Expedition," 51.

48. Ibid., 51–52.

49. One wonders if this was the brother of Core Tom or of Sam. Hancock was not at Barnwell's second attack on the fort, so his brother would stand in his place. But where was Core Tom? He may have been killed in earlier actions, such as the Yamasee attack on Core Town. Or, and this is conjecture, he may have already been spirited out of the area by his Seneca allies.

50. Barnwell, "Tuscarora Expedition," 52–54; Milling, *Red Carolinians*, 126–27.

51. Quotes from Barnwell, "Tuscarora Expedition," 53–54; Johnson, *Tuscaroras*, 2:121; Gallay, *Indian Slave Trade*, 274 ; Parramore, "With Tuscarora Jack," 132–33.

52. *Boston News-Letter*, no. 426, June 9 to June 16, 1712.

53. Barnwell, "Tuscarora Expedition," 53–54.

54. Quote from *CVGA*, 244–45; Spotswood to the Council, Virginia, July 26, 1712, *CSPCAWI*, 27:1–20 (#25); A True Copy of a Letter to the Lords Proprietor, Sept. 20, 1712, *CRNC*, 1:873–76.

55. A True Copy of a Letter to the Lords Proprietor, Sept. 20, 1712, *CRNC*, 1:873–76. Historians accusing Barnwell of attacking the Cores include Thomas Parramore, "With Tuscarora Jack," 133–36, 135 n. 78; Lee, *Indian Wars*, 31; and Byrd and Heath, "The Country," 103. Those believing in Barnwell's innocence include Lefler and Powell, *Colonial North Carolina*, 77–78; and Gallay, *Indian Slave Trade*, 274–76, 408

n. 71. Those exonerating Barnwell say that the attack on the Cores started another round of attacks and so on June 2, when North Carolina asked South Carolina for additional help, their message did not mention Barnwell's attack on Core Town. And neither did any of Barnwell's men mention the attack on Core Town.

56. Hyde to Rainsford, May 30, 1712, *CRNC*, 1:850.

57. Spotswood to Council, Virginia, July 26, 1712, *CSPCAWI*, 27:1–20 (#25).

58. Map of Southeastern North America by John Barnwell, Map Collection, Box 15, Folder 16, Columbia, South Carolina Department of Archives and History; House Minutes, May 15, 1712, SCCHJ; House Minutes, Aug. 9, 1712, SCCHJ; Barnwell's Letter to Governor Hyde, Aug. 18, 1712, *CRNC*, 1:903; *Boston News-Letter*, no. 438, Sept. 8 to Sept. 15, 1712.

59. Quote from House Minutes, Aug. 8, 1712, SCCHJ; House Minutes, Aug. 9, 1712, SCCHJ.

CHAPTER 6

1. Spotswood to Council of Trade, Virginia, July 26, 1712, *CSPCAWI*, 27:1–20 (#25); Mooney, *Siouan Tribes*, 75.

2. Klingberg, *Le Jau*, 113–14.

3. Quote from DGM, 956; Gallay, *Indian Slave Trade*, 276–77; Lee, "Fortify, Fight, or Flee," 738–39; Parramore, "With Tuscarora Jack," 138.

4. Quotes from Rainsford letter to Chamberline, July 25, 1712, *CRNC*, 1:860; Spotswood to Council of Trade, July 26, 1712, ASP, 34; Lee, *Indian Wars*, 32; Gallay, *Indian Slave Trade*, 277.

5. Pollock to the Governor of South Carolina, c. Oct. 1712, *CRNC*, 1:881–82.

6. *Boston News-Letter*, no. 433, June 28 to July 4, 1712.

7. Quote from Council Journal, Sept. 12, 1712, *CRNC*, 1:870; Council Journal, May 10, 1712, *CRNC*, 1:843–44; A True Copy of a Letter to Lord Carteret, Sept. 20, 1712, *CRNC*, 1:876–78; Soldiers were impressed for the Indian War, 1711–1712, *NCHGR* 3 (Apr. 1093): 274–75; Hyde to Capt. Palin, Aug. 3, 1712, *NCHGR* 1 (July 1900): 438; Johnson, *Tuscaroras*, 2:126.

8. Quote from Hyde to [Earl of Dartmouth], North Carolina, July 20, 1712, *CSPCAWI*, 27:1–20 (#18); Council Minutes, July 31, 1712, *CRNC*, 1:866; A True Copy of a Letter to Lord Carteret, Sept. 20, 1712, *CRNC*, 1:876–78; Lee, *Indian Wars*, 32.

9. Quote from Pollock's Letterbook, Sept. 9, 1712, *CRNC*, 1:869; Council Minutes, Sept. 12, 1712, *CRNC*, 1:869; Council Minutes, Oct. 22, 1712, *CRNC*, 2:64–65; DGM, 966–68.

10. Urmston to the Bishop of London, Sept. 29, 1712, *CRNC2*, 10:148.

11. Quote from DGM, 971; Spotswood to Board of Trade, Feb. 8, 1712, *CRNC*, 1:835; Spotswood to the Council, Virginia, May 8, 1712, *CSPCAWI*, 26:272–93 (#408); Spotswood to the Council, Virginia, July 26, 1712, *CSPCAWI*, 27:1–20 (#25); Powell, *Dictionary*, 2:328.

12. Quote from Council Journal, June 2, 1712, *CRNC*, 1:852; Council Minutes, May 10, 1712, *CRNC2*, 7:18–19; Council Journal, Oct. 22, 1712, *CRNC*, 2:64; Council Minutes, Jan. 9, 1713, *CRNC2*, 7:33.

13. Council Minutes, July 31, 1712, *CRNC2*, 7:24.

14. Quote from Governor Hunter to the Council of Trade, New York, June 23, 1712, *CSPCAWI*, 26:293–310 (#454); Foster's Instructions, June 2, 1712, *CRNC*, 1:901; Spotswood to the Council, Virginia, July 26, 1712, *CSPCAWI*, 26:1–20 (#25); Fenton, *The Great Law*, 382–83; Gallay, *Indian Slave Trade*, 277–78.

15. Quote from Foster's Instructions, June 2, 1712, *CRNC*, 1:900; Council Journal, June 2, 1712, *CRNC*, 1:851.

16. Council Minutes, Sept. 12, 1712, *CRNC*, 1:871; Pollock to Governor of South Carolina, c. Oct. 1712, *CRNC*, 1:881.

17. Council Journal, May 10, 1712, *CRNC*, 1:843.

18. Quote from House Minutes, Dec. 11, 1712, SCCHJ; House Minutes, Dec. 3, 1712, SCCHJ.

19. House Minutes, Dec. 12, 1712, SCCHJ.

20. Pollock Letter Book, c. Oct. 1712, *CRNC*, 1:884.

21. House Minutes, Aug. 7, 1712, SCCHJ.

22. Quote from Spotswood to the Council, Virginia, July 26, 1712, *CSPCAWI*, 27:1–20 (#25); Spotswood to Board, May 8, 1712, *CRNC*, 1:839–41; Byrd, *Secret Diary*, 526.

23. Journal of the Virginia Council, Feb. 20, 1712, *CRNC*, 1:836–37; Spotswood to the Council of Trade, Virginia, May 8, 1712, *CSPCAWI*, 26:272–93 (#408); Byrd, *Secret Diary*, 501, 516–18, 520–21, 572.

24. Vestry Meeting, Dec. 15, 1702, *CRNC*, 1:560; Johnson, *Tuscaroras*, 2:162–64; Powell, *Dictionary*, 1:185–86.

25. Pollock Letter Book, Nov. 16, 1713, *CRNC*, 2:75.

26. Council Minutes, June 3, 1712, *CRNC2*, 7:20; Pollock to the Governor of Virginia, Oct. 5, 1712, *CRNC*, 1:880–81.

27. Pollock's Letter Book, c. Oct. 1712, *CRNC*, 1:883.

28. Quotes from Pollock's Reply to Spotswood, Dec. 28, 1712, *CRNC*, 1:896; Letter to Governor Pollock, Dec. 13, 1712, *CRNC*, 1:891; Johnson, *Tuscarora*, 2: 133; Powell, *Dictionary*, 1:186.

29. Thomas Pollock's 1712 Tuscarora Treaty, JDP. The historian Thomas Parramore in his article "With Tuscarora Jack on the Back Path to Bath" has been the most vocal supporter of the idea that the towns of Torhunta, Kenta, Neoheroka, Innennits, and Caunookehoe had not supported Hancock and the war. In fact, that they were more allied with King Blount than with King Hancock, and that they had been mistakenly attacked by Barnwell as they had played no part in the September 22 attacks.

30. Thomas Pollock's 1712 Tuscarora Treaty, JDP.

31. Ibid.

32. Lords Proprietor, Jan. 26, 1713, *CRNC*, 2:8, 9; Council Journal, Aug. 7, 1713, *CRNC*, 2:56.

33. Quote from Rainsford to Secretary, Feb. 17, 1713, *CRNC2*, 10:158; Rainsford to Jno. Chamberline, July 25, 1712, CR 1:858; Urmston to the Secretary, Sept. 22, 1714, *CRNC2*, 10:185–86.

34. *Boston News-Letter*, no. 426, June 9 to June 16, 1712.

35. Urmston to Mr. Hodges, Oct. 22, 1712, *CRNC*, 1:884–85; Towles, "Cary's Rebellion," 52–53.

36. Council Journal, Sept. 12, 1712, *CRNC*, 1:872; Executive Council Minutes, Nov. 5, 1712, *CRNC2*, 7:30–31; Higher-Court Records, Nov. 4, 1712, *CRNC2*, 5:470.

37. *CPCNC*, 1, 2 4, 9; Edwards, "Indians Massacre"; Dew, "Descendant of Koonce Family."

38. Council Minutes, Apr. 14, 1713, *CRNC*, 2:35.

39. Council Journal, May 8, 1713, *CRNC*, 2:44.

40. Council Minutes, Aug. 7, 1713, *CRNC2*, 7:41.

41. Council Journal, Aug. 9, 1712, *CRNC*, 1:867; Council Journal, Sept. 12, 1712, *CRNC*, 1:872; Council Journal, Mar. 10, 1715, *CRNC*, 2:171.

42. Copy to Mr. Hart, Sept. 1, 1713, *CRNC*, 2:61; Higher-Court Records, Feb. 23, 1714, *CRNC2*, 5:478–80; Pollock's Letter Book, Feb. 10, 1715, *CRNC*, 2:166–67.

43. Higher-Court Records, Feb. 23, 1714, *CRNC2*, 5:479.

44. Pollock Letter Book, Oct. 20, 1714, TPP.

45. Petition of the Palatines, July 13, 1747, *CRNC*, 4:954–59.

46. Ibid.; Laws of North Carolina, 1765, *CRNC*, 25:491; *NCHGR* 1 (Jan. 1900): 121, 122, 125.

47. A True Copy of a Letter to My Lord Carteret, Sept. 20, 1712, *CRNC*, 1:867–78; Council Minutes, Jun. 2, 1712, *CRNC2*, 7:19.

CHAPTER 7

1. Message of Charles Craven to the House, Aug. 6, 1712, SCCHJ.

2. Milling, *Red Carolinians*, 127–28.

3. House Minutes, Aug. 7, 1712, SCCHJ.

4. House Minutes, Aug. 7 and 8, 1712, SCCHJ.

5. Edgar and Bailey, *Biographical Directory*, 2:468; Klingberg, *Le Jau*, 135 n. 180; Oatis, *Colonial Complex*, 35.

6. *PRSC*, 1:58 n. 53.

7. *PRSC*, 1:34, 34 n. 10, 44, 58, 58 n. 53; Edgar and Bailey, *Biographical Directory*, 2:466–68; Letter by 150 of the Inhabitants, June 26, 1705, *CRNC*, 2:904; Wright, *Only Land*, 111–15; Oatis, *Colonial Complex*, 47.

8. Edgar and Bailey, *Biographical Directory*, 2: 468–69; Klingberg, *Le Jau*, 18, 26, 35, 40 n. 49; Gallay, *Indian Slave Trade*, 210; Book June 5, 1707–July 19, 1707, *JCHASC*, 27–28.

9. Quote from House Minutes, Apr. 9, 1712, SCCHJ; South Carolina House of Assembly, 1712, *CRNC*, 1:897–98; Council Journal, Nov. 5, 1712, *CRNC*, 2:72.

10. Quote from House Minutes, Nov. 20, 1712, SCCHJ; Johnson, *Tuscaroras*, 2:130.

11. Quote from Klingberg, *Le Jau*, 122–23; Barnwell, "Second Tuscarora Expedition," 35, 37, map; Milling, *Red Carolinians*, 128–29.

12. Johnson, *Tuscaroras*, 2:131; Barnwell, "Second Tuscarora Expedition," 34–35.

13. Sent by Lieutenant Woodhouse and Thomas Johnson, Oct. 3, 1712, *CRNC*, 1:879.

14. Quote from Governor Pollock in Reply on the Same Subject, Dec. 23, 1712, *CRNC*, 1:893.

15. Council Minutes, Jan. 9, 1713, *CRNC2*, 7:32; Thomas Pollock Letter, Mar. 6, 1713, *CRNC*, 2:23–25; Johnson, *Tuscaroras*, 2:131.

16. Quote from *Boston News-Letter*, no. 454, Mar. 2 to Mar. 9, 1713; Thomas Pollock Letter, Mar. 6, 1713, *CRNC*, 2:23–25; Spotswood to Pollock, Mar. 8, 1713, *CRNC*, 2:25–26; Spotswood to Council of Trade, Virginia, June 2, 1713, *CSPCAWI*, 27:184–94 (#355); Lee, *Indian Wars*, 33–35; Boyce, "Tuscarora Confederacy," 33–34; Lee, "Fortify, Fight, or Flee," 744.

17. Quote from Council Minutes, Aug. 7, 1713, *CRNC*, 2:56; Lee, *Indian Wars*, 33.

18. Council Minutes, Aug. 19, 1713, *CRNC2*, 7:41.

19. Petition of Certain Persons to the Honb. Grand Court, Mar. 26, 1713, *NCHGR* 2 (Jan. 1901): 111.

20. Johnson, *Tuscaroras*, 2:127, 131; Barnwell, "Second Tuscarora Expedition," 35.

21. Pollock Letter Book, Jan. 1713, *CRNC*, 2:7.

22. Governor Pollock in Reply on the Same Subject, Dec. 23, 1712, *CRNC*, 1:892.

23. *NCHGR* 1 (July 1900): 438–39; List of Bushels Received, Dec. 29, 1712, ACP; Rainsford to Secretary, Feb. 17, 1713, *CRNC*, 2:16–18; Spotswood to the Lords Proprietor, Feb. 11, 1713, *CRNC*, 2:14–16; Barnwell, "Second Tuscarora Expedition," 37; Lee, *Indian Wars*, 33–35; Johnson, *Tuscaroras*, 2:137.

24. Quote from Klingberg, *Le Jau*, 131; Pollock to Craven, Feb. 20, 1713, *CRNC*, 2:20; Barnwell, "Second Tuscarora Expedition," 36–37; Milling, *Red Carolinians*, 128–29; Lee, *Indian Wars*, 35.

25. Pollock in Reply on the Same Subject, Dec. 23, 1712, *CRNC*, 1:892–94; Stannard, "Examination of Indians," 272–75.

26. Pollock in Reply on the Same Subject, Dec. 23, 1712, *CRNC*, 1:894; Pollock to Craven, Feb. 20, 1712, *CRNC*, 2:19; Letter from Pollock, Feb. 24, 1713, *CRNC*, 2:21–22.

27. Quote in Boyce, "Tuscarora Confederacy," 33; Spotswood to Pollock, Mar. 19, 1713, *CRNC*, 2:26–27.

28. Spotswood to Pollock, Mar. 19, 1713, *CRNC*, 2:27.

29. Stannard, "Examination of Indians," 272–75.

30. Ibid.

31. Spotswood to Council of Trade, Virginia, July 26, 1712, *CSPCAWI*, 27:1–20 (#25); Spotswood to Council of Trade, Virginia, Oct. 15, 1712, *CSPCAWI*, 27:58–70 (#99); Spotswood to the Earl of Dartmouth, Virginia, Feb. 11, 1713, *CSPCAWI*, 27:130–52 (#273).

32. Quotes from To the Honble Alexander Spotswood, c. Nov. 1712, *CRNC*, 1:888–89; Pollock in Reply on the Same Subject, Dec. 23, 1712, *CRNC*, 2:892–94; Council Minutes, Jan. 12, 1713, *CRNC2*, 7:34; Pollock to Spotswood, c. Jan. 21, 1713, *CRNC*, 2:6–8.

33. Spotswood to Pollock, Jan. 21, 1713, *CRNC*, 2:5–6; Pollock to Spotswood, c. Jan. 21, 1713, *CRNC*, 2:6–8; Virginia Council Journal Nov. 6, 1713, *CRNC*, 2:73.

34. Pollock to Spotswood, c. Jan. 21, 1713, *CRNC*, 2:6–8.

35. Quote from Spotswood to Council of Trade, Virginia, Feb. 11, 1713, *CSPCAWI*, 27:130–52 (#272); Virginia—Journal of the Council, Mar. 5, 1713, *CRNC*, 2:22–23.

36. Letter to Governor Pollock on Indian Affairs, Dec. 13, 1712, *CRNC*, 1:890–91; To Governor Pollock, Dec. 22, 1712, *CRNC*, 1:892.

37. Barnwell, "Second Tuscarora Expedition," 37; Neoheroka Fort Site [31GR4], Jan. 31, 2009, NPS; Byrd and Heath, "The Country," 118; Holloman, "Fort Nohoroco," 18; A New and Accurate Map.

38. Noo-He-Roo-Ka Fort, map. c. 1713 (SCHS 32-5-9), SCHS; Barnwell, "Second Tuscarora Expedition," map, no page; Lee, "Fortify, Fight, or Flee," 714, 740–43; Holloman, "Fort Nohoroco," 18; Neoheroka Fort Site.

39. Lee, "Fortify, Fight, or Flee," 740–43.

40. Noo-He-Roo-Ka Fort, map.

41. Ibid.; Lee, "Fortify, Fight, or Flee," 743; Barnwell, "Second Tuscarora Expedition," 37.

42. Barnwell, "Second Tuscarora Expedition," 37.

43. Quotes from ibid, 38; James Moore Letter, Mar. 27, 1713, *CRNC*, 2:27.

44. Barnwell, "Second Tuscarora Expedition," 38; Lee, "Fortify, Fight, or Flee," 743–44.

45. Quotes from Barnwell, "Second Tuscarora Expedition," 38; Lee, "Fortify, Fight, or Flee," 743–44.

46. Quotes from Barnwell, "Second Tuscarora Expedition," 37–40; James Moore Letter, Mar. 27, 1713, *CRNC*, 2:27; Lee, "Fortify, Fight, or Flee," 743–44; *Boston News Letter*, no. 473, May 4 to May 11, 1713.

47. Letter of Thomas Pollock, Apr. 2, 1713, *CRNC*, 2:29–31.

48. Spotswood to the Council of Trade, Virginia, June 2, 1713, *CSPCAWI*, 27:184–94 (#355).

49. Klingberg, *Le Jau*, 134.

50. *Boston News-Letter*, no. 473, May 4 to May 11, 1713.

51. Barnwell, "Second Tuscarora Expedition," 40; Pollock's Letter Book, May 25, 1713, *CRNC*, 2:47; Gallay, *Indian Slave Trade*, 285.

52. Quote from Klingberg, *Le Jau*, 132; Clark, *Indian Massacre*, 15; Gallay, *Indian Slave Trade*, 283–84.

53. Pollock to Spotswood, Apr. 2, 1713, TPP, 9–10.

54. Quote from Letter of Thomas Pollock, May 25, 1713, *CRNC*, 2:45; Letter of Thomas Pollock, Mar. 31, 1713, *CRNC*, 2:27–29; Letter of Thomas Pollock, April 25, 1713, *CRNC*, 2:38; Thomas Pollock Letter, Apr. 30, 1713, TPP, 10–11.

55. Spotswood to Council of Trade, Virginia, Feb. 11, 1713, *CSPCAWI*, 27:130–52 (#272); Spotswood to Council of Trade, Virginia, Sept. 14, 1713, *CSPCAWI*, 27:231–43 (#473); Treaty of Peace between Spotswood and Tuscoruro Nations, Virginia, Feb. 27, 1714, *CSPCAWI*, 27:302–25 (#603i); Johnson, *Tuscaroras*, 2:147.

56. Letter to Pollock, Apr. 1713, *CRNC*, 2:31–32.

57. Letter of Thomas Pollock, Apr. 25, 1713, *CRNC*, 2:37–38.

58. Pollock to Spotswood, Apr. 25, 1713, TPP, 10.

59. Spotswood to Pollock, May 1713, *CRNC*, 2:47–48; Journal of the Virginia Council, Aug. 12, 1713, *CRNC*, 2:57.

60. Ransford to the Secretary, July 13, 1713, *CRNC2*, 10:160–61.

61. Quote from Copy to Mr. Hart, Sept. 1, 1713, *CRNC*, 2:61–62; Wetmore, "Role of the Indian," 168.

62. Letter of Pollock, Nov. 16, 1713, *CRNC*, 2:74; Council Journal, June 25, 1713, *CRNC*, 2:51–52.

63. Chicken, "A Letter from Carolina," 321; Letter of Pollock, June 25, 1713, *CRNC*, 2:252–53; Copy to Mr. Hart, Sept. 1, 1713, *CRNC*, 2:61; Barnwell, "Second Tuscarora Expedition," 40.

64. Thomas Pollock Letter, June 8, 1713, TPP, 11; Council Journal, Apr. 7, 1714, *CRNC*, 2:124; Chicken, "Letter from Carolina," 348 n. 2.

65. Council Minutes, Jan. 23, 1714, *CRNC2*, 7:44.

66. Quote from Copy to Mr. Hart, Sept. 1, 1713, *CRNC*, 2:62; Letter of Pollock, Sept. 1, 1713, *CRNC*, 2:59–60; To Capt. Edward Bellenger, Sept. 1, 1713, *CRNC*, 2:62–63; Barnwell, "Second Tuscarora Expedition," 40; Milling, *Red Carolinians*, 132.

67. House Minutes, Dec. 3, 1713, SCCHJ.

68. House Minutes, Dec. 5, 1713, SCCHJ.

69. Treaty of Peace Concluded between Spotswood and the Deputys from That Part of the Tuscarora Nation, Virginia, Feb. 27, 1714, *CSPCAWI*, 27:302–25 (#603, 603i, 601ii, 603iii).

70. Spotswood to the Council of Trade, Virginia, July 20, 1714, *CSPCAWI*, 27:362–79 (#726).

71. Urmston to the Secretary, Aug. 7, 1714, *CRNC*, 2:183.

72. Urmston to the Secretary, Sept. 22, 1714, *CRNC2*, 10:185.

73. Klingberg, *Le Jau*, 141 (quote), 144.

74. Council Journal, Dec 17, 1714, *CRNC*, 2:147; Council Minutes, May 29, 1714, *CRNC2*, 7:47; Council Minutes, Nov. 15, 1716, *CRNC2*, 7:66.

75. Council Minutes, May 29, 1714, *CRNC*, 2:129.

76. To the Earl of Dartmouth, June 18, 1713, *CRNC*, 2:50–51; Duke of Beaufort to Francis Brooke, Aug. 13, 1713, *CRNC*, 2:58; Council Journal, Feb. 14, 1715, *CRNC*, 2:170; Letters from Proprietors, Feb. 19, 1717, *CRNC*, 2:299.

77. Council Minutes, Aug. 11, 1714, *CRNC*, 2:141.

78. Council Minutes, Dec. 17, 1714, *CRNC2*, 7:51; Council Minutes, Feb. 11, 1715, *CRNC*, 2:168; Lefler and Powell, *Colonial North Carolina*, 79.

CHAPTER 8

1. Pollock's Letter Book, Oct. 20, 1714, *CRNC*, 2:145.

2. *CPCNC*, 16–18, 69, 71.

3. Barnwell, "Second Tuscarora Expedition," 40–41; Lee, *Indian Wars*, 39; Gallay, *Indian Slave Trade*, 328; Wright, *Only Land*, 121.

4. Oatis, *Colonial Complex*, 112–39; Wright, *Only Land*, 121–25.

5. Lee, *Indian Wars*, 39–42; Oatis, *Colonial Complex*, 132–39.

6. Council Journal, May 25, 1715, *CRNC*, 2:180–81; Milling, *Red Carolinians*, 13–33; Gallay, *Indian Slave Trade*, 329.

7. Lee, *Indian Wars*, 39–49.

8. Quote from Lee, *Indian Wars*, 42; South Carolina House Records, Mar. 8, 1716, *CRNC*, 2:256–9; Chicken, "A Letter from Carolina," 325; Wright, *Only Land*, 121–25; Gallay, *Indian Slave Trade*, 335–38; Oatis, *Colonial Complex*, 135–36.

9. Gallay, *Indian Slave Trade*, 338–41.

10. *JCIT*, ix–x; Gallay, *Indian Slave Trade*, 341–44.

11. Edgar and Bailey, *Biographical Directory*, 2:52–54; Wright, *Only Land*, 125; Extracts from 'Sketch of John Barnwell," Barnwell Family Papers, SCHS, 9.

12. Edgar and Bailey, *Biographical Directory*, 2:52–54; Will of Coll. John Barnwell, June 16, 1724, BDC; Will of John Barnwell, 1724, Barnwell File, SCHS; Presgraves and Presgraves, *Old Churchyard Cemetery*, 1; McDowell, "John Barnwell," BDC.

13. House of Assembly, Feb. 13, 1720, *CRNC*, 2:417–18; *NCHGR* 3 (Apr. 1903): 221–22; Wolf, "Patents and Tithables," 267–68; Neoheroka Fort Site; Colonel Maurice Moore Historical Marker.

14. Quote from McDowell, Mar. 21, 1718, *JCIT*, 262; May 23, 1718, *JCIT*, 277; Milling, *Red Carolinians*, 132–34.

15. Chicken, "A Letter from Carolina," 325; Barnwell, "Second Tuscarora Expedition," 34 n. 2; Edgar and Bailey, *Biographical Directory*, 2:468–69.

16. Colonial Laws, 1715, *CRNC*, 23:3.

17. Quote from Pollock's Letter Book, Nov. 13, 1717, *CRNC*, 2:296; Franklin, "Agriculture in Colonial North Carolina," 571–72.

18. Gallay, *Indian Slave Trade*, 299.

19. Council Journal, May 8, 1713, *CRNC*, 2:41–44; Edwards, "Indians Massacre"; Parramore, "With Tuscarora Jack," 117 n. 5; Earnest, *John and William Bartram*, 6–7.

20. Council Journal, Nov. 4, 1713, *CRNC*, 2:68; Council Journal, June 7, 1715, *CRNC*, 2:181–82.

21. General Court, July 18, 1716, *CRNC2*, 5:124.

22. Council Journal, Nov. 4, 1713, *CRNC*, 2:67.

23. Council Journal, Nov. 4, 1713, *CRNC*, 2:66.

24. Council Minutes, Apr. 14, 1713, *CRNC*, 2:31–35.

25. *CPCNC*, 36.

26. Council Journal, Apr. 7, 1714, *CRNC*, 2:124–25.

27. Council Minutes, Mar. 10, 1715, *CRNC*, 2:171; Council Journal, Nov. 23, 1715, *CRNC*, 2:204; Petition of Aaron Tyson, Nov. 13, 1735, *CRNC2*, 8:49.

28. Council Journal, Nov. 10, 1719, *CRNC*, 2:352–53.

29. Council Minutes, Apr. 14, 1713, *CRNC*, 2:31–35.

30. Letter to Charles Eden, Mar. 26, 1715, *CRNC*, 2:173–74.

31. Council Journal, Nov. 6, 1714, *CR*, 2:147; Spotswood to the Council of Trade, Virginia, July 20, 1714, *CSPCAWI*, 27:362–79 (#726); Council Journal, May 4, 1742, *CRNC*, 4:618; Council Journal, Mar. 29, 1743, *CRNC*, 4:632; Petition of the Palatines, July 13, 1747, *CRNC*, 4:954–59; Gabriel Johnston to the Board of Trade, May 17, 1748, *CRNC*, 4:868–70; Petition of the Palatines, 1749, *CRNC2*, 8:236–37.

32. *CVGA*, 95; Byrd, "Letters of William Byrd, 2d," 240; Powell, *Dictionary*, 2:328.

33. Quote from Haun, *CPCNC*, 19; see also 11, 12, 13, 21, 22, 24, 35, 42, 61; A Book of the Claim Paid in Craven Precinct out of Three Lists of William Brice, 1714,

ACP, 1:111; *NCHGR* 1 (July 1900): 444; An Act for Establishing the Church, 1715, *CRNC*, 2:207–13.

34. *CPCNC*, 26–27, 36–38, 47, 76, 81–83, 87–88.

35. *CPCNC*, 22, 25, 31, 35–37, 57; Higher-Court Records, Oct. 28, 1713, *CRNC*, 2:109, 149; Higher-Court Records, Mar. 29, 1718, *CRNC2*, 5:158; Pollock's Letter Book, July 15, 1720, *CRNC*, 2:388.

36. Quote from Pollock's Letter Book, Feb. 16, 1718, *CRNC*, 2:298; Council Minutes, Aug. 4, 1716, *CRNC*, 2:242–43; Council Minutes, Aug. 23, 1716, *CRNC*, 2:246–47; Journal of Virginia Council, Nov. 3, 1716, *CRNC*, 2:247; Lee, *Indian Wars*, 44–45.

37. Will of William Brice, Nov. 16, 1718, Carteret County Wills, E, F, G [Microfilm] MF129, 1745–1948, North Carolina State Archives, Raleigh, N.C.

38. Higher-Court Records, July 1723, *CRNC2*, 5:418; Higher-Court Records, May 1731, *CRNC*, 3:244; Higher-Court Records, Sept. 25, 1735, *CRNC*, 4:64–65; Council Minutes, Feb. 5, 1740, *CRNC*, 4:493; Higher-Court Records, Mar. 12, 1741, *CRNC*, 4:589; Nov. 16, 1718, *NCHGR* 1 (Jan. 1900): 33; Grimes, "Abstract," 46.

39. Council Minutes, Sept. 13, 1715, *CRNC2*, 7:57.

40. An Act Relating to the Biennial and Other Assemblies, c. 1715, *CRNC*, 2:213–16.

41. Ibid.; Oath of Allegiance, c. 1716, *NCHGR* 1 (Apr. 1900): 267; Styrna, "Winds of War and Change," 186–92.

42. Ibid., 191–92, 196, 240.

43. Ibid., 223–24, 227, 237, 282, 331, 350.

44. Council Journal, Jan. 21, 1715, *CRNC*, 2:217; Council Journal, June 7, 1715, *CRNC*, 2:181; Council Journal, Aug. 3, 1716, *CRNC*, 2:239–41; Council Journal, Dec. 30, 1718, *CRNC*, 2:323.

45. Land Grants, Folder 3, TPP; Council Minutes, Nov. 11, 1718, *CRNC*, 2:316–17; Council Journal, Apr. 4, 1720, *CRNC*, 2:377–78; Pollock's Letter Book, July 15, 1720, *CRNC*, 2:386–88; Thomas Pollock Land Grant, Aug. 12, 1720, *NCHGR* 1 (Jan. 1900): 9; *NCHGR* 1 (Jan. 1900): 121, 122, 125; *NCHGR* 2 (Jan 1901): 81.

46. Copy of a Letter Sent to Sir Robert Pollock by Capt. Henderson's Kinsman, Apr. 3, 1717, *CRNC*, 2:276–78; Pollock's Letter Book, July 15, 1720, *CRNC*, 2:387–88.

47. Council Journal, Mar. 30, 1722, *CRNC*, 2:449–50; Council Journal, Apr. 4, 1722, *CRNC*, 2:454.

48. Court Records, Aug. 8, 1722, *CRNC*, 2:459; Special Court of Oyer and Terminer, Aug. 14, 1722, *CRNC*, 2:476–78.

49. Council Journal, Sept. 7, 1722, *CRNC*, 2:460; Towles, "Cary's Rebellion," 58.

50. Will of Col. Thomas Pollock, Aug. 8, 1721, *CRNC*, 22:290–94; Queries and Answers, *NCHGR* 3 (Jan. 1903): 156–59; Apr. 18, 1727, *NCHGR* 2 (July 1901): 471; *NCHGR* 2 (Jan. 1901): 131–32, 302; *NCHGR* 2 (Apr. 1901): 192, 297; *NCHGR* 3 (July 1903): 428; Laws of North Carolina—1765, *CRNC*, 25:491; Powell, *Dictionary*, 5:117; Grimes, "Notes," 139–40, 143, 146; Wolf, "Patents and Tithables," 267–68, 270. The Pollock Genealogy in the Thomas Pollock Papers says Thomas Pollock Jr. died January 1, 1733, and George died November 28, 1733.

51. Thomas Pollock's 1712 Tuscarora Treaty, JDP; Garrow, *Mattamuskeet Documents*, 22.

52. Quotes found in Fenton, *Great Law*, 386, 389; Gallay, *Indian Slave Trade*, 266.

53. Hunter to Mr. Popple, New York, Sept. 10, 1713, *CSPCAWI*, 27:231–43 (#471); Shannon, *Iroquois Diplomacy*, 71–72; Boyce, "Iroquoian Tribes," 286–87; Gallay, *Indian Slave Trade*, 284; Neoheroka Fort Site.

54. Smallwood, "Three Cultures," 83–86, 95–96.

55. Hunter to Governor Nicholson, New York, Oct. 26, 1713, *CSPCAWI*, 27:253–21 (#524iii).

56. Fenton, *Great Law*, 381, 383; Shannon, *Iroquois Diplomacy*, 71–72.

57. Lee, *Indian Wars*, 46–46; Garrow, *Mattamuskeet Documents*, 19.

58. Council Minutes, Sept. 13, 1715, *CRNC*, 2:200; Council Minutes, Aug. 4, 1716, *CRNC*, 2:243–44; Council Minutes, July 31, 1718, *CRNC*, 2:308–9; General Court, Oct. 28, 1718, *CRNC2*, 5:188; Council Minutes, Oct. 30, 1718, *CRNC2*, 7:76; Council Minutes, Nov. 11, 1718, *CRNC2*, 7:76–77; Watson, Latham, and Samford, *Bath*, 21–22.

59. Council Minutes, Aug. 24, 1725, *CRNC*, 2:570–71; Journal of Mr. Watis' Mission to the Indians, Charles Town, May 10, 1731, *CSPCAWI*, 39:266–78 (#490iii); Petition to the Governor and Council, Oct. 13, 1749, *CRNC2*, 8:461.

60. Council Minutes, Jan. 9, 1713, *CRNC*, 2:2; General Court Minutes, Mar. 31, 1713, *CRNC*, 2:95–96; Council Minutes, Aug. 7, 1713, *CRNC*, 2:55; Complaint of John Durant, Apr. 27, 1714, *CRNC2*, 5:481; Complaint of John Blish, Apr. 27, 1714, *CRNC2*, 5:482–83; Commission Minutes, May 20, 1714, *JCIT*, 57; Moore v. Stone, Mar. 1718, *CRNC2*, 5:161–62; Council Minutes, July 31, 1724, *CRNC*, 2:534; Council Minutes, Oct. 24 and 28, 1724, *CRNC2*, 7:146–47; Council Minutes, Aug. 3, 1725, *CRNC2*, 7:159; *NCHGR* 1 (Oct. 1900): 615–16; *NCHGR* 3 (Apr. 1903): 285–86; Gallay, *Indian Slave Trade*, 298–305; Grimes, "Notes," 103–4.

61. Stevenson, "Indian Reservations," 28–30.

62. Quote from Council Journal, June 5, 1717, *CRNC*, 2:283; Pollock's Letter Book, July 8, 1717, *CRNC*, 2:288–89; Stevenson, "Indian Reservations," 29; Smallwood, "Three Cultures," 9–11, 19–20; Byrd and Heath, "The Country," 104; Boyce, "Iroquoian Tribes," 288; Powell, *Dictionary*, 1:186.

63. Brickell, *Natural History*, 283–85; Lee, *Indian Wars*, 46

64. Quote from Council Journal, Oct. 31, 1725, *CRNC*, 2:573; Burrington to the Duke of Newcastle, July 2, 1731, *CRNC*, 3:153; Boyce, "Iroquoian Tribes," 287–88.

65. Quote from Diary of Bishop Spangenberg, Sept. 13, 1752, *CRNC*, 5:1; Burrington to Newcastle, July 2, 1731, *CRNC*, 3:153; Indians in North Carolina, Jan. 4, 1755, *CRNC*, 5:320–21; Smallwood, "Three Cultures," 91–94; Boyce, "Iroquoian Tribes," 287–88; Byrd and Heath, "The Country," 99.

66. Quote from Byrd, *Dividing Line*, 290–92; Council Minutes, Apr. 4, 1720, *CRNC*, 2:380; Council Minutes, Apr. 5, 1722, *CRNC*, 2:456; Council Minutes, June 14, 1722, *CRNC*, 2:458; Council Minutes, Apr. 9, 1724, *CRNC2*, 7:141; Council Minutes, May 28, 1725, *CRNC2*, 7:155; Council Minutes, July 30, 1725, *CRNC*, 2:568; Council Minutes, Aug. 25 and 26, 1726, *CRNC*, 2:640; House Minutes, Oct. 2, 1736, *CRNC*, 4:237; House Minutes, Feb. 26, 1740, *CRNC*, 4:529; Council Minutes, May 4 and 5, 1742, *CRNC*, 4:615–17; Council Journal, Nov. 29, 1758, *CRNC*, 5:994–95.

67. Council Minutes, Nov. 11, 1718, *CRNC*, 2:316; Council Minutes, Oct. 14, 1736, *CRNC*, 4:224; Council Minutes, Mar. 28 and 29, 1753, *CRNC*, 5:31, 35.

68. Council Minutes, Nov. 23, 1715, *CRNC*, 2:204; Stevenson, "Indian Reservations," 27–30; Garrow, *Mattamuskeet Documents*, 20, 45; Aug. 2–4, 1733, *NCHGR* 1 (Jan. 1900): 106.

69. Petition of James Blount, Oct. 1, 1748, *CRNC2*, 8:221; Land Indenture, July 12, 1766, and Dec. 2, 1775, Folder 1, 1723–1798, LTP; Speech of Thomas Basket, Nov. 11, 1766, *CRNC*, 7:361; Order in Council, Jan. 11, 1769, *CRNC2*, 9:617–20; A Letter Concerning the Lands Formerly Held by the Tuscaroras Indians in Bertie County, North Carolina Secretary of State, Apr. 5, 1911, Cp970.03 N87s, NCC; Stevenson, "Indian Reservations," 29; Smallwood, "Three Cultures," 34; Powell, *Dictionary*, 1:186.

70. Quote from Abstracts from the Returns from the Several Counties, c. Dec. 1754, *CRNC*, 5:161–63; Indians in North Carolina, Jan. 4, 1755, *CRNC*, 5:320–21.

71. Gallay, *Indian Slave Trade*, 208; Wetmore, "Role of the Indian," 170–71; Perdue and Oakley, *Native Carolinians*, 53; Oakley, *Keeping the Circle*, 18–35.

72. Byrd and Heath, "Tuscarora Homeland," 12–13; Lefler and Powell, *Colonial North Carolina*, 80; Grimes, "Notes," 103; Watson, Latham, and Samford, *Bath*, 22; McIlvenna, *Very Mutinous People*, 158–60.

73. Dowd, *A Spirited Resistance*.

74. Lee, "Fortify, Fight, or Flee," 714, 744–45.

Bibliography

PRIMARY SOURCES

Archival Sources

Beaufort County, N.C.—Land & Deed Records. http://files.usgwarchives.net/nc/
    beaufort/deeds/p1–50.txt. Accessed September 8, 2010.
Beaufort County Library, S.C.
    Beaufort District Collection
Proceedings of the Council of Maryland. Archives of Maryland Online. 848 total
    online vols. http://aomol.net/html/volumes.html.
North Carolina Division of Archives and History, Raleigh, N.C.
    Albemarle County Papers, Miscellaneous Records, 1678–1737, C.002–10001,
        2 vols. Microfilm.
    Carteret County Wills, E, F, G [Microfilm] MF129, 1745–1948.
    John Devereux Papers, 1712–1883. PC.34.1.
    Francis Lister Hawks Papers, Private Collections, P.C. 574.1.
    Thomas Pollock Papers, 1708–1859, 1711–1842, P.C.31.1.
    Alexander Spotswood Papers, PC 24.1, Letterbook.
South Carolina Historical Society, Charleston, S.C.
    Barnwell Family Papers.
    Barnwell File, 30-04.
South Carolina Department of Archives and History, Columbia, S.C.
    South Carolina Commons House Journal.
Wilson Library, University of North Carolina, Chapel Hill, N.C.
    North Carolina Collection, Cp970.03 N87s.
    Lewis Thompson Papers, Southern Historical Collection, Collection Number
        716, Series 1.1, Folder 1, 1723–1798.

Newspapers

Boston News-Letter
London Gazette

Published Primary Sources

Archdale, John. *A New Description of That Fertile and Pleasant Province of Carolina:
    With a Brief Account of Its Discovery, Settling, and the Government Thereof to
    This Time, with Several Remarkable Passages of Divine Providence during My*

Time. London: John Wyat, 1707; Ann Arbor, Mich.: University Microfilms International, 1979.

Barlowe, Arthur. "Captain Arthur Barlowe's Narrative of the First Voyage to the Coasts of America." In *Early English and French Voyages: Chiefly from Hakluyt, 1534–1608*, edited by Henry S. Burrage, 227–41. New York: Barnes and Noble, 1906.

Barnwell, Joseph W. "The Second Tuscarora Expedition." *South Carolina Historical and Genealogical Magazine* 10 (Jan. 1909): 35–48.

———. "The Tuscarora Expedition: Letters of Colonel John Barnwell." *South Carolina Historical and Genealogical Magazine* 9 (Jan. 1908): 28–54.

Brickell, John, *The Natural History of North-Carolina*. Dublin: James Carson, 1737; Murfreesboro, N.C.: Johnson Publishing Company, 1968.

Byrd, William. "Letters of William Byrd, 2d, of Westover, Va." *Virginia Magazine of History and Biography* 9 (Oct. 1901): 113–30; 9 (Jan. 1902): 225–51.

———. *The Secret Diary of William Byrd of Westover, 1709–1712*. Edited by Louis B. Wright and Marion Tinling. Richmond, Va.: Dietz Press, 1941.

———. *William Byrd's Histories of the Dividing Line betwixt Virginia and North Carolina*. Edited by William K. Boyd. Raleigh: North Carolina Historical Commission, 1929.

Calendar of State Papers, Colonial, America and West Indies, 1574–1739. 46 vols. Edited by Cecil Headlam. London. *British History Online*. http://www.british-history.ac.uk/catalogue.aspx?gid=123&type=3. Accessed August 2009.

Chicken, George. "A Letter from Carolina in 1715, and Journal of the March of the Carolinians into the Cherokee Mountains, in the Yemassee Indian War, 1715–1716, from the Original Ms. [of Col. George Chicken]." In *Year Book—1894: City of Charleston, S.C.*, edited by Langdon Cheves, 313–54. Charleston, S.C.: Walker, Evans and Cogswell, 1894.

Christoph von Graffenried's Account of the Founding of New Bern: Edited with an Historical Introduction and an English Translation. Edited by Vincent H. Todd. Raleigh: Edwards and Broughton Printing Company, 1920.

Colonial Records of North Carolina. 24 vols. Edited by William L. Saunders. Raleigh, N.C.: P. M. Hale, 1886; Wilmington, N.C.: Broadfoot Publishing, 1993.

Colonial Records of North Carolina. 2nd series. 11 vols. Edited by Mattie Erma Edwards Parker and Robert J. Cain. Raleigh, N.C.: Department of Cultural Resources, Division of Archives, 1968–2007.

Craven Precinct-County North Carolina, Precinct-County Court Minutes, 1712 thru 1715, Book 1. Edited by Weynette Parks Haun. Durham, N.C.: Private Printing, 1978.

"De Graffenried's Manuscript, copied for *The Colonial Records of North Carolina* from the Original Mss. In the Public Library at Yverdon, Switzerland, and Translated by M. Du Four." In *The Colonial Records of North Carolina*, edited by William L. Saunders, 1: 905–85. Raleigh: P. M. Hale, 1886; Wilmington, N.C.: Broadfoot Publishing, 1993.

Grimes, J. Bryan, *Abstract of North Carolina Wills*. Raleigh, N.C.: E. M. Uzzell, 1910.

Harriot, Thomas. "A Briefe and True Report." In *The Roanoke Voyages, 1584–1590: Documents to Illustrate the English Voyages to North America under the Patent*

Granted to Walter Raleigh in 1584, edited by David Beers Quinn, 1:317–87.
London: Hakluyt Society, 1955.

Journal of the Commons House of Assembly of South Carolina. Edited by A. S. Salley.
Columbia: Historical Commission of South Carolina, 1937.

Journals of the Commissioners of the Indian Trade: September 20, 1710–August 29, 1718.
Colonial Records of South Carolina. Edited by William L. McDowell Jr. Columbia:
South Carolina Department of Archives and History, 1955 (reprint, 1992).

Klingberg, Frank J., ed. *Carolina Chronicle: The Papers of Commissary Gideon
Johnston, 1707–1716*. Berkeley: University of California Press, 1946.

———, ed. *The Carolina Chronicle of Dr. Francis Le Jau, 1706–1717*. Berkeley:
University of California Press, 1956.

Lawson, John. *A New Voyage to Carolina*. 1709. Edited by Hugh Talmage Lefler.
Chapel Hill: University of North Carolina Press, 1967.

Ludwell, Philip, and Nathaniel Harrison. "Boundary Line Proceedings, 1710."
Virginia Magazine of History and Biography 4 (July 1896): 30–42; 5 (July 1897): 1–21.

Minutes of the Provincial Council of Pennsylvania. Published by the State. 16 vols.
Philadelphia: Jo. Severns, 1852.

North Carolina Historical and Genealogical Register. 3 vols. Edited by J. R. B.
Hathaway. Edenton, N.C., 1900–1903.

Proprietary Records of South Carolina. 3 vols. Edited by Susan Baldwin Bates and
Harriott Cheves Leland. Charleston, S.C.: History Press, 2005.

Stanard, William, ed. "Examination of Indians, 1713 (?)." Miscellaneous Colonial
Documents, *Virginia Magazine of History and Biography* 19 (July 1911): 272–75.

———, ed. "Letters of William Byrd, First." *Virginia Magazine of History and
Biography* 26 (Jan. 1918): 17–31; 26 (Apr. 1918): 124–34; 26 (July 1918): 247–59;
26 (Oct. 1918): 388–92; 27 (Apr. 1919): 167–68; 27 (July–Oct. 1919): 273–88; 28
(Jan. 1920): 11–25.

Yeardley, Francis. "Francis Yeardley's Narrative of Excursions into Carolina,
1654." In *Narratives of Early Carolina, 1650–1708*, edited by Alexander S.
Smalley Jr., 25–38. New York: Barnes and Noble, 1911.

Maps

Map of Southeastern North America by John Barnwell. Map Collection, Box 15,
Folder 16, Columbia: South Carolina Department of Archives and History.

A New & Accurate Map of the Province of North & South Carolina, Georgia
&c. Eman. Brown. 1747. http://www.history-map.com/picture/002/Carolina-
Georgia-North-South.htm. Accessed February 2011.

Noo-He-Roo-Ka Fort. Map. c. 1713 (SCHS 32-5-9), South Carolina Historical
Society, Charleston, S.C.

SECONDARY SOURCES

Allred, Fred J., and Alonzo T. Dill. "The Founding of New Bern: A Footnote."
North Carolina Historical Review 40 (Summer 1963): 361–74.

Aquila, Richard. "Down the Warrior's Path: The Causes of the Southern Wars of the Iroquois." *American Indian Quarterly* 4 (Aug. 1978): 211–21.

Ashe, Samuel A. *Biographical History of North Carolina: From Colonial Times to the Present*. 8 vols. Greensboro, N.C.: Charles L. Van Noppen, 1905–17.

Barnwell, Stephen B. *The Story of an American Family*. Marquette, Mich.: Private Printing, 1969.

Bennett, D. Gordon, and Jeffrey C. Patton, eds. *A Geography of the Carolinas*. Boone, N.C.: Parkway Publishers, 2008.

Boyce, Douglas W. "Did a Tuscarora Confederacy Exist?" In *Four Centuries of Southern Indians*, edited by Charles M. Hudson, 28–45. Athens: University of Georgia Press, 1975.

———. "Iroquoian Tribes of the Virginia–North Carolina Coastal Plain." In *Handbook of North American Indians, Northeast*, 17 vols., edited by William C. Sturtevant and Bruce G. Trigger, 15:282–89. Washington, D.C.: Smithsonian Institution, 1978.

Byrd, John E., and Charles L. Heath. "'The Country here is very thick of Indian Towns and Plantations . . .': Tuscarora Settlement Patterns as Revealed by the Contentnea Creek Survey." In *Indian and European Contact in Context: The Mid-Atlantic Region*, edited by Dennis B. Blanton and Julia A. King, 98–125. Gainesville: University of Florida Press, 2004.

———. "The Rediscovery of the Tuscarora Homeland: A Final Report of the Archaeological Survey of the Contentnea Creek Drainage, 1995–1997." Report submitted to the National Park Service and the North Carolina Division of Archives and History, Raleigh, N.C., 1997. Greene County Surveys, #4153, Raleigh, N.C.: Office of State Archaeology.

Camp, Cordelia. *The Influence of Geography upon Early North Carolina*. Raleigh, N.C.: Carolina Charter Tercentenary Commission, 1963.

Cecelski, David S. *The Waterman's Song: Slavery and Freedom in Maritime North Carolina*. Chapel Hill: University of North Carolina Press, 2001.

Clark, Walter. *Indian Massacre and Tuscarora War, 1711–1713*. Raleigh, N.C.: Capital Printing Company, 1901.

Clonts, F. W. "Travel and Transportation in Colonial North Carolina." *North Carolina Historical Review* 3 (Jan. 1926): 16–35.

Colonel Maurice Moore Historical Marker, http://www.hmdb.org/marker. asp?marker=6510. Accessed March 27, 2012.

Dew, Allen Powell. "Descendant of Koonce Family." Allen Dew Genealogy, http://www.apdew.com/koo/koonmoo1.htm. Accessed September 30, 2011.

Dill, Alonzo Thomas, Jr. "Eighteenth Century New Bern: A History of the Town and Craven County, 1700–1800." *North Carolina Historical Review* 22 (Jan. 1945): 1–21; 22 (Apr. 1945): 152–75; 22 (July 1945): 293–319.

Dowd, Gregory Evans. *A Spirited Resistance: The North American Indian Struggle for Unity, 1745–1813*. Baltimore: Johns Hopkins University Press, 1992.

Earnest, Ernest. *John and William Bartram, Botanists and Explorers*. Philadelphia: University of Pennsylvania Press, 1940.

Edgar, Walter B., and N. Louise Bailey, eds. *Biographical Directory of the South Carolina House of Representatives.* 5 vols. Columbia: University of South Carolina Press, 1974–92.

Edwards, Bonnie. "Indians Massacre Neuse and Trent River Settlers." *Olde Kinston Gazette,* March 1998. Reprinted in RootsWeb, Ancestry.com, www.rootsweb. ancestry.com/~ncbertie/tscnews.htm. Accessed December 2011.

Eid, Leroy V. "'A Kind of Running Fight': Indian Battlefield Tactics in the Late Eighteenth Century." *Western Pennsylvania Historical Magazine* 71 (1988): 147–71.

Eilers, Hazel Kraft. "Barnwell Coat-of-Arms." *Hobbies—The Magazine for Collectors,* April 1977, 146–47.

Fenton, William N. *The Great Law and the Longhouse: A Political History of the Iroquois Confederacy.* Norman: University of Oklahoma Press, 1998.

Fischer, Kirsten. *Suspect Relations: Sex, Race, and Resistance in Colonial North Carolina.* Ithaca, N.Y.: Cornell University Press, 2002.

Franklin, W. Neil. "Agriculture in Colonial North Carolina." *North Carolina Historical Review* 3 (Oct. 1926): 539–74.

Gallay, Alan. *The Indian Slave Trade: The Rise of the English Empire in the American South, 1670–1717.* New Haven, Conn.: Yale University Press, 2002.

Garrow, Patrick H. *The Mattamuskeet Documents: A Study in Social History.* Raleigh: North Carolina Department of Cultural Resources, 1975.

Grimes, J. Bryan. "Some Notes on Colonial North Carolina, 1700–1750." *North Carolina Booklet* 5 (Oct. 1905): 90–149.

Herndon, G. Melvin. "Indian Agriculture in the Southern Colonies." *North Carolina Historical Review* 44 (1967): 283–97.

Heyward, Barnwell Rhett. *Genealogical Chart: Barnwell of South Carolina.* Albany, N.Y.: Private Printing, 1898.

Holloman, Charles R. "Expeditionary Forces in the Tuscarora War." *We the People: Official Publication of the North Carolina Citizens Association* 23 (Mar. 1966): 15–30.

———. "Fort Nohoroco: Last Stand of the Tuscaroras." *We the People: Official Publication of the North Carolina Citizens Association* 23 (Dec. 1965): 15–31

———. "Palatines and Tuscaroras." *We the People: Official Publication of the North Carolina Citizens Association* 23 (Jan. 1966): 21–29.

———. "Tuscarora Towns in Bath County." *We the People: Official Publication of the North Carolina Citizens Association* 23 (Feb. 1966): 16–30.

Hudson, Charles. *The Southeastern Indians.* Knoxville: University of Tennessee Press, 1976.

Jennings, Francis. *The Ambiguous Iroquois Empire: The Covenant Chain Confederation of Indian Tribes with English Colonies from Its Beginning to the Lancaster Treaty of 1744.* New York: W. W. Norton, 1984.

Johnson, F. Roy. *The Tuscaroras: Mythology—Medicine—Culture.* 2 vols. Murfreesboro, N.C.: Johnson Publishing Company, 1967.

Kelton, Paul. *Epidemics and Enslavement: Biological Catastrophe in the Native Southeast, 1492–1715.* Lincoln: University of Nebraska Press, 2007.

Kupperman, Karen Ordahl. "English Perception of Treachery, 1583–1640: The Case of the American Savages." *Historical Journal* 20 (June 1977): 263–87.

Lee, E. Lawrence. *Indian Wars of North Carolina, 1663–1763*. Raleigh, N.C.: Division of Archives and History, 1963 (reprint, 1997).

Lee, Wayne E. "Fortify, Fight, or Flee: Tuscarora and Cherokee Defensive Warfare and Military Culture Adaptation." *Journal of Military History* 68 (July 2004): 713–70.

Lefler, Hugh T., and William S. Powell. *Colonial North Carolina: A History*. New York: Charles Scribner's Sons, 1973.

LeMaster, Michelle. "Into the 'Scolding Houses': Indians and the Law in Eastern North Carolina, 1684–1670." *North Carolina Historical Review* 83 (Apr. 2006): 193–232.

———. "The Tuscarora Massacre Revisited: These Were Not 'Random Acts of Violence.'" Paper presented at the New Voyages to Carolina: The First North Carolina conference, East Carolina University, Greenville, N.C., February 3, 2012.

McCain, Paul M. *The County Court in North Carolina before 1750*. Durham, N.C.: Duke University Press, 1954.

McDowell, Rebecca DesChamps. "John Barnwell and the Tuscaroras." Paper presented at the Beaufort County, S.C., Historical Society, June 29, 1965. Beaufort District Collection, Beaufort County Library, Beaufort, S.C.

McIlvenna, Noeleen. *A Very Mutinous People: The Struggle for North Carolina, 1660–1713*. Chapel Hill: University of North Carolina Press, 2009.

Milling, Chapman J. *Red Carolinians*. 1940; Columbia: University of South Carolina Press, 1969.

Moody, Robert Earle. "Massachusetts Trade with Carolina, 1686–1709." *North Carolina Historical Review* 20 (Jan.-Oct. 1943): 43–53.

Mooney, James. *The Siouan Tribes of the East*. Washington, D.C.: Government Printing Office, 1894; New York: Johnson Reprint Corporation, 1970.

Neoheroka Fort Site [31GR4], Greene County, N.C., National Register of Historical Places Registration Form, January 31, 2009, National Park Service, United States Department of the Interior, Washington, D.C.

Oakley, Christopher. "The Indian Slave Trade in Coastal North Carolina and Virginia." M.A. thesis, University of North Carolina Wilmington, 1996.

Oakley, Christopher Arris. *Keeping the Circle: American Indian Identity in Eastern North Carolina, 1885–2004*. Lincoln: University of Nebraska Press, 2005.

Oatis, Steven J. *A Colonial Complex: South Carolina's Frontiers in the Era of the Yamasee War, 1680–1730*. Lincoln: University of Nebraska Press, 2004.

Oberg, Michael Leroy. "Gods and Men: The Meeting of Indian and White Worlds on the Carolina Outer Banks, 1584–1586." *North Carolina Historical Review* 77 (Oct. 1999): 367–90.

Otterness, Philip L. *Becoming German: The 1709 Palatine Migration to New York*. Ithaca, N.Y.: Cornell University Press, 2004.

Parramore, Thomas C. "With Tuscarora Jack on the Back Path to Bath." *North Carolina Historical Review* 64 (Apr. 1987): 115–38.

Perdue, Theda. *Cherokee Women: Gender and Culture Change, 1700–1835.* Lincoln: University of Nebraska Press, 1998.

———. *Slavery and the Evolution of Cherokee Society, 1540–1866.* Knoxville: University of Tennessee Press, 1979.

Perdue, Theda, and Christopher Arris Oakley. *Native Carolinians: The Indians of North Carolina.* Raleigh: North Carolina Department of Cultural Resources, 2010.

Powell, William S. *Dictionary of North Carolina Biography.* 6 vols. Chapel Hill: University of North Carolina Press, 1979–96.

———. *The Proprietors of Carolina.* Raleigh, N.C.: Carolina Charter Tercentenary Commission, 1963; Raleigh, N.C.: State Department of Archives and History, 1968.

Presgraves, James Cawood, and S. Louise Presgraves. *Old Churchyard Cemetery of St. Helena's Episcopal Church, Beaufort, South Carolina.* Beaufort, S.C.: James Cawood Presgraves and S. Louise Presgraves, 1987.

Reed, C. Wingate. *Beaufort County: Two Centuries of Its History.* N.p.: private printing, 1962.

Richter, Daniel K. *The Ordeal of the Longhouse: The Peoples of the Iroquois League in the Era of European Colonization.* Chapel Hill: University of North Carolina Press, 1992.

Rights, Douglas L. "The Trading Path to the Indians." *North Carolina Historical Review* 8 (Oct. 1931): 403–26.

Roper, L. H. *Conceiving Carolina: Proprietors, Planters, and Plots, 1662–1729.* New York: Palgrave Macmillan, 2004.

Rountree, Helen C. *Pocahontas, Powhatan, Opechancanough: Three Indian Lives Changed by Jamestown.* Charlottesville: University of Virginia Press, 2005.

Salley, A. S., Jr., ed. "Barnwell of South Carolina." *South Carolina Historical and Genealogical Magazine* 2 (Jan. 1901): 46–88.

Saraydar, Stephen C. "No Longer Shall You Kill: Peace, Power and the Iroquois Great Law." *Anthropology and Humanism Quarterly* 15 (Feb. 1990): 20–28.

Seaman, Rebecca M. "John Lawson, the Outbreak of the Tuscarora Wars, and 'Middle Ground' Theory." *Journal of the North Carolina Association of Historians* 18 (Apr. 2010): 9–33.

Shannon, Timothy J. *Iroquois Diplomacy on the Early American Frontier.* New York: Viking, 2008.

Silver, Timothy. *A New Face on the Countryside: Indians, Colonists, and Slaves in South Atlantic Forests, 1500–1800.* New York: Cambridge University Press, 1990.

Smallwood, Arwin D. "A History of Three Cultures: Indian Woods, North Carolina, 1585 to 1995." Ph.D. diss., Ohio State University, 1997.

Stevenson, George, Jr. "Indian Reservations in North Carolina." *Carolina Comments* 57 (Jan. 2009): 26–31.

Styrna, Christine Ann. "The Winds of War and Change: The Impact of the Tuscarora War on Proprietary North Carolina, 1690–1729." M.A. thesis, College of William and Mary, 1990.

Towles, Louis P. "Cary's Rebellion and the Emergence of Thomas Pollock." *Journal of the Association of Historians in North Carolina* 4 (Fall 1996): 36–58.

Watson, Alan D., with Eva C. Latham and Patricia M. Samford. *Bath: The First Town in North Carolina*. Raleigh, N.C.: Office of Archives and History, 2005.

Wetmore, Ruth Y. "The Role of the Indian in North Carolina History." *North Carolina Historical Review* 56 (Apr. 1979): 162–76.

Whitford, Sara. "Case #1: On the Trail of Tom; or, A New Look at the Tuscarora War." Coastal Carolina Indian Center, 2007, http://www.coastalcarolinaindians.com. Accessed July 30, 2009.

Wolf, Jacquelyn H. "Patents and Tithables in Proprietary North Carolina, 1663–1729." *North Carolina Historical Review* 56 (July 1979): 263–77.

Wright, J. Leitch, Jr. *The Only Land They Knew: The Tragic Story of the American Indians in the Old South*. New York: Free Press, 1981.

Acknowledgments

Though my name will be put down as the author, all historians know that a book is an endeavor done by so many more people. First and foremost, I would like to thank Dr. Alan Watson, my colleague at the University of North Carolina Wilmington, whom I consider the best and most knowledgeable historian of North Carolina's colonial period. A kind man and a true gentleman, he allowed me to pester him constantly over the years with questions and willingly read several drafts of this book. I could not have done it without him and my gratitude to him is great. I can only hope that my foray into North Carolina colonial history will please him. I also want to thank UNCW and its College of Arts and Sciences for a Faculty Research Reassignment that allowed me to finish researching and writing this book. It took much more time than I imagined, and I could not have done it without the help of that reassignment. Others at UNCW who helped pave my way to publication include Dr. Paul Townend, the chair of the Department of History; Professor Emeritus Dr. Melton McLaurin; and my friend, Dr. Chris Fonvielle, himself a descendant of William Brice. I also want to thank Sara Whitford of the Coastal Carolina Indian Center. It was Sara who first introduced me to the idea of Core Tom as an agent provocateur and we held many discussions on this. She is a fine historian and I look forward to more creative thinking from her. I also want to thank the referees whose critiques were not only insightful but kept me from making mistakes and so made this a much better book. Much gratitude goes to Mark Simpson-Vos at the University of North Carolina Press who saw the value of the manuscript and wanted it for the Press. Paul Betz and Zach Read at the University of North Carolina Press helped much in ushering this manuscript into the light of publication, while copyeditor Petra Dreiser did invaluable work, her edits making the book all the stronger.

Down in South Carolina, I would like to thank Karen Stokes and Neil Polhemus of the South Carolina Historical Society in Charleston; Wade Dorsey and Marion Chandler at the South Carolina Department of Archives and History in Columbia; and Grace Morris Cordial and Charmaine Seabrook Conception at the Beaufort County Library in Beaufort. In North Carolina, much thanks goes to Vann Evans, William Brown, Sarah Koonts, and Mathew Waehner of the State Archives in Raleigh; Dolores Hall at the North Carolina Office of State Archaeology in Raleigh; Stephen Fletcher, Barbara Ilie, and Keith Longiotti at the Wilson Library at the University of North Carolina at Chapel Hill; Linda Eure of the Historic Edenton State Historic Site; and to David French of the Family History Society of Eastern North Carolina in New Bern, who strongly encouraged me to tell stories of his group's ancestors. Thanks also go to David Norris of Wilmington, who made the maps for me; Kip Shaw of Edenton for some pictures; Rita Bucher-Jolidon at the

Burgerbibliothek Bern, Switzerland, also for photographs; and to Matthew Thick, a graduate student at Wayne State University in Detroit, for some summer research assistance.

Of course, I owe much to friends and family who encouraged my writing and who listened, always patiently, to my stories about the Tuscarora War. These friends include the late Paco Strickland and his wife, Connie Nelson; Patricia Peters; Alan and Lynn Williams; and Bob and Annis Ross, who live up on "The Point" on High Rock Lake and enjoyed hearing history stories. Much gratitude also goes to Jack Fryar, who read a draft of the manuscript; and to Dr. Paul Kelton at the University of Kansas who also read a draft. I would be nowhere without the overwhelming support of my family. Thanks go to my mother, Ann, and my late father, Dick, who instilled in me a strong appreciation of history. This carries over to my sisters: Tracy and her partner, Karen, and my youngest sister, Rhonda, who always keeps me on my toes. My in-laws have always been supportive, and I cannot thank enough Jack and Carol Mills, my father- and mother-in-law, who always come to hear my talks and seem delighted to have a historian in the family. They also read a draft of the manuscript and gave excellent notes. They are the best in-laws ever. A shout-out also goes to my sister- and brother-in-law, Barb and Mark Courtney, and my niece and nephew, Alyson and Travis Courtney. I want to thank my stepson Charles Pynch and his fiancé, Annie Craven; and my stepdaughter Jordyn, her husband, Mark Zimmerman, and best of all, my granddaughter Mycah Mae, who was just a gleam in her father's eye when I started working on the book but was a toddler by the time I finished. Thankfully, she often pulled me away from my work, coming into my home office, grabbing my hand, saying "Come on, Fessor, let's go walk." And away we would go. I love that girl. And finally, my greatest appreciation goes to my sweet wife, Caryn. Without her, none of this would be possible. She understands how solitary the writing of history can be, but she never complains and always encourages. She is the light of my life, and I love her more than she knows. Thanks to you all. This is your book as well.

Index

Nottoway town, 81–82
Nusoorooka (Tuscarora town), 43
Nyasauckhee (Tuscarora), 175

Occaneechi Indians, 47
Old settlers (political faction), 7–9, 13,
    15, 17, 75, 149, 150, 192, 206
Oneida Indians, 40, 54, 196–97. *See also*
    Five Nations of the Iroquois
Onondaga Indians, 40, 54, 56, 196. *See*
    also Five Nations of the Iroquois
Ooneroy (Tuscarora town), 44, 147, 201
Opessa (Shawnee), 53
Ouskininorese (Machapunga). *See*
    Squire Hooks
Overman, Ephraim, 93–94

Pagett, John, aka Nonrontisgnotkau
    (Core), 148, 176, 196, 198
Palatine settlers, 16; attacks on, 73, 149;
    and Barnwell, 119, 123; Catechna
    expedition, 79, 88–89; joins Brice,
    88; land loss, 151–52, 187; North
    Carolina settlement, 20–28, 51, 93;
    opposes De Graffenried, 27–28,
    89–92; orphans, 71, 150; peace treaty,
    80
Pamlico Indians, 1, 3, 15, 45, 60, 147,
    185, 207; attacks by, 69–73; destruc-
    tion of, 173, 197; peace treaty, 80
Pamlico River, 4, 14, 34, 60, 87; attacks
    along, 68, 70, 72, 73, 77, 93, 136;
    Barnwell on, 110–13, 119, 120, 128;
    destruction on, 72–73, 196; forti-
    fications along, 119, 120, 136, 138;
    Indians on, 43, 44, 59, 82, 143, 146,
    148, 172, 173; Moore on, 160; patrols
    along, 180; settlements on, 9, 12, 15,
    32, 39, 84, 144, 159
Pasquatank Indians, 3, 15, 60
Pearce, Mrs., 125
Pedee Indians, 104, 105
Peterba King (Indian), 107
Peterson, Thomas, 186
Pierce, Capt., 156

Pollock, Cullen, 114, 194–95
Pollock, Esther, 116–17, 193
Pollock, George, 114, 194–95
Pollock, Margaret, 114
Pollock, Martha (daughter), 114, 194
Pollock, Martha (mother), 114, 116, 194
Pollock, Thomas, 2, 34, 36; as acting
    governor, 137, 150–51, 160, 194;
    attacks Meherrins, 50, 116; and
    Barnwell, 112, 119, 120, 127, 133, 135,
    136, 140–42, 159; and Brice, 86, 87,
    119, 189; Cary's Rebellion, 14, 28–29,
    118; and Gov. Craven, 155, 170, 173;
    death, 194; and De Graffenried, 25,
    27, 151, 187, 188; early life, 113–14;
    and Gov. Eden, 176, 180, 191; Es-
    ther's will, 117, 193; family, 114, 116,
    117; Hancock's execution, 146–47;
    and King Blount, 146–48, 161,
    171–74; lands, 14, 50, 74, 114, 116,
    164, 151–52, 191, 194; as lawyer, 115;
    leads war effort, 88, 93–94, 112, 119,
    127, 129, 138–39, 150–51, 209–10; as
    merchant, 114; and Moore, 160, 170,
    171; Palatine lands, 151–52, 187; as
    planter, 115; as politician, 117; post-
    war, 185, 191–94; and Quakers, 75,
    118; and Senecas, 157–58; September
    1711 attacks, 73–74, 83; slave owner,
    51, 115; and Spotswood, 94, 147,
    163–65, 171–72; treaties, 146–48, 151,
    171–72, 176–77, 234 (n. 29); Yamasee
    War, 180
Pollock, Thomas, Jr., 114, 194–95
Pompey (Indian), 198
Porter, John, Jr., 70, 160, 189
Porter, John, Sr., 75
Porter, Sarah, 70
Poteskeet Indians, 3, 15, 60, 176, 197,
    199, 203
Poythress, Peter, 77–78, 82, 108
Proprietary men (political faction), 9,
    12, 75, 117, 138, 149, 191–92

Quakers, 7; beliefs, 8, 118, 192; Cary's

Rebellion, 14; fear Ashley River Indians, 158; and Old Settlers, 8–9; in politics, 13, 118, 178; and Pollock, 75, 118; and Tuscarora War, 75, 84, 93–94, 127, 137, 150, 158–60. *See also* Dissenters

Qualks Hooks (Seneca), 64, 196

Queen Anne (Britain), 13, 24

Rainsford, Rev. Giles, 136, 149, 173

Rarocaithee (Tuscarora town), 175

Raruta (Core town), 58

Raudauquaquank (Bear River Indian town), 59

Reading, Lyonell, 34, 72, 112, 119, 136, 138, 148, 160

Reading's Fort. *See* Reading, Lyonell

Resootka (Tuscarora town), 44, 147, 201

Richman, Hodman, 150

Richman, Lees, 150

Roanoke Island, 4, 47, 171

Roanoke River, 16, 43, 116, 147, 162, 164, 175, 193

Roper, Thomas, 186

St. Augustine, Fla., 98, 103, 154

Sam (Core), 59

Santee Indians, 32, 98, 104, 180

Saponi Indians, 32, 57, 139, 204

Sarooka (Tuscarora), 147

Savannah Indians, 52, 98–99, 155, 179

Saxapahaw Indians, 57, 104, 105, 155

Seneca Indians, 40, 47, 54, 56; attack Carolinas, 33, 56–57, 198; blamed for September 1711 attacks, 76, 109, 207; at Conestoga council, 53–54; as English enemies, 96; influence Tuscaroras, 57–58, 109, 125, 144–45, 172; and Moore, 157–58; reject war, 161, 197; suspected Tuscarora allies, 139, 158, 176. *See also* Five Nations of the Iroquois

Sewee Indians, 32, 33, 52, 98

Shackleford Plantation, 72, 138

Shrieve, Robert, 85, 198

Siouan Indians. *See* Cape Fear Indians; Catawba Indians; Cheraw Indians; Congaree Indians; Eno-Shakorie Indians; Esaw Indians; Hoopeng Indians; Keyauwee Indians; Occaneechi Indians; Pedee Indians; Santee Indians; Saponi Indians; Saxapahaw Indians; Sugeree Indians; Waccamaw Indians; Wareere Indians; Wateree Indians; Waxhaw Indians; Winyaw Indians

Slavery, 11

—African American, 37, 51, 96, 115, 116, 199; Indian relations, 67–68, 70, 80, 123

—Indian, 11, 51, 115, 198–99

—slave taking, 16, 51, 156, 173, 180, 185; by Barnwell, 108, 210; by Brice, 87, 89, 92–93; at Core Town, 133–34; by Moore, 157, 169

—in South Carolina, 52–53, 97–99, 154–55, 179, 181

Slocum, Samuel, 150

Slocumb, John, 94

Smith, Hannah, 32, 150

Sothel, Seth, 115, 117

South Carolina, 3, 6, 57; appeals by North Carolina, 76, 96, 139–40; assistance to North Carolina, 99–100, 139–42, 153–54; Barnwell expedition, 100–112, 119–34; Barnwell's return, 134; founding of, 96–97; Indian allies, 98–99, 101, 140, 170, 179; Moore expedition, 155–61, 165–74; Moore's return, 174–75; slave raiding, 11, 16, 51–53, 97–99, 154–55, 179, 181; slavery in, 96–99; Tuscaroras in, 183–84; war casualties, 107–8, 124, 169; Yamasee War, 179–83, 209

Spanish, 98, 102–3, 154–55

Spellman, John, 10

Spotswood, Gov. Alexander (Virginia), 73, 88, 163, 195; on Barnwell, 133, 163; and Blount, 78, 81–83, 94–95,

Carolina, 76, 94, 142–43; and Blount, 81–83, 94–95, 175; and Pollock, 94, 118; Tuscarora refugees in, 161–63, 171, 175; Tuscarora treaties, 94–95, 175; Yamasee War, 180

Waccamaw Indians, 98, 153, 179
Wareere Indians, 104
Warfare, 46, 55–57, 69–73, 213; North Carolina militia, 119, 121–22, 124, 129, 137, 139, 190; plunder, 72, 77, 108, 110, 120, 121, 186; strategy, 72, 109, 112, 123, 126, 156, 166, 208; torture, 46–47, 56, 121, 125; Yamasee War, 179–83
—captives: European, 72, 77, 125, 128; Indian, 11, 16, 51–54, 92–93, 132–33, 135, 154–56
—fortifications: English, 72, 112, 119, 120, 138, 167; Indian, 78, 95, 107, 109, 121–26, 128–32, 135, 156–57, 165–66, 208–9
Wateree Indians, 32, 33, 47, 52, 57, 98; Barnwell expedition, 104, 107; Yamasee War, 179–80
Waxhaw Indians, 104, 135
Weetock Indians, 1, 3, 49, 185, 207; as Cores, 59–60; disappearance, 197; enslaved, 51; September 1711 attacks,

69–73; as Tuscaroras, 43, 45
Westo Indians, 52, 98–99
Wharton, David, 127, 186
Whitby, John, 186
White Oak River, 12, 15, 27, 28, 30, 60; attacks along, 70, 76; Barnwell on, 134; destruction along, 72–73
Wilkinson, William, 87, 116, 117
Wilkinson's Point, 80, 152
Winyaw Indians, 104, 105, 155
Women, 10–11; Anglo, 71–72, 116–17; Indian, 33, 40–42, 52, 79, 107, 165; as slaves, 99, 156; "Trading Girls," 33
Wull, Anna, 28

Yamasee Indians, 98, 209; and Barnwell, 102–3, 181–82; Barnwell expedition, 103, 107–8, 111, 124, 128; Moore expedition, 156, 166; remain in North Carolina, 136, 137, 170; as South Carolina allies, 52, 57, 99, 103; Yamasee War, 179–83
Yamasee War, 179–83, 209
Yeopim Indians, 3, 15, 44, 49, 50, 60, 61, 199–200, 203
Yuchi Indians, 103, 179

Zant, Anna, 27
Zionien, Benedict, 28